Video Games and Spatiality in American Studies

Video Games and the Humanities

Edited by
Nathalie Aghoro, Iro Filippaki, Chris Kempshall,
Esther MacCallum-Stewart, Jeremiah McCall
and Sascha Pöhlmann

Advisory Board
Alenda Y. Chang, UC Santa Barbara
Katherine J Lewis, University of Huddersfield
Dietmar Meinel, University of Duisburg-Essen
Ana Milošević, KU Leuven
Soraya Murray, UC Santa Cruz
Holly Nielsen, University of London
Michael Nitsche, Georgia Tech
Martin Picard, Leipzig University
Melanie Swalwell, Swinburne University
Emma Vossen, University of Waterloo
Mark J.P. Wolf, Concordia University
Esther Wright, Cardiff University

Volume 5

Video Games and Spatiality in American Studies

Edited by Dietmar Meinel

DE GRUYTER
OLDENBOURG

ISBN 978-3-11-135330-2
e-ISBN (PDF) 978-3-11-067518-4
e-ISBN (EPUB) 978-3-11-067523-8
ISSN 2700-0400

Library of Congress Control Number: 2021948841

Bibliographic information published by the Deutsche Nationalbibliothek
The Deutsche Nationalbibliothek lists this publication in the Deutsche Nationalbibliografie;
detailed bibliographic data are available on the Internet at http://dnb.dnb.de.

© 2023 Walter de Gruyter GmbH, Berlin/Boston
This volume is text- and page-identical with the hardback published in 2022.
Cover image: Maxiphoto / iStock / Getty Images Plus
Printing and binding: CPI books GmbH, Leck

www.degruyter.com

Acknowledgements

This volume developed out of the international conference "Playing the Field II: Video Games and Space in American Studies" hosted in 2019 at the Kulturwissenschaftliches Institut in Essen, Germany. As the title suggests, the event was a follow-up to the first "Playing the Field" conference organized by Sascha Pöhlmann in 2018 at the Ludwig-Maximilian University in Munich, Germany. Without his initial motivation to bring American Studies in conversation with the study of video games, this volume would not exist. Sascha has done pioneering work not only in bringing together a variety of scholars to engage with video games as a meaningful object of study. In asking scholars to explore the interconnections between American Studies and Video Game Studies, his intellectual vision and ideas also inform the theoretical premise of this volume. But Sascha has been more than an intellectual inspiration for the following pages. When I first approached him with the idea for a follow-up event to his inspired conference, he has been incredibly gracious by sharing his knowledge, experience, and resources. His scholarly ingenuity, professional generosity, and spirit of collegiality made this volume possible.

This volume would also not have been possible without the pioneering intellectual work of Barbara Buchenau. Her scholarship about urban, rural, and transitional spaces in American culture have defined this endeavor from the outset. Her scholarship about scripts (together with Jens Martin Gurr) provided me with a critical vocabulary to think about video games in the first place and eventually inspired the theme of the volume. As a keynote speaker, Barbara also shaped the theoretical debates surrounding the intersections of American Studies, Video Games Studies, and spatiality as her lecture constituted one of the high points of a stimulating conference. Her unwavering support for this endeavor from its inception to its conclusion should also not go unmentioned. As every project faces organizational hurdles, scheduling conflicts, or financial difficulties at times, her enthusiasm sustained this endeavor during its most challenging moments.

Lastly, I thank the Global Young Faculty program for its generous funding of the "Playing the Field II" conference. The Global Young Faculty is an initiative of Stiftung Mercator in cooperation with the University Alliance Ruhr and is coordinated by the Mercator Research Centre Ruhr in Essen. The program brings together outstanding and dedicated young researchers from universities and non-university research institutions based in the Ruhr area. It supports them in their efforts to forge new professional contacts and share ideas beyond institutional and disciplinary borders. I also thank the Kulturwissenschaftliche Institut

Essen and its director, Julika Griem for hosting the three-day conference in their beautiful spaces and for graciously extending their support.

Table of Contents

Dietmar Meinel
Video Games and Spatiality in American Studies: An Introduction —— 1

Part I

Sören Schoppmeier
Notes on the State of Montana: The U.S. American Spatial Imagination and the Retrotopia of *Far Cry 5* **—— 33**

Felix Zimmermann
Ethical Boredom in the Wilderness: Treating *Red Dead Redemption 2* **as an Ambience Action Game —— 51**

Nathalie Aghoro
On Postapocalyptic Frontiers in *Horizon Zero Dawn* **—— 71**

David Callahan
Owning Global Spaces and the Frontier in *Uncharted 4: A Thief's End* **—— 85**

Andrei Nae
From Male to Colonial Gaze: The Intersection of Patriarchy and Colonial Discourse in the Rebooted *Tomb Raider* **Video Game Series —— 101**

Hanne Nijtmans
The Inevitable Fate of the "Dragonborn:" Selling Player Agency in *The Elder Scrolls V: Skyrim* **—— 117**

Part II

Damien B. Schlarb
Filling Out the Map: The Anxiety of Situatedness and the Topological Poesis of Cartographic Maps in Video Games —— 137

Juliane Borosch
Detroit: Become Human – Orientational Mapping in the City and (Hi)Story —— 153

Stefan Schubert
'Playing for Space:' Negotiating and Narrativizing Space in *One Hour One Life* —— 167

Greta Kaisen
There is no Place like *Gone Home:* Exploring Gothic Settings in Video Games —— 181

Florian Deckers
Exploring the Digital Land of the Dead: Hybrid Pan-Latinidad in *Grim Fandango* —— 193

Part III

Michael Nitsche
Breaking Worlds Three Ways —— 209

Maria Sulimma
Surviving the City: *Zombies, Run!* and the Horrors of Urban Exercise —— 223

Elisabeth Haefs
"#Gameüse:" Planting the Digital Garden —— 241

Kirsten Möller and Anna Kpok
Performative Playground: Narrative Spaces in Theater Games —— 253

Lauren Kolodkin and Ryan Linthicum
Museum Space Invaders: Video Gaming at the Smithsonian American Art Museum —— 263

Soraya Murray
Coda: Disoriented in the Field of Play —— 275

Contributors —— 285

Index —— 291

Dietmar Meinel
Video Games and Spatiality in American Studies: An Introduction

This volume aims to bring the methodological richness of American Studies to the study of space in the medium of video games. The essays assembled here map out conversations about spatiality in video games from the vantage point of American Studies, exploring the digital spaces players experience, navigate, and manipulate within games and beyond. Following this approach, video games are not understood as forms of digital literature or as an interactive or playable media (although they certainly are) but first and foremost as a medium of space. Games, we argue, are defined by their spatiality. While this introduction conceptualizes video games as a medium inherently characterized by its various modes of spatial production, the present volume examines a particular kind, one that is keyed to the history and formation of U.S. culture.

From its inception, the experience of space in video games marked the decisive quality of the medium. In one of the earliest video games, *Tennis for Two* (1958), for example, players had to hit a simulated tennis ball on a court at a precise moment to either gain an advantage over their opponent or avoid hitting the ball into the net. Understanding the position of the ball on the digital tennis court (seen from the side) was crucial. Similarly, *Spacewar!* (1962) required players to understand the space – in this case the gravity well of a star in the universe – in which their spaceships moved. Players had to manipulate the simulated gravitational push and pull of the star to gain an advantageous position over the other player to shoot down their ship. Consequentially, Michael Nitsche sees the "representational form and their interactive design" of these early video games as originating from their "spatial realization" (18). Likewise, the popular text-adventure-game genre of the late 1970s and early 1980s also followed less a literary tradition and foregrounded experiences of space. While players encountered the game world only as a written text on a screen and could only interact with that world by typing in commands, text-adventure games, Henry Jenkins reminds us, "centered on enabling players to move through narratively compelling spaces" ("Narrative Spaces" 56).

With the ubiquitous use of 3D graphics today, space and movement in space have become an inherent part of the visual, auditory, and haptic gaming experi-

---

Note: I thank Damien Schlarb and Lara Ullrich for their invaluable critique of this introductory essay.

ence as navigating a digital world continues to be an essential feature of all genres. From vast open worlds to small one-screen challenge rooms, the play of video games takes place in and produces space. At the same time, space also functions as one of the quintessential narratological forms of video games since the medium tells its stories, Sebastian Domsch asserts, by way of "the experience of navigating through space" (104). Indeed, in the words of Alenda Y. Chang, "[a]lmost by definition, all computer and console games are environments" (58). In the digital spaces and environments of video games, questions about the medium, its mode of narration, its aesthetics, and its form coalesce.

Video Game Studies shares this interest in the function and meaning of spaces with American Studies which possesses an even longer tradition of thinking about space. Historically, notions of space have been crucial in describing the experiences of white settlers in North America and in the development of U.S. culture. While notions of a "wilderness," a "virgin land," a "garden," the "frontier," or a "city upon a hill" date to the colonial period, these ideas have played an instrumental role in shaping the making of a national culture in the nineteenth century. Since the 1950s, American Studies has wrestled with these ideas whether as myths and symbols, as ideological constructions, or as methodological frameworks of the field. Yet, even when American Studies scholars began to challenge conceptions of North America as a "virgin land" (Perry Miller) or a "garden" (Leo Marx) as a narrow perspective, these interventions tended to deploy a spatial vocabulary, nonetheless. The following introduction aims to provide an overview of the spatial discourse in Video Game Studies and in American Studies. As both fields have undergone a spatial turn in thinking about their subject of study, their distinct theoretical approaches and methodologies provide a critical vocabulary to interrogate the productions of space.

In bringing the two fields into a dialogue about their notions of space, this volume continues a conversation Sascha Pöhlmann initiated with his volume *Playing the Field* (2019). In his introduction, Pöhlmann wonders how conceptions of American Studies change by studying video games. He advocates to "systematically discuss ways in which the study of video games may present a challenge to the methods that are current in the loose interpretative community of American Studies, how it might demand new methods, or how it might reinvigorate those methods that have become unfashionable but are still part of the field's historical repertoire of cultural criticism" (4). Spatiality, I argue, may offer one such systematic approach to thinking about video games and American Studies.[1]

---

[1] The interest in the role of space developed out of Pöhlmann's inquiry and led to the organization of the conference "Playing the Field II: American Studies, Video Games, and Space" at the

Consequentially, the following passages trace the development of the role of space in Video Game Studies as one of the defining features of the medium. Similarly, the introduction will then look at the long history of the use of space and spatial vocabulary in American Studies from its early myth-and-symbol school to the(ir) fundamental revisions in the field and present scholarship following a spatial turn in American Studies.[2]

In tracking the meanings and functions of space in Video Game Studies and American Studies, this introduction sketches the plurality of conceptual and methodological approaches to space in both fields as well as their various intersections. The first part of the introduction examines the development of spatiality and discourses of space in Video Game Studies. This section provides a theoretical framework for the essays in this volume as they adopt the spatial vocabulary of Video Games Studies to critically examine the production of North American spaces in their material. The second part of this introduction provides a history of American Studies, albeit with a particular interest in the role of a spatial vocabulary since the inception of the field. This section thereby aims to demonstrate the centrality of spatiality in the theoretical conceptualizations of American Studies and in its programmatic shifts. By placing spatiality in Video Game Studies in proximity to similar debates in American Studies, the latter part of the introduction furthermore hopes to indicate a path for future explorations. As Video Game Studies moves beyond thinking about space as merely representative or representational to understand the production of space also as an act of playing, American Studies may similarly expand its notions of space as a practice or a form of doing. The introduction hence concludes with the idea of scripting as a current example of spatiality in the field; its interest in the scripted scenarios and the prescriptive actions of physical environments not only illustrates a performative sense of space but may offer novel approaches to thinking about video game spaces as well. Eventually, the individual contributions to the volume expand this overview and provide concrete examples of studying space in video games from an American Studies perspective while si-

---

Kulturwissenschaftliches Institut (KWI) in Essen, Germany, in May 2019. This collection of essays grew out of the event.

2 In some regard, this volume takes its cue from *Gamer Nation* (2019). In his book, John Wills provides "an analysis of video games within American culture; their presentation of America past, present, and future; and their potential to reframe American experience" (18). By examining gameplay mechanics as well as the production of space, this introduction and the following essays expand on Wills approach of looking at the "representation in (and the narrative geography of) games" (14).

multaneously questioning some of the theoretical premises introduced. In the following pages, I hope to provide a context for these conversations.

Space and Spatiality in Video Game Studies

Early Video Game Studies wrestled with a seemingly simply question: what are video games? Or rather, how should we analyze video games? In the 1990s, these questions were mostly answered with reference to literary theory and narratology. Video games were seen as "interactive narratives, procedural stories or remediated cinema" (Eskelinen). By the end of the millennium, this view of video games came under intense scrutiny as scholars increasingly foregrounded elements of play in their studies. Even as video games tell stories, video game scholar Jasper Juul maintains, "if we were to *play* only a single game session of a hypothetical game and end up performing exactly the same sequence of events that constitute *Hamlet*, we would not have had the same experience as had we *watched* Hamlet performed" ("Games Telling stories?"; emphasis in the original). Furthermore, the enjoyment of a video game may be completely detached from any story it attempts to tell (if, indeed, a game tries to tell a story in the first place). Scholars eventually transcended debates about the narrative or ludic quality of games as they shifted their exploration of the uniqueness of video games to questions of space, among other issues.

In Video Game Studies, three interrelated notions of space developed over the years. First, literary and media scholar Janet H. Murray describes the uniqueness of digital texts in general as the experience of moving in space. Second, theme park designer Don Carson and video game scholar Henry Jenkins further conceptualize this quality of video games as a form of narrativizing space to argue for their storytelling and worldbuilding potentials. A third strand of thinking, found in the work of video game scholars Espen Aarseth and Michael Nitsche, concentrates less on the narrative potential of space and instead theorizes what kind of space video games produce or how space functions as a digital environment. Stephan Günzel eventually describes this period in the 2000s as a "spatial turn" in the field. By conceptualizing video games as "active navigation through a pictorial space" (Günzel, "The Spatial Turn" 148), hence, scholars (and players) are asked to both read and interact with digital environments (see Günzel, "The Spatial Turn" 147). Lastly, this spatial turn also expanded the vocabulary to engage critically with the politics of representations at work in the medium. Spaces, landscapes, and environments are never empty or merely scenery, a Cultural Studies approach to space argues, but always possess meaning whether in service of various ideologies or as subversive sites thereof.

All these approaches to video game spaces ascribe meaning to the digital environments players experience. For Sebastian Domsch this act of "semanticizing space" (104) is a common occurrence in everyday life but is made particularly prominent in video games. "As we experience spaces," he explains, "we read them for their meaning and the stories they contain, and as we perform these spaces through movement and interaction, we inscribe our own narrative into them" (104). The narrativization of space through movement stands in stark contrast to sequential forms of storytelling most prominently found in literature and film and constitutes a defining feature of video games (see Domsch 105). Eventually, video game scholars have drawn from insights into the narrative potential of physical spaces to conceptualize virtual ones.

In her pioneering work about digital texts, Janet H. Murray plants the seeds for thinking about digital texts as spatial phenomena (even though she is often considered a proponent of a narratological approach to video games). In *Hamlet on the Holodeck* (1997),[3] Murray ascribes the unique means of telling stories in the digital medium to the immersive quality of experiencing the digital world as a "navigable space" (79). Murray does not have video game spaces but hypertext novels of the early 1990s in mind when she argues that whereas "[l]inear media such as books and films can portray space, either by verbal description or image, [...] digital environments can present space that we can move through" (79). She underscores that the spatial quality of the digital medium does not derive from its graphical capabilities or its ability to connect far-flung places in a global communication system. Instead,

> [t]he computer's spatial quality is created by the interactive process of navigation. We know that we are in a particular location because when we enter a keyboard or mouse command the (text or graphic) screen display changes appropriately. We can verify the relation of one virtual space to another by retracing our steps. (Murray 80; emphasis added)

This sense of movement in space is furthermore intimately tied to an experience of the narrative since the "navigation of virtual space has been shaped into a dramatic enactment of the plot" (Murray 83). Her conceptualization of digital media foremost as a navigable space refers to hypertext novels but eventually extends to include video games.[4]

---

[3] Her book spawned vivid responses as seen in the earlier quote by Juul. For further critical assessment of her work, see Ryan "Beyond Myth and Metaphor" (2001).
[4] For a detailed mapping of spatial forms in digital media of which the neologism "cyberspace" coined by William Gibson in his 1984 novel *Neuromancer* is probably one of the most famous instances, see, for example, Ryan "Cyberspace, Cybertexts, Cybermaps" (2004).

Theme-park designer Don Carson was one of the first to bring architectural thinking of physical spaces into conversation with video game spaces. For Carson in "Environmental Storytelling" (2000), a ride in a theme park tells its narrative or story through "the physical space a guest walks or rides through" (Carson). In his view, the physical environment "does much of the work of conveying the story the designers are trying to tell" as "[c]olor, lighting and even the texture of a place can fill an audience with excitement or dread" (Carson). Thanks to environmental storytelling, a narrative is not a linear procession of plot points but the immersive experience of an entire fictional world. Drawing from his work, Carson asserts that video game players should ultimately "come to a conclusion" about the fictional world "through their experience of the physical space and random encounters with peripheral game characters" (Carson).[5]

In the early 2000s, space seemed a particularly enticing concept for video game scholars, as environmental storytelling connects video games to early forms of play and allowed scholars to segue from fruitless debates about the status of narratology and ludology in the field. In "Game Design as Narrative Architecture" (2004), Henry Jenkins proposes to move the study of video games away from questions about their narratological or ludic quality and instead center the field around spatiality. Jenkins argues "for an understanding of game designers less as storytellers and more as narrative architects" (121) as the production, designing, or sculpting of space stands at the heart of video games. For example, the first text-based adventures, although devoid of visual depictions of space, "centered around enabling players to move through narratively-compelling spaces" (Jenkins 121).[6] As the graphic capabilities of gaming devices advanced, video games did not appeal to players because of their narrative form. On the contrary, early "Nintendo games have simple narrative hooks – rescue Princess Toadstool – but what gamers found astonishing when they first played them were their complex and imaginative graphic realms" (Jenkins 122). Instead of appreciating or analyzing video games exclusively for their narrative complexity or

---

[5] In his essay, Carson provides some concrete suggestions for the production of video game spaces from a "set of rules that will guide, the design and the project team to a common goal" to giving players a first sense of their placement in and their relationship to an environment, "Storytelling Through Cause and Effect," "The Power of Designing the Familiar," "Using Contrasting Elements to Your Advantage," and "Remember, This is a Theatre!" (Carson). While Carson hopes to inform and educate designers, his list also represents a set of useful analytical tools.

[6] Jenkins even harkens back to early table-top role-playing games, an inspiration for the text, noting that a play started "with designing the space – the dungeon – where the players' quest will take place" (121).

their ludic functionality, Jenkins suggests focusing on the critical examination of gamespaces since "the core narratives behind many games center around the struggle to explore, map, and master contested spaces" (122).

Thinking about video game spaces as "narrative architecture," "narrative space," or indeed "environmental storytelling" allows Jenkins to theorize video games as a unique form of cultural texts differing from literature and visual media. Jenkins conceptualizes "environmental storytelling" (which he adapts from the essay by Carson) by distinguishing four interrelated features: spatial storytelling references established narratives, spatial storytelling relates its narratives as movement in space, spatial storytelling communicates information in its setting, and spatial storytelling emerges out of the experience of space (see Jenkins 123). The digital environment, in this view, shapes the experience of the game narrative and world. To tell their stories, for one, video games draw from and evoke a "larger narrative system in which story information is communicated through books, film, television, comics and other media" to immerse players in a world they can "wander through and interact with" (Jenkins 124). Secondly, they enact stories through their spaces. These gamespaces privilege "spatial exploration over plot development" by structuring their narratives as "a matter of designing the geography of imaginary worlds so that obstacles thwart and affordances facilitate the protagonist's forward movement towards resolution" (Jenkins 125). Consequently, the traversal of a gamespace becomes an inherent aspect of the narrative experience because the accessibility of digital environment is tied to advancement in the plot of a game. Simply put: the plot is often organized around movement in space (see Jenkins 125–126). Thirdly, developers embed narrative components in the interactions with the digital world when designing a game. Players must locate and recognize these storytelling elements as games distribute "information across the game space" (Jenkins 126). This requires players to properly read and decipher the digital environment to advance the narrative. Lastly, narratives can be "mapped onto game space" (Jenkins 128) as the narratives emerge from the ways in which players can interact with and thereby produce space. These gamespaces then hold a potential for telling multiple stories or even allowing for player-driven narratives (see Jenkins 128–129). Instead of following a pre-written story, players write their narratives as they traverse a space or find their actions imprinted on the landscape of the game. From the perspective of environmental storytelling then, space moves to the fore of understanding video games.[7]

---

[7] Following Carson and Jenkins, Celia Pearce foregrounds the possibilities an architectural approach holds for the study of video games in her essay "Narrative Environments" (2007).

A third strand in Video Game Studies concentrates less on the narrative potential of space and instead theorizes the kind of digital environments video games produce. An early work to conceptualize space is Espen Aarseth's "Allegories of Space" (2001).[8] In his view, space in video games poses a dilemma since no physical realms exist which a person can actually enter (as the idea of the holodeck suggests). To solve the quandary of describing digital spaces, he borrows the notions of representational space and represented space from the work of Henri Lefebvre instead.[9] Aarseth understands computer games as "spatial practice[s]" which are "both representations of space (given their formal systems of relations) and representational spaces (given their symbolic imagery with a primarily aesthetic purpose)" (163). Aarseth moves beyond reading digital environments only as narratives to understand

> spatial representation in computer games as a reductive operation leading to *a representation of space that is not in itself spatial, but symbolic and rule-based*. The nature of space is not revealed in this operation, and the resulting product, while fabricating a spatial representation, in fact uses the reductions as a means to achieve the object of gameplay, since the difference between the spatial representation and real space is what makes gameplay-by-automatic-rules possible. (Aarseth 163; emphasis added)

Although gamespaces are representational, Aarseth foregrounds their "automatic rules" as the fundamental element of these digital environments. Obviously, digital environments simulate physical landscapes: anyone who set foot into the New York of *GTA IV* (2008) or the Washington DC of *The Division 2* (2019) will attest to the realist qualities of these depictions of space. Yet, video game spaces "are not exclusively focused on representation since the representation is always serving the primary purpose of gameplay" (Aarseth 47). Indeed, few players have complained about the inability to shop for groceries, sit at a café to read the daily paper, or the absence of the need to sleep, eat, and hydrate in these games since "[g]ameworld design must defer to gameplay design" (Aarseth 47). Consequentially, Aarseth proposes to understand games as "allegories of space" because "they pretend to portray space in ever more realistic ways but

---

[8] The essay by Espen Aarseth has seen several reprintings. I will be referring to its initial publication but also to a shortened version of his essay from the volume *Space Time Play: Computer Games, Architecture and Urbanism: The Next Level* (2007) edited by Friedrich von Borries, Steffen P. Walz, and Matthias Böttger.

[9] The spatial turn, of course, signals an interest in the exploration of culture with the help of notions of space and place. *La Production de L'Espace* (1974) and its English publication *The Production of Space* (1991) by Henri Lefebvre have become foundational texts in this regard (see Günzel 13).

rely on their deviation from reality in order to make the illusion playable" (169). The scholarship following this sense of space encounters the challenge of how to adequately analyze digital environments as narratives and symbols (representational spaces) but also as experienceable or playable (representations of space).

In his *Video Game Spaces* (2008), Michael Nitsche provides a toolbox for engaging with the narrative and architectural qualities of digital environments. His work furthermore expands the sense of spatiality in the study of video games by considering the physical places where people play and the social spaces playing produces. Similar to Aarseth, Nitsche does not understand video game spaces merely "as foregrounded spectacles based on visual cues such as perspective and parallax but as presented spaces that are assigned an architectural quality" (3).[10] While his work would echo the writing of Henri Lefebvre in conceptualizing 3D space as representation and representational, Nitsche also draws from narratology and aesthetic theory to explore the making of video game spaces.

To understand (the production of) video game spaces, Nitsche first examines the ways in which the narrative of a video game fosters a sense of space and movement therein. Comparable to the sense of navigable space in digital texts Murray describes, Nitsche also understands storytelling in video games first and foremost as movement in space. When completing a quest in a role-playing game, for example, players experience its narrative not merely as a story told by a non-player character but by comprehending "the events a player causes, triggers, and encounters inside a video game space" (Nitsche 7). Secondly, the aesthetic presentation of a video game world complements this narratological approach as the audiovisual production of space often borrows heavily from cinema to organize the game world and the possible interactions with that environment through a "narrative filter" (Nitsche 7). From (digitally simulated) camera positions and movement to sound design and music, video games produce their spaces by adopting the aesthetic conventions of other audiovisual media (see also Bolter and Grusin *Remediation*). Lastly, Nitsche borrows from architectural theory and design to explore the ways in which video games create a sense of presence and immersion in their spaces (see 159–202). As the production of video games increasingly necessitates to design three-dimensional spaces, their creators become a kind of "'spacemaker'" or even "'narrative architect'" and players the "explorer and conqueror of space" (Nitsche 20).[11]

---

10 Despite the rich history of space in video games, Nitsche concentrates on 3D navigational space in his work because he sees "fundamental differences among a space described in a written text, a cinematic space, and an interactive navigable virtual world" (5–6).
11 In addition to offering a set of tools to analyze the multi-layered production of space in video games – the mediated space and the fictional space of video games – Nitsche further draws at-

In his introduction to the essay collection *Ludotopia* (2019), co-edited with Espen Aarseth, Günzel would further expand this thinking about video game spaces. With his emphasis on video game space as "symbolic space" (21), Günzel aims to move away from questions about "the *what?* of space or the *where?* of place" and towards the "*how?* of space" (22; emphasis in the original). Rather than merely using spatial theories to analyze video games as previous scholarship has done, however, he suggests "look[ing] at computer games themselves *as spatial concepts*" (13; emphasis in original). At times, video games are instances of spatial theory.

Whether "environmental storytelling," "narrative environments," "spatial narrative," or "narrative architecture," all these concepts describe the role of space in video games as narrative elements, as aesthetic features, and as part of the gameplay mechanics. Yet, the "highly spatialized storytelling techniques" (201) of video games, as Celia Pearce reminds readers in her essay "Narrative Environments" (2007), create a sense of place that is tied to concrete identities, communities, and various forms of agency. Rather than thinking about how video games produce spaces, then, a Cultural-Studies-inspired approach to these digital landscapes explores the politics of their representation.

From a Cultural Studies perspective, as media scholar Soraya Murray asserts, the production of space in video games implicitly or explicitly "naturalize[s] a certain set of relations through a highly curated framing of the playable environment" (142) as every digital rendering of land eventually "make[s] claims about space, place and landscape" (180). In *On Video Games* (2017), she therefore conceptualizes "*landscapes as ideology*" (142, emphasis in the original). Drawing from the work of W.J.T. Mitchell, Murray eventually situates video game spaces in the broader history of landscape art to conceptualize their ideological work as a cultural practice or a form of doing (see 143–144). This doing includes an examination of the perspective on space, its uses and values within the logic of the game, the ways in which space produces meaning, and the gameplay mechanics to experience space (see Murray 180).[12] Murray, for example, reads the

---

tention to the role of digital environments as a "social space" within a "narrative landscape" (7). *Video Game Spaces* includes a theorization of the locations in which people consume video games, the "*play space*" and the social landscapes games produce as "actions in the virtual world can affect the spaces of other players" (Nitsche 16; emphasis in the original). For another interdisciplinary approach to the study of video game spaces, particularly with an interest in their epistemological potential, see Fraser "Why the Spatial Epistemology of the Video Game Matters" (2011).

12 For an earlier engagement with the ideologies of digital spaces, see Magnet "Playing at Colonization" (2006).

depiction of 1980s Afghanistan in the open-world game *Metal Gear Solid V: The Phantom Pain* as "startlingly devoid of local people, eliminating the possibility of friendly fire or collateral damage;" instead "[t]he land yields resources like medicinal plants and raw diamonds, but is just as easily a site of unexpected danger, such as animal attacks or passing Soviet trucks filled with enemy soldiers" (148–149). While Murray explores the production of space from a critical whiteness perspective in one instance, *Metal Gear Solid V*, Souvik Mukherjee provides a postcolonial look into the spatial ideologies of the medium in general.

With concepts such as Third Space (see Bhabha) and an-Othered space (see Soja), it should not come as a surprise that Postcolonial Studies offer a language to critically engage with spaces in video games.[13] In his *Videogames and Postcolonialism* (2017), Mukherjee connects the study of video games with a postcolonial perspective through the lens of spatiality. For Mukherjee, the history of colonialism and imperialism and the playing of empire in video games share an interest in "the acquisition of geographical space" (29). Mukherjee underscores the imperial logic of spatial expansion, conquest, and exploitation in (some) video games by looking at their gameplay mechanics of "spatial expansion" (29) and by interrogating "who the player is and whose maps are being represented" (31) in these scenarios. As players engage with, shape, and eventually conquer "the maps that *perpetuate* the logic of colonialism instead of challenging it," their "personal [experiences and] histories are intertwined with and constructed out of a colonialist logic" (Mukherjee 31; emphasis in the original). Consequentially, many video games – Mukherjee pays particular attention to the 4X and real-time strategy genres with prominent examples being the *Colonization* and the *Total War* series – provide an experience of space akin to the logic of imperialism by situating players at the helm of European empires at the start of their global expansion. In these games, space is something to be conquered, its natural resources and inhabitants exploited for further expansion by military, diplomatic, and religious means (see Mukherjee 40).[14]

---

13 Despite their rich analytical vocabulary, however, Postcolonial Studies have not found their way into the study of video games on a larger scale. For an overview of Postcolonial approaches to the study of video games see Mukherjee 8–9.

14 Mukherjee also locates various challenges to any straightforward sense of ideological interpellation in playing empire in video games. In real-time strategy games and 4X games, players have the opportunity to re-write history and create alternate versions as they lead the nation of their choice (and these games tend to organize human cultures alongside national identities) to global dominance. Yet, even within the "expansionist logic of empire" video games tend to provide moments, scenarios, and non-player characters who (try to) resist and even challenge the control of the player. Mukherjee sees a "thirdspace of protest" (45) at work when non-player groups or settlements hinder player expansion or challenge their seamless authority as non-

Whereas Mukherjee acknowledges the imperial logic informing the gameplay mechanics in real-time strategy and 4X games, Alenda Y. Chang examines similarly exploitative relations to gamespaces from an ecocritical perspective. In "Games as Environmental Texts" (2011) and *Playing Nature* (2019), Chang describes three principal roles nature and ecological environments play in video games, namely as "background scenery," as "stereotyped landscapes," and as "natural resources" ("Environmental Texts" 58). Digital landscapes in video games often consist simply of hazards and obstacles players need to surpass while their visual portrayal is limited all too often to clichés of an untouched wilderness or a pastoral ideal lacking any regional detail. Possible interactions with these environments furthermore boil down to what use value they have for players (see Chang, "Environmental Texts" 59–60). Consequentially, in-game interactions with the environment script player agency and expression as forms of "dominance," "manipulation," and "mastery of the external environment" (Chang, "Environmental Texts" 60).

The examples of the postcolonial and eco-critical approaches to the study of space showcase the development of the earlier spatial interest in Video Game Studies. The notion of space has been at the heart of the field from early attempts to understand the unique quality of digital texts as a form of movement in space to the spatial turn with its conceptualization of space as a narrative, aesthetic, and interactive feature of the medium. This theoretical tradition and its methodological toolbox inform an essential part of the critical work in this volume. Interest in the production of digital spaces, the experiences of the environments, and their politics of representation, however, also resonate with similar interests in the critical examinations of the production of North American spaces in American Studies.

Space and Spatiality in American Studies

Comparable to the spatial turn in Video Game Studies, American Studies underwent a similar change in recent years. While this shift opened novel perspectives bringing the interdisciplinarity of the field into proximity with, for example, Urban Studies, American Studies possesses a long history of thinking about notions of space. These ideas have been essential in characterizing the experiences

---

player populations protest, revolt, and even acquire independence in various scenarios – a tug-of-war between players pursuing an imperialist logic of expansion and exploitation (even when leading a subaltern group) and moments of resistance to their imperial authority (see 49).

of white settlers in North America and in the development of U.S. culture. Notions of a "wilderness," a "virgin land," a "garden," the "frontier," or a "city upon a hill" date to the early colonial period, continued to shape the making of a national culture in the nineteenth century, and stood at the center of early American Studies in the mid-twentieth century. From the 1950s to the 2010s, the conceptualization of space and spatiality in American Studies shifted from being understood as myths and symbols mediated in U.S. literature and history (North America as a new garden of Eden) to being used as a geo-political framework to debate the nation-state, American exceptionalism, and the transnational turn in the field.[15]

As video game scholars adapted the work of Lefebvre to formulate a spatial understanding of their medium, so can the competing roles of space in American Studies also be described fruitfully with his concepts. The framing of space in the myth-and-symbol school of the 1950s articulates, to borrow from *The Production of Space* (1991) by Lefebvre, a representational sense of space, i.e. "space as directly lived through its associated images and symbols" (39). For Lefebvre, representational space is less concerned with the built or physical environment; instead, it is "making symbolic use of its objects" (39). The myth-and-symbol approach to spatiality in U.S. literature therefore shares with the notion of representational space a tendency "towards more or less coherent *systems of non-verbal symbols and signs*" (39; emphasis added). In the wake of the myth-and-symbol school, American Studies scholars challenged the representational power of the chosen myths and symbols as too narrow to encapsulate the diverse literary (and cultural) production of the nineteenth century.[16] Revisionist interventions within the field since the 1970s also foregrounded, in the words of Lefebvre, the multiple spatial practices in North America to adjust, critique, or even dismiss notions of "the garden" or "the frontier." In highlighting the possibilities of the borderland or in linking U.S. culture and literature to U.S. imperialism and advocating for transnational perspectives in the field, American Studies scholars explore the multiple local, national, and global "spatial sets characteristic of [their] social formation" (Lefebvre 33). Recent years have also seen attempts to

---

15 For an introduction to the development of the video game industry and digital play in the United States, see, for example, *The Video Game Explosion* (2007), *From Playgrounds to PlayStation* (2016), *Atari Age* (2017), or *Gamer Nation* (2019).
16 Revisionist approaches to American Studies questioned whether a set of tropes, such as "virgin land" or "the machine in the garden," could be representative of American society – and whether canonical authors could actually offer a "radical resistance" against the rationalization of human life as the "[h]ighbrow writers in the tradition of the American Renaissance [...] [were] described as racist, sexist, imperialistic and complicit with the system" (Fluck 79).

bridge the divide between a representational view of space and the representation of space when thinking about the ways in which texts as well as built environments script stories and actions. In the following, I will spotlight some of the moments when notions of space shifted in American Studies.

Scholarship about the early colonial period in North American has shown the long history of European spatial concepts informing perceptions of North America. Oliver Scheiding, for example, examines the reorganization of Christian maps of the world from the Middle Ages to incorporate the North American continent after 1492. Scheiding reads early mappings of and storytelling about North America as cultural practices shaping "the colonial imagination of British America" (1). Scheiding refers to a "geography of salvation" in the writing of Richard Hakluyt about North America which fostered "the colonial imagination of British America and serves as a point of departure for understanding the global dynamics of empire building" (2). Similarly, the maps of Theodor de Bry – depicting North American spaces and people – framed Native Americans as "the descendants of Noah who have only forgotten social virtues as they turned into hunters over time" (Scheiding 14). Through maps, illustrations, and paintings, sixteenth- and seventeenth-century Europeans wrote North America into their perception of the world. For Ralph Bauer, the mapping of the North American continent complicated and ruptured European systems of knowledge production. More importantly, his *The Cultural Geography of Colonial American Literatures* (2003) argues that "the transformations in the organization of early modern knowledge must in part be understood as a response to the distinct geo-political questions raised by European settler colonialism in the Americas" (3). Knowledge and knowledge production in the colonial period should not only be understood as an expression of social hierarchies informing the political organization of the European empires. Epistemic systems were also organized "in geographic space in early modern settler empires;" Bauer understands colonial notions of science or "the early modem scientific paradigm" as "territorialized economies of knowledge production, 'empires of truth' that were structured by a geo-political order that might be characterized as forms of epistemic mercantilism" (4). In addition to placing the formation of knowledge within frameworks of historical developments and change – i.e. time – Bauer underscores "the spatial dialectics that were foundational in the making of modernity" (12).

Although indebted to European notions of space, the nineteenth century experienced a popularization of spatial language in an attempt to formulate a decidedly U.S. American perspective. One of the most (in)famous examples, the essay "The Significance of the Frontier in American History" (1893) by Frederick Jackson Turner, describes the process of becoming a U.S. American as a practice of westward movement into a frontier. For Turner, life on the frontier remade European immigrants into U.S. Americans through a form of rebirth fostered by the unique qualities of that space. Initially, the frontier experience overwhelmed the European immigrants, depriving them of their heritage, and forcing them to adopt the ways of the Natives for survival. As the frontier wilderness changes the settler completely, "the outcome is not the old Europe, not simply the development of Germanic germs, [...] [but] a new product that is American" (Turner 61). By stripping the settlers of their past, as historian Richard White explains, the frontier gives "them a new and uniform set of American characteristics [individualism and democracy]" (26). Writing from and about a white Eurocentric perspective (even as he hoped to substitute the former with a white U.S. American perspective), Turner was not the first and would not be the last scholar to link the search for an American national character to space.

Well into the twentieth century, notions of a "virgin land," a "wilderness," a "garden," or the "frontier" continued to indicate the centrality of spatial conceptions in American Studies. I am particularly thinking of Henry Nash Smith's *Virgin Land* (1950), Perry Miller's *Errand into the Wilderness* (1956) and Leo Marx' *The Machine in the Garden* (1964). While these scholars are usually subsumed under the label of the myth-and-symbol school, strikingly, their work refers to and revolves surprisingly often around notions of space in U.S. literature.[17] Space in the myth-and-symbol thinking is mostly an imagined landscape – the pastoral for example – with "symbolic power" in that these spaces bring "the political and the psychic dissonance associated with the onset of industrialization into a single pattern of meaning" (Marx 30). Rather than embracing earlier ideas of space uncritically, these scholars bemoaned that the myth of a wilderness, a virgin land, or said frontier, in the words of Nash Smith, "ceased very early to be useful in interpreting American society as a whole because they offered no intellectual apparatus for taking account of the industrial revolution" (259). Eventually, the myth-and-symbol school engaged (not only) with spatial myths about the United States in nineteenth-century literature because the frontier, the garden, or the virgin land, i.e. the agrarian myth in U.S. culture, have "appeared with increasing frequency in the service of a reactionary or false ideology, thereby helping to mask the real problems of an industrial civilization" (Marx 7). The myth-and-symbol school hence cared little for a theorization of physical environments. They preferred to explore the mythologization of spaces in nineteenth-

---

17 Even the last publication in the spirit of this first generation of American Studies scholars, *Brooklyn Bridge: Fact and Symbol* (1965) by Alan Trachtenberg, refers to a distinct space to think about U.S. culture.

century literature in order to formulate a critique of mid-twentieth-century capitalism.[18]

Revisionist scholars of the 1970s and 1980s would formulate their challenge of the myth-and-symbol consensus with attention to spatial language. Indeed, even as numerous scholars from Annette Kolodny to Gloria Anzaldúa, Patricia Limerick, and Marie Louise Pratt have highlighted the countless experiences complicating frontier stories of westward expansion, notions of a virgin land, or gardens endangered by technology, their works also introduce novel spatial conceptions of North America and the United States as a contact zone or borderland, thereby exemplifying the persistence of a spatial language. Conceptually speaking, however, these revisions also challenged the merely allegorical understanding of space as a symbol for ways of writing (and reading) North American landscapes. While the feminist intervention of the 1970s would still operate under the paradigm of space as an allegory albeit one of gender, revisionist scholars of the 1980s would increasingly ask what other spaces and experiences thereof exist in the United States to question the function of national boundaries and frameworks altogether. Spaces, as video game scholars would later maintain, did not merely tell stories and were not only representational.

In the 1970s, Annette Kolodny criticized the prevailing notions of space in U.S. literature and in American Studies as predominantly male-centered metaphors and fantasies. In *The Lay of the Land* (1975), Kolodny traces the myth of the garden to early colonial writings about North America underscoring its gendered connotations. The idea of North America as a lost garden of Eden and its use as metaphor for a "regression from the cares of adult life and a return to the primal warmth of womb or breast in a feminine landscape" (Kolodny 6) first appeared in promotional texts hoping to lure settlers to the continent. Kolodny situates this framing of the North American landscape within the broader colonial project of the sixteenth and seventeenth centuries and the westward expansion

---

[18] Since the 1970s, however, scholars have similarly emphasized the "reactionary or false ideology" embedded within the myth-and-symbol approach. Examining the status of space in the myth-and-symbol school, Richard Slotkin complicates the notion of the frontier in proposing a wider, more inclusive perspective in his *Regeneration Through Violence* (1973). Instead of focusing entirely on the function of the myth of the frontier (or, by extension, of a virgin land or the garden) in U.S. literature, his work points to the importance of thinking about the implied assumptions and perspectives – or social structures – operating in these concepts. In his view, (canonical) literature was not merely using the myth of the frontier to formulate a critique of the longing for a pastoral past in an industrialized society but failed to acknowledge the history of economic exploitation, the racism of slavery and Segregation, environmental destruction, and Native American genocide (see Slotkin 5). For another early critique of the myth-and-symbol school, see Sklar "American Studies and the Realities of America."

of the eighteenth and nineteenth centuries to ask rhetorically whether a need existed "to experience the land as a nurturing, giving maternal breast because of the threatening, alien, and potentially emasculating terror of the unknown?" (9). Indeed, the depiction of the North American landscape in literature and culture, Kolodny maintains, constitutes "probably America's oldest and most cherished fantasy: a daily reality of harmony between man and nature based on an experience of the land as essentially feminine" (4). In her feminist reading, Kolodny interrogates the male premises informing the literary and scholarly productions of space.

In the 1980s, various scholars continued to follow this path of questioning the prevalent ideas about U.S. American space. In *The Legacy of Conquest* (1987), for example, historian Patricia Limerick challenges not only the Turnerian notion of the frontier as a "civilizing" process but the entire idea of westward movement as progress. For Limerick, Turner and his frontier thesis privileged the perspective of "English-speaking white men" (21) and "agrarian settlement and folk democracy in the comparatively well watered Midwest" (21) at the expense of a plurality of other people, spaces, and experiences. Limerick therefore prefers to understand the American West as an intersection of multiple cultures all shaped by the pursuit of conquest (see 27). In *Borderlands/La Frontera* (1987), Gloria Anzaldúa places the movement (and displacement) of indigenous and Mexican people at the heart of the history of the North American continent. For Anzaldúa, borders do not separate two irreconcilable opposites as Western historians tended to rationalize European colonial and imperial conquest but are products of cultural, economic, political, and social struggles. Consequently, indigenous and Mexican people (not only) in the U.S. American South have been and continue to inhabit a borderland (see Anzaldúa 3). Where Turner depicted the frontier as a vast and uninhabited space of immense transitory power but also in need of cultivation by white settlers, Anzaldúa challenges this clear-cut distinction foregrounding the conceptual work the frontier vocabulary does: "Borders are set up to define the places that are safe and unsafe, to distinguish *us* from *them*" (Anzaldúa 25; emphasis in the original). Lastly, in her essay "Arts of the Contact Zone" (1991), Mary Louise Pratt introduces the notion of the contact zone to expand on what Anzaldúa labeled borderlands. For Pratt, the contact zone also refers to "social spaces where cultures meet, clash, and grapple with each other, often in contexts of highly asymmetrical relations of power, such as colonialism, slavery, or their aftermaths" (34), but she extends the contact zone to all parts of the world. Also, whereas Anzaldúa proposed a new conceptualization of border spaces, Pratt foregrounds the modes of expression constitutive of the contact zone or, its "literate arts" (37). These arts include "[a]utoethnography, transculturation, critique, collaboration, bilingualism, mediation, parody, denunciation, imaginary dialogue, vernacular expression" (Pratt 37).[19]

Alongside these interventions, scholarship further complicated notions of space in literature, culture, and American Studies as expressions of an imperial ideology. The essay collection *Cultures of United States Imperialism* (1993) edited by Donald Pease and Amy Kaplan, for example, faults the myth-and-symbol school for its formulation of an American exceptionalism and early American Studies for contributing to the dissemination of U.S. imperialism.[20] Whereas reformulations of the role of space in American Studies in the 1970s and 1980s underlined the plurality of experiences and perspectives within North America, the early colonies, and the nation state, Kaplan formulates her critique by embedding the United States and its history in a global network of European colonialism and Western slavery (see 6).

In this critique of American Studies, the conception of space constitutes the central focus of debate. The myth-and-symbol school not only omitted a plurality of perspectives in centering their study of U.S. literature and culture around the garden, the wilderness, or the frontier; the approach also situated the (history of the) United States outside of global networks of exchange and exploitation. Spatiality, then, as Klaus Benesch asserts in his introduction to *Space in America* (2005), is "perhaps the most important single driving force not only to build a new nation but to imagine one" (18). Given the debates surrounding the premises of American Studies, one may add that spatiality is also "the most important single driving force" to critically interrogate (the idea of) the nation.

---

[19] In *The New American Studies* (2002), John Carlos Rowe develops a comparative approach towards American Studies by discussing the works of Bhabha, Lauter, and Pratt. However, Rowe, ultimately, finds the concept of the "contact zone" most intriguing for a comparative perspective because it avoids the traps of multicultural pluralism, melting-pot assimilationism, and a total fragmentation of evaluation (one culture, one evaluation system). The curriculum of courses should thus focus on texts "through which cultural confrontations have been negotiated historically in the United States" (Rowe 14). Rowe also argues that in all major research fields dealing with U.S. culture and society the contact zone presents a useful tool (Rowe names African American Studies, Chicana/o Studies, Native American Studies, Asian-American Studies specifically) (see 15–16).

[20] For further critique of American exceptionalism, see, for example, David M. Wrobel *The End of American Exceptionalism* (1993), Daniel T. Rodgers "Exceptionalism" (1998), Rowe *Post-Nationalist American Studies* (2000), Donald E. Pease and Robyn Wiegman *The Futures of American Studies* (2002), Deborah Madsen "American Exceptionalism and Multiculturalism" (2003), Amy Kaplan "The Tenacious Grasp of American Exceptionalism" (2004), William V. Spanos *American Exceptionalism in the Age of Globalization* (2008), Donald E. Pease *The New American Exceptionalism* (2009), Winfried Fluck *Romance with America?* (2009).

Benesch captured the quintessential role of space at a moment when American Studies would further expand its spatial vocabulary. Following the critique of imperialist premises within the field, American Studies scholars increasingly situated their analyses of U.S. literature and culture in hemispheric and transnational contexts. This approach invited critical exploration of the United States and its cultures from a global perspective in order to de-center the nation-state. In her presidential address to the American Studies Association, "Crossroads of Cultures" (2004), Shelly Fisher Fishkin advocated for a transnational shift in the field to enable scholars to comprehend American culture and literature "from vantage points beyond its borders" (20) and within broader networks.[21] While a post-nationalist conceptualization of American Studies continues to be a widely shared understanding of the field, not all scholarship embraced the challenge to the nation-state as optimistically as Fisher Fishkin did. A critical view of globalization, the post-national, and the transnational cautions, in the words of Donald Pease, to "enshroud the structural injustices of the contemporary global economic order within the cosmopolitan ethos of a transnational democracy that had not yet materialized" (15). The spatial vocabulary of borderlands, crossroads, and the transnational asks American Studies, to borrow from Janice Radway's 1998 presidential address, what is in its name.[22]

So far, my overview has indicated a tension at the heart of the notion of space in American Studies. Some perspectives foreground the representational or symbolic potential of spatial vocabulary within literary and cultural texts; others may prefer to approach issues of space with an understanding of "their formal systems of relations," i.e. their lived experiences and ideological formations, in mind. Recent years have seen attempts to bridge this divide. In doing, the work by Barbara Buchenau and Jens Gurr offers a conceptual language to think productively about video game spaces as representational, as representative, and as practices.

---

[21] For further transnational interventions see also Walter D. Mignolo's *Local Histories/Global Designs: Coloniality, Subaltern Knowledges, and Border Thinking* (2000) or Ramón Saldívar's *The Borderlands of Culture* (2006).
[22] In the early 2000s, for example, contributors to the volume *Post-Nationalist American Studies* (2000) cautioned that the national "cannot be easily wished away by the application of the *post-* prefix" (Curiel et al. 2; emphasis in the original). Similarly, a critical view of globalization, the post-national, and the transnational would find articulation, for example, in the edited volume *Re-Framing the Transnational Turn in American Studies* (2011). In his introduction, Pease formulates a cautionary assessment of the transnational turn in American Studies when he writes that "no isomorphic relation [exists] between the transnational as a signifier and what it is made to signify" (6).

The examination of the mediated, the lived, and the representational qualities of space is at the heart of the urban scholarship Buchenau and Gurr pursue.[23] Their approach to space lends itself most explicitly to a study of spatiality in video games. In their essay "City Scripts" (2016), Buchenau and Gurr inquire into the "prospects of bringing American studies' current focus on media, materiality and knowledge into a structured conversation with" the narrative turn in Urban Studies, i.e. its "increasing attention to story, narrative and space" (397). Buchenau and Gurr therefore not only examine the mediations of urban spaces but also explore the narratives that built environments tell as they connect a spatial turn in American Studies with a story turn in Urban Studies (see "City Scripts" 395–398).[24] To do so, they introduce the notion of "scripting." Scripts are, Buchenau and Gurr explain, "pieces and systems of writing" but can also designate "social roles" or function "as theatrical and cinematic manuscripts and typescripts, maps and other visual media" ("City Scripts" 409). As scripting describes a variety of literary and cultural practices, the concept eventually "permits further insights into literature's ability to tentatively build scenarios and thereby preview future actions" (Buchenau and Gurr, "City Scripts" 409). This scripting of scenarios or prescription of actions, however, not only applies to literary and cultural texts. The notion of "scripting" also indicates a horizon of possible interactions with and within urban environments as scripts provide insights into the ways in which built environments "predicate human behavior and social interactions" (Buchenau and Gurr, "City Scripts" 396, 409).[25] Video games, with their imaginary yet simultaneously built environments and their pre-

---

[23] The research group *Scripts for Postindustrial Urban Futures: American Models, Transatlantic Interventions* explores the imaginative strategies and narrative scenarios which the centers of old industries (steel, coal and cars) in the United States and Germany are devising to forge paths into their futures. *City Scripts* is a joint endeavor of the American Studies Departments of the University Alliance Ruhr (Duisburg-Essen, Bochum, Dortmund). The research group is led by Prof. Dr. Barbara Buchenau.

[24] Buchenau and Gurr call for greater scholarly attention "to questions of form and shape as they affect both, narrativity and the built environment" with particular interest in the development of "a better understanding of the conjunctions between matters of materiality and matters of media, narrative and representation" ("City Scripts" 398).

[25] In their essay "On the Textuality of American Cities and Their Others" (2018) they further elaborate that scripts function "as powerful unconscious or semi-conscious guides of individual and collective human behavior" (136). Although many daily practices, such as a restaurant visit, prescribe social interactions, Buchenau and Gurr are particularly interested in the various ways the infrastructure of urban environments and the "detailed guidelines about proper usage of standard urban commodities and amenities [...] script what urban dwellers do and don't do" ("Textuality" 136) – as architectural and urban scripts "initiate various sets of action" ("Textuality" 148).

scribed interactions with the game world (and other players), exemplify this conception of scripting.

The story turn in Urban Studies and the spatial turn in American Studies resonate with the understanding of space in video games sketched earlier. For one, video game spaces tell stories. Whether video games simulate concrete cities or draw on imagined worlds from science fiction to the fantastic, as the notion of environmental storytelling argues, space is the essential element of narration. Spaces are furthermore not merely digital approximations of built environments or imaginative worlds to escape to but carry complex cultural connotations as the Cultural Studies approach to video games demonstrates. Digital spaces are never empty; they possess meaning. Comparable to literature, cinema, and other media, video games furthermore "build scenarios" and allow players to "preview future actions." Cultural and social scripts find playful expression in digital spaces.

Yet, through their gameplay mechanics, video games also script the possible interactions players have with their environments (and other players). Comparable to the usage of physical spaces, video games prescribe concrete interactions with the game world – whether as minute reproductions of urban spaces or in the form of a hostile extraterrestrial wilderness. This scripting of player action via the gameplay mechanics may be limited to running and jumping to complete a level as fast as possible or may follow scripts empowering players to re-shape their digital environments completely.[26]

To think about spatiality in video games necessitates and fosters interdisciplinary approaches. Video games have been about space from their inception. Video Games Studies have been similarly wrestling with space as scholars continue to develop their critical vocabulary. American Studies not only shares some of that vocabulary for studying space but possesses a long history of thinking about the production of space. In exploring the complexity of video game spaces and by drawing from Video Games Studies, this volume also hopes to deepen the understanding of spatiality in American Studies.

---

26 Games, however, not only script the proper modes of interacting with the game world, players also re-script these possible interactions for their advantages or pleasure. For example, speedrunning – the attempt to complete a game as fast as possible while using any means available – may include ignoring most of the existing game mechanics or adopting them to further progression. Most notably may be the deliberate killing of the player character to advance in the speedrun or to exploit glitches (programming errors) in the game.

Contributions

This volume is divided into three parts. Each section engages with a concrete feature of video game spaces from an American Studies perspective. Whether traditional spatial tropes, environmental storytelling, or the performative uses of physical space, each part also revolves around a distinct set of video games. The first section focuses exclusively on contemporary mainstream games by AAA companies, while the second part expands its scope to include independent and smaller scale productions. The last section moves away from traditional video games to examine gaming apps as well as the artistic use of video game spaces in stage design and puppetry, in the theater, and the museum.

The first section collects essays critically engaged with traditional notions of space in American Studies. The frontier myth plays a central role here as contributions interrogate its nostalgic, imperial, and gendered dimensions in a variety of contemporary video game franchises. Similarly, video game companies advertise the agency to traverse and shape such vast spaces as an empowering experience for players while narrowing the possible interactions to exploitative practices so intimately tied to the spatial history of the United States. The expansive and post-apocalyptic frontier spaces of recent open-world games, however, also create moments of introspection allowing for critical reflections of the digital landscapes and their relationships with the player character as well as the player.

The first part opens with Sören Schoppmeier and his engagement with the nostalgic quality of the frontier myth in contemporary video games. In "Notes on the State of Montana: The U.S. American Spatial Imagination and the Retrotopia of *Far Cry 5*," Schoppmeier focuses on the depiction of spaces and interactions with places that never existed in the romanticized video game version of Montana, thereby exemplifying the retrotopian character of *Far Cry 5*.

Felix Zimmermann also focuses on the frontier as a playable space. "Ethical Boredom in the Wilderness: Treating *Red Dead Redemption 2* as an Ambience Action Game" not only reads the frontier as a narrative device as well as a site of violence and settler colonialism in the Western game. The essay also understands the frontier as a space of introspection since its vast traversable landscape asks for little engagement from players, thereby fostering an experience of ethical boredom.

Nathalie Aghoro continues this cluster of essays about the mediation of the frontier myth in video games. In "On Postapocalyptic Frontiers in *Horizon Zero Dawn*," Aghoro argues that the projection of the frontier myth onto a postapocalyptic landscape in the video game undermines its hegemonial status as the spatial knowledge players acquire in their exploration of the game world foregrounds the ecological precarity stemming from the exploitation inherent in Western expansionism.

David Callahan expands discussions of the frontier myth by examining its imperial dimension in "Owning Global Spaces and the Frontier in *Uncharted 4: A Thief's End*." Callahan critically probes the function of non-European spaces as playgrounds of masculine bravado by situating the protagonist of *Uncharted 4* within the long Euro-American history of imperial adventure stories and the frontier myth from James Fenimore Cooper to Frederick Jackson Turner and Edgar Rice Burroughs in particular.

Andrei Nae continues the examination of imperial themes of the frontier myth in video games Callahan began but shifts from a critical assessment of masculinity to femininity. In "From Male to Colonial Gaze: The Intersection of Patriarchy and Colonial Discourse in the Rebooted *Tomb Raider* Video Game Series," Nae questions whether the most recent incarnation of Lara Croft in the *Tomb Raider* series presents a progressive femininity by foregrounding the imperial discourse encoded in the gamespaces the heroine traverses.

Lastly, the ideological premises of adventuring in a world of seemingly endless opportunities stand at the center of "The Inevitable Fate of the 'Dragonborn:' Selling Player Agency in *The Elder Scrolls V: Skyrim*." In her essay, Hanne Nijtmans questions the promise of player agency *Skyrim* advertises by foregrounding the absence of any meaningful action players can take in the game and the limited possibilities they have in shaping this expansive game world. This kind of agency, Nijtmans argues, fosters an exploitative relationship with the gamespace.

Part II of this volume shifts from long-standing spatial myths in U.S. culture to an exploration of video games and their ability to narrate stories through their spaces. Contributions examine the role of in-game maps to make spaces readable and to shape the understanding of the landscape they symbolize. Mapping, however, is not only a cartographical practice but can also serve as a tool to navigate the sprawling and multi-nodal plots of contemporary video games. Although historically maps and mapping have often functioned as means of conquest, contributions in this section shift attention from the exploitative to the collaborative potential of gamespaces. The stories inscribed in these digital environments can derive from player interactions, but modes of environmental storytelling similarly draw from long-standing literary traditions and discourses. This section hence also sees contributors examining the role of the Gothic mode in video games or the potential of digital spaces to create culturally-hybrid environments. Given its interest in unconventional spatial modes of storytelling, this section shifts away from the most popular mainstream games and sees an increased interest in smaller, independently produced titles.

Maps, mapping, and their role in telling stories are intimately linked to the exploration of open-world games, Damien Schlarb shows in his contribution. Drawing on scholarship about cultural geography in Early American Studies, "Filling Out the Map: The Anxiety of Situatedness and the Topological Poesis of Cartographic Maps in Video Games" examines the ways in which in-game maps render space legible, demarcate playable areas, encourage exploration, and express spatial politics.

While also examining the role of mapping in video games, Juliane Borosch moves from spatial to narrative mapping. In "*Detroit: Become Human* – Orientational Mapping in the City and (Hi)Story," she explores the ways in which Detroit is re-imagined in an alternate, science fiction future not only through its landmarks but also through a sprawling narrative that players are able to map with the help of various in-game tools. Eventually, *Detroit: Become Human* presents its various stories as navigable spaces.

A similar interest in the ideologies of space guides Stefan Schubert's "'Playing for Space:' Negotiating and Narrativizing Space in *One Hour One Life*." In his contribution, however, Schubert examines practices of spatial exploration and management not as conflict and struggle but as cooperation. As player-characters only exist for a single hour, *One Hour One Life* fosters collaboration within the game and communication outside leading to communal spatial practices.

In contrast to the interest in mapping and collaborative spaces as narrative practices, Greta Kaisen examines the use of the Gothic mode in *Gone Home* as players discover the haunting past of a mansion by exploring the various spaces of the house. In "There is no Place like *Gone Home*: Exploring Gothic Settings in Video Games," Kaisen not only reads the setting as a defining feature of Gothic texts but also scrutinizes the restrictions to movement, the haunting presence players leave behind in the game world, and the nostalgic tone of the locations as part of a digital American Gothic.

Florian Deckers looks at the spatial design of *Grim Fandango* and its depiction of a culturally-hybrid urbanity rarely present in video games. "Exploring the Digital Land of the Dead: Hybrid Pan-Latinidad in *Grim Fandango*" analyzes the hybrid formations of various North American cultures in the built environment of a metropolis for the dead located in the architecture of its buildings, the character design of its inhabitants, and the sound design of its scenes.

Part III concludes the exploration of spatiality in video games by moving away from the TV or computer screen. Contributions focus on the intersection of digital play and physical space as people use apps to exercise in urban environments or plant vegetables in virtual gardens only to harvest actual produce.

Essays not only critically interrogate the cultural tropes embedded in these spatial practices but simultaneously examine the ways in which video games spaces shape our perception of the world around us. More explorative in nature than the previous parts, contributors sketch the various uses of video game spaces as a workshopping tool in stage design or a training ground for puppetry. Similarly, this section introduces the perspective of artists creating experimental theater inspired by jump-and-run games and curators offer insights into their decisions when arranging museum spaces for video game exhibitions. All essays share a desire to move beyond an analysis of virtual gamespaces to explore the manyfold adaptions and creative uses of digital landscapes in artistic, commercial, institutional, and urban spaces. Consequentially, Part III brings American Studies into conversation with other disciplines, most notably Urban and Performance Studies, foregrounding the interdisciplinary nature of the field and the study of space.

In "Breaking Worlds Three Ways," Michael Nitsche explores the potential of video game spaces for artistic and creative work. They function as workshops in stage design but also help to conceptualize the blending of the physical and the digital world in everyday life as social environments or they become performance spaces for non-human agents such as virtual puppets. In his examples, Nitsche fuses video game spaces with Performance Studies, new materialism, or the posthuman to indicate the potentialities of the medium.

Maria Sulimma continues to explore the intersection of physical and digital spaces, albeit with a critical look at the commercialization of these spaces in fitness apps. "Surviving the City: *Zombies, Run!* and the Horrors of Urban Exercise" particularly discusses the liberating potential the running app *Zombies, Run!* possesses for female runners by re-scripting physical urban spaces as fictional post-apocalyptic environments in its narrative, design, and interface.

The entanglement of production, marketing, and consumption inscribed at the intersection of physical and digital spaces moves to the center of the next contribution as Elisabeth Haefs looks at the gamification of gardening and small-scale agriculture. In "'#Gameüse:' Planting the Digital Garden," Haefs interrogates the use of the pastoral ideal in the marketing of *IPGarten*, a start-up provider of all-inclusive gardening services, as well as the digital interface consumers use to manage and surveil the cultivation of their parcels.

Drawing from a performative approach to digital gamespaces, Kirsten Möller's "Performative Playground: Narrative Spaces in Theater Games" introduces the work of the artist collective AnnaKpok and their use of the narrative and interactive features of video games for the theater. Möller particularly details the ways in which space shapes the creative process of adapting video games to the traditional stage as well as to unconventional sites of performance such as repurposed buildings.

In a related manner, Lauren Kolodkin and Ryan Linthicum conclude this section by examining the intersections of video game worlds and physical space in the museum. In "Museum Space Invaders: Video Gaming at the Smithsonian American Art Museum," they present their curatorial work in the *The Art of Video Games* exhibition at the Smithsonian American Art Museum, detailing the design decisions going into the exhibition as well as discussing their choices of exhibited games.

Soraya Murray concludes this volume with her coda "Disoriented in the Field of Play." Murray brings together the various intellectual threads addressed throughout the chapters to describe possible future trajectories for the study of video game spaces. Central to her intervention is an invitation to scholars engaging with digital environments not only to critically examine familiar spatial tropes as this volume attempts to do. In addition, Murray calls for an engagement with unfamiliar, disorientating, possibly uncomfortable digital environments and the affective, phenomenological, or contemplative frictions they produce. Eventually, her coda asks to move beyond the all too familiar comfort zone of critical distance and encourages scholars to "point us someplace else."

Works Cited

Aarseth, Espen. "Allegories of Space: The Question of Spatiality in Computer Games." *Cybertext Yearbook 2000*, edited by Markku Eskelinen and Raine Koskimaa, Research Center for Contemporary Culture, Jyväskylä, 2001, pp. 152–171.

Aarseth, Espen. "Allegories of Space: The Question of Spatiality in Computer Games." *Space Time Play: Computer Games, Architecture and Urbanism: The Next Level*, edited by Friedrich von Borries, Steffen P. Walz, and Matthias Böttger, Birkhäuser, Basel, 2007, pp. 44–47.

Aarseth, Espen and Stephan Günzel, eds. *Ludotopia: Spaces, Places and Territories in Computer Games*. Transcript, 2019.

Anzaldúa, Gloria. *Borderlands/La Frontera: The New Mestiza*. Aunt Lute Books, San Francisco, 1987.

Bauer, Ralph. *The Cultural Geography of Colonial American Literatures: Empire, Travel, Modernity*. Cambridge University Press, 2003.

Benesch, Klaus. "The Concept of Space in American Culture: An Introduction." *Space in America: Theory, History, Culture*, edited by Klaus Benesch and Kerstin Schmidt, Rodopi, 2005, pp. 11–24.

Borries, Friedrich von, Steffen P. Walz, and Matthias Böttger, editors. *Space Time Play: Computer Games, Architecture and Urbanism: The Next Level*. Birkhäuser, Basel, 2007.

Bolter, Jay David and Richard Grusin. *Remediation: Understanding New Media*. The MIT Press, 2000.

Buchenau, Barbara, and Jens Martin Gurr. "City Scripts: Urban American Studies and the Conjunction of Textual Strategies and Spatial Processes." *Urban Transformations in the USA.: Spaces, Communities, Representation*s, edited by Julia Sattler, transcript, 2016, pp. 395–420.

Buchenau, Barbara, and Jens Martin Gurr. "On the Textuality of American Cities and Their Others: A Disputation." *Projecting American Studies: Essays on Theory, Method, and Practice*, edited by Frank Kelleter and Alexander Starre, Universitatsverlag Winter, 2018, pp. 135–54.

Carson, Don. "Environmental Storytelling: Creating Immersive 3D Worlds Using Lessons Learned from the Theme Park Industry." *Gamasutra*, 1 March 2000.

Chang, Alenda Y. "Games as Environmental Texts." *Qui Parle: Critical Humanities and Social Sciences*, vol. 19, no. 2, 2011, pp. 57–84.

Chang, Alenda Y. *Playing Nature: Ecology in Video Games*. University of Minnesota Press, 2019.

Curiel, Barbara Brinson, David Kazanjian, Katherine Kinney, Steven Mailloux, Jay Mechling, John Carlos Rowe, George Sánchez, Shelley Streeby, and Henry Yu. Introduction. *Post-Nationalist American Studies*, by John Carlos Rowe, University of California Press, 2000, pp. 1–22.

Domsch, Sebastian. "Space and Narrative in Computer Games." *Ludotopia: Spaces, Places and Territories in Computer Games*, edited by Espen Aarseth and Stephan Günzel, transcript, 2019, pp. 103–123.

Eskelinen, Markku. "The Gaming Situation." *Game Studies*, vol. 1, no. 1, 2001, no page. www.gamestudies.org/0101/eskelinen/. Accessed 3 July 2020.

Fisher Fishkin, Shelley. "Crossroads of Cultures: The Transnational Turn in American Studies – Presidential Address to the American Studies Association, November 12, 2004." *American Quarterly*, vol. 57, no. 1, pp. 17–57.

Fluck, Winfried. *Romance with America? Essays on Culture, Literature, and American Studies*, edited by Laura Bieger and Johannes Voelz, Winter, 2009.

Fluck, Winfried, Donald E. Pease, and John Carlos Rowe, editors. *Re-Framing the Transnational Turn in American Studies*. Dartmouth College Press, 2011.

Fraser, Benjamin. "Why the Spatial Epistemology of the Video Game Matters: Metis, Video Game Space and Interdisciplinary Theory." *Journal of Gaming and Virtual Worlds*, vol. 3, no. 2, 2011, pp. 93–106.

Günzel, Stephan. Introduction. *Ludotopia: Spaces, Places and Territories in Computer Games*, by Espen Aarseth and Stephan Günzel, transcript, 2019, pp. 7–12.

Jenkins, Henry. "Game Design as Narrative Architecture." *First Person: New Media as Story, Performance, and Game*, edited by Noah Wardrip-Fruin and Pat Harrigan, MIT Press, 2004, pp. 118–130.

Jenkins, Henry. "Narrative Spaces." *Space Time Play: Computer Games, Architecture and Urbanism: The Next Level*, edited by Friedrich von Borries, Steffen P. Walz, and Matthias Böttger, Birkhäuser, Basel, 2007, pp. 56–60.

Juul, Jesper. "Games Telling stories? A Brief Note on Games and Narratives." *Game Studies*, vol. 1, no. 1, 2001, no page. www.gamestudies.org/0101/juul-gts/. Accessed 3 July 2020.

Kaplan, Amy. Introduction. *Cultures of United States Imperialism*, edited by Amy Kaplan and Donald E. Pease., Duke University Press, 1993, pp. 3–21.

Kaplan, Amy. "The Tenacious Grasp of American Exceptionalism: A Response to Djelal Kadir, 'Defending America against its Devotees'." *Comparative American Studies*, vol. 2, no. 2, 2004, pp. 153–159.

Kaplan, Amy and Donald E. Pease, editors. *Cultures of United States Imperialism*. Duke University Press, 1993.

Kolodny, Annette. *The Lay of the Land: Metaphor as Experience and History in American Life and Letters*. University of North Carolina Press, 1975.

Lefebvre, Henri. *The Production of Space*. Blackwell, 1991.

Limerick, Patricia. *The Legacy of Conquest: The Unbroken Past of the American West*. W. W. Norton, 1987.

Lipsetz, George. *How Racism Takes Place*. Temple University Press, 2011.

Madsen, Deborah. "American Exceptionalism and Multiculturalism: Myths and Realities." *Representing Realities: Essays on American Literature, Art and Culture*, edited by Beverly Maeder, Gunter Narr Verlag, 2003, pp. 177–188.

Magnet, Shoshana. "Playing at Colonization: Interpreting Imaginary Landscapes in the Video Game *Tropico*." *Journal of Communication Inquiry*, vol. 30, no. 2, 2006, pp. 142–62.

Marx, Leo. *The Machine in the Garden: Technology and the Pastoral Ideal in America*. 1964. Oxford University Press, 2000.

Mignolo, Walter D. *Local Histories/Global Designs: Coloniality, Subaltern Knowledges, and Border Thinking*. 2000. Princeton University Press, 2012.

Miller, Perry. *Errand into the Wilderness*. The Belknap Press of Harvard University Press, 1956.

Mukherjee, Souvik. *Videogames and Postcolonialism: Empire Plays Back*. Palgrave Macmillan, 2017.

Murray, Janet H. *Hamlet on the Holodeck: The Future of Narrative in Cyberspace*. The MIT Press, 1997.

Murray, Soraya. *On Video Games: The Visual Politics of Race, Gender and Space*. I.B. Tauris, 2017.

Newman, Michael Z. *Atari Age: The Emergence of Video Games in America*. The MIT Press, 2017.

Nitsche, Michael. *Video Game Spaces: Image, Play, and Structure in 3D Game Worlds*. The MIT Press, 2008.

Pearce, Celia. "Narrative Environments: From Disneyland to *World of Warcraft*." *Space Time Play: Computer Games, Architecture and Urbanism: The Next Level*, edited by Friedrich von Borries, Steffen P. Walz, and Matthias Böttger, Birkhäuser, 2007, pp. 200–204.

Pease, Donald E. *The New American Exceptionalism*. University of Minnesota Press, 2009.

Pease, Donald E. Introduction. *Re-Framing the Transnational Turn in American Studies*, by Winfried Fluck, Donald E. Pease, John Carlos Rowe, Dartmouth College Press, 2011, pp. 1–48.

Pease, Donald E. and Robyn Wiegman, editors. *The Futures of American Studies*. Duke University Press, 2002.

Pratt, Mary Louise. "Arts of the Contact Zone." *Profession*, 1991, pp. 33–40.

Pursell, Carroll. *From Playgrounds to PlayStation: The Interaction of Technology and Play*. Johns Hopkins University Press, 2015.

Radway, Janice. "What's in a Name? Presidential Address to the American Studies Association, 20 November 1998." *American* Quarterly, vol. 51, no. 1, 1999, pp 1–32.

Rodgers, Daniel T. "Exceptionalism." *Imagined Histories: American Historians Interpret the Past*, edited by Anthony Molho and Gordon S. Wood, Princeton University Press, 1998, pp. 21–40.

Rowe, John Carlos, editor. *Post-Nationalist American Studies*. University of California Press, 2000.

Rowe, John Carlos. *The New American Studies*. University of Minnesota Press, 2002.

Ryan, Marie-Lauren. "Beyond Myth and Metaphor: The Case of Narrative in Digital Media." *Game Studies*, vol. 1, no. 1, 2001, no page. www.gamestudies.org/0101/ryan/. Accessed 3 July 2020.

Ryan, Marie-Lauren. "Cyberspace, Cybertexts, Cybermaps." *Dichtung Digital: Journal für Kunst und Kultur digitaler Medien*, vol. 31, 2004, www.dichtung-digital.org/2004/1/Ryan/index.htm. Accessed 10 June 2020.

Saldívar, Ramón. *The Borderlands of Culture: Américo Paredes and the Transnational Imaginary*. Duke University Press, 2006.

Scheiding, Oliver. "Mapping America and the Colonial Imagination." *A Companion to American Cultural History: From the Colonial Period to the End of the Nineteenth Century*, edited Bernd Engler and Oliver Scheiding, WVT, 2009, pp. 1–26.

Sklar, Robert. "American Studies and the Realities of America." *American Quarterly*, vol. 22, no. 2, 1970, pp. 597–605.

Slotkin, Richard. *Regeneration through Violence: The Mythology of the American Frontier, 1600–1800*. Wesleyan University Press, 1973.

Smith, Henry Nash. *Virgin Land. The American West as Symbol and as Myth*. Harvard University Press, 1950.

Spanos, William V. *American Exceptionalism in the Age of Globalization: The Specter of Vietnam*. State University of New York Press, 2008.

Trachtenberg, Alan. *Brooklyn Bridge: Fact and Symbol*. University of Chicago Press, 1965.

Turner, Frederick Jackson. "The Significance of the Frontier." *History, Frontier, and Section*. University of New Mexico Press, 1993, pp. 60–90.

White, Richard. "Frederick Jackson Turner and Buffalo Bill." *The Frontier in American Culture: An exhibition at the Newberry library, August 26, 1994—January 7, 1995*, edited by James R. Grossman, University of California Press, 1994, pp. 7–66.

Wills, John. *Gamer Nation: Video Games and American Culture*. Johns Hopkins University Press, 2019.

Wrobel, David M. *The End of American Exceptionalism: Frontier Anxiety from the Old West to the New Deal*. University Press of Kansas, 1993.

Wolf, Mark J.P. *The Video Game Explosion: A History from PONG to PlayStation and Beyond*. Greenwood Press, 2008.

Part I

Sören Schoppmeier
Notes on the State of Montana: The U.S. American Spatial Imagination and the Retrotopia of *Far Cry 5*

"Montana. Big Sky Country. The Treasure State. People got a lot of names for it. I just call it home" (*Far Cry 5*). These are the first words heard by the player in Ubisoft's first-person, open-world shooter *Far Cry 5* (2018). Uttered by Mary May Fairgrave, a bar owner and resident of the game's fictional Hope County, they do not just introduce the game's setting. They also establish an affective contrast to the violent events surrounding the militant, Christian-fundamentalist cult called Project at Eden's Gate, which constitute the basis for the game's central conflict. A particular sense of place, then, permeates the gameworld and combines with a larger notion of space that emerges from a long history and tradition of a decidedly U.S. American spatial imagination. This conception of space, in turn, is imbued with a temporal dimension unequivocally oriented toward the past, which is exemplary for a line of reactionary political thinking that has grown in prominence over the past decade.

In his 2017 book *Retrotopia*, Zygmunt Bauman theorizes the recent surge in populist, reactionary, and nationalist political movements in many Western democracies. Bauman locates the visions of society and community guiding these rising political forces in a disfigured appropriation of the utopian tradition, which has been inverted and reoriented from a progressive, ideal future-in-the making to a return to a past experienced as lost but worthy of resuscitation (see 8–9). In Bauman's words: "From that double negation of More-style utopia – its rejection succeeded by resurrection – 'retrotopias' are currently emerging: visions located in the lost/stolen/abandoned but undead past, instead of being tied to the not-yet-unborn and so inexistent future, as was their twice-removed forebear" (4–5). One could say, then, as I argue in a comparable context, that "retrotopia constitutes a longing for a better future in the image of an idealized, if not outright imagined, past" (Schoppmeier 18). This longing, one may add, evidently hampers efforts to envision alternative futures not based on a presumed state of a better past, which may be better equipped to solve empirically real, global, and unprecedented challenges – such as human-caused climate change – which are rooted precisely in the past romanticized here.

Drawing on Bauman's concept of "retrotopia" (8), this chapter argues that *Far Cry 5*'s spatial imaginary betrays a distinctly reactionary view of the United States. Even though the game seemingly attempts to stay clear of (explicit) polit-

https://doi.org/10.1515/9783110675184-003

ical statements, its rendering of contemporary Montana as a place suffused with a nostalgic longing for an imagined, bygone state that never was exemplifies the "retrotopian romance with the past" (9) delineated by Bauman.

I begin with a brief summary of *Far Cry 5* in order to contextualize its setting, plot, and gameplay. My argument then unfolds across three sections. First, I examine *Far Cry 5*'s organization of gamespace against the background of U.S. American traditions of imagining space on the North American continent, focusing particularly on the ways in which gameplay is structured around and informs the gamespace in this context. This consideration of gameplay continues in the second section, which zooms in on specific notions of place in relation to the shared cultural history of the venues depicted in the game. Finally, the third section weaves together the threads from the preceding parts and explicates the reactionary temporal imagination underlying *Far Cry 5*'s depiction of Montana *qua* its fictional proxy Hope County, illuminating the game's cultural work with regard to questions of space, time, and American culture.

Out of Montana: An Overview of *Far Cry 5*

Released in March 2018 for PC, PlayStation 4, and Xbox One, Ubisoft's *Far Cry 5* both follows established routines and breaks new ground for the *Far Cry* series. Staying true to the franchise's blueprint, gameplay revolves around exploring a vast, freely traversable gamespace of varying terrain and conquering its sections by force. Whereas the familiar *Far Cry* formula continues to structure the ludic experience of *Far Cry 5*, however, its setting marks a turning point in the history of the series. Previous titles were set in remote and decidedly exoticized regions such as Micronesia, central Africa, an archipelago somewhere between the Indian Ocean and the Pacific Ocean, and the Himalayas. In contrast, *Far Cry 5* is the first entry to take place in the United States, specifically rural Montana. Populated, as were its predecessors, not only by hostile factions but also an assortment of habitat-appropriate wildlife, *Far Cry 5*'s gameworld evokes the recurring function of nature in the U.S. American cultural imagination – not without consequence for its cultural work vis-à-vis ideas about time and space in the United States, as I elaborate in the following pages.[1] Before returning to the question

---

[1] From the myth of the wilderness and the frontier to the myth of the garden, and from the transcendentalists' appreciation of nature as the source of truth to the continuing allure of finding enlightenment in nature in postmodernity: the American wilderness has played a central role in how Americans have imagined themselves and their country from the colonial era to the present. For some key texts on these evolving conceptions of 'untamed' spaces on the North American

of the American wilderness, however, a few words on *Far Cry 5*'s central plot are in order.

Set in Hope County, a fictional blend of recognizable Western landscape, rural industry, and small-town clichés, players take on the role of an unnamed deputy of the United States Marshals Service on an assignment with the goal of ending the activities of an apocalyptic, Christian cult called 'Project at Eden's Gate' and arresting its charismatic leader Joseph Seed. The mission ends in a disaster, with Seed escaping and the cult, which operates like a paramilitary militia, capturing all members of the squad except for the protagonist and the local Sheriff. The remainder of the game revolves around taking Hope County back from the cult by expunging its members and rallying the scattered resistance around the county. Throughout the game, players help the locals, rescue hostages, destroy cult property, and, most importantly, liberate cult outposts, which are essentially various businesses hijacked by the cult. The fact that Hope County is finally devastated anyways in *Far Cry 5*'s final scene does not take away from the dominance of acts of retaking throughout the duration of the game.

First announced in 2017, *Far Cry 5* entered a political moment in the United States that had just seen former real estate mogul and reality TV star Donald Trump win the American presidential election for the Republican Party. Against this background, the populist right-wing resurgence in the United States immediately became a lens through which some interpreted *Far Cry 5*'s plot and setting when the game was revealed. Once the game was released, however, nearly all allusions to the political reality in the United States had been subdued either by not engaging with issues evoked by the game or by keeping them contained in smaller, often inconsequential parts of the game. Nonetheless, as I will argue in the following sections, *Far Cry 5*'s conceptions of space and place and their relation to longer traditions of thought in American culture betray a reactionary vision of the United States intimately related to that underlying Trump's election and presidency.

---

continent from wilderness to garden, see Henry Nash Smith's *Virgin Land: The American West as Symbol and Myth* (1950), Perry Miller's *Errand into the Wilderness* (1956), Leo Marx's *The Machine in the Garden: Technology and the Pastoral Ideal in America* (1964). For a transcendentalist treatise on nature and truth, see especially Ralph Waldo Emerson's *Nature* (1836). For two widely received non-fiction accounts of solitary journeys into U.S. American nature, one successful and one resulting in a young man's untimely death, see Cheryl Strayed's *Wild: From Lost to Found on the Pacific Crest Trail* (2012) and Jon Kracauer's *Into the Wild* (1996).

Big Sky Country: Gamespace and the American Spatial Imagination

The first thing players see in *Far Cry 5* after the failed mission to arrest Joseph Seed is the inside of a high-tech bunker, where the protagonist wakes up after having been rescued by a local prepper. Upon leaving the bunker for the first time, players are momentarily blinded by sunlight before witnessing what appears like a placid forest. Players now find themselves surrounded by lush and seemingly unspoiled nature, which exudes a sense of tranquility and regeneration. From this point onward, open spaces and idyllic landscapes dominate the visual and spatial experience of playing *Far Cry 5*, while also providing a recurring contrast between the enclosed and the open, between the technological and the natural – in other words: between the 'civilized' and the 'wild.' As the third-least populated state of the United States, Montana epitomizes a region prone to evoke sensations of a vast, untamed continent even today. The game's audiovisual representation, I argue, combines this geographical focus to imbue the structural organization of the gamespace and the rhythms of open-world gameplay with cultural connotations linked to a particular history of thought concerned with 'uncivilized' space on the North American continent.

From a purely formal perspective, the game not only follows its predecessors in the *Far Cry* franchise, it also epitomizes a spatial distinction regularly found in video games. Particularly in the genres of role-playing games and open-world shooters, the most fundamental segmentation of gamespace is the differentiation between safe zones, where the player character cannot be attacked or at least is not attacked without provocation, and conflict zones, where the player character is continuously exposed to potential harm by other entities in the gameworld.[2] The former often serve as opportunities for the player to save the game state, regenerate the player character's health, purchase in-game goods, and learn about and accept quests. The latter, in turn, provide the space for the game's ludic challenges as well as the ensuing rewards. While safe zones generally come in the guise of towns or even houses, conflict zones are often decidedly marked as a kind of wilderness regulated by little other than the 'law of the jungle.' In other words: it is commonly a representation of 'civilization' that grants players safety, while it is the 'wilderness' that puts them in peril at the same time as it also promises material rewards and character growth.

---

[2] Christopher W. Totten has theorized this using the terms *"prospects* and *refuges"* (211; emphasis in the original) for conflict zones and safe zones, respectively (see 210–221).

In the history of the U.S. American spatial imagination, few ideas have proven as powerful as that of the wilderness on the North American continent. A central figuration of this idea has been the myth of the frontier, whose core argument is that the Western frontier, the line which separates the civilization embodied by settlements east of the frontier from a perceived wilderness beyond, has decisively shaped the American people and nation. Throughout the various forms of the myth, exceptional individuals of originally European origin leave civilization, venture into the wilderness, endure hardships, and eventually return to civilization as new, stronger, and wiser men, now distinctly U.S. American.[3] The most famous formulation of the myth has been historian Frederick Jackson Turner's 1893 paper "The Significance of the Frontier in American History." Turner viewed the frontier experience as the single most important influence in the emergence of an original U.S. American nation. In his view, the pioneers' contact with wilderness forced them into a struggle with a hostile environment for which they were not prepared. Yet they endured and eventually overcame this ordeal, during the course of which they were remade as U.S. Americans at the same time as the wilderness was transformed into a place of civilization (see Turner 1–4).[4]

A more pertinent conceptualization of the frontier thesis as a myth can be found in Richard Slotkin's study *Regeneration through Violence: The Mythology of the American Frontier 1600–1860* (1973). What Turner considered a historical development, Slotkin identifies as a myth originating in Puritan writing and perpetuated through numerous works of U.S. American literature. What is absent in Turner's hypothesis, however, becomes the central force defining the American experience of westward expansion in Slotkin's study: violence. The regeneration allegedly afforded by the mythic space of the frontier appeared to necessitate violence, generally directed at Native Americans: "The first colonists saw in America an opportunity to regenerate their fortunes, their spirits, and the power of their church and nation; but the means to that regeneration ultimately became the means of violence, and the myth of regeneration through violence became the structuring metaphor of the American experience" (Slotkin 5). Throughout its many figurations, the myth of regeneration through violence simultaneously

---

[3] The myth of the frontier has been a decidedly gendered myth, propagated chiefly by male writers, in which men acted, conquered, and remade the North American continent.
[4] This wilderness/civilization dichotomy, which has not lost its allure in U.S. American culture, remains oblivious to the erasure of the native populations who, for centuries, had been living in the very spaces imagined as pristine before they were violently removed from whichever area of land was deemed expedient by settler colonists and the U.S. American government.

has produced *and* justified the violence characterizing the colonization of the continent and the westward expansion of the United States.

In *Far Cry 5*, the lush nature of Hope County dominating the visual landscape is significant for the relation between gamespace and the U.S. American spatial imagination. Adapting the work of Soraya Murray, who conceptualizes video games as *"playable representations"* (*On* 25; emphasis in the original), one can consider this aspect of *Far Cry 5*'s gameworld as playable wilderness. Drawing on W. J. T Mitchell's work on landscape and power, Murray reminds us that

> [v]ideo games that render land make claims about space, place and landscape. As the many forms of landscape that came before them, games are tools of power, and particularly in relation to lived spaces, may be thought of as connected to imperialist expansion. As 'practiced' forms of place, the spaces of games in which players move often tend toward a predatory vision of landscape, in the sense that the space is observed from a privileged position, and often assessed in an ongoing, activated manner for its use-value or exploitability for success within the rule-based system of play. (*On* 180)

This assessment of both the constructed nature of landscape and its instrumentalist appropriation in video games equally applies to the spatial imagination of *Far Cry 5*.

Although most of the action in *Far Cry 5* takes place in human-made environments, the gameworld is dominated by nature. Players repeatedly cross forests, meadows, and rivers populated by a variety of wildlife and they are frequently presented with captivating vistas of an almost sublime Western mountain landscape. If one stays away from the action, *Far Cry 5* can feel like taking a walk through Yellowstone or Yosemite. Players regularly cross the ways of the region's fauna. Ranging from herbivores like hare and caribou to predators like cougars and wolves, wildlife is a prominent feature of the game's *"ambience act"* (Galloway 10; emphasis in the original). Coined by Alexander R. Galloway, this term refers to all the things that continue to happen in the gameworld without input from players. The protagonist can be attacked by these animals, but players can also choose to hunt them, which is even formalized in hunting and fishing challenges.

While hunting is a common feature in many video games, it also signifies more than the activity itself, at least in a U.S. American context. In Slotkin's account of the frontier myth, the hunter, best embodied by the mythical figure of Daniel Boone, is a principal agent of regeneration through violence (see Slotkin 294–312). As the mythical hero equally versed in the ways of the natives and the settlers, the hunter figure in American literature regularly ventures into the unknown and opens up new territories. Hunting in *Far Cry 5* may not fulfill the same function, yet it cannot be divorced from the myths evoked by the gamespace and the logic of regeneration through violence that the game embeds in it. Killing animals in *Far Cry 5* facilitates character growth by generating experience points, and Hope County's native species exist predominately as a resource for personal gain; pelts can be sold for in-game money, which can be exchanged for weapons, health kits, and other equipment. Wildlife as a resource, furthermore, cannot be exhausted in the game since it continually respawns. This endless replenishment aligns with the idea of a continent of seemingly limitless resources bound to be exploited for economic gain. Ultimately, one can find, then, at least a residue of the mythical hunter figure in *Far Cry 5*, which lingers in the player character's repeated engagement with the gameworld's natural environment.

In settlements and buildings held by the resistance, as indicated earlier, *Far Cry 5*'s protagonist is mostly out of harm's way. As soon as players go 'into the wild,' whether that is Hope County's forests or the violence-ridden locations controlled by the cult, however, players are left to their own devices and often find themselves in danger. This movement virtually reenacts that of the pioneer in Turner's and Slotkin's accounts, who regularly crosses the line between civilization and wilderness and consequently undergoes a personal transformation.[5] Like the mythical heroes of American literature, every time the player character returns from the wilderness, they come back changed, having gained resistance points and often also perk points, which may be invested in special abilities for the protagonist that further facilitate progress in the game. Similarly, the player's mastery of *Far Cry 5* likely improves with each endeavor, too. But most importantly, Hope County itself is being remade with each effort, from a space permeated by savagery into a civilized area. This process amounts to a regeneration through violence enacted by the player. In contrast to its mythical-historical forebear, however, nature itself is not transformed in *Far Cry 5* but, at best, preserved (see fig. 1).[6]

---

[5] Parts of *Far Cry 5* even reenact the genre of the captivity narrative, as I have argued elsewhere (see Schoppmeier 16).

[6] Fittingly, *Far Cry 5* players regularly visit places ostensibly aimed at both preserving nature and commodifying it. Examples include the F.A.N.G. Center animal sanctuary, the Whitetail State Park, and the Mastodon Geothermal Park. The preservation aspect underlines a conservative logic of maintaining a state of affairs, in this context certainly laudable, and thus points beyond the present and into the past, to a time when what is deemed worthy of preservation now was presumably unspoiled. Such a view of nature reserves naturally aligns with a retrotopian mindset.

Fig. 1: Nature preserved and commodified in Hope County's Whitetail State Park (*Far Cry 5*, Ubisoft).

The combination of *Far Cry 5*'s audiovisual and procedural representations of the American West, then, align the game with the enduring myth of the frontier and with its ideological implications. While the larger gamespace replicates this mythic structure, the individual places that serve as focal points for the game's missions and plot come with their own cultural histories, which also betray a particularly nostalgic, even reactionary, view of the American heartland, as the next section elaborates.

The Treasure State: American Places and their Cultural History

Far Cry 5's Hope County appears as a collage of U.S. American places with distinct cultural histories, all of which have developed to allow mythical images to supplant their material histories. While the game aspires to a seemingly realistic depiction of rural Montana in its graphical and sound design, the audiovisual verisimilitude actually throws into relief the archetypal shape of Hope County and its individual places. Graphical realism comes at the expense of historical realism at the same time as narratives and histories about westward expansion and settler colonialism permeate *Far Cry 5* below the surface. The game's Montana setting is a case in point here.

One of Montana's common nicknames, also mentioned in *Far Cry 5*'s opening cut-scene, is the Treasure State. The nickname hails from the state's historically rich deposits of gold and silver, which have even become Montana's state motto: *oro y plata*. Evidently, the prospective fortunes of gold mining played their part in the settlement of Montana and the accompanying displacement and slaughter of the region's indigenous population throughout the second half of the nineteenth century.[7] In *Far Cry 5*, players can discover the residues of this history in the form of the Catamount Mines, an old gold mine in Hope County.

The treasures of the Treasure State, however, include more than precious metals. The mining of coal, the pumping of petroleum and gas, the production of lumber, mineral extraction, and farming have been equally important to Montana's economy. These industries connect the past, specifically the expansion of the United States in the nineteenth century, with the present. They were central to industrialization and economic growth in the past and they continue to play a role in the Montana economy and self-perception today, even though their share of the overall economy has radically declined (see "Montana Economy at a Glance").

With the exception of farming, these industries share a common feature: they are all extractive and, thus, exhaustive industries. Mining and its kin epitomize an economic model based on the exhaustion of finite natural resources. Here the primitive accumulation of American settler colonialism and its land grab from the native populations continues in the literal extraction of resources from the same stolen grounds (see Marx, *Capital* 915). Additionally, with their indispensability to industrial capitalism, the extractive industries of Montana and similar states are intrinsically tied to carbon dioxide emissions, which have been identified as a major catalyst to an ever-accelerating human-caused climate change headed towards catastrophe.

---

[7] In the process, Montana saw the perhaps most mythologized battle of the war against the indigenous people of the Great Plains fought on its ground. In the Battle of the Little Bighorn in 1876, George Armstrong Custer's cavalry regiment was defeated by Lakota, Northern Cheyenne, and Arapaho forces. For a long time, this battle has been remembered in American culture under the myth of "Custer's Last Stand." Its commemoration has mostly concentrated on mourning the fallen U.S. troops rather than remembering this rare victory of the victims of American settler colonialism and the genocide against indigenous people. It was also one of the last major victories of Native American forces before large-scale resistance was principally subdued by the end of the century, not incidentally coinciding with Turner's declaration of the closing of the frontier.

Fig. 2: Driving through the sublime mountain landscape of Hope County, powered by fossil fuels, past the Baron Lumber Mill and the Golden Valley Gas Station, both of which represent extractive industries (*Far Cry 5*, Ubisoft).

The point here is that the Treasure State of Montana in *Far Cry 5* represents an economic model of the past and one that is at odds with Montana's much more diverse and healthy contemporary economy (see "Montana Economy at a Glance"). It is not only a fact that "[t]he specter of exhaustion always hovers over a mine" (Studnicki-Gizbert 99) and other extractive industries. With a global community slowly but steadily realizing the threat of the impending climate catastrophe, the key measure to combat climate change is the reduction of carbon emissions. Although the United States are among the most reluctant countries in this respect, even here unsustainable energy sources will become less and less lucrative in the long run. Employment in the U.S. American coal industry has steadily declined throughout the twentieth and twenty-first centuries even as overall coal production grew well into the new millennium, before starting to shrink severely in recent years (see "Coal Mining Fatality Statistics"; "Coal Production, 1949–2019"). Coal mining as a stable source of employment, then, does not seem to have a viable future in the United States.

This is relevant to understanding *Far Cry 5*'s gameworld in relation to a U.S. American spatial imagination because it connects the Montana setting with the specific places around which the game centers its action, characters, and narratives. Hope County is a decidedly rural area dominated by vast stretches of nature interspersed with roads, small businesses, and a single town called Fall's End (see fig. 3). The cult outposts in want of liberation mainly comprise business-

Fig. 3: A view of Fall's End, Hope County, with its small businesses and the seemingly unspoiled nature on the horizon (*Far Cry 5*, Ubisoft).

es from the three sectors agriculture, processing and manufacturing, and preservation and recreation. Over the course of *Far Cry 5*'s missions, players liberate farms, ranger stations, shops, a lumber mill, a packing facility, a hotel, a youth camp, a brewery, a garage, a rail yard, a fertilizer company, and more. While all of these places simply fit the Montana setting, they are significant for at least two reasons.

First, nearly all of these places are businesses in the sense that they are commercial enterprises. There are no schools, libraries, community colleges, parks, or public swimming pools in need of liberation in Hope County. While some of the businesses appear to be somewhat larger companies, like the Green-Busch Fertilizer Company, several are distinctly small businesses, such as Lorna's Truck Stop and Nolan's Fly Shop. In fact, the characters who serve as intermediaries sending the protagonist on quests often relate their own personal involvement in these businesses, how their owners established them, or how they have been run by local families and long-time community members for years. These narrative vignettes authenticate the businesses as belonging to the community, as the result of hard work, and as the deserved reward for individual effort.

Second, *Far Cry 5*'s places are not significant in themselves but, rather, in their common denominator: their temporal dimension. All of the places mentioned point to an idealized American past which is easily contrasted with a present that bears no resemblance to such idealizations. As Antje Kley and Heike

Paul assert, "the rural connotes notions of the past" (3) in itself, and Hope County is no exception here, especially in the composition of its economy. Businesses appear entirely family-owned, with strong ties to the community; retailers, for example, are exclusively independent, small shops. Fall's End conforms to the ideal of Main Street, whose "dual reality [...] as place and as idea," as Miles Orvell argues, has "[given] it its centrality in American culture" (3). In the words of Richard V. Francaviglia, "'Main Street' has come to symbolize a place close to the people, people who have few pretenses and honest aspirations; and because it fuses images of place and time, it also symbolizes their past" (xviii). In Fall's End, there is no mall in sight, no Walmart, no Google data center. In terms of its economy and the nature of its businesses, Hope County truly appears like a place frozen in the past, particularly since these kinds of places have become rarities in the contemporary United States. The small, family-owned business is not only no longer the norm that Main Street America, as embodied by *Far Cry 5*'s Fall's End, represents; it is, in fact, a species threatened by extinction (see Orvell 47–71). Rural and small-town America, as David B. Danbom asserts, is "a remnant that is shrinking, demographically, economically, culturally, and politically" (31), even as its people "consider their communities the heartland of America" (Wuthnow 3).[8]

The places central to *Far Cry 5*'s gameworld and story, therefore, stand for a cultural history of American economic growth after World War II, the attainability of middle-class status and business ownership through hard work, and strong ties between businesses and the communities in which they were located. Comparable to the extractive industries of Montana, this ideal of small-town America is a remnant of the past and increasingly hard to find in rural regions in the present.

Being set in the Treasure State, then, *Far Cry 5* relates to both the historically important extractive industries in Montana and to an idealized image of rural, small-town America in the ways in which space and place work in concert on a representational level. Both space and place here reveal a temporal dimension that signifies a prosperous past rather than the present, which has momentarily become unbearable, or the future. The way in which the Montana setting and the specific places of Hope County are integrated into the game's "procedural level" (Sicart 51), its gameplay mechanics, furthermore accords both a distinct meaning, as I elaborate in the next and final section. It addresses the cultural work performed by the move from the actual to the imagined in relation to *Far Cry*

---

[8] For a recent survey of the challenges rural America faces, see Robert Wuthnow's *The Left Behind* (2018).

5's spatial imagination, its temporal dimension, and the historical context of the game's release.

Calling It Home:

Retrotopian Delusions and the Cultural Work of *Far Cry 5*'s Spatial Imagination

Far Cry 5's depiction of American spaces and places, especially in light of the Trump presidency, exhibits retrotopian sentiments throughout. The gamespace incorporates the logic of the frontier myth in the way it stages missions in spaces structured around a wilderness/civilization dichotomy; in the process, parts of the wilderness are remade into civilized spaces. Hope County's selection of places, in turn, seems to signify an American past rather than the present in which *Far Cry 5* is supposedly set. The game, therefore, revels in an imagined, foregone America seemingly lost but desirable to revive, at least in its spatial vision.

The only thing that disturbs this idealized American space is the Project at Eden's Gate. The cult members are the intruders who have ruined Hope County, taken its citizens and businesses hostage, and corrupted its communities. Gone is Main Street, gone is the lumber mill, gone are freedom and security – at least as long as the cult resides in Hope County. This state of affairs, the starting premise of *Far Cry 5*, signals two related things: the 'good life' of rural and small-town America still exists, it has only been suspended by the cult, and one only needs to remove the cult to return to that blessed state of the past. Since there is no other way to expel the Project at Eden's Gate than with deadly force, players are literally proceeding by exterminating unwanted populations from the area.[9] "The player actively saves small-town America from a lurking threat," John Wills summarizes the game's central thrust, but "there is always a sense of righteousness and patriotic duty on display." Hope County's residents and the player character here appear similar to the "moral communities" of rural America described by Robert Wuthnow, which he views in the "sense of a place to which and in which people feel an obligation to one another and to up-

---

[9] For an insightful reading of the Project at Eden's Gate's motivation and appeal as expressed through *Far Cry 5*'s music, especially the cult's hymns, in which the author identifies "a collective whose concerns align with many of today's real-world concerns" behind the cult's violent surface, see Eli Badra's "Folk-Music, Radical Politics, and Bliss: *Far Cry 5*'s Music as Western Hymnody" (2019).

hold the local ways of being that govern their expectations about ordinary life and support their feelings of being at home and doing the right things" (4).

As the cult is repeatedly marked as savage and evil, the ideological work of progressing through *Far Cry 5*'s story and gamespace ties in with an imagination that is connected to the myths outlined earlier. On one level, gameplay in *Far Cry 5* exemplifies the trope of regeneration through violence described by Slotkin in its purest form. Hope County is literally restored through consecutive waves of violence. Although the violence starts with the cult's intrusion, it is then reflected by the player-led resistance, which appears to reinstate a previous condition – a deceptive reversal of the historical developments of U.S. American settler colonialism that formed both the material and ideological basis of said previous condition, the rural idyll. "I just call it home," says Mary May Fairgrave of Montana in the game's opening cut-scene. Yet players do not actually get to see what she calls home, as they enter Hope County only after the Project at Eden's Gate has already taken over. In this sense, the "home" Mary May speaks of is presumed but no longer existent at the moment the game sets in. Hope County is only made home *again* for characters like Mary May through the process of regeneration through violence in the game.

Similarly, all of the businesses only become functional again after the player has expelled the cult from each premise by killing all cult members present. This is the second and more significant level of *Far Cry 5*'s ideological work. Reinstating Hope County's businesses is nothing short of the fulfilment of the retrotopian fantasies guiding the rhetoric and subsequent success of reactionary political actors like the Trump administration and the Republican Party under it. Elsewhere, I have argued that "the politics of 'making America great again' reverberate strongly in the central rhetoric of *Far Cry 5*" (Schoppmeier 19). The regeneration of local businesses in Hope County is perhaps the most explicit overlapping of the video game and the retrotopia that has formed parts of the basis for Trump's success in rural and small-town America (see Wuthnow 1). One of the recurring talking points of Trump during his campaign were the numerous pleas to bring business back to the United States, especially to the regions left behind by the structural changes that have resulted from the ongoing period of deindustrialization since the second half of the twentieth century. Particularly his advances to coal miners are exemplary for the retrotopian delusions underlying Trump's appeal since this is an industry that, as outlined before, is more likely to die out altogether than to generate any considerable number of new jobs (see Cohn).

Far Cry 5, in contrast, keeps that promise. By reinstating one business after the other, the regional economy is indeed revitalized, and there is not a trace of chain stores, malls, or big box stores, let alone twenty-first-century corporations like Amazon and Google. Hope County's economy is entirely local, which is to say it is entirely U.S. American, and it is able to thrive (again). There is agriculture, there is industry, and there is recreation. But most importantly, there is independence and self-determination for the residents and small enterprises of Hope County once more, as the cult is expelled along with the decline associated with it. Ultimately, however, "the cult is nothing more than a scapegoat, a whipping boy for all of the problems of Hope County and America writ large," as Austin Walker asserts in his review of *Far Cry 5* before denying the game the integrity that warrants such an interpretation. The game remains oblivious to the concerns and challenges brought about by the shift to a postindustrial society that has played a significant role in the decline of rural and small-town economies and communities in the United States and instead casts an intruding, outside force as the root of Hope County's current problems.

The discourse of calling it home, epitomized by Mary May Fairgrave's statement quoted earlier, comes full circle here. As Adi Robertson describes it, *Far Cry 5*'s "most straight-faced and important storylines are generally about pastors, veterans, farmers, and other positive rural American archetypes protecting their way of life." Under the cult's presence, Hope County's residents feel like "strangers in their own land" (Hochschild 219) just like the disillusioned Louisiana Tea Party supporters surveyed by Arlie Russell Hochschild in her book of the same title have done after the societal shifts of the past 50 to 60 years. These are the sentiments, in turn, on which the Trumpian rhetoric and appeal have operated since his first bid for the Republican presidential candidacy – successfully so, one must add, until the 2020 election – while deflecting from the structural root causes of the problems faced by such communities. Similarly, "[m]uch of *Far Cry 5* feels less like a game about a modern world in crisis, and more like a stock conservative fantasy about the triumph of small-town America" (Robertson). In this light, the State of Montana *qua* its proxy Hope County is the retrotopia of America under the Trump presidency come true in *Far Cry 5*. Progressing in the game means realizing the retrotopian vision one business at a time.

Conclusion

As I elaborated in this chapter, *Far Cry 5*'s utilization of space and place within its Montana setting draws on a rich tradition of a U.S. American spatial imagination, more specifically the cultural histories of imagining nature, wilderness, and the rural small-town. Whereas the first two aspects lend meaning to the gamespace, the latter elicits a particular sense of place. The cultural work of the game's spatial imagination can ultimately be located in the reactionary logic that emerges when Hope County is coupled with gameplay revolving predominately around conquering, liberating, and restoring. Space in *Far Cry 5*, thus, actually signifies time: it constantly points to an imagined past and urges players to reinstate that past. By securing the places central to Hope County's community, players really turn back time to an undifferentiated but supposedly better past. This impetus is not unlike the one encapsulated by Trump's slogan "Make America Great Again," which, like the political rhetoric around Trump's candidacy and presidency more generally, similarly posits a more prosperous past but never really pinpoints what exactly it refers to or what it looked like. The return to such idealized, imaginary pasts, whether in the gameworld of *Far Cry 5* or in the political vision of the U.S. American President, blanks out past and continuing realities of violence and oppression in a distinctly reactionary view of the United States.

This does not mean that *Far Cry 5* actively supports reactionary politics. Nonetheless, as Murray asserts, "the constructed landscape models a particular kind of relationship between player and the in-game space, which is in turn connected to the lived-world reality that informs it" ("Landscapes" 172). It does concern us that the logics sketched out above structure not only the spatial imagination but the entire gameplay of a video game that appears to have no real interest in politics or social issues (see Robertson). Imagined spaces, like imagined pasts, have consequences; it is our responsibility to work toward different imaginations of the past, the present, and, most importantly, the future. Here, *Far Cry 5* has it the wrong way around. Perhaps this is where the game's strange, apocalyptic ending, in which Hope County is annihilated by an atomic bomb, acquires a meaningful dimension: holding on to the past, especially an imagined one, may literally usher in the end of the world. While the game thus unwittingly hints at its misguided imaginary, drawn from the long history of U.S. American culture, it simultaneously concedes its impotence in envisioning a different future. In this view, *Far Cry 5*'s ending is not subversive or even clever; it is cynical at best, and cynicism is ill-equipped to prevent catastrophe.

Works Cited

Badra, Eli. "Folk-Music, Radical Politics, and Bliss: *Far Cry 5*'s Music as Western Hymnody." *First Person Scholar*, 10 April 2019, www.firstpersonscholar.com/folk-music-radical-politics-and-bliss-far-cry-5s-music-as-western-hymnody. Accessed 29 December 2020.

Bauman, Zygmunt. *Retrotopia*. Polity, 2017.

"Coal Mining Fatality Statistics: 1900–2019." *Mine Safety and Health Administration*, United States Department of Labor, www.arlweb.msha.gov/stats/centurystats/coalstats.asp. Accessed 30 December 2020.

"Coal Production, 1949–2019." *U.S. Energy Information Administration*, 5 Oct. 2020, www.eia.gov/coal/annual/pdf/tableES1.pdf. Accessed December 2020.

Cohn, Scott. "Trump's Pledge to Save US Coal Is Failing, Leaving Coal Country in Crisis." *CNBC.com*, 8 October 2019, www.cnbc.com/2019/10/08/trumps-pledge-to-save-us-coal-is-failing-leaving-wyoming-in-crisis.html. Accessed 19 December 2019.

Danbom, David B. "Americanism Distilled: The Place of the Countryside in American Thought." *Rural America*, edited by Antje Kley and Heike Paul, Winter, 2015, pp. 13–34.

Emerson, Ralph Waldo. *Nature*. Munroe, 1836. *Internet Archive*, 10 Feb. 2006, www.archive.org/details/naturemunroe00emerrich/page/n5/mode/2up. Accessed 30 December 2020.

Far Cry 5. Ubisoft, 2018.

Francaviglia, Richard V. *Main Street Revisited: Time, Space, and Image Building in Small-Town America*. University of Iowa Press, 1996.

Hochschild, Arlie Russell. *Strangers in Their Own Land: Anger and Mourning on the American Right*. New Press, 2016.

Kley, Antje, and Heike Paul. Introduction. *Rural America*, edited by Kley and Paul, Winter, 2015, pp. 1–11.

Kracauer, Jon. *Into the Wild*. Villard, 1996.

Marx, Karl. *Capital: A Critique of Political Economy*. Translated by Ben Fowkes, vol. 1. Penguin, 1976.

Marx, Leo. *The Machine in the Garden: Technology and the Pastoral Ideal in America*. Oxford University Press, 1964.

Miller, Perry. *Errand into the Wilderness*. The Belknap Press of Harvard University Press, 1956.

"Montana Economy at a Glance." *Montana Department of Labor and Industry*, August 2019, www.lmi.mt.gov/Portals/193/Publications/LMI-Pubs/Labor%20Market%20Publications/EAG-0819.pdf. Accessed 19 December 2019.

Murray, Soraya. "Landscapes of Empire in *Metal Gear Solid V: The Phantom Pain*." *Critical Inquiry*, vol. 45, no. 1, 2018, pp. 168–198.

—. *On Video Games: The Visual Politics of Race, Gender and Space*. I. B. Tauris, 2018.

Orvell, Miles. *The Death and Life of Main Street: Small Towns in American Memory, Space, and Community*. University of North Carolina Press, 2012.

Robertson, Adi. "*Far Cry 5* Wasn't a Game for the Trump Era, but It Tried to Be One Anyway." *The Verge*, 6 April 2018, www.theverge.com/2018/4/6/17202546/ubisoft-far-cry-5-politics-social-commentary-irrelevance. Accessed 29 December 2020.

Schoppmeier, Sören. "Playing to Make America Great Again: *Far Cry 5* and the Politics of Videogames in the Age of Trumpism." *COPAS: Current Objectives of Postgraduate American Studies*, vol. 20, no. 1, 2019, pp. 6–23.

Sicart, Miguel. *Beyond Choices: The Design of Ethical Gameplay*. The MIT Press, 2013.

Slotkin, Richard. *Regeneration through Violence: The Mythology of the American Frontier, 1600–1860*. University of Oklahoma Press, 1973.

Smith, Henry Nash. *Virgin Land: The American West as Symbol and Myth*. 1950. Harvard University Press, 1978.

Strayed, Cheryl. *Wild: From Lost to Found on the Pacific Crest Trail*. Knopf, 2012.

Studnicki-Gizbert, Daviken. "Canadian Mining in Latin America (1990 to Present): A Provisional History." *Canadian Journal of Latin American and Caribbean Studies*, vol. 41, no. 1, 2016, 95–113.

Totten, Christopher W. *An Architectural Approach to Level Design*. CRC Press, 2014.
Turner, Frederick Jackson. "The Significance of the Frontier in American History". *The Frontier in American History*. 1920. Dover, 2010, pp. 1–38.
Walker, Austin. "'*Far Cry 5*' Tries to Do It All, but Fails to Be Much of Anything." *Vice*, 26 March 2018, www.vice.com/en/article/qvxbeb/far-cry-5-review. Accessed 29 December 2020.
Wills, John. "*Far Cry 5:* Cults, Radicalism and why this Video Game Speaks to Today's Divided America." *The Conversation*, 13 April 2020, www.kar.kent.ac.uk/80170/1/far-cry-5-cults-radicalism-and-why-this-video-game-speaks-to-todays-divided-america-95000. Accessed 29 December 2020.
Wuthnow, Robert. *The Left Behind: Decline and Rage in Rural America*. Princeton University Press, 2018.

Felix Zimmermann
Ethical Boredom in the Wilderness: Treating *Red Dead Redemption 2* as an Ambience Action Game

When the ever-present violence of *Red Dead Redemption 2* (Rockstar Games 2018)[1] and its ludic realization as repetitive and monotonous shoot-outs have drained players of their energy to continue, they can find refuge under the trees of the Big Valley in West Elizabeth, a fictive scenery referring to real-world landscapes in California, U.S.A. (fig. 1). West Elizabeth is only one of five states you can traverse in *RDR2* while trying to find your place as Arthur Morgan in a world that increasingly condemns his lifestyle as an outlaw. Clinging to the only life he has ever known, Arthur rides, robs, and kills on a quest to score that one last big heist that will finally allow him to retire from this dangerous line of work. As an open world game *RDR2* allows players to follow this storyline at their own pace or, if they prefer, spend their time with side activities like playing poker or hunting one of the 166 huntable animals (see GTABase). *RDR2* has been particularly praised for its implementation of a "dynamic and interactive ecosystem" (Ali).[2] In his review of the game Kirk Hamilton writes that *RDR2* "contains the most bracingly beautiful depictions of nature I have ever seen in a video game" and jokingly describes it as an "Open World Human Nature Simulator" (Hamilton, "The *Kotaku* Review"). It does not seem far-fetched to claim that the game's depiction of a lush frontier landscape is one of the reasons for its success.

To explore this assumption, I visited the review aggregator metacritic.com and compared the much-debated "Metascore" based on critic reviews to the "User Score" of user reviews. The discrepancy I found between professional assessments of the game and user impressions was more noticeable than expected. While user reviews are "generally favorable", the PlayStation 4 version displays a "User Score" of 'only' 8.4 of 10 while the Xbox One version shows a "User Score" of 7.8 of 10 at the time of writing this essay. This is of interest in that the game shows an impressive score of 97 of 100 for both the PlayStation 4

---

[1] From here on referred to as *RDR2*.
[2] Similarly, Alenda Y. Chang notes that Rockstar Games "has taken positive steps" towards "seriously [considering] the goal of environmental realism – not solely in terms of visual rendering, but also in sound design, weather, species density and distribution, and the arrangement of organic and inorganic actors in complex interrelation" (22).

https://doi.org/10.1515/9783110675184-004

Fig. 1: A typical view of the Big Valley region in *Red Dead Redemption 2*. All pictures in this article taken by the author with the in-game camera (except stated otherwise) and used courtesy of Rockstar Games.

and Xbox One version based upon 99 (PlayStation 4) and 33 (Xbox One) included critic reviews (see Metacritic "PlayStation"; Metacritic "Xbox"). The clarity of this discrepancy motivated me to take a closer look at the user reviews in search for an explanation. One major complaint apparent in many responses to the game – also suggested in many professional reviews – concerns the controls of the game. The user "MisterLupus" for example writes in one of the more serious reviews that "[t]he controls are clumsy and bad – needlessly hard to navigate, often unresponsive – and both movement as well as combat are clunky to say the least and also unimaginative" (Metacritic "User Reviews"). The user "theTRUTHson" adds that "[i]t is a slow game with lots of waiting and little action" (Metacritic "User Reviews") while user "NuSix3" points out that "the controls are convoluted and it feels very slow and clunky" (Metacritic "User Reviews").[3]

However, I argue in this chapter that the undeniably unresponsive controls as well as the general slowness of *RDR2* enable an experience vastly different from recent blockbuster open world games. Because of the way in which a game of such enormous production value undermines the conventions of con-

---

[3] I have picked three of the user reviews here that other user found "[m]ost helpful" according to Metacritic (see Metacritic "User Reviews"). Of course, other reviews could be quoted here, but the reviews claiming the game is mediocre or bad all paint a similar picture (see Metacritic "User Reviews").

temporary game design I will describe *RDR2* as an Ambience Action Game. This genre term is an epistemological tool which enables scholars to put emphasis on specific elements of games. "As an umbrella term, referring to games in which presence in awareness spaces is central to the experience" (Zimmermann and Huberts 38) it was originally coined by Christian Huberts and me to do justice to games misrepresented by the reductionist term "Walking Simulators." We see the term as a description of "a specific mindset which changes the way players of digital games play" (Zimmermann and Huberts 46) rather than an attempt to replace the commonly used term "Walking Simulator." Therefore, it is productive not to claim that something categorically *is* an Ambience Action Game but rather to *treat* something *as* an Ambience Action Game and gain a fresh perspective on existing material. Treating a game as an Ambience Action Game emphasizes if and how a game reduces player agency to produce awareness spaces which allow for experiences different from the usual player-action based gameplay.

The "ambience act" has been defined by Alexander R. Galloway as "the machine's act" (10). While "[t]he user is on hold [...] the machine keeps on working" (10). By this, Galloway suggests that when an ambience act occurs the player acts to a lesser degree than the machine (that is the computer and the game) does through the game world (see also Chang 96). The spaces, in which these ambience acts occur, must therefore be of a specific kind in that they reduce the "operator actions" (Galloway 5), i.e. the player actions, to a minimal level. Consequently, and to distinguish them from possibility spaces – that is a functional space which serves the player in that it enables certain action (see for example Sicart 2008) – Huberts and I have termed such spaces "awareness spaces" (32) and the games in which they are prominently found "Ambience Action Games" (38–39). Using this term as an epistemological lens, I want to treat *RDR2* as an Ambience Action Game and claim that the unresponsive controls and the slowness of the protagonist's movements inhibits the player agency in such a way that they become susceptible to perceiving the ambience acts of the game world. I understand especially the wilderness areas of the game, which are mostly devoid of non-player characters, quests, bandits, or any other elements which force the player to act, as awareness spaces.

'Wilderness,' as I will show utilizing Marc Bonner's concept of "striated wilderness" (1), is common in the open world games of recent years and realized in specific, ludified ways. However, a reading of the wilderness areas in the game as awareness spaces is complicated by the Western setting of *RDR2*. Oftentimes, in the predominantly positive critic reviews of the game I found on Metacritic, the virtual landscape is praised in light of this tradition-rich setting of the game. For example, in one review by the Swedish tech website "M3" it is called "the ultimate Wild West sandbox-experience" (Metacritic "PlayStation") while the games blog "Hardcore Gamer" calls it "the single most immersive Wild West game yet" (Metacritic "PlayStation"). Therefore, wilderness in *RDR2* has to be regarded considering how it utilizes mythologies of the frontier so closely intertwined with popular Wild West iconographies. I will draw from the work of Leo Marx on the *Machine in the Garden* (1964), in which he identifies the "pastoral idea of America" (73) as the pivotal manifestation of a machine-nature dichotomy. Wilderness, in this sense, is not only a space presumably untouched by humans but also a space ever in danger of becoming assimilated by the machine, of ceasing to be wilderness and becoming something else as the frontier is pushed westward. Hence, what is of interest for a reading of *RDR2*'s wilderness areas in light of its Western setting is how the relationship between machine and nature is negotiated in the cultural tradition of the American West and in one of the most recent entries into this tradition, namely *RDR2*.

Finally, the strands of my argument will coalesce as I will argue that in its slowness and even sometimes boringness *RDR2* opens up a special connection to its highly sophisticated depictions of nature which makes it possible for players to achieve a state of "embodied empathy" (op de Beke 5) for the ecosystem of the game. As Hans-Joachim Backe points out, "ecocritical studies of computer games would benefit from taking the long and rich history of mainstream computer games into consideration more frequently and systematically" (41). By offering an ecocritical reading of *RDR2*, I will do so and show that apart from its conventional Western narrative the game can be seen as an intriguing approach to wilderness experience which is of value in the geologic age of the Anthropocene.

Red Dead Redemption 2 as a Cinematic Western

Let me begin by explaining how *RDR2* is not special. The tradition of digital Western games can be traced back as far as the arcade machines of the 1970s like *Gun Fight/Western Gun* (1975) or *Boot Hill* (1977) (see Wills; Buel). While these earliest games differ significantly from titles like *RDR2* in the quality of their presentation or the complexity of their gameplay, they are very much comparable to these recent games in how they cater to "expectations of the Wild West" and how they, therefore, "include [their] fair share of cowboys, outlaws, and Indians" (Wills 278). As John Wills notes, these Western games – and this has not changed in the last 50 years – are "simulacra of simulacra" (277) as they display an image of North American frontier space which never existed in such a manner but has always been infused by fiction, mythology, and ideology.

More than anything else digital Western games draw upon the fantastical iconography of the cinematic Western which "helped cultivate and mythologize much of the imagery of the American West through presenting concrete, larger-than-life visuals" and thereby embedded "the image of the cowboy, the choreography of the gunfight, the sweeping vistas, and the horizontal expanses of desert" (Buel 50) into popular culture. As Esther Wright points out, Rockstar Games, the developer of *RDR2*, rigorously uses these cinematic influences in their marketing efforts. By publishing blog posts in which they make their cinematic influences explicit, for example, Rockstar Games "attempt[s] to orient potential players toward a specific way of reading or accessing cinematic history" (Wright 154). In these blog posts "'Rockstar Recommends' certain films that could be watched before playing" (143), for example *Once Upon a Time in the West* (1968), *The Wild Bunch* (1969) or *Unforgiven* (1992) (see 146–147). In doing so, Wright claims, Rockstar Games tries to produce "cinematic authenticity" (143) to verify their version of the Wild West.

This version of the Wild West in *RDR2* and in its predecessor *Red Dead Redemption* (Rockstar Games 2010)[4] draws heavily from such popular cinematic influences but struggles to provide critical commentary on the tropes it inherits from them. Buel goes so far as to attest that *RDR1* is a "revisionist Western in terms of its narrative genre as it romanticizes the West and views it nostalgically" but simultaneously points out that "[t]he audience is encouraged to take a critical look at the underlying ideologies of the American West mythology of power and entitlement" (53). What is described here for *RDR1* still holds for *RDR2*. It is true that the central role of "the cowboy figure, the rugged individual" (Humphreys 200) is contrasted in both games by the inevitable death of the protagonist who is unable to withstand the pressure of modernization or, as Humphrey puts it, "neoliberalism that is euphemistically described in frontier narratives as progress and freedom" (200). This narrative certainly encompasses the possibility "to get players to think critically and reflect upon violence within games and within Westerns" (Buel 56). Considering that players will have killed hundreds of non-player characters until the protagonists, Arthur Morgan and John Marston respectively, meet their untimely demise and that they can then continue the killing with a different character, *RDR1* and *RDR2* still fall short of being a critical commentary on Wild West mythology. Even with the addition of the so-called "honor system" in *RDR2* which reacts to unlawful and ethically questionable behavior by players (see Hoffmann), *RDR2* still stages the West "as violence par excellence" (Wills 303). It is in this vein, to borrow from Wills, that RDR2 "use[s]

---

4 From here on referred to as *RDR1*.

fresh technology to preserve an old chimera" (295) – at least on the level of narrative, characters, and overall gameplay.[5]

Arthur Morgan and Pastoral Hope

In light of the game's narrative this "old chimera" comes forcefully into view when turning to Leo Marx' work on "the machine in the garden," a trope he discusses in his literary critique of influential works of U.S.-American authors like Henry David Thoreau or Mark Twain. For Marx, the trope of "the machine in the garden" refers to "the contrast between the industrial machine, say a steam locomotive, and the green landscape" – that is, the disruption of the pastoral idyll by "iron, fire, steam, smoke, noise, speed" (374) of the engine. This trope, as I have pointed out in the introduction, is intertwined with what Marx calls the "pastoral idea of America" (226). This idea entails that when the machine enters the garden – the "conquest of the wilderness" (226) – something is at stake of being lost, namely a "rural happiness" (226). As Marx points out, "[i]n this sentimental guise the pastoral idea remained of service long after the machine's appearance in the landscape" (226) in the sense that the "pastoral hope" (355) endured. The incarnation of this hope is the "middle landscape" (226), a space of balance between nature and civilization that is to be created to preserve a pastoral way of living. Thereby, the trope of "the machine in the garden" is as much about the "machine's increasing domination of the visible world" (364) as it is about the "pursuit of rural happiness while devoting itself [the American nation] to productivity, wealth, and power" (226). In this lies the "contradiction" (226) of trying to bring the dominator and the dominated into a state of balance, of harmony even. "[P]astoral fables" (364), therefore, deal with exactly this contradiction between nature and machine and the protagonist's struggle to solve it.

RDR2 appears to be a faithful rendition of this trope. Arthur Morgan, as part of a gang of outlaws, clings to an ideal of life in communion with nature. As part of the "Van der Linde-Gang," Arthur lives in a small camp under the trees just outside the small town of Valentine – at least at the beginning of the story. He sleeps in a tent next to the gang's homestead wagons, hunts for food, and only seldom gets in contact with the townsfolk. Meanwhile, industrialization

---

[5] This is not to say that *RDR2* does not warrant a more thorough analysis in terms of its narrative strands and characters (e.g. considering Arthur's illness in the game or the role of Sadie Adler). However, such analysis is reserved for future scientific engagements with the game.

Fig. 2: The locomotive in Red Dead Redemption 2. Picture taken in the so-called "cinematic mode" of the game.

and productivism push from the east and try to take this way of life away from him. The symbolism is clear and enacts the trope of "the machine in the garden:"[6] The untouched wilderness is disrupted by the locomotive (fig. 2); the calm and slow life in the gang's camps (fig. 3) is contrasted with the bustling activity in the easternmost town of Saint Denis and the smoke rising from the factories (fig. 4). Beyond that, the "Pinkerton National Detective Agency" – always in pursuit of the gang – symbolizes order and control and a subjugation of a free way of living under the code of law that modernization brings with it.[7] While the relationship to the other members of the gang is ambiguous and changes during the game, the Pinkerton detectives are the definite antagonist of the game.

What is at stake, now, for Arthur Morgan is the "pastoral hope" (Marx 355), the hope of running away from the conforming pressures of civilization and of finding peace in a "middle landscape," a space "neither wild nor overcivilized,

---

[6] Also, as Dietmar Meinel criticizes in his engagement with Leo Marx' work, the latter "continues to validate the idea of the (white, male, heterosexual) American hero – whether triumphant, tragic, or disrupted – as the essential figure through which increasing industrialization, urbanization, and commercialization are negotiated" (197). *RDR2* reinforces this problematic dynamic of "the machine in the garden" trope by employing Arthur Morgan as the lens through which the confrontation between wilderness and civilization is observed.

[7] Of course, it is not the Van der Linde-Gang's way of life in communion with nature that forces the detectives to prosecute but rather the gang's inclination to rob and murder.

Fig. 3: An encampment of the "Van der Linde-Gang" in RED DEAD REDEMPTION 2.

Fig. 4: A typical view of the town of Saint Denis in RED DEAD REDEMPTION 2.

where the dream of harmony between humanity and nature might be attainable" (Marx 377). In its narratives *RDR2* reveals this "middle landscape" to be a fantasy.[8] Arthur Morgan fails in his attempt to conserve his pastoral lifestyle. He tries to keep the gang together and preserve their living in harmony with "undefiled, bountiful, sublime Nature" (Marx 228) but has to witness the gang falling apart in the course of the narrative. He is unable to dissolve this contradiction of wanting to live a rural life while also profiting – by stealing – from the wealth and power of the modernized world. The "middle landscape" that seems so nearly perfect in the first hours of the game emerges as unsustainable. "[I]n the end the American hero is either dead or totally alienated from society, alone and powerless" (364), writes Leo Marx, and this assessment holds true for *RDR2*.

Narratively, therefore, *RDR2* reproduces the trope of "the machine in the garden" while emphasizing the inescapability of the machine's triumph. In this sense, *RDR2* employs a "complex pastoral" which "acknowledge[s] the power of a counterforce" to the sentimental pastoral hope and thereby "acknowledges the reality of history" (Marx 362–363). On the level of gameplay and game world, however, *RDR2*'s engagement with the pastoral has to be regarded separately. On the one hand, the game adheres to the trope of "the machine in the garden" and showcases a futile "pastoral hope." *RDR2* thereby adds a narrative layer to its landscapes in that they come to represent a clash of nature and the machine, of the rural and the modernized. On the other hand, however, the gameplay invites an intimate involvement of the player into the wilderness areas in the game. Therefore, somewhat contrary to the incompatibility of nature and machine brought forth in the game's rendition of the trope, nature and machine appear to enter a symbiotic relationship in the virtual world.

Ambience Acts in Smooth Spaces

As I pointed out earlier, the virtual open world landscapes of *RDR2* function as awareness spaces that allow players to focus their attention on the ambience acts of the game world. These awareness spaces in *RDR2* are best understood in terms of what Marc Bonner has called a "striated wilderness" (1) that is designed to afford certain actions by the player and restrict others. This theory puts emphasis on the contrast between representations of seemingly untouched nature and the ludic subjugation, i.e. the 'playability' of natural landscapes. Thereby, it ties in with the cultural implications of *RDR2*'s setting in how nature

---

[8] Similar observations can be made regarding *RDR2s* predecessor *RDR1*. Especially, as *RDR1*'s plot takes place after *RDR2*'s, an intriguing dynamic comes to pass. Having played *RDR1* players can be reasonably sure of the futility of Arthur Morgan's pursuit of his "pastoral hope." However, for the sake of stringency of my argument, I will not go into detail about *RDR1* here.

and machine – the computer – find themselves in conflict on the level of gameplay. Finally, by connecting the notion of "striated wilderness" to the Ambience Action Game, it becomes visible that this conflict is also one between possibility spaces and awareness spaces.

"Striated wilderness" is defined by its two-layered structure, consisting of one layer of "polygon meshes and historical as well as cultural coined sign systems" and of another which Bonner calls a "practice of wildness" (8). In this sense, wilderness in a game always is an amalgam of reproduced iconographies of culturally well-grounded notions of wilderness as a unique type of place and a specific set of affordances for crossing this space, hence a practice (see 8). The simulacrum of wilderness which "has no antecedent, no original from which it has emerged" (Vidon et al. 66) and which acts "as a virtual panacea for social ills, a place of solitude, wholeness, and serenity" (66) is therefore striated by the ways in which it becomes ludically accessible.

According to Bonner, this process of striation becomes visible in the form of two types of spaces into which the totality of the open world gamespace can be divided. The "striated space" is the space which "enables a goal-oriented, ludic, crossing of the vast landscape" (Bonner 8) and which comes close to the aforementioned idea of a "possibility space" catering to the players' needs and enabling their actions. "In context of computer games this means following navigational points, overall goals of a quest or the NPCs' path routines" (8), as Bonner elaborates. While other open world games like *Assassin's Creed Odyssey* (Ubisoft 2018) or *Horizon Zero Dawn* (Sony Interactive Entertainment 2017) rely on more elaborate navigational systems such as a compass-like interface element at the top of the screen showing nearby points of interest and the way to the next quest, *RDR2* employs only a small map at the bottom left corner of the screen.

This, I would argue, eases the transition from "striated space" and its accompanying modes of exploration into "smooth space" (Bonner 9). The latter type "focuses on the stretch of way, the distance itself" and can be reached by "players turning a blind eye to maps, icons and markers of interfaces" (Bonner 9). This is why I see a game like *RDR2* with a more minimalistic interface as being more prone to having its space experienced as "smooth space." As Bonner notes, "[o]nly few open world games are brave enough to confront the players with wilderness as an empty vastness free of quests, hostile NPCs and other affordances" (4) while it is in this space that it becomes more likely that players enter a state of "free roaming" which is the mode of experiencing smooth space (see Bonner 10). Therefore, a game which is willing to offer such empty spaces specifically encourages free roaming practices.

RDR2 is such a game. Between the few human settlements in the world of *RDR2* there are vast spaces encouraging undirected exploration. The so-called fast-travel function prominent in almost every open world game is limited to only a few stagecoach stations in *RDR2*. The lush green meadows of the Heartlands (fig. 5) or the sticky marshes of Lemoyne (fig. 6) are therefore best traversed by yourself on horseback and their sheer size and emptiness invite a non-ludic – in this sense more paidiaic – way of experiencing this space.[9]

Fig. 5: A typical view of the Heartlands in Red Dead Redemption 2.

Still, at times the player is confronted with seemingly random events like a stagecoach robbery, an animal attack, or with a call for help from a stranger bitten by a snake. This is part of the "emergent events, rewarding prospects or rare items" (10) which Bonner identifies, and which are employed by designers to specifically encourage free roaming practices. But the farther the player travels to the north or west of *RDR2*'s world, the more uncommon these interventions by the game become. There were times when I camped in the western Big Valley area and just roamed the nearby forest areas without anything happening for hours. In this extreme form, the smooth spaces of *RDR2* come close to the idea of awareness spaces as a constituent part of the Ambience Action Game. "The frontier in open world games seems to shift with the players' agency by exploring, conquering and freeing designated places from hazards" (3), Bonner

---

[9] Roger Caillois coined "ludus" and "paidia" as "ways of playing" (53). Paidia, in his influential definition, is positioned as "active, tumultuous, exuberant, and spontaneous" (x) while ludus "represent[s] calculation, contrivance, and subordination to rules" (x).

Fig. 6: A typical view of the Lemoyne region in RED DEAD REDEMPTION 2 with two dead bandits sinking into the marshes.

writes, but these secluded spaces in *RDR2* cannot be conquered in this sense. Reaching them remains time-consuming for the entirety of the game, the ludic possibilities continue to be minimal.

One thing which is true, however, is, that the fauna in these areas still can be exploited by players. Bears, cougars, or stags can be forced "into tables of exchangeable data sets, into economies of XP and rupees" (Brown 398) as is common in open world games. The player who hunts perfect pelts of certain animals is rewarded with a new hat or an improved carry capacity for one of the protagonist's bags. At least, as Backe notes in his analysis of *RDR1*, "[h]unting is not trivialized" (50) as the process of skinning the dead animal is displayed in some detail. "Still," he adds, "the game makes hunting attractive through rewards, and the player will be motivated to explore the possibilities of this activity" (50). The same can be said for *RDR2*.

So while *RDR2* encourages free roaming and notably employs smooth spaces which display characteristics of awareness spaces more than other recent blockbuster open world game, it still takes an act of "transgressive play" (Aarseth 132) by players to really utilize the potential of these awareness spaces. "Transgressive play," as coined by Espen Aarseth, refers to "a symbolic gesture of rebellion against the tyranny of the game" (132) which, in the case of *RDR2*, would mean to resist the urge to exploit your surroundings for ludic purposes.[10] *RDR2*, however, makes it easy to be transgressive. As I mentioned, the game is criticized for its unresponsive controls and the general slowness of Arthur Morgan's movements. Players can control Arthur, yes, but they are never really *in* control.

In another article for *Kotaku*, Heather Alexandra opens up a different perspective on this critique by writing about "smaller and more subtle friction points" in *RDR2* and by coming to the conclusion that this game "is something you push against, something that you comb and scratch and brittly feel in your hands" (Alexandra). She therefore argues that *RDR2* has a certain feel to it and that even the clunkiness of the game adds to "the texture of the world" (Alexandra). I see two consequences following from the realization that the presumably unresponsive or uncomfortable controls of this game are not bad game design but a way to add to the illusion of world. Firstly, I argue that this "friction" bolsters the game's potential to offer awareness spaces as it haptically involves the player in the game world and therefore heightens awareness for the ambience acts of the game world as they become physically appreciable. Secondly, this "friction" – visible in the user scores of the game – still has the potential to be less fun than other open world games with their tight and responsive controls. This is why *RDR2* makes it easy to be transgressive. In the context of other recent games, the pure gameplay of *RDR2* is mediocre in the sense that it is not up to date to how other games are controlled and therefore played. This encourages players to experience *RDR2* differently, not only as an action game but also as ambience acts by taking a break at the campfire, contemplating their surroundings, and indulging in the game world's atmospheres at times because this corresponds well with the specific qualities of the game's controls. *RDR2* provides a special form of striated wilderness which encourages the player to experience it as smooth space. Ultimately, this leaves room for ambience acts to occur in these smooth spaces, turning them into awareness spaces for the players.

Pastoral Awareness Spaces

One could be inclined to call *RDR2*'s hyperreal wilderness environments a manifestation of a "postmodern pastoral" (77) as defined by Scott Hess. For him, the "postmodern pastoral" is a "popular pastoral of consumerism" which symboliz-

---

[10] The online mode for *RDR2*, which is not the focus of this paper, adds the highly interesting character of Harriet Davenport to the game. The naturalist Davenport actively encourages players to not exploit the game's fauna but to study it in the name of science (see Zimmermann).

es "the pursuit of happiness through leisure in a secular and sensual Utopia paradoxically claiming to be grounded in nature, even as it is refracted back at us through the massive proliferations of our technologies" (71–72). Based on the notion that increasing digitalization has changed the dynamic between machine and nature, authors like P. Saxton Brown (2014) or Dietmar Meinel (2014) have brought forth the proposal to rethink the trope as its inversion and therefore – as both the essay by Brown and Meinel are titled – "The Garden in the Machine" (see also Chang 158–163). As Hans-Joachim Backe makes clear, "there are absolutely no natural environments in computer games" but only "environments coded as natural" (43–44). Consequently, *RDR2*'s landscapes can be said to be "the machine's version of the garden" (Brown 386) and, finally, a "garden in the machine." In this sense, the wilderness of *RDR2* has already been tamed by the code which suddenly puts the fantasy of the "middle landscape" and therefore of "harmony between humanity and nature" into the player's reach.

One implication of this, then, could be to follow Hess' idea of a "postmodern pastoral" and see these beautiful, all-too-perfect landscapes in *RDR2* as a form of escapism, as "the perfect fulfillment of his or her 'natural' desires and thus the final realization of secular happiness" (78). In a pessimistic reading the smooth or even awareness spaces of *RDR2* can be said to "distract us from recognizing the impact of our daily lives both on the local and global environment" (Hess 92) and to "keep us from pursuing happiness in more profound and effective ways" (89), that is, in interacting with real-world natural environments and working to preserve them.

Therefore, one could come to the conclusion that *RDR2* does indeed, as I pointed out ealier, offer awareness spaces which afford meaningful interactions with nature-like environments. However, these spaces, which could be termed pastoral awareness spaces, afford a problematic kind of interaction because they offer an illusionary depiction of a seemingly untouched wilderness. Thereby, it "seduces the nature tourist with its siren song of authenticity" (Vidon et al.66) while failing to make the player aware of how nature is under siege in the real world through exploitation.

There are arguments for such a position. For one, the pastoral awareness spaces of *RDR2* are never really threatened by the expansion of industrialization so prominent in the narrative of the game. The environment does not change during the course of the game's narrative, so players could come to think that the threat to the game's wilderness is indeed not imminent. However, there are areas of the game world, for example the expanses of Annesburg in the eastern part of the map, where cleared woodlands signal what might happen to these pastoral awareness spaces in the future (fig. 7).

Fig. 7: A cleared area near the eastern coast of Annesburg in RED DEAD REDEMPTION 2.

Additionally, "as games present themselves as tempting vehicles for environmental escapism, the hard reality is that the games industry is a significant contributor to the demolition of our planet" (D'Anastasio). In the same vein, Brown points out that "[h]igh-tech, high-energy electronics like video games [...] are an important element of the same network of exploitation and exchange as such 'dirty oil' processing plants" (385). While it remains to be seen if these measures will have an effect, some of the biggest gaming companies, however, "formally committed to harness the power of their platforms to take action in response to the climate crisis" (Rukikaire). There at least seems to be a growing consciousness in the video game community of the detrimental effects of video game production on the environment.[11] That said, *RDR2* nonetheless affords a non-player-centric engagement with its environments. Similar to how Laura op de Beke engaged with the idea of pastoral landscapes in her research on "the environmental orientation of videogames" (5) and came to the conclusion that some games

---

11 Also, there have been alarming accounts of so-called "crunch" practices in the development of *RDR2*, meaning that a significant amount of people working on the game had to put in extra hours to finish the game while some even cracked under the pressure and had to leave the production for health reasons (see Schreier). One could argue that the hardships of these game workers are hidden behind the beauty of the game world. There are, however, efforts to unionize in the industry (see Game Workers Unite) but in this regard it also remains to be seen if this campaign will have an effect.

make possible an "embodied empathy for a virtual ecosystem" (74), I claim that *RDR2* is able to raise environmental consciousness.

Ethical Boredom and the Sustainable Pastoral

As a crucial addendum to the introduction of the Ambience Action Game earlier, it needs to be pointed out that being witness to an ambience act in the pastoral awareness spaces of *RDR2* is not a form of passivity. On the contrary, by offering these spaces *RDR2* "create[s] time and space for the contemplation of ways of being in the world" (Brown 387) and for "the appreciation of the atmospheres" of these spaces (Zimmermann and Huberts 36). Emphasizing awareness over action is not equivalent to forcing players into passivity. Rather, "[w]hen the ambience action game brings the player into a latent state of pause, it fills the emerging void with the action of the game world—the ambience act" (Zimmermann and Huberts 45). In her analysis of the game *Stardew Valley* (Chucklefish 2016) op de Beke comes to a similar conclusion. She points out that it would be wrong to speak of a "postmodern pastoral" (20) here. As Hess makes clear, a "[p]ostmodern consumer pastoral is almost completely passive" (87) and *RDR2* by no means puts players into a state of passivity in how it lets players engage with their environment. To the contrary, it can be said that "many of today's environmentalisms, such as community, slowness, and sense of place" (66) that op de Beke identified in her analysis can also be found in *RDR2*.

It is especially notable how through the slow and time-consuming traversal of the landscape the game reduces the possibilities for player action and thereby creates awareness spaces. One could go as far as to say that the pastoral awareness spaces of *RDR2* afford "ethical boredom" (401) as termed by P. Saxton Brown. "Boredom," as he elaborates, describes here "not the repetitive tasks of work Horkheimer and Adorno focus on as a central tenet of the 'culture industry,' but a cessation of goal-directed behavior" and thereby "might have a value for an environmental consciousness" (400). He adds that "[b]oring gameplay can be a resistant strategy" (400) comparable to what has been discussed as transgressive play in the context of *RDR2*. More than any other mainstream open world game of recent years *RDR2* not only offers ample opportunities to be bored but even encourages players to be bored while playing the game.

The boredom in *RDR2* can be called "ethical" in how it gives "rise to questions about the relationship between a technological-natural world and the presence of the (presumably) human user" (Brown 402). It negotiates whether the aforementioned "environmentalisms" and especially slowness might be a valid way for humanity to responsibly interact with the ecosystems on our planet.

In this ecocritical reading, the game is comparable to the so-called "Slow Movement" which "emphasizes slowness in the creation and consumption of products as a corrective to the frenetic pace of 21st-century life" (Green). To put it bluntly: *RDR2* produces slowness in times of the blazingly fast machine, the computer. It dares to bore the player in a time in which game makers work so hard to eradicate all traces of boredom by flooding their games with distractions. For example, in the context of open world games developed and published by Ubisoft, this "focus on busy work or mindless padding" (Frye) has been criticized as the so-called "Ubisoft Open World Formula" (Frye) while *RDR2* has been especially praised by critics for how it "rejects so many modern open-world game design mainstays" (Hamilton "Open-World Trends") like world maps filled to the brim with question marks showing potential activities for the player. This deviation from the norm has also informed many of the negative user reviews for the game. The user "MisterLupus," for example, concludes his aforementioned review by attesting that *RDR2* "treats you more like a spectator than a participant" (Metacritic "User Reviews") which encapsulates the perceived affront of *RDR2* well. It is in this vein that the pastoral awareness spaces of *RDR2* could be interpreted by some players as a humiliation, "being less important than the world around them" (Zimmermann and Huberts 45; see also Chang 71). In treating *RDR2* as an Ambience Action Game it becomes clear that in its ability to afford "ethical boredom" it is a powerful antidote to the anthropocentric perspective so common in video games.

It would be wrong, surely, to fall under the spell of *RDR2*s impressive landscapes and claim that it is an act of environmental activism. As I have shown by engaging with the critique of how the game still affords exploitation of its environment and how its very development causes harm to our real-world environment, *RDR2* is not. However, the game also challenges conventions of contemporary open world games and opens room for notable free roaming practices in pastoral awareness spaces which encode environmental consciousness through slowness and even boredom.

The environmental depictions of *RDR2* and especially its wilderness areas are hyperreal in their beauty, sure. Having built an intimate relationship to a digital notion of nature in *RDR2*, players might find that this environment is worth defending against the human exploitation – in the virtual as well as the physical world. *RDR2*, then, might be a step towards a "sustainable pastoral" in video games, "a pastoral that recognizes its relation to other forces, a pastoral that does not attempt to escape and drown out social and environmental tensions, contingencies, injustices, but which highlights tensions and provides a staging ground from which balances are readjusted, from which harmonies can be continuously and contingently restored" (Hess 95). The pastoral awareness spaces of

RDR2 have the potential to help in such an act of balancing. Since they encourage slowness in our engagement with the environment, they could become a staging ground for environmental discourse.

Conclusion

In this essay I have shown how *Read Dead Redemption 2* can be treated as an Ambience Action Game. I have introduced the concept of the Ambience Action Game as a lens which helps to emphasize how a game reduces player agency to achieve certain goals. Referring to Marc Bonner's concept of "striated wilderness" I conclude that *RDR2* emphasizes free roaming in smooth spaces which can even be described as awareness spaces. These spaces, then, encourage players to perceive the "ambience acts" (Galloway) of the environment by employing "friction points" (Alexandra) and therefore afford a slow playstyle. Hence, *RDR2* is an intriguing addition to the tradition of Western games even though its narrative hardly qualifies as daring. It sticks to the typical figure of the cowboy as the center piece for its rendition of the trope of "the machine in the garden." It is only on a gameplay level, then, that it puts an interesting spin on this established trope by producing ample opportunities for indulging in "ethical boredom" (Brown). In the twenty-first century, ironically, the "undefiled, bountiful, sublime Nature" (Marx) is accessible via the machine. Especially in its pastoral awareness spaces *RDR2* encourages players not to act and may thereby facilitate an "embodied empathy" (op de Beke) of the player for the game's environment. *RDR2*'s step away from the dominant anthropocentrism in video games hints at what role video games and their creators could be playing in the age of the Anthropocene.

Works Cited

Aarseth, Espen. "I Fought the Law: Transgressive Play and The Implied Player". *Proceedings of the 2007 DiGRA International Conference: Situated Play*, 2007, pp. 130–133, www.digra.org/digital-library/publications/i-fought-the-law-transgressive-play-and-the-implied-player/. Accessed 4 October 2019.

Alexandra, Heather. "*Red Dead Redemption 2*'s Mundane Tasks Bring the Game to Life". *Kotaku*, 11 May 2018, www.kotaku.com/red-dead-redemption-2s-mundane-tasks-bring-the-game-to-1830237192. Accessed 4 October 2019.

Ali, Umran. "*Red Dead Redemption 2:* Virtual Ecology is Making Game Worlds eerily like our own." *The Conversation*, 27 Nov. 2018, www.theconversation.com/red-dead-redemption-

2-virtual-ecology-is-making-game-worlds-eerily-like-our-own-107068. Accessed 16 September 2019.

Backe, Hans-Joachim. "Within the Mainstream: An Ecocritical Framework for Digital Game History." *Ecozona: European Journal of Literature, Culture and Environment*, vol. 8, no. 2, 2017, pp. 39–55.

Bonner, Marc. "On Striated Wilderness and Prospect Pacing: Rural Open World Games as Liminal Spaces of the Man-Nature Dichotomy." *Proceedings of the 2018 DiGRA International Conference: The Game is the Message*, pp. 1–18, www.digra.org/digital-library/publications/on-striated-wilderness-and-prospect-pacing-rural-open-world-games-as-liminal-spaces-of-the-man-nature-dichotomy/. Accessed 4 October 2019.

Brown, P. Saxton. "The Garden in the Machine: Video Games and Environmental Consciousness." *Philological Quarterly*, vol. 93, no. 3, 2014, pp. 383–407.

Buel, Jason W. "Playing (with) the Western: Classical Hollywood Genres in Modern Video Games." *Game On, Hollywood! Essays on the Intersection of Video Games and Cinema*, edited by Gretchen Papazian and Joseph Michael Sommers, McFarland & Company, 2013, pp. 47–57.

Caillois, Roger. *Man, Play and Games*. Translated by Meyer Barash, University of Illinois Press, 2001.

Chang, Alenda Y. *Playing Nature: Ecology in Video Games*. University of Minnesota Press, 2019.

D'Anastasio, Cecilia. "Video Game Companies Vow Action on Climate Change, but Critics Say They Need to Do More." *Kotaku*, 24 September 2019, www.kotaku.com/video-game-companies-vow-action-on-climate-change-but-1838420425. Accessed 4 October 2019.

Frye, Brendan. "The Ubisoft Open World Formula Is Feeling Dated." *CGMagazine*, 13 August 2020, www.cgmagonline.com/2020/08/13/the-ubisoft-open-world-formula-is-feeling-dated/. Accessed 23 November 2020.

Galloway, Alexander R. *Gaming: Essays on Algorithmic Culture*. University of Minnesota Press, 2006.

Game Workers Unite. *Game Workers Unite!* www.gameworkersunite.org/. Accessed 23 November 2020.

Green, Penelope. "The Slow Life Picks Up Speed." *The New York Times*, 31 January 2008, www.nytimes.com/2008/01/31/garden/31slow.html. Accessed 30 October 2019.

GTABase. *Red Dead Redemption II Wildlife Database*, www.gtabase.com/red-dead-redemption-2/animals/#sort=attr.ct77.frontend_value&sortdir=asc&attr.ct102.value=hunted&page=1. Accessed 23 November 2020.

Hamilton, Kirk. "*Red Dead Redemption 2:* The *Kotaku* Review." *Kotaku*, 25 October 2018, www.kotaku.com/red-dead-redemption-2-the-kotaku-review-1829984369. Accessed 4 October 2019.

Hamilton, Kirk. "*Red Dead Redemption 2* Defiantly Bucks Open-World Trends." *Kotaku*, 30 October 2018, www.kotaku.com/red-dead-redemption-2-defiantly-bucks-open-world-trends-1830101610. Accessed 23 November 2020.

Hess, Scott. "Postmodern Pastoral, Advertising, and the Masque of Technology." *Interdisciplinary Studies in Literature and Environment*, vol. 11, no. 1, 2004, pp. 71–100.

Hoffmann, Moritz. "The Moral of the Story: *Red Dead Redemption 2*." *Public History Weekly*, 4 April 2019.

www.public-history-weekly.degruyter.com/7-2019-12/red-dead-redemption-2/. Accessed 18 September 2019.

Humphreys, Sara. "Rejuvenating 'Eternal Inequality' on the Digital Frontiers of *Red Dead Redemption*." *Western American Literature*, vol. 47, no. 2, 2012, pp. 200–215.

Marx, Leo. *The Machine in the Garden: Technology and the Pastoral Ideal in America*. Oxford University Press, 2000.

Meinel, Dietmar. "The Garden in the Machine: Myth and Symbol in the Digital Age." *Rereading the Machine in the Garden: Nature and Technology in American Culture*, edited by Eric Erbacher, Nicole Maruo-Schröder, and Florian Sedlmeier, Campus, 2014, 190–210.

Metacritic. *Red Dead Redemption 2, PlayStation 4*, www.metacritic.com/game/playstation-4/red-dead-redemption-2. Accessed 23 November 2020.

Metacritic. *Red Dead Redemption 2, Xbox One*, www.metacritic.com/game/xbox-one/red-dead-redemption-2. Accessed 23 November 2020.

Metracritic. *Red Dead Redemption 2, User Reviews*, www.metacritic.com/game/playstation-4/red-dead-redemption-2/user-reviews?sort-by=most-helpful&num_items=100. Accessed 23 November 2020.

op de Beke, Laura. *Empathy for Ecosystems. On the Environmental Orientation of Videogames*. Research Master Thesis. Leiden University Repository, 30 November 2018, www.openaccess.leidenuniv.nl/handle/1887/67058. Accessed 4 October 2019.

Red Dead Redemption 2. Rockstar Studios, 2018.

Rukikaire, Keishamaza. "Video Games Industry Levels Up in Fight against Climate Change." *UN Environment Press Release*, 23 September 2019, www.unenvironment.org/news-and-stories/press-release/video-games-industry-levels-fight-against-climate-change. Accessed 4 October 2019.

Schreier, Jason. "Inside Rockstar Games' Culture of Crunch." *Kotaku*, 23 October 2018. www.kotaku.com/inside-rockstar-games-culture-of-crunch-1829936466. Accessed 4 October 2019.

Vidon, Elizabeth S., Jillian M. Rickly, and Daniel C. Knudsen. "Wilderness State of Mind: Expanding Authenticity." *Annals of Tourism Research*, vol. 73, 2018, pp. 62–70.

Wills, John. "Pixel Cowboys and Silicon Gold Mines: Videogames of the American West." *Pacific Historical Review*, vol. 77, no.2, 2008, pp 273–303.

Wright, Esther. "Marketing Authenticity: Rockstar Games and the Use of Cinema in Video Game Promotion." *Kinephanos: Journal of Media Studies and Popular Culture*, vol. 7, no. 1, 2017, pp. 131–164.

Zimmermann, Felix and Christian Huberts. "From Walking Simulator to Ambience Action Game: A Philosophical Approach to a Misunderstood Genre." *Press Start Journal*, vol. 5, no. 2, 2019, pp. 29–50.

Zimmermann, Felix. "A Love Letter to Harriet Davenport, the Maddest of Them All: The Life of a Naturalist in *Red Dead Online*." *Spiel-Kultur-Wissenschaft*, 27 August 2021. www.spielkult.hypotheses.org/3082. Accessed 1 November 2021.

Nathalie Aghoro
On Postapocalyptic Frontiers in *Horizon Zero Dawn*

An array of distinct time layers pervades the space of *Horizon Zero Dawn* and defines its topographic density. Published for Playstation 4 by Guerilla in 2017, the open-world action RPG is characterized by a sublime wilderness with animal populations and settlements that allude to the Neolithic as much as it resembles a future Earth largely reclaimed by nature and populated by machines after the annihilation of mankind. *Horizon Zero Dawn*'s postapocalyptic gamespace is riddled with residential sites marked by techno-tribal civilizations and unexplored remnants of an ancient world that invoke the state of the Earth at the beginning of the twenty-first century.

Spatial exploration drives the gameplay and the progressive uncovering of the map leads to discoveries that explain the interdependencies between nature, technology, and NPC settlements found in each region of the game. *Horizon Zero Dawn*'s game world is an interstitial space in which each site is simultaneously situated in the Neolithic present of its current settlers and the futuristic past of the Old Ones who triggered their own mass extinction. Moreover, players are encouraged to draw on their own geographical and historical knowledge while traveling through the gamespace. The video game not only fictionalizes actual places in North America and around the globe to produce an ecological science fiction setting rife with allusions to contemporary environmental and posthumanist debates. It also works with the idea of the American frontier as a culturally specific means to conquer space through the establishment of spatial and social dichotomies that order and subsequently transform contact zones into dominated areas. The frontier serves as a reference system and spatial device for the production of *Horizon Zero Dawn*'s temporally dense gamespace.

Spatial knowledge directly affects the power relations within the game world. While the player-character Aloy navigates the game's frontier space, the player encounters differing perspectives on the postapocalyptic contact zone that determine how characters understand the territory, how they treat natural and technological resources, and how they interact with others. Aloy's travels are motivated by her quest to find out where she comes from. As she moves along her increasing knowledge becomes crucial in assessing situations, positioning herself, and resolving conflicts. In this context, the main quest negotiates frontier-related ideas of conquest, colonization, and exploitation by complicat-

https://doi.org/10.1515/9783110675184-005

ing dichotomies along the lines of nature and technology as well as wilderness and civilization.

This chapter seeks to establish that *Horizon Zero Dawn* projects a reimagination of the American frontier onto a postapocalyptic environment while challenging the hegemonial characteristics of its imaginary. The video game positions players as explorers who can use both the geographical and historical knowledge that they bring to the game and the spatial knowledge they acquire through the exploration of the game world to fully experience the precarity of its ecosystem. *Horizon Zero Dawn* showcases a temporally layered game environment that alludes to a fictionalized historical past, to our contemporary present, and to possible futures through the postapocalyptic frontier that it generates. In a first step, a look at how the game deals with notions of order – with a focus on the relationship between wilderness and civilization – and ideas of technological progress will provide a conceptualization of the postapocalyptic frontier in the game. Then, an analysis of the game's virtual space shall explain how the mapping of temporal references onto the spatial plane drives the gameplay. Finally, this chapter will end on considerations about the functions of ecological aspects within *Horizon Zero Dawn*'s gamespace.

The Frontier in *Horizon Zero Dawn*

Nature, settlements, and machines forge close interdependencies within *Horizon Zero Dawn*'s ecosystem. Machines are inextricably connected to nature; the distinction between wilderness and civilization situates tribal principles of inclusion and exclusion on the map; local rituals and knowledge production respond to material remnants of preapocalyptic technology and natural conditions. Together, these interdependencies both replicate and contradict established dichotomies of frontier imaginaries.

Wildlife in form of machines represents technology and nature as simultaneously opposed and inseparably merged aspects of the game world. Machines are zoomorphic and populate the vast natural spaces that the player can explore. They are hunted like deer for their material components. To the heroine Aloy and the majority of non-player characters, their provenience is unknown since knowledge about the technology involved is lost. As a consequence, they are perceived as natural resources from an anthropocentric point of view. Because they look and behave like animals, machines are considered to be just another species alongside the natural fauna and flora, beasts alongside other animals "of the air, water, and earth" (*Horizon Zero Dawn*), as Rost – Aloy's guardian and father figure – states at the beginning of the game. They appear as part of an unpredictable natural environment to in-game characters and they render the locations in which they roam uninhabitable. Along the lines of the Wilderness Act signed by Lyndon B. Johnson in 1964, they emphasize the "primeval character" of *Horizon Zero Dawn*'s wilderness "as an area where the earth and its community of life are untrammeled by man, where man himself is a visitor who does not remain" (Section 2.c). The uninhabited spaces populated by machines can be traveled and visited but never fully tamed and conquered. To in-game populations they appear as wilderness while players recognize the presence of zoomorphic machines as an imprint of human-made technology onto the landscape that complicates clear distinctions between nature as unaffected by humankind and its constructions that shape natural spaces.

As naturalized technology or techno-nature, machines provide an interactive stimulus to the progressive deployment of the gamespace. Since Aloy is a hunter who collects machine components to sell them or to build and reinforce armor and weapons, the player's spatial exploration of *Horizon Zero Dawn* includes experiencing wilderness and civilization through the dynamic confrontation with techno-nature. Learning how to hunt machines with bow and arrow serves as an initiation into the tribal structure of the fictional society as well as the various cultures and rules that define these associations. At the same time, the weapon types as well as the differing costumes and armors of each tribe qualify the gamespace as an interstitial space in time simultaneously set in a post-industrial future and an early stage of human history. To use Edward Soja's words when he discusses the emplacement of social beings, one could argue that the player in *Horizon Zero Dawn* is "being actively emplaced in space and time in an explicitly historical and geographical contextualization" (11). The in-between character of *Horizon*'s time-space allows the procedural discovery and conquest of places unknown and their successive transformation into a multidimensional and temporally layered contact zone as players gain spatial knowledge throughout the main story arc and side quests.

Stormbirds, tallnecks, and other machines simultaneously reproduce and undermine the frontier myth of a virgin land waiting to be discovered. On the one hand, their robot appearance clearly implies that they are an advanced technological invention. On the other hand, they determine wilderness in opposition to settlements as they exhibit territorial behavior in contact with human characters who approach or attack them and, when they transgress the boundaries of populated areas, defend the demarcations of their settlements. The spatialization of adversarial relations between machines and human characters emulates Frederick Jackson Turner's description of the American frontier as the "the outer edge of the wave [of westward expansion] – the meeting point between savagery and civilization" (3). The erasure of oppression and extinction in the wake of territorial expansion in Turner's hegemonic, future-oriented master narrative of national progress determines his problematic definition: "American development has exhibited not merely advance along a single line, but a return to primitive conditions on a continually advancing frontier line, and a new development for that area. American social development has been continually beginning over again on the frontier" (2). According to him, the frontier is a border line with a clear-cut spatial and temporal teleology, not a space or contact zone of exchange and mutual connections. As *Horizon Zero Dawn* uses the techno-natural hybridity of zoomorphic machines for world building purposes, it explicitly counters the hierarchical idea of "a return to primitive conditions" (Turner 2) with the postapocalyptic premise of a highly technologized society that the machines are a sign of.

They signify to the player that neither is technological progress an unlimited upward movement, nor do new beginnings take place on a blank page. In *The Rhizomatic West* (2008), Neil Campbell notes the ideological perspective that transpires from Turner's historiographic take is an interpretation of America as "a nation forged out of the intense and diverse experiences of the so-called open, vacant frontier, transforming encounter and contact into a closed, destined relationship of evolution and progress toward the production of an essentially rooted American character" (2). For Campbell, this national imaginary encompasses the two contradictory experiences of

> mobility and migration existing both as ideas and as the material conditions that transformed the region [...] and the mythic quest for rootedness, settlement, and synthesis so often accepted as the outcome, the final point, and the essential identity of this fluid movement. The desire for fixity, belonging, and integration has an impressive presence in the narratives of the West. (1–2)

Hence, the frontier constitutes the nation by separating it from the openness of a world beyond. Migration and rootedness are strictly separated phenomena in terms of time and space as respectively appearing in places previously located outside of and situated inside the nation after a successful conquest.

Horizon Zero Dawn plays with this opposition by changing the outcome of gameplay and storyline from settlement to perpetual mobility. The gameplay focuses on generating spatial immersion through movement away from the place players are introduced to at the beginning, renewed exploratory stimuli throughout the game, and a resolution that does not end in a final arrival. Tribal principles of social inclusion and exclusion in the game drive the player's movement away from the apparent security of the settlements. Aloy is introduced as an outcast by birth from the Nora tribe. She is a foundling who was handed over to her outcast foster father Rost because her appearance appeared suspicious to some of the tribe's matriarchs. She was raised by him according to tribal customs on the outskirts of a Nora settlement. Aloy is allowed to participate in the tribe's initiation trials called the Proving and wins which qualifies her to become an accepted member of the Noras. Her repositioning within the social structure of the Nora results in her acquiring the special status of Brave with her victory, a role that makes it possible for her to go places other Noras are not allowed to explore. In combination with her early experiences at the fringes of the community, her double position as outsider and insider enables her to move back and forth between the open world and Nora settlements and to explore the in-between space of the frontier. She becomes traveler and cultural go-between who never settles, but, instead, learns to recognize the complex interconnectedness of the world on her travels.

As the player-character, Aloy extends her successively acquired spatial privileges to the player. In *The Art of Videogames* (2009), Grant Tavinor observes that in order to allow players to "adopt a role in the fictional world of a videogame, many videogames represent the player as character within that world, making the game world fictions [...] more [...] robust" (70). The interactive handling of Aloy's movement and actions allows players to become alternative pioneers together with her on her quests. Along the way, they experience how her main quest to search for clues about her roots almost accidentally intersects with a future-oriented survival narrative in a world threatened by a second destruction by an imperialist faction of the Carja tribe who seeks domination through conquest and war after the apocalypse that precedes the story of the game. As Keith Stuart remarks in his review of the game,

> Aloy, is not so much motivated by some grand mission to save humanity (though that sort of comes into it), she is motivated by intellectual curiosity. She is fascinated by the mechanised monsters roaming the landscape and the ruins of an ancient technological culture that she first discovers as a child, and she wants to learn more. Her interactions with the world, the characters and the wider narrative within it, are all personal rather than heroic. In short, she acts like a human being. (Stuart)

Along these lines, the protagonist's wish to learn motivates the action and serves as a catalyst for the player's movement around the map.

The contextualization of places is crucial for the player's immersion into the open space of *Horizon Zero Dawn*. While discussing the differences between space and place, Marie-Laure Ryan argues in *Narrative as Virtual Reality 2* (2015) with reference to Yi-Fu Tuan that spatial immersion requires a sense of place. She notes that "[t]he opposition is one of abstraction versus concrete environment invested with emotional value" (86). Accordingly, the initial storyline connects places to formative experiences for Aloy, in particular Rost's hovel where Aloy grew up and Mother's Heart, the Nora settlement where she succeeds in the initiation trials. However, one could argue that the opposition between abstract and concrete spatiality does not necessarily reside in emotional value per se but in the different kinds of affective needs that they fulfill. Ryan herself notes as she continues to contrast space and place that "[s]pace allows movement – and therefore freedom, adventure and danger – while place offers a sense of security but also of containment" (86). In other words, localized needs define places while the affective dimensions of spatial imaginaries like the reimagined frontier in *Horizon Zero Dawn* may entail the gratification of the above-mentioned curiosity, of bonds forged with new encounters, or of the potential relief from social pressure in transit.

The crossing of thresholds and the ensuing discovery of places the player can relate to through Aloy's mobility builds up spatial immersion. Her movement is the impetus for the player's discovery of a world imprinted with the frontier motif. Her interstitial perspective on the game world highlights its "global dimension as a geographical, cultural, and economic crossroads defined by complex connectivity, multidimensionality, and imagination" (3), to appropriate the phrasing that Campbell uses to describe the dense layers of signification embedded in the idea of the American West. The knowledge about the semantic layers that define it – a knowledge that is unevenly distributed among the characters one interacts with – transpires from the abundance of encounters and the continuous assembly of partial information shared along the way. Consequently, Aloy's in-depth understanding of the global dimensions of the gamespace she lives in helps her to avert the imperialist conquest. Moreover, the personal origin story that she discloses on her travels only strengthens her position as wanderer between worlds instead of pinning her down. In both cases, *Horizon Zero Dawn*'s main storylines do not provide closure in form of a final order or rootedness but the perpetuation of openness and continuous change.

Time-Space and Virtual Space

Architecture provides spatial and temporal information in the postapocalyptic setting of the gamespace. Ancient, ruined sites of concrete and metal disrupt and complicate the dichotomies of settlement and wilderness, nature and technology. They highlight that players do not venture out as settlers into virgin lands but rather travel through locations that nature has recovered after the extinction of preceding technological societies. Buildings and human-made sites function in relation to nature in *Horizon Zero Dawn*.

Together, architecture and nature establish a comprehensive and multilayered time-space. As Michael Nitsche writes, in-game architecture "relate[s] to natural spaces in three different ways" (161):

> They make the natural space more *precise* – including the visualization of the natural space, the understanding of it, and the resulting building in it [...]. They *complement* the natural space – adding what seems to be lacking in the natural space [...]. They *symbolize* the human understanding of nature – including the translation of acquired meaning of space into another medium. (161; emphases in the original)

In the game, settlements define nature more precisely as a wilderness that includes zoomorphic machines. It establishes clearly demarcated boundaries between their habitat devoid of buildings and the residential sites with their walls and fortifications. The player understands the space that constitutes the frontier because of the relationship between architecture and wilderness. Ancient, mid-twenty-first century human-made places like the abandoned urban agglomerations, bunkers, and military production sites one finds when leaving the tribal centers complement the natural space while qualifying this dichotomy between nature and culture as artificial, shifting, and unstable. Since they are not considered suitable housing for larger communities and because they are rank with weeds and populated with wildlife, they symbolize a historical perspective on the mutual relationship between nature and human life.

A significant example for the translation or remediation of spatial meaning simultaneously referencing time in the game is the former welcome center of a wildlife reserve that situates the gamespace on the Northern American continent. In the building, the hologram installation of extinct wildlife plays a sound file spoken by a male voice that includes the final commercial claim "Brought to you by Montana Recreations" (*Horizon Zero Dawn*). This is one of several instances in which the game offers what Nitsche calls "evocative narrative elements" to the players that "encourage [them] [...] to project meaning onto events, objects, and spaces in game worlds" (44). For Nitsche, these elements "help to infuse significance. Their value is not realized on the level of the element itself but in the way players read and connect them. Creating these connections, players can form narratives that refer to the game world" (44). In case of the commercial, the player understands that Montana Recreations is a place, while Aloy and the character on site, Enjuk, do not. Enjuk believes that it is the name of the man who built the digital installation of animals that no longer exist in the current time-space of *Horizon Zero Dawn*, like the black bear, the puma, and the mule deer. By referencing an actual place name and animals factually subject to species conservation at the beginning of the twenty-first century, the holograms function as symbols for a cultural conception of nature that is framed as U.S.-American. They allow the player to connect the game story to discourses of nature as national heritage that is preserved in national parks and wilderness territories, or, in other words, remainders of spaces that have undergone the transformation process of the frontier during the nineteenth-century westward expansion.

In *Horizon Zero Dawn*, architecture not only relates to nature in multiple ways. Pre- and postapocalyptic buildings are also set into relation to one another. They are spatial artifacts in which time sediments. For instance, the technological advances from an earlier age are integrated into the settlement space of All-Mother, the inner sanctum of the Nora tribe. Light comes in from a hole that a machine drilled before the apocalypse and the drill head remained stuck, probably because it ran out of power. In the background we can see a locked door that never opens since the knowledge about the necessary identification device is lost. The request for identification is spoken by an artificial intelligence with a female voice. Only the matriarchs interact with this central installment and they interpret the voice as a spiritual phenomenon. To them the speaking AI is All-Mother, the goddess. And since the leaders interpret what is said as prophecies, the site is recognized as a religious place of pilgrimage and consequently decorated with candles and handcraft. Hence, the gamespace is depicted as an assemblage of different layers of time, knowledge, technologies, and spatial usage.

In *Horizon Zero Dawn*, knowledge about cultural references from before the apocalypse is lost because most inhabitants do not know what caused the extinction of a previous civilization and how the technology of the Old Ones works. However, they trigger their imagination and therewith the production of stories and lore. These situated stories in turn change the meaning and purpose of particular locations that "acquire their status of being places through the stories that single them out from the surrounding space" (Ryan 86) as seen in All-Mother. The economic dimension of the welcome center is lost on Enjuk, but its function as a place of learning transpires through the virtual wildlife exhibition that is still functional. In correspondence with Aloy's intellectual curiosity, Enjuk envisions himself as "a student of the natural world" who seeks to "catalogue behaviors, preserve images" (*Horizon Zero Dawn*). His scientific interest cannot transcend the level of speculation or conjecture because of the technological threshold that prevents him from accessing further epistemic information.

Aloy, however, has access to the virtual archive hidden in the world. She exemplifies "the role of the player-character as an epistemic agent in the visuospatial worlds of videogames" (74) that Tavinor relates to the interactive characteristics of video games. She can both combine information from several sources into comprehensive spatial knowledge and facilitate the player's interactive access. Aloy and, consequently, the player is endowed with a device called Focus that enables her to navigate the various layers situated on the technological frontier. She finds the device by accident as a child and it virtually enhances her interactions with technological artifacts scattered around the world map. Through these interactions, she acquires more skills such as gathering information, hacking machines, and uncovering the map. She also learns more about the apocalypse and her own role in this world during her progression on the path of the main story. By activating the Focus, she can access a virtual space that adds privileged meaning to the overall space of exploration. As a consequence, sites become transitory and situated in different temporal layers when Aloy navigates between the time-space seen by all and the unseen layers that complement it. She shifts from one spatial layer to another. The Focus emphasizes her status as a fringe character in the game by turning her into a border crosser with advanced knowledge. Other characters recognize her special abilities to make connections, but do not necessarily understand how she makes them because the virtual space remains invisible to them.

In terms of gameplay, the Focus fulfills two functions: It is a navigation system that also provides access to a twenty-first century communication network that still works within the game. It is used by the faction of the Carja tribe engaged in a civil war for imperialist purposes and by Sylens, a rebel who eventually appears to support and guide Aloy through her main quest in order to prevent the destruction of the human population by a corrupted AI. Both functions, i.e. navigation and communication, steer the spatial immersion of the player because they facilitate the connection of in-game events with contemporary discourses and pop cultural references that the player knows more about than Aloy. As Nitsche argues, when discussing the player's involvement in a video game, "[u]ncovering the space, its drama, and meaning goes hand in hand with the gradual comprehension of events and objects into narrative context" (45). The Focus can therefore be considered as a tool for the mediation of temporal and spatial context. It provides the player with privileged knowledge about the meaning and significance of the heroine's quest.

In addition to Aloy's access to *Horizon Zero Dawn*'s archive, players bring their own perspectives to the fictional gamespace. They complement the virtual space with their understanding of the twenty-first-century technology represented in the gamespace, such as computer interfaces, holograms, interactive displays, and other technological equipment. Tavinor argues that in story-driven video games "the player has an epistemic interest in the fictional world: successfully playing the game, interacting with the simulation, or interpreting the narrative all demand that the participant is able to access what is fictional of the world" (74). Through the asymmetric distribution of knowledge between players,

NPCs, and protagonist, the game constructs a second, technological frontier in which the powers that arise from knowledge advantage are crucial to the interactive assembly of a cognitive map.

The technological frontier in the sense of an interstitial space is mapped onto the in-game surroundings once the Focus is activated by the player. While exploring the world of *Horizon Zero Dawn*, the player can search for vantage points, often situated on an elevation, mountain, or ruined skyscraper. Vantage points virtually display images of buildings or constructed sites that are now ruins directly on their former geographical location. Thereby they convey information about the building's past purpose. In combination with audio files that players can listen to while looking around the virtual rendering of architecture, vantage points allow the player-character to retrace the path of a traveler right in the early stages of the apocalypse when places designated as Mother's cradle or Devil's Thirst on the map had names players can situate in the United States, such as Colorado Springs or Denver.

Overall, information gathered with the Focus is site-specific. Datapoints can only be found in specific places and provide information about the explored space, the time of their recording, and their connections to other sites around the globe. This means that players build a joint archive of a near future from our perspective and Aloy's current gamespace as they assemble a cognitive map. "Cognitive maps are complex mental interpretations of a real or fictional environment, and its components that live in the fictional plane" (161), Nitsche observes. The assembly of information during the player's spatial exploration in *Horizon Zero Dawn* leads to a "resulting cognitive map [that] ties spaces together in a meaningful way, assembles events in a spatial order, and positions the human in relation to them" (Nitsche 162). Vantage points, found footage, and recordings in the game transform settlements, buildings, and wilderness into temporal nodes. The nodal structure of space makes switching timelines possible to compare the game's present renewal to its highly technologized past as well as to the possible futures that the game suggests through the references to actual twenty-first century environmental issues and technological advances.

The archive allows players to uncover the reason for the apocalypse that the game describes as a fatal malfunction of self-reproductive military machines and weapons causing an ecological crisis because of their consumption of biological material to fuel their progress. This insight reveals the ecocritical stance of *Horizon Zero Dawn*. The game's storyline gains its environmental perspective from the science fiction backstory that attributes the fault for the disaster to the greed for economic gain and military supremacy of a tech company with production sites around the globe. The solution is terraforming, which in science fiction most often means to alter the environment in order to make possible the support of terrestrial life forms on other planets. In *Horizon Zero Dawn*, however, the terraforming system is launched on Earth and not in space. Instead of sending humans on a quest to find new inhabitable space out there, the game positions this planet as the only viable solution for the survival of the biosphere. Thus, the reimagined frontier negotiates the material impact of a former militaristic and capitalist notion of unlimited progress as well as the altered relations between nature, society, culture, and technology. What has once failed can potentially fail again. Therefore, the threat of extinction remains inscribed in the open world of *Horizon Zero Dawn* and its successful prevention only seems tangible where flexibility and openness trumps the ordering pull of fixity and permanence.

The Frontier as Endangered Ecosystem

Ultimately, *Horizon Zero Dawn*'s eco-fictional resolution challenges imaginaries of unlimited spatial expansion that would allow to avoid the consequences of ecological wastage, such as climate change or – to come back to the idea of the frontier – the ruthless exploitation and conquest of territories. The problems caused by the damages to organic life and terrestrial ecosystems cannot be escaped but need to be dealt with right on location. By offering the player the experiences of repurposing machine components, and by extension, industrial waste, of exploring the temporally dense spaces of the game world, and of uncovering the main story arc through player-character interaction, the game constructs its gamespace as an ecology that remains precarious even after the first success of the terraforming system.

In "Games as Environmental Texts" (2011), Alenda Y. Chang underlines the relevance and potential of games that include ecological principles in their game design:

> Ecological specificity and accuracy may be neither necessary nor sufficient criteria for successful commercial games, but if we seek to measure games as instruments of public knowledge, it suddenly becomes worthwhile to make games that are more meaningfully local, games that take the goal of environmental realism seriously—not solely in terms of the visual rendering of environments, but also at the levels of sound design, weather, species density and distribution, and the arrangement of organic and inorganic actors in complex interrelations. (59–60)

Even if one could criticize *Horizon Zero Dawn* for "predicating player success on extraction and use of natural resources" (58) – a gameplay driver common for most blockbuster games that Chang identifies as anti-ecological –, its handling and contextualization within the gameworld must clearly be regarded as a successful development of ecological consciousness that takes known forms of play a step further into an ecocritical future.

In this sense, it is "meaningfully local." Its environments are subject to temporal change and a thick visual density that is not only rendered visible by traces of decay and overgrowth. It also becomes consistently accessible during player interaction with the environment through the Focus device, vantage points, and textual artifacts that are invariably tied to specific places in the gameworld. Locations clearly differ in terms of distinct climates, diverse social settings, and localized resources (if not finite throughout, at least scarce in appearance). Moreover, they are subject to dynamic weather and a night and day cycle. Finally, machines certainly are fair game and thus subjected to the game principles of domination and manipulation, their position in relation to other actors and to the player-character, however, is far more complex. The set of possible interactions is broad with alternative options that go beyond hunting for resources. The manipulation of tallnecks, for instance, resembles the marking of threatened species for conservation purposes. With overall five active tallnecks in the main game and one more in the *Frozen Wilds* DLC that the player can rescue and repair, their number is limited. Once Aloy discovers one of them, she interacts with the machine once and then leaves as the tallneck continues on its path, unimpaired. Other types of machines are available for alternative interactions as riding mounts or temporarily tamed protection. After a while, though, the manipulation effect fades, and they return to their flock or become a threat to Aloy once more. The immediate effect of these time-bound interactions is that the player cannot take these changes for granted but needs to remain vigilant and respectful of techno-nature at all times. In this sense, *Horizon Zero Dawn*'s postapocalyptic frontier calls for its populations to sustain an inherently fragile equilibrium and to embrace its cultural, social, and ecological richness and diversity instead of seeking to exploit nature and dominate the living environment.

Works Cited

Campbell, Neil. *The Rhizomatic West: Representing the American West in a Transnational, Global, Media Age*. University of Nebraska Press, 2008.
Chang, Alenda Y. "Games as Environmental Texts." *Qui Parle: Critical Humanities and Social Sciences*, vol. 19, no. 2, 2011, pp. 57–84.
Horizon Zero Dawn. Guerilla, 2017.
Nitsche, Michael. *Video Game Spaces: Image, Play, and Structure in 3D Game Worlds*. The MIT Press, 2008.
Ryan, Marie-Laure. *Narrative as Virtual Reality 2: Revisiting Immersion and Interactivity in Literature and Electronic Media*. Johns Hopkins University Press, 2015.
Soja, Edward W. *Postmodern Geographies: The Reassertion of Space in Critical Social Theory*. Verso, 1989.
Stuart, Keith. "Dawn of a new Era: Why the best video games are not about saving the World." *The Guardian*, 19 April 2017, www.theguardian.com/technology/2017/apr/19/horizon-zero-dawn-why-best-modern-video-games-are-not-about-saving-the-world. Accessed 30 December 2019.
Tavinor, Grant. *The Art of Videogames*. Wiley-Blackwell, 2009.
Turner, Frederick Jackson. *The Frontier in American History*. 1920. The University of Arizona Press, 1986.
Wilderness Act. Wilderness Connect, University of Montana, www.wilderness.net/learn-about-wilderness/key-laws/wilderness-act/default.php. Accessed 30 December 2019.

David Callahan
Owning Global Spaces and the Frontier in *Uncharted 4: A Thief's End*

Who has played Naughty Dog's *Uncharted 4: A Thief's End* (2016) and not enjoyed the madcap drive in a 4x4 down the long slope of the fictitious city of King's Bay in Madagascar, attempting to avoid an armored vehicle and to save one of the party at the bottom? The lack of time to make considered decisions adds to the frantic desperation and contributes to the sense of satisfaction when one arrives breathlessly at the harbor. Before being able to catch much of a breath, you are off again, this time on the horizontal, as you try to catch up to a convoy of enemy vehicles in order to rescue someone. And yet who has not also been aware, despite the concentration required to navigate, avoid obstacles and enemy fire, and shoot back, that your avatar Nathan Drake and his vehicle are mostly smashing their way destructively through people's properties, crops and livelihoods? Of course, no real people are seeing their fences flattened or leaping for safety as you come their way, and yet it must matter in representation that these things are being depicted as happening somewhere, in this place and not another one, in a named country even if the city is made up. Representation studies have insisted that "digital systems [...] operationalize and instrumentalize race" (Nakamura 209), whether race is their deliberate focus or not. This chapter will explore some of the ways in which the locations in *Uncharted 4* "operationalize and instrumentalize" discourses of ethnic, cultural, and gender formations in ways related to the ongoing relevance of Frederick Jackson Turner's "The Significance of the Frontier in American History" (1893). The chapter claims that the representation of spaces and locations, and what these places make possible within gameplay, reproduce sedimented hierarchies of cultural value, while simultaneously attempting to articulate an updated politics of gender more in tune with contemporary priorities.

One of the characteristics which most marks the *Uncharted* series (2007–2017) is its traversing of global spaces generally beyond most people's experience, spaces evoked in the game series' map-referring title. Nathan Drake and assorted family members and companions are involved in complicated quests for treasures of different types, and these quests take them through well-

---

Note: Funding for this chapter was provided by the project "Bodies in Transit 2: Difference and Indifference," Ministry of Science, Information & Universities, Spain (Reference FFI2017–84555-C2–2-P).

https://doi.org/10.1515/9783110675184-006

known adventure locations such as tropical jungles, far-flung islands, and remote countries. In the process the player has to work out how to traverse difficult terrain or cityscapes without attracting enemies' attention, eliminate these enemies when necessary, deal with puzzles designed to make access to the treasure difficult, and follow numerous cut scenes which stitch the narratives together. Individual differences in playthroughs come from how skillful the player is at managing the game's mechanics of movement, combat, and clues which enable puzzles to be solved: the common affordances of action-adventure games.[1]

Playing our way through the visually detailed locations does not just provide us with what Cara Ellison calls the "feedback candy" (19) of digital interaction, but reprises the classic tropes of imperial adventure stories in which the rest of the world is available for Euro-American quest narratives, masculinity-proving scenarios, and the establishment of hierarchies of value in which local inhabitants' priorities are written over by those of white males from the centers of metropolitan power. Martin Green sums this context up bluntly: "[T]he adventure tales that formed the light reading of Englishmen for two hundred years and more […] were, in fact, the energizing myth of English imperialism" (3). And Souvik Mukherjee in his *Videogames and Postcolonialism: Empire Plays Back* (2017) wearily points out how many adventure video games "seem to replay the narratives of empire from time immemorial" (55). As Edward Said would stress, "[u]nderlying social space are territories, lands, geographical domains, the actual geographical underpinnings of the imperial, and also the cultural contest" (93). Critical inquiry has only confirmed this assessment, from Mary Louise Pratt to English historian and novelist Miranda Carter who encapsulates contemporary thinking when she points out that "[m]any of these books are now unreadable. They were cheerleading for imperialism, and were imbued with an unthinking assumption of the racial superiority of the white colonial adventurer over the colonised native." In this dispensation, the world is a series of locations in which ranging through other people's territories is available to particular white, male characters and no-one else.

---

[1] In another sort of chapter, the need to dominate the protocols through which digital space itself encases gameplay might conceivably be highlighted. For example, games made by or with a high degree of input by Indigenous peoples intent on creating "space for Indigenous teachings that reconnect players with the land utilizing gameplay" (89), in the words of Métis scholar Elizabeth LaPensée, cannot avoid the movement across both digital space and represented space as a basic gameplay affordance. Thus, in the Inuit *Never Alone* (2014) we explore our relation to the natural world by way of moving ourselves across it and achieving certain things, or not, which enable us to keep moving. Whether this affordance in itself always implies extrapolation to scripts of dominance and hierarchy is beyond the intention of this chapter.

The Respawning Frontier Myth

The games may accordingly be seen as significant present-day iterations of the myth of the frontier which deserve serious attention from American Studies scholars and not simply from video game scholars. The analysis of the locations traversed in *Uncharted 4* in terms of the conflation of colonial adventure narratives and the frontier myth is licensed, in part, by the lineage which can be traced between two characters with closely related names, Nathan Drake from the *Uncharted* series, usually called Nate, and James Fenimore Cooper's Nathaniel Bumppo, usually called Natty. The latter is the crucial mythic figure in Cooper's series of five Leatherstocking novels, termed by Richard Slotkin "the seminal fictions of American literary history" (80). Cooper's ambiguous frontier hero, whose career throughout the novels sees him pushed to the edge of practical significance, but to the center of mythic significance, as the U.S. becomes ever more settled by Europeans, serves as one origin of Nate's traversal of wild and exotic spaces not at all in search of wealth or ownership (despite the treasures he is ostensibly hunting for), as of a sense of self-worth and valorization outside the settled spaces and structures of society.[2]

Frederick Jackson Turner's "The Significance of the Frontier in American History," enquiring into the closing of the American frontier as an arena for free actions by white males had, then, already been amply predicted and explored in the Leatherstocking novels written by Cooper in the second quarter of the nineteenth century. In fact, Cooper's first novel in the series, *The Pioneers* in 1823, focused on a then-settled New York town in which order has been imposed on local space but in which order still has to be imposed on individuals who behave as if frontier options still remained. Hunting is no longer the simple choice of the individual, for example, but is legislated upon and controlled by the authorities. And two characters at first intended to be bit-players in the drama, former frontier roamers on either side of the European and Indigenous divide, Natty Bumppo and Chingachgook, both elderly and hemmed in by restrictions which they are unable to adapt to, so began to intrigue Cooper that

---

[2] Another origin, of course, is flagged in Nathan's surname, "Drake," associated with maritime frontiers as Natty is of landbound ones. It is a surname proposed by Nate's brother Sam in *Uncharted 4* as an aid to evading the authorities after the possibility arises that the brothers might be wrongly charged with the murder of their dead mother's former employer. It is not a name plucked out of nowhere but associated by Sam with their mother's suggestion that Sir Francis Drake did have heirs, as yet unknown to history. The fantasy remains unproven at the end of the games. It might be noted that Nathan's original surname, Morgan, is also that of a famous pirate, Sir Henry Morgan.

Natty was elevated to central status in the remaining four books in the series (see Franklin xxvi), and Chingachgook became a major character in three of them. While Cooper redefined many aspects of the adventure novel in his career, he has been most remembered for the creation of what David Reynolds calls "[h]is central likeable pariah, Natty Bumppo" (185). Natty, however, is not shown venturing beyond the American space, apart from brief approaches to now Canadian territory in *The Pathfinder* (1840), while that other "likeable pariah" Nate is almost always anywhere but America. Most of the nations he traverses are not now politically colonized, but most of them throughout the game series are places typically associated with subjugation to European power and priorities at some time in their history.

Just as England could almost never do duty as the location of a British quest narrative in the colonial period, so also the United States, after the end of the frontier myth, became less available for American adventure narratives set in the present. In Turner's essay, still the most influential assessment of American history despite the priorities and interests of everyone other than white males being absent, the frontier had presented such a structuring factor in American culture that even when it was perceived to have closed – as in there being no more Native American lands to appropriate – its impact in American history had been such that the national character had been shaped by it, and this had had permanent effects on American culture. One effect Turner did not immediately predict was that the rest of the world would become, in displaced form, the frontier at which American males could continue to prove themselves and expand their wealth, particularly the world associated with what the nineteenth century had classified as "inferior peoples" (Horsman 272), cognate to some extent with Indigenous Americans.

By the time of Turner's 1910 speech on "Social Forces in American History" he had rectified this, recognizing that now the national project had led to the U.S. having become "an imperial republic [...] with a potential voice in the problems of Europe, Asia, and Africa" (315). Since Turner's first essay, the defeat of Spain in the brief war of 1898 had seen the U.S. effectively gain colonies or protectorates beyond the nation's borders, those of Cuba, Puerto Rico, the Philippines and Guam. Even so, the expansion of the potential scenes of action of American heroes should hardly have been surprising, given the nineteenth-century history of American consideration of annexing or taking over or purchasing a range of nearby territories. The Louisiana Purchase in 1803 from France, the takeover of Mexican territories in 1846–48, the purchase of Alaska from Russia in 1867, not to mention the relentless annexation of Native lands, took place in an America in which, as Paul Frymer details in *Building an American Empire* (2017), many lawmakers seriously debated taking over such places as the Dominican Republic, the Yucatán, Cuba, or even the whole of Mexico, well before the War of 1898.

In comparison to European colonial possessions, the offshore spaces directly controlled by the U.S. were and are few, offering a limited range of exotic spaces to serve as national frontier adventure locations. To remedy this lack of direct or official colonial connections, which would provide innumerable British adventure heroes with reasons to travel to far-flung territories around the world, American storytellers were thus freed up to consider nothing less than the whole world as the possible stamping ground of American adventurers. In terms of U.S. cultural mythology then, the *Uncharted* series may be seen in part as a post-Frederick Jackson Turner revisiting of the never dead frontier myth.

From Natty to Nate: The Persistence of Frontier Heroes

With respect to the imaginative effects of the vanishing of the American frontier associated with Turner's essay (but actually announced by the Superintendent of the U.S. Census in 1890), American spaces became for a time less available as the sites of male quest adventures. Symptomatically, when Edgar Rice Burroughs published the first of his adventure novels, *A Princess of Mars* (1912 in serial form), the action is not set in Burroughs' present but in the period immediately after the American Civil War, the 1860s and 1870s, when expansion into American Indian frontier territories became the central relation to space in the American culture of the time. Writing of such a location in the twentieth century was to write of a known and supposedly bygone past, and although adventure narratives set in well-trodden pasts remained popular, Burroughs was restless for something more surprising to his readers, so that his prospector protagonist, chased by Apaches, transits a mysterious Arizona cave to find himself on Mars. After all, readers knew what the end result of settler-invader conflict with the Apaches was. Freed from the limitations of a nation which defined itself as a nation of frontier-explorers and frontier-dominators, but now without a frontier, *A Princess of Mars* was able to trade in as many colonial, racist, and masculinist tropes as occurred to Burroughs, transferred into a realm beyond most of the constrictions of realism. After the spectacular success of this series – eventually to total nine novels – Burroughs supposedly came back down to earth with *Tarzan of the Apes* in 1914. Once again though, *Tarzan* was not set in America except for its use of romantic novel conventions towards the end. Set in West Africa, most of its central characters were not American either, but

British or French. The space of adventure was no longer North America, and the specifically American transmutation of this myth into the renewed adventure of the road trip had yet to occur.

Naughty Dog's use of the geography of faraway does not need to go as far as Mars, after a century in which the rest of the world increasingly became a frontier to the U.S., and neither is the frontier of Cooper's myth mapped simplistically onto the *Uncharted* games, while Nathan Drake is not exactly Nathaniel Bumppo. Firstly, Nate's frontier is not a settling one but an adventuring one, although this was also what Natty desired the frontier to be, and what the narrative movement of the Leatherstocking novels evidences. Natty Bumppo himself was not a settler but a roamer, a frontier impulse which Turner somewhat fudged by insisting that at one and the same time the frontier was peopled by those who "viewed governmental restraints with suspicion as a limitation on their right to work out their own individuality" (303) and by those whose frontier freedom outfitted them for "constructing democratic society" (302). Both Natty and Nate are not conspicuously community-minded, which nevertheless does not prevent them from displaying "instinctive honesty, courage and generosity" (75) in Deborah Madsen's description of Natty. Like Natty, Nate appears to live in a world in which frontiers are an affective location rather than an official one, given that he is able to travel the globe without troubling himself overmuch about borders, passports, and local authorities.

That Nate goes to some of the most obscure parts of the world over the four games may be attributed to the fact that the application of the word "uncharted" to the United States has become increasingly impossible in the present, although it is not inconceivable that Alaska could serve such a desire. Even so, in the conventions of an *Uncharted* plot in which various locations need to be traversed as enigmatic clues are followed up in the search for an ultimate objective that lies somewhere beyond the familiar space, it is also not inconceivable that a location in the United States could serve as one of these waystations. Potential locations could have been generated in acceptably remote areas on the one hand, of which the United States has many, both in the experience of most individuals and in myth: locations in the desert Southwest, for example, or even mysterious houses at the end of a forested road in populated New England, to evoke another mythic location.[3]

---

[3] Symptomatically, the sequence in *Uncharted 3* in non-remote France takes place in a ruined chateau which appears to be completely external to either the operations of power and order in the country, or indeed any version of daily life in France in any sphere. Lost in a forest, and completely stripped of any local inhabitant, this is a location derived from fable and adventure stories in which the knowledge that it is in France does not provide any links to French cultural

In *Uncharted 4*, however, the contemporary U.S. serves largely as a space of safety, routine, and order. Nathan Drake's salvaging of sunken copper wire in New Orleans, and doing legitimate business paperwork, plus brief moments of nostalgia in his attic with mementos of past adventures, are all explicitly presented near the beginning of the game as having reduced the scope and drama of his life. This is amply proven by his wife Elena's beating him at the video game *Crash Bandicoot*, symptomatically a jump-and-run platformer in which mastering various types of spatial challenge is the key to success. In order to rectify this reversal of conventional gender power in the mastery of video game space, Nate leaves the domestic space – both that of the family and that of the nation – to prove himself in the spaces of others.

In *Uncharted 4*, as Nate reaches the geographical limit of his journey in the game, an important subtext emerges which offsets private questing against intimations of more general thinking about human beings, social organization, and responsibility. This subtext comes into view via the gradual uncovering of the history of Henry Avery, the pirate whose treasure Nate is on the track of. Henry Avery supposedly only plundered and murdered the non-British, which, in Nate's brother Sam's eyes, makes him a "good thief." Sam, however, is noticeably not the moral center of the game, not just because we do not play as him, but in the sense that the much more self-serving nature of his agenda is always apparent. This is shockingly revealed at the point when he admits that the story of needing to find Avery's treasure in order to escape death at the hands of a Latin American crime lord, a story which has led Nate to put his marriage and his life at risk, had been made up in order to manipulate Nate's sentiments and get him to help. When they finally find Avery's pirate community called "Libertalia," it is seen to have been an attempt at an egalitarian society well before the American Revolution, but one which failed on account of the inability of the community's leaders to distribute wealth fairly. This thematic strand is interestingly ambiguous, in that it can be read as a critique of the acquisitive selfishness which has characterized Sam, not to mention mainstream American political ideologies, or it can be read as a suggestion that the desire to establish a fair society as a commune beyond official structures is doomed to failure on account of inevitable human selfishness. That is, individualism is revealed to be destructive and not joyfully liberating at all. In this, the thematic strand both denies the supposed positive effects of the frontier, and serves as one more vehicle for

---

flows other than through certain details of its architecture. It could of course be claimed that after all what we encounter are the "playful geographies of video games" (Lammes and DesMale, 4), and that expecting documentary attention to detail in such a genre is unreasonable.

Nate's maturation story in which the attractions of the freedom of uncharted locations are ultimately rendered secondary to the attractions of family and the rejection of male swashbuckling in which he damages almost everywhere he goes outside the U.S.

If the game's quest for the treasure of Libertalia ends up revealing the story of the failure of the dream of the just society beyond the frontier and beyond the reach of official authorities, it might be asked whether the game supports any vision of social organization at all. The frontier myth typically privileges individuals distant from the control of any organizing authority. Although considered an American cultural myth, and in Turner's view a promoter of democratic thinking and practices, it is also a general utopian myth of escaping the state and rules and regulations of any kind. The self-policing community beyond the purview of official control remains a vision suspicious of the intentions and efficacy of a central authority, whether democratically elected or not, as does the Wyoming redoubt in one of Naughty Dog's other narrative games, *The Last of Us*. *Uncharted 4: A Thief's End* enacts a trajectory in which the protagonist is initially subject not so much to the domestication of the home space to the rule-bound routines of employment. Nate's job is as much taken up with paperwork as with the reduced excitement of the underwater salvage of material which the capitalist, consumerist society needs, within the city boundaries.

From U.S. Order to Madagascar

Beyond the safe boundaries of Nate's life, the principal non-American locations transited during the game are Italy, Scotland, and, by far the largest in terms of gameplay, Madagascar. In addition, in a prelude to the adventure, Nate and his brother Sam negotiate a Panamanian prison and particularly the Spanish-colonial ruins which lie just outside the prison. In the ruins which Nate has to investigate as part of a scheme to track down an old pirate treasure, two typical patterns can be observed. On the one hand, wherever Nate goes he destroys ruins or elaborate structures. It does not matter how complex or old they are, as soon as he starts jumping, climbing, and exploring he begins doing everything from breaking bits off them to seriously damaging or even completely destroying structures. His very first handhold as he climbs the ruin in Panama broke off in my playthrough (although no doubt it did not in that of more competent players).

In the other prelude, when Nate is a child taken by his brother Sam on an illicit roam outside the children's home in which he is placed, parentless, the suburban American space explored remains as undestroyed at the end of the experience as at the beginning. American locations are apparently too well-made to be affected by the actions of Nate and Sam within them, even when transgressive, such as breaking out of the institution and, in a continuation of this flashback later in the game, breaking into a house which contains records of their mother. Or, in another reading, as implicitly representatives of order and resistance to disorder, American spaces remain resistant to the destruction evidenced in other countries. The principal locations in these American segments of the game are those of large, long-established houses or the house-like institution in which the child Nate is being kept, quiet streets and roads, tree-lined and calm. Even though Sam and Nate introduce disorder into these scenarios, it is the temporary disorder of their challenge to the institutional control of the home, and the social control enabling people with a lot of possessions to hold onto them over against social inequality. At the end of the sequence in the home of a woman whom the brothers' mother used to work for, they escape the police and nothing physical is destroyed. Moreover, while they mow down large numbers of people in non-American spaces, they do not kill people in these sequences in the United States but merely run away from them.

The other pattern in the game with respect to the locations traversed is an implicit critique of local people, who have not cared for their heritage, are not present in or on it, and who are read by the game as having no stake in it, in a possible metonymy of how the whole world belongs to America and Americans. In Panama, it takes an American to explore the ruins, despite the fact they are adjacent to the prison. No local person apparently has the knowledge or intelligence to have worked out that there might be useful information to be decoded within the ruins, or the physical ability to access and manage the space of the ruin. After all, the whole of Central and South America are ideologically "uncharted" in U.S. terms. That is, while maps exist which portray these areas, their mythic existence in the American imaginary as disorder enables them to serve as types of frontier after all. The jail in Panama seems as if it is at the very edge of civilization, not merely because of its murderous prison culture and official corruption, but geographically. No town or city is visible beyond the jail walls, and only the overgrown and crumbling ruins of colonial history lie adjacent.

One of the origins of this staging ground of entitled action is not specifically American, but rather the colonial hierarchy in which local people do not deserve their land on account of their not having developed it according to European frameworks of appropriate development. This viewpoint was taken up with vicious efficiency by settling-invading Americans, for whom Native Americans' land use patterns were destroyed because they did not enact settled agricultural practices, let alone technologically aided industrial development or the circulation of capital as driver of individual and community wealth. To such beliefs were added racial hierarchies if Native Americans showed they were in fact quite capable of adaptation to, say, settled agriculture, and even Christianity. The shameful event of the Trail of Tears in the 1830s is only the most notorious example of the implacable opposition of settler-invaders to any ownership of territory by people classified as racially Other.

After Panama and the United States, the action shifts to Scotland. Scotland is not an undeveloped country, and one of the key cultural origins of the United States itself. Nevertheless, the Scottish ruins are treated mercilessly, dynamited at the drop of a hat both by Nate when he feels he needs to, and of course by the mercenaries they are in conflict with, hired by their American enemy, Rafe. As Nate says in this location at one point with fine sensitivity: "Let's desecrate some graves," while his brother Sam tells him: "You have a real knack for breaking things, especially cliffs." This could be seen as a fairness in destructiveness: Europe as well as everywhere else gets trashed in the quest for the treasure. But there is a difference between this remote Scottish coast and the largest space in the game, that of Madagascar. The location Nate and Sam smash their way around in Scotland is called in the game a "forgotten coastline," given that all its former inhabitants have decided there is no future in remaining there and there is nobody living in the area. Once again local people are not present in their own heritage space, seemingly do not know there might be useful or valuable information there, and it is left for white American men to treat it as they will in the service of their acquisitive quest.[4]

In Madagascar, on the other hand, local people live and conduct daily life around many locations in the game, such as the belltower in the middle of a busy urban market, not to mention the houses and smallholdings which Nate and Sam crash through as they flee the made-up city of King's Bay and head for a more rural location. The chapter "Hidden in Plain Sight," which takes place in King's Bay, is characteristically disturbing. The old tower is locked,

---

[4] Thus it is that we get impressive attention to visual details in the representation of the black-market auction house in Italy and the cliff it is built on, but no details at all with respect to where exactly it is (although evocative of the Amalfi coast), or what connection it has to Italy other than the nationality of lowly employees such as waiters and security guards. This Italian mansion is largely an exception to the pattern of visiting destruction upon the spaces and built environments of others, with minimal damage being inflicted, perhaps because it is not the type of heritage building which signifies a culture's history. From a distance, some of it looks too new, like a Las Vegas Italian palace rather than an Italian palace with a rooted relation to local history. Even so, it is a space whose secrets and its promise of wealth are unable to be left to locals.

with the surrounding people paying it so little attention that our heroes are able to swing up the side and enter with no-one noticing. As is usual in action-adventure media texts, no local people, no bored and agile children, no disaffected youth, are hanging out in the monument, even though the city and its busy market are right up against its walls. The idea that splendid ruins could exist anywhere and not be exploited by the tourist industry and/or used in spatial discourses of local identities and achievements is disruptive even of the thin realism of the adventure narrative. Moreover, this building is unkempt inside and out, iterative of the established belief that non-white peoples cannot take care of either their space or their time, either their geography or their history. At the end of this sequence, Nate destroys the complex cog mechanism which has apparently remained functional for centuries, and for good measure brings the main giant bell in the tower crashing down through the structure and on through the floor.

At this point, Nate and his friend Sully rush out and nobody in the market appears outraged, frightened, or anything much, as Nate and Sully are immediately launched into a firefight with the Shoreline mercenaries, who are also not locals, with whom they are in competition throughout the game. Where local law enforcement might feature in this scenario was clearly too much for the game designers to factor in. At least Sully has the decency to say: "We can never ever come back to this city," to which Nate replies: "Add it to the list." This is about as close as the game comes with respect to the destructiveness of Nate's movement through other people's spaces to what Grant Tavinor calls "a reflective component that would make the moral context obvious to the player" (161).

Even so, this is a conversation in the fine tradition of Indiana Jones and related heroes for whom the spaces of others may be trashed almost as a boyish prank, echoing a more sinister sense of entitlement running through American history evidenced initially in the destruction of Native American settlements. This entitlement was not just confined to the borders of the United States or adjacent American Indian territories felt to be destined to satisfy the desires of invader-settlers. With the 1823 Monroe Doctrine having unilaterally claimed that the Americas as a whole were a zone in which the United States had the right and even duty to intervene to preserve American interests, nowhere at all in the vicinity was safe during the rest of the century. Already in 1857, the infamous burning to the ground of the city of Granada in Nicaragua by would-be expansionist American William Walker inaugurated a series of high-handed American destruction of other people's spaces outside the imagined natural boundaries of the U.S. which continues into the present.

Walker's actions were retaliation against acts by local inhabitants, but Nate's actions are not directed intentionally at local people. It is noticeable throughout the games that local people tend to suffer at the hands of the mercenaries Nate is fighting against, so that local inhabitants of the locations portrayed are not treated as foreign obstacles to Nate's actions on the frontier. Nate's human enemies are not from the spaces he is crashing through but are mercenaries from elsewhere – in *Uncharted 4* they tend to be South Africans, given that Shoreline is a South African company led by South African Nadine Ross. By not having Nate's enemies culturally implicated in the locations he traverses in this game leads to the sensation that, as Stephanie Patridge surmises in her article on "The Incorrigible Social Meaning of Video Game Imagery" (2011): "In many cases, the representational violence that we find in video games is presented so that it does not directly implicate our shared, moral reality" (310). Mercenaries are not defending their own land or society and visit even more disruption on local inhabitants than Nate and his friends; mowing them down is more acceptable than would be the uncomfortably colonial mowing down of local people who are defending their own spaces and heritage. Unlike mostly nameless non-playable characters, named locations, on the other hand, cannot be so easily subtracted from our consideration of their roles in narrative development. One way to evade the cultural weight of named locations, of charted locations one might say, is to avoid spaces which are too well known, spaces which are "marked with disparate anchors of locations and places, each carrying meaning, temporal significance and past memories" (Hameed and Perkis 325). Madagascar may be a real place, but in a world in which everywhere has now been charted, it may still serve in a game called *Uncharted* as it is obscure enough that it presumably does not possess either significance or memories for almost all of its players.

One significance that a distant place from the U.S. such as Madagascar would have had in the nineteenth century is as the location of ethnic subalterns. This highlights another difference from Cooper's world in that overt issues of race are sidelined in *Uncharted*, issues which had been crucial to settling-invading America, but which are only implicit in the games. That is, Nate does not spend time reflecting and commenting upon race and ethnicity, unlike Natty. This does not mean the games are post-racial, given that the central group of adventurers associated with Nate are white (only in *Uncharted: The Lost Legacy*, the last game in the series, is this aspect challenged by having two mixed-heritage women as the central characters rather than Nate[5]), and almost all of the un-

---

[5] Such a game has been called a "spiritual sequel, where an affinity between different and autonomous [...] video games may be identified and acknowledged by developers (usually in the case of video games with a cult following or a previously cultivated brand" (Kudláč 195).

charted territories passed through over the course of the game series are occupied by those traditionally identified by white Americans as racial others. White American entitlement becomes implicit rather than explicit. This is perhaps the most significant difference between Cooper's myth and Naughty Dog's transmutation of it, for the frontiers which the games explore are not made up of American spaces and the desire to conquer the people already occupying them is not an issue.

Updating the Male Frontier

The part of Nate's wife, Elena, in *Uncharted 4* further indexes a significant difference from the world of Cooper, that of the relation of the masculine hero to women. Where Cooper consistently included women on his frontiers, incorporating memorable and strong figures such as Cora in *The Last of the Mohicans* (1826), in the end Natty is unable to settle down with anyone, and fails in his one attempt at persuading a woman to ally herself with him, in *The Pathfinder* (1840). In this he becomes a type of isolate male American hero, outside the domestication which female characters in nineteenth-century fiction tended to represent, his priority being to remain beyond the control of any authorities.

Uncharted 4 reprises precisely this aspect of Nate as he lies to his wife and disappears with his brother and a close male friend in order to pursue adventure far beyond the United States, but in the end the game rejects male attempts to evade domesticity and local boundaries as insufficient. It is Elena who comes to Nate's aid at a crucial point and underlines the value of the teamwork of their relationship. Near the end of the game, she is the one who reenables the possibility of continuing to traverse global spaces as affirmation of American desires when she arranges a permit to legitimately explore treasure possibilities in Malaysia, together, and takes the initiative to buy out the salvage company Nate has been an employee of. This supposed throwaway detail, in which the woman encourages and allies herself to the man's frontier-dreaming, serves importantly to insert American roaming over the world's spaces into a legally approved framework, accepted by local authorities and in conjunction with their priorities. Elena is an example of the evolution in the representations of women in all types of cultural production, including video games, confirming what Audrey Anable underlines throughout her book *Playing With Feelings: Video Games and Affect* (2018): "[I]t seems increasingly important to understand how video games are more than just containers for nonideological aesthetic experiences" (121). This evolution, however uneven as it is, is one of the marks of the present, and a sign that video game producing companies as large as Naughty Dog do pay attention to cultural critique and do not simply reenact hoary myths of male actions on or beyond the frontier.[6]

At the end of *Uncharted 4*, in the game's coda, we are back with the domesticity of the marriage, but it is noticeable that it is not the same safe suburban house as before. This house, at least, is situated on an exotic beach in an unspecified location. There are no other houses visible. It is a type of frontier after all, the hope of a location which is un-charted, off the grid, and thus where the American hero can truly find personal realization. From one angle this revisits Natty Bumppo's doomed search for a location in the continental U.S. where he could be free, free from the control of others, free from the control of official institutions such as the law. The game's epilog allows Nate this freedom even as it implicitly recognizes how doomed this desire is in its termination of his story arc; "the original Myth of the Frontier," in Slotkin's words, "held that history promised a career of unending youth expressed in interminable conquests of inexhaustible frontiers" (207). But youth can never be interminable, and Naughty Dog's bringing of Nate's story to a close as a (somewhat late) growing up narrative acknowledges this in elegiac mode. Natty is pushed farther and farther from settled locations as he gets older until he has to realize that there is nowhere else to go. In Cooper's work this is felt as a loss, as the price to pay for American expansion. The nation may succeed, but the (male) individual loses the possibility of immersion in spaces beyond formal control, this control partly symbolized by the company of a woman. Nate's journey finds, well before he gets old, that in fact there is somewhere else to go, something that Natty never did, and that marks Nate's journey as having explored the frontier myth and then having brought it into the present via a companionship of equals with a woman. Despite the geographic range of the game, and its reminders of the entitlements of colonial fiction, it is this personal relationship which lies at its moral center. The success of this relationship is marked at the end by their child, who is, again symptomatic of contemporary interventions in mythic conventions, not a boy but a girl. One with her own American dreams of frontiers to traverse, but in her case stirred by the now legal career of archaeological exploration her parents went on to enjoy when Nate abandoned treating everyone else's spaces as an unregulated frontier.

---

[6] The structural success of the game and its general narrative outline is all the more noteworthy given the departure of the creative director, Amy Hennig halfway through the production process (see Schreier for an absorbing account of this).

Works Cited

Anable, Audrey. *Playing with Feelings: Video Games and Affect*. University of Minnesota Press, 2018.
Burroughs, Edgar Rice. *A Princess of Mars*. 1912. Fall River Press, 2011.
Burroughs, Edgar Rice. *Tarzan of the Apes*. 1914. Penguin, 1990.
Carter, Miranda. "British Readers and Writers Need to Embrace their Colonial Past." *The Guardian*, 23 January 2014. Accessed 19 October 2019. www.theguardian.com/books/2014/jan/23/british-readers-writers-embrace-colonial-past
Cooper, James Fenimore. *The Pioneers; or, the Sources of the Susquehanna*. New York, 1823.
Cooper, James Fenimore. *The Last of the Mohicans: A Narrative of 1757*. Philadelphia, 1826.
Cooper, James Fenimore. *The Pathfinder; or, The Inland Sea*. Philadelphia, 1840.
Ellison, Cara. *Embed with Games: A Year on the Couch with Game Developers*. Polygon, 2015.
Franklin, Wayne. *James Fenimore Cooper: The Early Years*. Yale University Press, 2007.
Frymer, Paul. *Building an American Empire: The Era of Territorial and Political Expansion*. Princeton University Press, 2017.
Green, Martin. *Dreams of Adventure, Deeds of Empire*. Routledge & Kegan Paul, 1980.
Hameed, Asim and Andrew Perkis. "Spatial Storytelling: Finding Interdisciplinary Immersion." *Interactive Storytelling: International Conference on Interactive Digital Storytelling*, edited by Rebecca Rouse, Hartmut Koenitz and Mads Haahr, Springer, 2018, pp. 323–332.
Horsman, Reginald. *Race and Manifest Destiny: The Origins of American Racial Anglo-Saxonism*. Harvard University Press, 1981.
Kudláč, Martin. "Transmedia Storytelling: The Many Faces of Video Games, Fluid Narratives and Winding Seriality." *Body and Text: Cultural Transformations in New Media Environments*, edited by David Callahan and Anthony Barker, Springer 2019, pp. 191–203.
Lammes, Sybille and Stephanie de Smale. "Hybridity, Reflexivity and Mapping: A Collaborative Ethnography of Postcolonial Gameplay." *Open Library of Humanities*, vol. 4, no. 1, 2018, pp. 1–31.
LaPensée, Elizabeth. "Transformations and Remembrances in the Digital Game *We Sing for Healing*." *Transmotion*, vol. 3, no. 1, 2017, pp. 89–108.
Madsen, Deborah. *American Exceptionalism*. University Press of Mississippi, 1998.
Mukherjee, Souvik. *Videogames and Postcolonialism: Empire Plays Back*. Palgrave Macmillan, 2017.
Nakamura, Lisa. *Digitizing Race: Visual Cultures of the Internet*. Minnesota University Press, 2008.
Never Alone. E-Line Media, 2014.
Patridge, Stephanie. "The Incorrigible Social Meaning of Video Game Imagery." *Ethics and Information Technology*, vol. 13, 2011, pp. 303–312.
Pratt, Mary Louise. *Imperial Eyes: Travel Writing and Transculturation*. Routledge, 1992.
Reynolds, David. *Beneath the American Renaissance: The Subversive Imagination in the Age of Emerson and Melville*. Harvard University Press, 1988.
Said, Edward. *Culture and Imperialism*. Chatto & Windus, 1993.
Schreier, Jason. *Blood, Sweat, and Pixels: The Triumphant, Turbulent Stories Behind How Video Games are Made*. Harper, 2017.

Slotkin, Richard. *The Fatal Experiment: The Myth of the Frontier in the Age of Industrialization, 1800–1890*. 1985. University of Oklahoma Press, 1998.
Tavinor, Grant. *The Art of Videogames*. Wiley-Blackwell, 2009.
Turner, Frederick Jackson. *The Frontier in American History*. 1920. University of Arizona Press, 1986.
Uncharted 3: Drake's Deception. Naughty Dog, 2011.
Uncharted 4: A Thief's End. Naughty Dog, 2016.
Uncharted: The Lost Legacy. Naughty Dog, 2017.

Andrei Nae
From Male to Colonial Gaze: The Intersection of Patriarchy and Colonial Discourse in the Rebooted *Tomb Raider* Video Game Series

Since the release of the first *Tomb Raider* video game in 1996, Lara Croft has become a cultural icon present in virtually all mainstream visual media: video games, feature films, and comics. Her global popularity has inevitably turned Lara Croft into a research interest for many scholars, which has resulted in a significant body of literature (see Brown; Carr; Schleiner; Han et al.; Kennedy; Murray; Mikula; Pape; du Preez; Shaw). Although the *Tomb Raider* series has benefitted from constant academic attention, most works have focused primarily on the issue of gender and have downplayed or sometimes even ignored that of colonialism (see Breger). In addition to this, it is usually the first instalment of the series that is most often analyzed, while more recent games have so far not benefitted from the same amount of scholarly attention. This essay contributes to existing scholarship on the *Tomb Raider* franchise by investigating how patriarchy and colonial discourse intertwine in the rebooted origin story consisting of *Tomb Raider* (Crystal Dynamics, 2013), *Rise of the Tomb Raider* (Crystal Dynamics, 2015), and *Shadow of the Tomb Raider* (Eidos Montréal, 2018).

In the 1990s, action-adventure games were a privileged site of masculinity where the position of women was restricted to marginal roles such as those of passive victim or ludic reward. Although a few female playable characters had already been featured in action game series such as *Street Fighter* (Capcom, 1987-present) or *Mortal Kombat* (Midway et al., 1992-present), Core Design's 1996 release, *Tomb Raider*, was initially regarded by many as a breath of fresh air that would finally open up action-adventure games to non-male, non-heterosexual playable characters (see Kennedy; Schleiner 222). Unfortunately, as critics would soon show, the franchise's first two series do not challenge the patriarchal assumptions that inform the representation of femininity in mainstream action-adventure games. Although Lara enjoys a level of empowerment atypical for female characters (see Mikula 80), because of the young male audience of action-adventure video games (see Brigit), Lara Croft has to compensate for

---

Note: This work was supported by a grant from the Romanian Ministry of Education and Research, CNCS – UEFISCDI, project number PN-III-P1–1.1-PD-2019–0898, within PNCDI III.

https://doi.org/10.1515/9783110675184-007

her ludic and narrative agency by adopting a hypersexualized representation which satisfies the male gaze of the games' intended audience (see Carr 171; Han et al. 35; du Preez, 20; Schleiner 222; Kennedy). Some critics go one step further and argue that her exaggerated sexuality coupled with her violent dominance over her adversaries lend Lara Croft the image of a dominatrix (see; Han et al. 40), which can engender masochistic pleasures for the male audience. In her survey of the male reception of the early *Tomb Raider* games, Schleiner observes that "players likely derive masochistic pleasure from Lara's repeated destruction of her enemies and their consequent death cries and throes of agony" (224).

After completing two series comprising of nine major games released between 1996 and 2008, the franchise entered a new era in 2013 when Square Enix released *Tomb* Raider, the first instalment of what was to become a three-part rebooted origin story. The new series of the franchise sought to accommodate the criticism regarding the objectification and hypersexualization of Lara Croft and attempted to add narrative depth to the character in the reboot. My aim in this essay is to show that, despite downplaying the caricatural fetishization of the playable character, Lara Croft's story is still one of voluntary submission to patriarchy. I furthermore argue that her acceptance of the patriarchal framework also shapes her experience of different cultures. In the game, assuming the norms of patriarchy determines Lara to adopt a colonial gaze that constructs its subject in accordance with the tropes and stereotypes of modern colonialism. Consequently, my second goal is to highlight the manner in which the game's narrative is indebted to colonial discourse and how Lara Croft, the explorer-archaeologist, is, in fact, a colonizer of foreign territories.

In conveying its critique of the game's race and gender politics, this chapter sheds light upon the ideological assumptions that frame the simulation of space in mainstream action-adventure games. As non-linear media, video games challenge conventional models of narrative based on temporality and, instead, foreground a narrative experience which is first and foremost spatially structured (see Jenkins "Game Design as Narrative Architecture"). The understanding of space and spatiality implicit in the *Tomb Raider* games pays tribute to a Eurocentric framework that equates being in space with asserting control and mastery over space. Given this propensity towards territorial entitlement, it should come as no surprise that *Tomb Raider*'s narrative of voluntary subjugation to patriarchy is framed within a broader narrative of the civilizing mission.

Before going on with my argument, I would like to mention that my essay investigates the recent *Tomb Raider* games as rhetorical and political interactive texts, which means that my analysis is geared towards showing the political dimension of these games in relation to their implied young heterosexual male target audience. The manner in which actual players may appropriate the meaning of these games falls outside the scope of this endeavor.[1] Moreover, my deconstruction of the strategies of othering that features especially in the latter part of this essay does not assume that the representation of indigenous peoples can be correct or incorrect, right or wrong. Although misrepresentation is an issue to be dealt with in Cultural Studies, I am mostly interested in how subjects of colonialism are rhetorically constructed by the games and how the various identities are ethically valued in the storyworld of the games.

Lara's Submission to Patriarchal Authority

As already mentioned, the new Lara Croft differs from her earlier incarnations in terms of body shape and outfit. While early games featured a playable character with oversized breasts, an unnaturally slim waist, and a revealing outfit that is by no means adequate for the actions simulated by the game, the new Lara Croft has more natural bodily proportions (see Han et al 34). Although Lara's outfits can be changed in-game, her default attire is featured on the advertising material which show Lara wearing a more climate appropriate gear that covers her body instead of gratuitously revealing it. Moreover, Toni Pape points out that the core stealth mechanics of the game draw the player's attention away from Lara's body as an object of fetish to the environment which must be analyzed for potential hiding spaces. Lara's body is primarily viewed in relation to the environment with the goal of making the body imperceptible to her enemies (see Pape 641).

Despite the game's renouncing of hypersexualization, some critics have pointed out that gameplay nonetheless enmeshes Lara Croft in a patriarchal discourse that renders women vulnerable objects of male fantasies. In the early stages of *Tomb Raider*, Lara is presented as a weak and insecure character who constantly ponders her possible failure. During many stages, Lara is stripped of her weapons and must survive wounded in the middle of a jungle with little to no resources at hand. *Rise of the Tomb Raider* and *Shadow of the Tomb Raider* feature Lara in similar positions of vulnerability in their incipient stages. Given the intended young male audience and the history of the representation of women in Western visual culture, Soraya Murray claims that the games normalize a masculine predator/protector position (see 174). On the one hand,

---

[1] Schleiner and Kennedy observe that in the first game, Lara is sexually ambiguous enough to leave room for a queer reading of the game. However, this avenue of reception will soon be closed by the film adaptations that disambiguate her sexuality and impose a heterosexual reading (see Carr 178; Kennedy; Shaw 87; Schleiner 221–6).

the presumably heterosexual male player has privileged access to Lara Croft's body and control over her outfit (the game allows the player to choose even the now canonic tank top and short tight trousers), on the other hand, by successfully completing the challenges of the game, the player interactively saves Lara from her ordeal.² Although the game design choice to strip the playable character of weapons and items is very common in survival horror video games featuring both male and female characters, *Tomb Raider*, *Rise of the Tomb Raider*, and *Shadow of the Tomb Raider* are more standard action-adventure games, a genre which usually reinforces the hyperpotency of its playable characters. It would seem that the choice to highlight Lara's vulnerability in a genre marked by strength and belief in one's abilities bespeaks a patriarchal conception of femininity as weak and in need of rescuing.

Lara's vulnerability is also supported by a controversial sexual assault scene which Adrienne Shaw criticizes as follows:

> To include the threat of sexual assault [...] demonstrates an assumption that players of the game have never feared or been the targets of sexualized violence, at least to the extent that it would deter them from purchasing the game. Furthermore, it is questionable that when the series is inviting players to identify with Lara, her strength is being framed in relation to a victimization narrative. Marketing logics presume that a strong woman is not a character with which male players could connect. (72–73)

Both Murray and Shaw are right to criticize the representation and simulation of gender at a microlevel, but their analyses do not take into consideration how the wider narrative arc frames the entire gameplay of the rebooted franchise as an enactment of patriarchal norms and desires, despite the ludic and narrative centrality of Lara Croft.

From the very onset of the first game of the reboot, entitled simply *Tomb Raider*, Lara Croft is constructed in relation to her father, the late Richard Croft. The evolution of the character implies a transition from a rejection of Richard Croft's authority to acceptance. The game's first cut-scene depicts Lara's internal monologue in which she asserts her desire to become a famous archaeologist on her own, implying an independence from her father's teachings. Lara says to herself: "A famous explorer once said that the extraordinary is in what we do, not who we are. I'd finally set out to make my mark to find adventure. But instead, adventure found me" (*Tomb Raider*).

---

2 Murray's observation with respect to the savior position of the player only concerns *Tomb Raider* but is applicable to the entire video game franchise (see Han et al. 36).

A few hours of gameplay later, the game further substantiates Lara's desire to be independent from her father by referring to their disagreement with respect to the factuality of myths. In an in-game cut-scene, Lara clarifies her disbelief in the authenticity of myths claimed by her father. She mentions that "myths are usually based on some version of the truth" (*Tomb Raider*). However, by the end of the game, Lara will have accepted that myths are real and agreed to carry out her father's quest of finding and understanding them. In the final cut-scene of *Tomb Raider*, Lara is convinced that "I've been so blind ... so naïve. For years I resented my father, doubted him like the rest. But he was right about so much. I just wish I could tell him that now. There are so many mysteries that I once dismissed as mere stories. But the line between our myths and truth is fragile and blurry. I need to find answers ... I must understand" (*Tomb Raider*)

Lara's evolution from a rejection of patriarchal authority to submission is further mitigated by the ending of *Rise of the Tomb Raider*, the next instalment in the trilogy. At one point during the gameplay, the game cuts to a scene in the Croft manor where Lara is listening to an audio tape of her father encouraging her to follow her own path and make her own impact on the world. It turns out that the anonymous famous explorer who inspired Lara to be autonomous and self-reliant in *Tomb Raider* had been her father all along. "[Lord Croft:] My dearest Lara, I often think about how my father would turn over in his grave if he knew the shame I had brought upon our family's name. Croft ... what does it even mean? I just hope you can make your own mark on this world someday. Remember that the extraordinary is in what we do, not who we are" (*Rise of the Tomb Raider*). Consequently, the evolution of the character in the first game from an independent explorer to a submissive daughter is relativized. The ending of *Rise of the Tomb Raider* reveals that Lara had been enacting her father's will all along with the difference that she had not fully acquiesced to her father's conception of myths.

Although Richard Croft is seminal for Lara's identity in the storyworld and the events she is engaged in, *Tomb Raider* features another male character who constitutes a source of patriarchal authority, namely Roth, captain of the ship on which Lara is sailing. Roth had been a father-figure for Lara and contributed to the training that would eventually turn her into a female hero after Richard Croft's death (see Han et al. 39). The father-daughter relation between the two is important for the way rules and narrative blend in the game's storyworld and sheds a new light upon the vulnerability of the playable character which, according to Murray, situates the male player in a savior position. The mechanics that enable the player to control Lara and ensure her survival are narratively framed as having been taught to Lara by Roth. In the early stages of the game when Lara is stranded without any help, she relies on patriarchal counsel in the form of her memories of Roth's training. For instance, when Lara finds a bow and wants to test it, the game represents her memory of Roth via internal monologue. "Let's see if this thing still works. Just remember Roth's training. *[Roth] You can have the best form and technique in the world, but it won't mean a thing if you can't focus. The key to using any weapon is focus*" (*Tomb Raider*; italics in original).

Roth plays an important role not only because he gives a diegetic explanation to the mechanics that govern gameplay, but also because his authority is essential for the inciting moment of the plot. In one of the game's early cut-scenes, the team of researchers are debating where to sail next. Lara proposes an island called Dragon's Triangle but is dismissed. It is only after Roth backs Lara's proposal that the crew sails to the island where the events of the game would eventually take place. The narrative logic of the game seems to suggest that Lara, the female protagonist, lacks the authority to dramatically alter the storyworld. In order for this to happen, the presence of a patriarchal figure is crucial.

Rise of the Tomb Raider offers a similar example of how patriarchy must sanction Lara's choice at crucial moments in the plot. As I explain at greater length in the following section, the plot in this game revolves around the Divine Source, an artefact able to grant immortality. During the final moments of the game, Lara manages to grasp the artefact. Given the immediate danger of being seized by an army maintained alive by the Divine Source and the artefact's ability to corrupt its users, she eventually decides to destroy it. However, before smashing the object, she seeks the approval of Jacob, the patriarch of a local community of natives. It is only after Jacob gives his approval that Lara destroys the object.

Colonization in the Name of the Father

As suggested by *Tomb Raider* and *Rise of the Tomb Raider*, the trilogy's plot is to be read as a fulfilment of Richard Croft's legacy. Because Lara follows her father's will, through his daughter, the deceased Richard Croft vicariously maintains narrative agency in the storyworld. His agency is framed in a colonial discourse that informs Lara's experience of foreignness, ensuring that the playable character's encounter with otherness is filtered through a colonial gaze.[3] One

---

3 In a manner similar to John Rieder, I use the term colonial gaze in order to highlight the manner in which Lara's perception of otherness is always already determined by her Western knowl-

manner in which colonial discourse manifests itself in the *Tomb Raider* games is cartography. According to Bill Ashcroft et al,

> [c]olonization itself is often consequent on a voyage of 'discovery,' a bringing into being of 'undiscovered' lands. The process of discovery is reinforced by the construction of maps, whose existence is a means of textualizing the spatial reality of the other, naming or, in almost all cases, renaming spaces in a symbolic and literal act of mastery and control. [...] Maps also inscribe their ideology on territory in numerous ways other than place-names. The blank spaces of early maps signify a literal *terra nullius*, an open and inviting (virginal) space into which the European imagination can project itself and into which the European (usually male) explorer must penetrate. (28)

As Souvik Mukherjee points out, real-time strategy games that are thematically related to imperialism and colonialism employ a procedural rhetoric that uses the same strategies of othering and appropriation characteristic to colonial cartography. The virtual gamespace and its cartographic representation constitute a territory covered by what players call fog or darkness, which can be dispelled if the player sends a unit to explore. Once a particular parcel has been explored, it is graphically rendered on the map as belonging to the player with all its resources ready to be harvested or extracted. The assumption of these mechanics is that of the playable entity's manifest destiny, i.e. it is the duty of the collective entity commanded by the player (which in many cases is either the center of a former colonial empire, or an entity akin to such a center) to expand onto the unexplored territories of gamespace.[4]

The *Tomb Raider* games discussed in this chapter employ somewhat different cartography mechanics, but they amount to an ideological effect similar to the one of the real-time strategy games discussed by Mukherjee. Maps in the *Tomb Raider* games show the terrain but offer no game relevant information. Both from a ludic and a narrative perspective, gamespace is a previously unexplored territory filled with secrets ready to be uncovered. Therefore, the more the

---

edge, a body of knowledge which is created so as to favor the position of the Westerner and which reduces the subject of colonialism to a silent object: "The colonial gaze distributes knowledge and power to the subject who looks, while denying or minimizing access to power for its object, the one looked at" (Rieder 7).

4 The concept of manifest destiny was coined in 1845 by John L. O'Sullivan and entailed that it was the duty of the United States to dominate North America. This belief rested on a sense of moral and political superiority of the United States that enabled them to impose their civilizational model on the region. In this chapter I use the term in relation to the European colonization of foreign territories based on similar ideological grounds – the idea that it was modern Europe's duty to bring the light of reason and salvation to the presumably primitive and savage territories of the world (see Miller 115–120).

player explores the gamespace, the richer and denser the maps become, offering the player a variety of means to interact with the game world: resources, animals for hunting, documents, and, most importantly, tombs to raid. It is only through the gaze of the British playable character that space exists ludically and diegetically.

If colonization is fundamentally "the conquest and control of other people's land and goods" (Loomba 8), then the *Tomb Raider* games provide a faithful simulation of colonization. The game imposes no limits on the extent to which players can use, appropriate, or even steal artefacts. In the game, colonialism seems to be the natural assumption which entitles Lara Croft to interact with the game world in any way she, or the player controlling her, pleases. The way the games naturalize colonialism (and its implicit power relations that favor the colonizer) is most obvious during Lara's exploration of populated native settlements. In *Rise of the Tomb Raider* and *Shadow of the Tomb Raider*, the player gains access to two villages of native populations: the Remnants' village and Paititi, respectively. When exploring the two communities, Lara can enter any open house, shop, or building and take whatever resource available without the owners of the respective establishment reacting in any way. The AI governing the native non-playable characters is procedurally blind to the enactment of colonialism, which renders it implicit and natural. This blind and mute acceptance of colonialism is typical of the way colonial discourse constructs its subjects as subaltern others, i.e. voiceless subjects who cannot speak for themselves (see Spivak "Can the Subaltern Speak?").

As a result, space in the storyworld of the *Tomb Raider* games is strictly the construct of Lara's colonial gaze which she assimilates from her father and to which the voiceless natives have no contribution. The three games abound in orientalist clichés that vacillate between savagery and nobility: the native societies are underdeveloped, but the natives show signs of ingenuity; the territories inhabited by the natives are filled with dangers but are at the same time noble as a result of the absence of modernity. This colonial bias filtering Lara Croft's gaze can be observed, for example, when the playable character faces complex puzzles. She marvels at the engineering skills of the natives, which indicates the assumption that natives are expected to lack the skills to build complex contraptions. Lara's reaction when faced with the Orrery in *Rise of the Tomb Raider* or the mechanism underpinning the Trial of the Eagle puzzle in *Shadow of the Tomb Raider* are just two of the many instances when Lara's interaction with otherness confirms her colonial gaze.

The Polarization of Colonial Discourse: Modern Imperialism vs. Neo-Imperialism

As Edward Said points out in his seminal work *Orientalism* (1978), colonial discourse is marked by an ambivalent attitude of fascination and horror with respect to otherness. This ambivalence is most obvious in the representation of indigenous people which vacillates between the savage and the noble savage. However, unlike nineteenth-century colonialism, the representation of otherness in the *Tomb Raider* games is determined not only by Western colonial knowledge but also by more recent anxieties related to the Cold War and globalization.

In *Rise of the Tomb Raider*, most of the action is set in Siberia in the remains of a former gulag. The soviet infrastructure used for forced labor is employed by Trinity, the antagonist organization of the game, in their search for an artefact called the Divine Source with which they aim to remake the world into a utopia free from sin and vice. Trinity is competed by Lara Croft who is on a quest to find the same artefact in order redeem her father's name.[5] The region of Siberia where the action is set is populated by a native population called the Remnants whose ancient-old duty has been to prevent anyone from obtaining the Divine Source. Although both Lara Croft and Trinity are colonial explorers who pursue the Divine Source for individual goals, the Remnants evince a radically different attitude with respect to the two. On the one hand, they are relentless in fighting off Trinity, on the other hand, they quickly embrace Lara and soon after help her attain the Divine Source. The rhetoric of the game amounts to a polarization of colonial discourse. The British Lara Croft is rendered the 'good' providential colonizer whose intervention is a priori acceptable, while the transnational paramilitary organization Trinity is rendered the 'bad,' intrusive colonizer.

The game text suggests that colonialism is acceptable if it is conducted by the 'right' colonizer. The opposition between Lara Croft and Trinity is in fact an opposition between modern imperialism and neo-imperialism, with the game favoring the former. Modern imperialism is defined by the existence of one territorially defined metropole, a nation-state, which has control over a distant territory in the form of colonialism (see Loomba 11–12; Hardt et al. xii). The principal moral justification of modern imperialism is that of the civilizing mission, the idea that foreign intervention is required so that the colonized territories be saved from savagery (see Ashcroft et al. 114–115). In the new *Tomb Raider*

---

[5] Richard Croft had lost his reputation after devoting his work to the mythical artefact called the Divine Source.

trilogy, Lara Croft epitomizes modern imperialism. First of all, she is a British explorer-colonizer whose national identity is constantly reinforced: she was born to an archaeologist in an aristocratic English family, she is keen on her ancestry, she speaks standard British English, and her default weapon – whose use brings most ludic rewards – is the longbow, one of the hallmark weapons of English medieval and early modern armies (see DeVries et al. 38). Secondly, her intervention in the internal affairs of foreign territories is deemed not only necessary but also salutary. In fact, one aspect of Lara Croft's evolution as a character in *Rise of the Tomb Raider* is the gradual acceptance of her manifest destiny.[6]

In the initial stages of the game, Lara's motivation to find the Divine Source is strictly personal (redeeming her father's name by proving the existence of the Divine Source), but as the game progresses she concedes to her manifest destiny of saving the Remnants from Trinity. Crucial for Lara's change of attitude is her conversation with Jacob, the leader of the Remnants, shortly after they both escape incarceration. Jacob beseeches Lara to help him and his people repel Trinity. At a later point of the game, Jacob even discloses the whereabouts of the Divine Source for Lara to obtain, lest Trinity should find it and use it for their own goals. In addition to this, Lara's acceptance of her manifest destiny is framed as a successful assent to patriarchy. Before dying, Jacob, himself a patriarch, reassures Lara that she had made a difference as her father had ordained in *Tomb Raider:* "[Lara] All I wanted was to make a difference. [Jacob] You already have… you already have" (*Rise of the Tomb Raider*).

The relation between the colonizer and the colonized in this case once again points out the manner in which colonial discourse fashions the identity of its subjects. The natives go as far as to ask for the providential intervention of the colonizer and try to convince the colonizer of her manifest destiny. *Rise of the Tomb Raider* suggests that it is not only the manifest destiny of the British to colonize foreign populations, but it is also the manifest destiny of the respective populations to be colonized. Colonization is represented as a mutual effort in which both the colonizer and colonized are agentive in establishing the colonial hierarchy.

Counterbalancing Lara's British imperialism is the transnational organization Trinity, which stands for the new global institutions that exercise colonial-

---

[6] One could further argue that Lara Croft's commitment to manifest destiny amounts to an Americanization of the protagonist. This should not come as a surprise since the international dimension of the character and its appeal to North American audiences adds an imagological dimension to the game. To some extent, Lara Croft's Britishness has to be recognizable to North American players, which is why her identity is constructed in keeping with American colonial knowledge and American national stereotypes.

ism through neo-imperialism as theorized by Ashcroft (see 147). While modern empires exerted their rule from nation-states, neo-imperialism refers to the new forms of colonialism which are exercised by decentered and deterritorialized international organizational bodies (see Hardt et al. xii). According to Neil Lazarus, examples of such bodies are international financial institutions such as the World Bank, the International Monetary Fund, or the World Trade Organization. He accuses these institutions of using financial aid programs to usher in neoliberal reforms in the beneficiary countries (see 8–10). In the case of postcolonial states, this amounts to "domesticating them and rendering them subservient to the needs of the global market" (Lazarus 9). Although the purpose of Trinity is not that of increasing the wealth of its owners by means of deregulating target markets, it shares two important similarities with Lazarus's prototypical neo-imperial institutions. Firstly, it is a decentered, deterritorialized organization with greater similarity to a present-day transnational institution than to a public colonial company typical of modern imperialism. Secondly, it reiterates the former colonial power relations whereby foreign territories are disciplined and domesticated so as to help Trinity in accomplishing its goals. At the same time, it must be acknowledged that Trinity also retains traits of modern imperialism. As I explain at greater length in the next section, Trinity's mission is a utopian religious one, namely that of purging the world of sin.

The *Tomb Raider* games seem to exert a critique of neo-imperialism by framing Trinity's project as traumatic (in opposition to the benevolent modern imperialism represented by Lara). In order to achieve this, *Rise of the Tomb Raider* relies on Cold War rhetoric and associates Trinity's colonialism with communism. While making their way out of the former Soviet facility where they had been incarcerated by Trinity, Lara and Jacob come across a room with a slide projector showing pictures of the Soviet's endeavor to find the Divine Source. When seeing the images, Jacob remembers how his people had been enslaved by the Soviets and forced to work in the camp. The implication is that the subjects of Trinity's colonialism are just as traumatized as the subjects of Russian communism were in one of communism's most atrocious forms, namely forced labor in the gulag. If communism was a corrupt version of modernity, then its association with Trinity suggests that the latter can only perform a corrupt version of colonialism.

The colonial discourse in which *Rise of the Tomb Raider* is enmeshed is by no means an inclusive one. While the game remediates colonial tropes of Western, in particular British superiority and the Westerner's providential duty to civilize underdeveloped peoples, it is very skeptical of the new forms of colonialism produced by globalization. The game text implies that colonialism is a valid project only inasmuch as it mirrors the hierarchies and power relations of modern empires founded by nation-states. In opposition to modern empires, neo-imperialism is seen as a threat to indigenous populations, a threat that once again calls for the intervention of the modern empire.

Contending Versions of Hybridity in *Shadow of the Tomb Raider*

The conflict between modern imperialism and neo-imperialism remains central in the final instalment of the rebooted origin trilogy, yet this time the game attempts to relativize the clear-cut opposition between the two colonial agents. In *Shadow of the Tomb Raider,* Trinity is still pursuing the goal of cleansing the world of sin and, after the destruction of the Divine Source in *Rise of the Tomb Raider*, is now interested in a new artefact with similar powers. The new artefact is the Silver Box of Chak Chel which can be used only with the Dagger of Ix Chel. In the game's initial stages, Lara is in Cozumel, Mexico where she manages to find the Dagger before Trinity. Despite the warnings that its removal would cause a series of cataclysms, Lara eventually takes the artefact. Shortly thereafter, a tsunami hits, thus confirming the warnings ignored by Lara. As the game simulates Lara's struggle to survive the tsunami, it also highlights the suffering of the local Mexican population affected by the cataclysm thereby stressing the culpability of Lara's reckless behavior as a colonizer. The moral justification to fulfil her father's legacy and to stop Trinity (in other words, to reaffirm patriarchy and fight neo-imperialism) seems no longer to vouchsafe Lara's actions.

In the scripted narrative of *Shadow of the Tomb Raider,* Lara's taking of the dagger functions as an inciting moment which disrupts the equilibrium of the storyworld. The main narrative agents of the game, Lara and Trinity (led by Dr. Pedro Dominguez), must now commit themselves to reinstating the initial balance, which implies finding the Silver Box of Chak Chel and using it to stop the series of extreme natural phenomena that would otherwise lead to the destruction of the world. Although both seek to prevent the Mayan apocalypse, Dr. Dominguez also wants to use the two artefacts to remake the world into a utopia.

Unlike *Rise of the Tomb Raider, Shadow of the Tomb Raider* simulates a less intrusive version of colonialism in the sense that the explorer-colonizers now have to blend in with the local native populations. This form of soft intervention coerces Lara and Dr. Dominguez to position themselves in the liminal space between modern culture and the culture of the native populations and in doing so to become colonial hybrids (see Bhabha *The Location of Culture*).

The hybridization of cultures occurs in the legendary city of Paititi where, in her quest to find the Silver Box, the female protagonist must immerse herself into otherness. When in Paititi, the playable character may wear only local Paititian attire and is not allowed to use any modern weapons she is in one of the city's public spaces. The adoption of a foreign culture does not bring any change to Lara's manifest destiny as providential colonizer, yet it does alter the means used to save the native population and the world. If in *Rise of the Tomb Raider* Lara brings the conflict to its resolution by destroying the mythical artefact, now the artefacts are used correspondingly in a ritual that would end the apocalypse. The ritual presupposes that the leader of Paititi and the leader of Yaaxil (a mythical population in charge of protecting Paititi from foreigners) symbolically take up the roles of the two primordial gods, Ix Chel and Chak Chel, respectively. In order for the ritual to be consummated, the latter, also known as the Crimson Fire, must symbolically sacrifice the former. In *Shadow of the Tomb Raider*, the role of the Paititian leader is assumed by Lara who is symbolically stabbed with the Dagger of Ix Chel by the Crimson Fire.

The manner in which Lara accomplishes her manifest destiny and saves the world seems to rest on two important pillars: the ideal colonial leader provided by the modern imperialist framework and contemporary views on imperceptibility in today's globalized world. As far as the former is concerned, the conflict between Lara and Dr. Dominguez can be construed as confrontation between two opposing notions of hybrid colonial leaders: the Western-born and the native-born.[7] Lara's hybridity tunes in with what modern imperialism saw as an appropriate leader of native populations. Given the fear of miscegenation which pervaded modernity especially in the context of nineteenth-century racialism, colonial discourse maintained that "the combination of racial superiority and local knowledge constructs an image of the ideal ruling figure for the colonial world in which being native-born can be achieved without the fear of racial contamination" (Ashcroft et al. 143). This image of the ideal colonial leader fits Lara's hybrid condition and is confirmed by the unfolding of the events. Dr. Dominguez is defeated by Lara who assumes the role of the providential leader of Paititi in the ritual that saves the world.

As far as the latter pillar is concerned, according to Toni Pape, in today's surveillance culture visibility is no longer politically empowering and power lies in imperceptibility understood as the subject's existence below or around the threshold of perceptibility (see 630–631). This notion of empowerment is very

---

[7] When players enter Paititi, they soon learn that Dr. Dominguez is also the leader of the local community and that he was born in Paititi where he was given the name Amaru.

much at play in *Shadow of the Tomb Raider* where intervention in a foreign culture is buttressed by the invisibility of the colonizer's otherness to the native population. The inhabitants of Paititi are keen on remaining hidden from the modern world and do their best to keep outsiders away. In order for Lara to act, she must conceal her otherness and blend in with the cultural environment, lest she should re-enact the aggressive logic of penetration which characterizes the *Tomb Raider* games of previous series (see Breger 51–53). Hybridity is therefore a strategy of becoming imperceptible which empowers Lara to act as the providential colonizer in a game that attempts to be more sensitive with respect to colonialism.

Lara's experience of otherness as a hybrid has an important bearing on her evolution as a character in the game. If *Tomb Raider* and *Rise of the Tomb Raider* present Lara's gradual submission to her father's authority and the acceptance of her manifest destiny, the events of *Shadow of the Tomb Raider* convince her that "I had it all wrong. I thought that taking control of my life meant venturing out to do something extraordinary. I thought I had to fix everything. But the mysteries of the World are to cherish, more than to solve. I am just one of their many protectors" (*Shadow of the Tomb Raider*). Lara's new understanding of her manifest destiny still calls for her intervention in foreign territories but this time as a guardian against disenchantment.

The disenchantment of the world is a critique of modernity from within. It deplores the fact that "with the rise of instrumental reason, the gradual alienation of humanity from nature, and the production of a bureaucratic and technological life, [the] world [was] stripped of mystery and wonder" (Josephson-Storm 4). Lara Croft suggests that her activity as an explorer who employs her Western knowledge of foreign cultures has yielded the same effect of robbing the world of mystery and after her experience of Paititi she is committed not to repeat the mistake. Nevertheless, her new goal to maintain the allegedly enchanted nature of cultures is the product of the same colonial discourse which she claims to reject.

Jason Ā. Josephson-Storm argues that not only had the modern world not rid itself of myth and magic as it purported, but that the very idea that modernity was involved in an endeavor to dispel myth altogether is itself a Western myth (see 10). Consequently, the final point in Lara's evolution as a character, i.e. her assuming the mission of protecting mystery from a disenchanting modernity, presupposes projecting a Western myth onto other cultures. By adhering to the new version of manifest destiny, she finds herself within the same colonial logic that reifies otherness and reduces the subaltern to silence. Additionally, Lara's new manifest destiny is still framed within patriarchy. The above quotation is an excerpt from a letter which Lara wrote to her friend and sidekick Johan at her father's desk. Her return to the ancestral mansion and her decision to continue her endeavors from her father's workspace implies that she still follows in his footsteps and that she will further act as a ludic and diegetic ersatz for Richard Croft in the *Tomb Raider* games to come.

Conclusion

In this essay I have shown how patriarchy and colonial discourse work together in molding the evolution of Lara Croft in the rebooted origin trilogy. The evolution of the character can be separated into three stages: the submission to her father's authority whereby she fully acquiesces to his understanding of myths, the acceptance of her manifest destiny as a providential colonizer who must save subaltern populations from globalization and neo-imperialism, and, finally, a refinement of her manifest destiny which now entails saving foreign native cultures from the danger of disenchantment.

My analysis has pointed out that all three stages of her evolution presuppose an intertwining of patriarchy and colonialism. Lara's agency in the storyworld amounts to the exertion of mastery over a gamespace which functions as a colonial playing ground where the player can safely enact the role of the colonizer-explorer via the white female protagonist. This explorer-colonizer role is framed within Lara's desire to fulfil her father's legacy and, in doing so, she acts as a substitute for her father. Therefore, through colonialism Lara reinstates patriarchal order while, at the same time, patriarchy functions as the foundation for Lara's colonial project. Patriarchy and colonialism are two co-dependent power structures that reinforce one another and determine Lara's agency in the games.

Works Cited

Ashcroft, Bill, et al. *Post-Colonial Studies. The Key Concepts*. 2nd ed. Routledge, 2007.
Bhabha, Homi K. *The Location of Culture*. Routledge, 1994.
Breger, Claudia. "Digital Digs, or Lara Croft Replaying Indiana Jones: Archaeological Tropes and 'Colonial Loops' in New Media Narrative." *Aether: The Journal of Media Geography*, vol. 11, 2008, pp. 41–66.
Brown, Jeffrey A. *Dangerous Curves: Action Heroines, Gender, Fetishism, and Popular Culture*. University Press of Mississippi, 2011.
Carr, Diane. "Playing with Lara." *ScreenPlay: Cinema/Videogames/Interfaces*, edited by Geoff King and Tanya Krzywinska, Wallflower Press, 2002, pp. 171–180.
du Preez, Amanda. "Virtual Babes: Gender, Archetypes and Computer Games." *Communication*, vol. 26, no. 2, 2000, pp. 18–27.

DeVries, Kelly, et al. *Medieval Military Technology*. 2nd ed. University of Toronto Press, 2012.
Han, Hye-Won, and Se-Jin Song. "Characterization of Female Protagonists in Video Games: A Focus on Lara Croft." *Asian Journal of Women's Studies*, vol. 20, no. 3, 2014, pp. 27–49.
Hardt, Michael, and Antonio Negri. *Empire*. Harvard University Press, 2000.
Jenkins, Henry. "Game Design as Narrative Architecture." *First Person: New Media as Story, Performance, and Game*, edited by Noah Wardrip-Fruin and Pat Harrigan, The MIT Press, 2004, pp. 118–130.
Josephson-Storm, Jason Ā. *The Myth of Disenchantment: Magic, Modernity, and the Birth of the Human Sciences*. The University of Chicago Press, 2017.
Kennedy, H. W. "Lara Croft: Feminist Icon or Cyberbimbo? On the Limits of Textual Analysis." *Game Studies*, vol. 2, no. 2, 2002.
Lazarus, Neil. *The Postcolonial Unconscious*. Cambridge University Press, 2011.
Loomba, Ania. *Colonialism/Postcolonialism*. 2nd ed. Routledge, 2005.
Mikuila, Maja. "Gender and Videogames: The Political Valency of Lara Croft." *Continuum: Journal of Media & Cultural Studies*, vol. 17, no. 1, 2003, pp. 79–87.
Miller, Robert J. *Native America, Discovered and Conquered: Thomas Jefferson, Lewis & Clark, and Manifest Destiny*. Prager, 2006.
Mukherjee, Souvik. *Video Games and Postcolonialism: Empire Plays Back*. Palgrave Macmillan, 2017.
Murray, Soraya. *On Video Games. The Visual Politics of Race, Gender and Space*. I. B. Tauris, 2018.
Pape, Toni. "The Aesthetics of Stealth: Towards an Activist Philosophy of Becoming-Imperceptible in Contemporary Media." *Feminist Media Studies*, vol. 17, no. 10, 2017, pp. 630–645.
Pretzsch, Birgit. *A Postmodern Analysis of Lara Croft: Body, Identity, Reality*. 1999. Women's Studies, Trinity College Dublin, Ireland, PhD dissertation. www.cyberpink.de/laracroft/LaraCompleteTextWOPics.html. Accessed 29 October 2020.
Rieder, John. *Colonialism and the Emergence of Science Fiction*. Wesleyan University Press, 2008.
Rise of the Tomb Raider. Square Enix, 2015.
Said, Edward. *Orientalism*. 1978. Vintage Books, 1979.
Schleiner, Anne-Marie. "Does Lara Croft Wear Fake Polygons? Gender and Gender-Role Subversion in Computer Adventure Games." *Leonardo*, vol. 34, no. 3, 2001, pp. 221–226.
Shadow of the Tomb Raider. Square Enix, 2018.
Shaw, Adrienne. *Gaming at the Edge: Sexuality and Gender at the Margins of Gamer Culture*. University of Minnesota Press, 2014.
Spivak, Gayatri C. "Can the Subaltern Speak?" *Marxism and the Interpretation of Culture*, edited by Carl Nelson and Lawrence Grossberg, Macmillan Education, 1988, pp. 271–313.
Tomb Raider. Square Enix, 2013.

Hanne Nijtmans
The Inevitable Fate of the "Dragonborn:" Selling Player Agency in *The Elder Scrolls V: Skyrim*

As this edited volume shows, applying an American Studies perspective to the study of video games proves a fruitful way to reveal how video games are intertwined with questions of American identity and American culture in the twenty-first century. The interdisciplinary nature of American Studies offers a rich field of theoretical, historical, and political resources to situate games within the culture from which many of them originate, thus supplementing the medium-focused field of Game Studies. What American Studies approaches share is not a set of canonical texts or predefined methods but rather a common set of inquiries into the nature of American identity.

Space has been one of those central concepts. As David Noble argues in his impressive work *Death of a Nation: American Culture and the End of Exceptionalism* (2002), space has been formative in the self-conceptualization of the United States. Tracing the larger intellectual, ideological, and social structures throughout American history, Noble observes that the fundamental ideals of American identity were predicated on the metaphor of two worlds: the "European Old World" where hierarchies, conventions, and traditions entrapped the individual, and the "American New World," "where the individual could be free from those oppressive conventions" (xxx). Focusing on some of the most influential historians of the nineteenth century, George Bancroft and Frederick Jackson Turner, Noble suggests that in the American imagination, the U.S. was considered a "timeless space" (1). In spaces characterized as 'virgin land' or 'the frontier,' (Protestant, male, Anglo-)Americans had the theoretical liberty to own private property, which made them equal citizens in one of the first modern democracies, separate from the oppressive histories of the "Old World" (see 5–8). We can find an analogous ideology of space in open-world sandbox games like *The Elder Scrolls V: Skyrim* (2011). There, the player is offered a rich landscape in which she can explore the gamespace, cultivate the land, and defeat 'enemies,' thus marking out the territory as her own private property. This

Note: I gratefully acknowledge Kathryn Roberts for her critical advice and guidance. Tim Jelfs and Nick Bowman are warmly thanked for their helpful suggestions. I thank Raquel Raj for her inspiration and helpful discussions. I thank Keith Richotte Jr. for helping me understand this project as an American Studies project.

conception of space depends on a set of claims about agency. In order to navigate, cultivate, or conquer the gamespace, the player needs to have the power to make a meaningful change within the game's landscape.

To Janet Murray, one of the most influential Game Studies scholars, agency is a pivotal feature of video games, something to which games should aspire. In *Hamlet on the Holodeck* (1997) she defines agency as "the satisfying power to take meaningful action and see the results of our decisions and choices" (126). Murray's definition raises an important question: what constitutes meaningful action? According to Murray, one of the aspects that makes playing a video game meaningful is spatial navigation, as she mentions that "the movement forward has the feeling of enacting meaningful experience" (132). Furthermore, her preoccupation with choices implies that making choices is a meaningful action, but what are the choices a video game can offer? As Murray suggests herself, these choices will always be limited to the game's rules. Nonetheless, the promise of agency in video games has become a preoccupation among gamers as well as theorists. On the forum Gamers with Jobs, a post in January 2010 by TheArtOfScience observes that "agency is the latest buzzword in gaming reviews and gaming podcasts. Over the past year I've heard it used with increased frequency" (TheArtOfScience).

Scholars seem to agree that the video game industry is preoccupied with giving the player more agency.[1] David Thue, Vadim Bulito, Marcia Spetch, and Trevon Romanuik, for example, render agency not only a vital aspect of video games but consider "[m]uch of the games industry [to be] concerned with providing more agency to its players" (91). Matthew Fendt, Brent Harrison, Stephen Ware, Rogelio Cardona-Rivera, and David Roberts, on the other hand, focus more on audience perceptions of agency writing that "[o]ne important way video games, especially role-playing video games, are appraised is on how much control the player has over the story content" (114). Karen and Joshua Tanenbaum furthermore call agency a basic premise for pleasure: "Agency has long been considered one of the core pleasures of interacting with digital games. Recent treatments of agency in games culture and game design [have grown] increasingly concerned with providing the player with limitless freedom to act" (12).

The recent obsession with agency among game makers, players, and commentators coincides with the prevailing neoliberal political economy that causes

---

[1] In Game Studies, the rise of the concept of agency is often linked to Janet Murray. Gonzalo Frasca even argues that game producers started considering agency because of Murray's views: "Encouraged by authors like Brenda Laurel and Janet Murray, video game designers have been taking for granted that a high level of agency and immersion are desirable effects" (1).

increasing isolation and social insecurity for workers, while it sells itself under the guise of agency and freedom to choose where one works and what one consumes. Journalist Keith Stuart recently addressed this, speculating that "the satisfaction [of gaming] comes from having a sense of control that real life doesn't afford us" (Stuart). One largely under-documented aspect of this obsession is how U.S. game company Bethesda, the producer of open-world role-playing games like *Skyrim*, uses the promise of agency as a marketing strategy to attract players. Even though the fantastic setting of *Skyrim* with its dragons and medieval castles may not connote American spaces visually, the procedural rhetoric of the game is deeply imbedded in North American spatial discourses. On the *Elder Scrolls* website, Bethesda describes its game as "reimagin[ing] and revolutioniz[ing] the open-world fantasy epic, bringing to life a complete virtual world open for you to explore *in any way you choose*" (emphasis added). For Bethesda, agency is a marketing strategy, as the company promises players large open worlds they can explore and exploit. Agency sells: *Skyrim* has sold over 30 million copies in the first five years after its release, which makes it one of the best-selling role-playing games of all time (see Suellentrop). The focus on agency and extensive interactive gamespaces benefits large video game corporations such as Bethesda, as these games require a vast starting capital to fund the resources and the hundreds of programmers necessary to build these virtual worlds.[2]

This paper concentrates on the role of agency and space in open-world role-playing games, using *Skyrim* as a case study. This type of game seems to provide players with agency: the player is given the possibility to create a character and personality of their desire and can solve problems in numerous ways by playing as warriors, wizards, or thieves, and the open-world game environment hardly restricts player movement. This single-player game makes use of a non-linear gameplay system, also known as a sandbox game. In a sandbox game "[p]layers are offered big, open, full of life worlds where they have a high degree of freedom to choose what they want to do to progress through the game" (Ocio and Brugos 70). However, I argue that while *Skyrim* promises its players agency, the procedural rhetoric dictates a limited form of agency predicated on mandatory spatial exploration and quasi-choices. Quasi-choices resemble what Max Horkheimer and Theodor Adorno call the illusion of choice. As they say of Hollywood movies in *The Dialectic of Enlightenment* (1947), "the advantages and dis-

---

[2] Executive producer of *Skyrim*, Todd Howard, stated in Bethesda's podcast that roughly a hundred people worked on the *The Elder Scrolls V: Skyrim* ("Episode 6: Enter the Dragon," 6:00 – 6:11).

advantages debated by enthusiasts serve only to perpetuate the appearance of competition and choice" (97). The choices *Skyrim* offers have a similar function, as they are aimed at giving players an illusory sense of agency. Indeed, when playing any (video) game, the player will always be constricted by the game's rules. Nevertheless, *Skyrim*'s procedural rhetoric and Bethesda's marketing perpetuate the idea of player agency. The focus on procedural rhetoric opens up a new way of thinking about agency and spatial exploration in games such as *Skyrim*, renegotiating Murray's conceptualization of meaningful action.

Moreover, this critical analysis of *Skyrim* interrogates the ideological effects of the focus on agency in video games. Firstly, this focus on agency aligns with a particular neoliberal ideology in which individual agency is valued over more collective forms of organization. Secondly, *Skyrim*'s use of quasi-choices highlights a consumerist (and limited) idea of choice where one can choose between different consumer products. Finally, linking agency and the game environment promotes an imperial logic in which the players' aim is to exploit the game environment and those who inhabit it. In doing so, this paper follows Nick Dyer-Witheford and Greig De Peuter in their critical assessment of agency when they caution that "[c]ontra enthusiasts for game 'empowerment,' interactivity does not mean virtual play is free from ideology; rather, it intensifies the sense of free will necessary for ideology to work really well" (192). In other words, the player's perception of agency is necessary for them to believe for the ideology to work.

This chapter has two primary objectives. First, I map out how technological developments and changes in the material conditions in the lives of U.S. Americans since the 1970s have contributed to the centering of agency in current academic and public discourse. Secondly, I illustrate how *The Elder Scrolls V: Skyrim*, a video game that markets agency as its main appeal, sells its players an illusion of agency. My analysis shows that in *Skyrim* agency is often limited to quasi-choices. I aim to put pressure on the tendency to use agency as a one of the core pleasures to evaluate video games.

Agency in the Neoliberal State

While the scholarship discussed so far illustrates the prominent position agency has taken in game discourse, they do not elaborate on how agency has become such a celebrated term. This section maps out changes in the political economy and the video game industry that have contributed to this contemporary focus on agency. From the 1970s onward, changing material conditions have increasingly moved public discourse towards an appreciation and centering of human agency. The mid-1970s mark what American Studies scholar Tim Jelfs has called the "triumph of neoliberalism" (23), initiating a decisive change in the social and political lives of Americans. David Harvey suggests in *A Brief History of Neoliberalism* (2005) that neoliberalism redirected the course of political economy towards a policy of liberating the markets from its governmental restraints. Harvey describes neoliberalism as a theory of political economic practices that "proposes that human well-being can best be advanced by liberating individual entrepreneurial freedoms and skills within an institutional framework characterized by strong private property rights, free markets, and free trade" (2). According to Harvey, neoliberalism promises "[g]reater freedom and liberty of action in the labor market [that] could be touted as a virtue for capital and labour alike" (53). However, this neoliberalism "converted into a highly exploitative system of flexible accumulation" is key to explaining "why real wages, except for a brief period in the 1990s stagnated or fell [...] and benefits diminished" (Harvey 53). Harvey as well as other scholars like Luc Boltanski and Eve Chiapello maintain that the shift to neoliberalism is not beneficial for workers, as it weakens their position to negotiate wages and take political action: increasing competition among workers, de-unionization, and the loss of social security make it more difficult to organize.

In *The New Spirit of Capitalism* (2007), Boltanski and Chiapello trace how the move from a Fordist mode of production towards a neoliberal system was justified in the 1970s. Specifically, Boltanski and Chiapello contend that capitalism, which to them is inherently a system of exploitation, is always accompanied by an ideological justification that they call "the spirit of capitalism." This "spirit of capitalism" changes as modes of production change and are able to adapt to various critiques. With the shift towards neoliberalism, Boltanski and Chiapello show that the more flexible "network" (326) structure of neoliberalism sells itself on the premise providing workers with more autonomy, freedom, and creativity. The new spirit of capitalism moves discussions away from systematic problems and oppression, because, as Harvey mentions "individual success or failure are interpreted in terms of entrepreneurial virtues or personal failings" (64). The new spirit of capitalism thus shifted the public discourse away from collective forms of action towards an appreciation of individual agency.

Malcolm Harris' book *Kids These Days: Human Capital and the Making of Millennials* (2017) shows that the neoliberal political economy still dictates the material conditions in the twenty-first century. Harris writes that capitalism has become "the single dominant mode for organizing society," and that "[l]ately, the system has started to hyperventilate: It's desperate to find anything that hasn't yet been reengineered to maximize profit, and then it makes those changes as quickly as possible" (4). According to Harris, capitalism's drive to maximize profit has millennials invest unprecedented amounts of time and money to acquire a job which does not offer them their desired security because of the increased demand for flexibility, lower wages, the increasing reliance of employers on internships (free labor), de-unionization, and the precarity of the nature of work (see 3–63, 104–156).

In conjunction with these economic and social shifts, video games became a prominent form of entertainment during the 1970s and 1980s.[3] In "A Short History of Video Games" (2010), Robert T. Bakie gives a comprehensive account of how the video game industry has moved from engineers experimenting with software in 1959 (*Tennis for Two*) to the full-fledged industry it is today (see 4). Despite the success of *Tennis for Two*, Bakie shows it was not until the 1970s that video games would be available for broader audiences. The introduction of game consoles like the Atari, according to Bakie, "helped launch the entire video games industry" (7–8). The following decades saw a surge of technological changes and innovations, and U.S. American (Microsoft) and Japanese (Nintendo, Sega, and Sony) companies took the lead in the mass production of consoles and games (see 9–15). With the introduction of the home computer in the 1980s and 1990s, many families in the U.S. also gained access to video games.

With the consolidation of the video game industry and increasing technological advances, the spirit of capitalism and its centering of agency found its way into video game discourse. Bakie notes in his "Games in Society" (2010) that "[w]hile video games are ostensibly about fun and entertainment, every published video game is, at its core, a business venture designed to make money. As such, it is targeted toward a particular audience or demographic" (45). By the end of the 1980s, the focus of game designers shifted towards giving players agency – exemplified by the popularity of 'God' games like Will Wright's *Sim City* (1989) and Sid Meier's *Civilization* (1991) in which players are granted control over cities and worlds. Sid Meier explains in the documentary *The Rise of the Video Game* (2007) the appeal of his game: "The perspective that the players have in the game is that they're omniscient, that they're all powerful, that they can make all the important decisions. A lot of people don't have that ability in real life, and to give that to them is entertaining and fun" (hauntdos).

The technological shift from a 2D game environment towards a 3D environment further helped anchor how a focus on player agency had become a way to market games in subsequent years. *The Rise of the Video Game* gestures to this

---

[3] The demographics of the millennial generation Harris talks about – those born between 1980 and 2000 – overlap with those who play video games, as this year's survey by the Entertainment Software Association states that the average age of gamers is 33 years old (see "2019 Essential Facts About the Computer and Video Game Industry").

development as paving the way for game designers to create virtual worlds in which players can experience their own stories. The complexity of the design process of virtual worlds coupled with the large amounts of money needed for development led to a change in the production process. According to James Newman, author of *Videogames* (2004), "[t]he complexity and diversity of such games demands a more formalized, managed development strategy and effectively prohibits the 'one man band' operations in the 1970s and 1980s" (33). The focus on agency leads to more expansive game worlds, and as such helped to drive the corporate consolidation of the commercial game development world. Consider, for example, the contemporary game *Red Dead Redemption II* (2019), which enlisted over 3,000 workers and faced public backlash for the 100-hour work weeks its programmers reported (see Goldberg). There is an irony here: in the production process of the open-world games that seemingly grant their players maximal agency, the people involved as workers lose a lot of agency.

The Encoding and Decoding of Agency

Agency is a loaded term, particularly in Video Game Studies. Game scholars have been trying to define and redefine agency in different ways, intricately making the concept more complex with every redefinition. Tanenbaum and Tanenbaum illustrate how agency has been defined as "choice," "freedom," or "commitment" (6–8). I will structure some of these different definitions of agency along the lines of the encoding/decoding model as posed by Stuart Hall, building towards a new definition. Hall's model is useful due to the two processes he identifies for the transmission of a message, encoding and decoding.

Hall's theory explains how messages are produced and disseminated, arguing there are two processes of meaning-making involved: encoding and decoding (see 90–95). Encoding deals with message construction and is not an isolated process: it is informed by the producer's ideology and by audience input (see 92). At the same time, the way in which a message is perceived by its audience depends on another process: decoding. Hall states that "[b]efore a message can have an 'effect,' satisfy a 'need' or be put to a 'use,' it must first be appropriated as meaningful discourse and be meaningfully decoded" (93). The decoding process is performed by the audience and entails the ways in which the audience interprets the message based on their own ideological background and frameworks of knowledge, as such creating a particular understanding of what the message means. According to Hall, "production and reception of the television message are not, therefore, identical, but they are related: they are differentiated moments within the totality formed by the social relations of the communicative process as a whole" (93). Both the encoding, or production process, and the decoding, or reception process, are thus equally important for understanding how ideas are communicated in a medium.

While Hall's model initially was intended for television, Adrienne Shaw translates his model to the study of video games. Shaw argues:

> A video game, for example, simply cannot function without a measure of activity and involvement beyond that which is required in other media. This makes video games activities as much as they are texts. The interactive properties of the texts, however, do not define the experience of game play. Understanding their reception, thus, must interrogate what actions these texts invite and how players actually use them. (597)

Shaw's emphasis on "actions that these texts invite and how players actually use them" moves Hall's model of a linear message towards a more action-centered approach. "All interactive media technologies," Shaw claims, "can be looked at in terms of what they allow users/audiences to do" (597). With this statement Shaw emphasizes that the decoding process for interactive media technologies is dependent upon the affordances of these particular media forms: what do they allow the users/audiences to do? Essentially, Shaw suggests that the decoding process is dependent upon the kind of agency that the digital medium affords.

In Game Studies, the debate of agency's definition usually focuses only on one of Hall's meaning-making processes, either encoding or decoding. One scholar that focuses specifically on the encoding process is Janet Murray. To her, agency is, "the satisfying power to take meaningful action and see the results of our decisions and choices" (126). However, she emphasizes the limitations of this power as she contends that "interactors can only act within the possibilities that have been established by the writing and programming" (152). Likewise, Katie Salen and Eric Zimmermann focus on the encoding aspect of Hall's model as they argue that playing a game "occurs within a game-system designed to support meaningful kinds of choice-making" (31). Lately, game scholars Tanenbaum and Tanenbaum have offered a different, more decoding-focused definition of agency. Their perspective is that agency is "the process by which participants in an interaction commit to meaning" (13). Similarly, Thue et al. claim that it is not the amount of agency that is given to the player that is crucial, but "what matters most is the amount of agency each player perceives" (91). This essay takes a more holistic approach towards agency by including both encoding and decoding processes. After all, in video games, agency is both the freedom encoded by the designer that allows players to make decisions and the freedom to make decisions as decoded by the player.

Paying attention to both the encoding and the decoding process sheds light not only on how the open-world rpg (role-playing game) *Skyrim* sells its players an illusion of agency, it also opens up a new way of understanding agency. To analyze how video games encode agency, I use Ian Bogost's concept of procedural rhetoric as a heuristic. Bogost's definition of procedural rhetoric is, in short, "[the] practice of using processes persuasively" (3). According to Bogost, games can make ideological claims about how the world works, not through text or visuals, but through the game's processes, mechanisms, and systems of rules. The procedural rhetoric is thus always encoded in the game, and an analysis of the game's mechanisms and systems of rules can expose a particular ideology. Mechanisms and rules eventually decide how the game *should* be played, as such demanding a particular playing style necessary to advance in the game. In this context, I suggest that in addition to making a meaningful intervention to the game environment, what agency in an open-world rpg means that the player can deviate from the preferred playing style that the producers have encoded, without this deviation frustrating or even prohibiting making progress in the game. To analyze the decoding process, I use reviews of *The Elder Scrolls V: Skyrim* from different newspapers and magazines and player reviews from Metacritic.com. When players of a particular game perceive a large amount of agency while the encoded agency is limited, that game creates an illusion of agency.

Agency in *The Elder Scrolls V: Skyrim*

The Elder Scrolls V: Skyrim is widely celebrated for its perceived agency. Reviews indicate that players of *Skyrim* perceive this degree of freedom in the game. For example, Nick Cohen writes in *The Guardian* that "the amount of things to do in Skyrim makes the player feel like they're a living, breathing part of its world" (Cohen). Journalist for *Virtual Gamer 24/7* Steve Clark adds: "The game's pull is the ability to go anywhere, do anything" (Clark).

A form of procedural rhetoric that provides players with a sense of agency in *Skyrim* is the process of avatar creation. The avatar is the player character used to navigate the gamespace and therefore can define the player's aesthetic experience in the game world if she chooses to play in third-person, but *Skyrim* can also be played in first-person perspective. Selen Turkay and Charles K. Kinzer assert that "[d]irect control over their character can imbue players with a sense of agency" (4). They conclude that "[a]vatar-based customization played an important role in the player's identification with their characters by increasing their sense of autonomy" (22). In *Skyrim*, avatar creation is an elaborate process, and the only stable variable is that the player character is known as the Dragonborn, because of his or her ability to absorb the souls of dragons. The Dragonborn's race, which includes human-like races but also fantasy races like Orcs and Elves, gender, weight, and aesthetic qualities like hair color and even battle scars are up to the player. The customization process is concluded by giving the character his or her name. Clark describes these features in *Skyrim* as the possibility to "develop a unique personality" (Clark). Avatar creation therefore promises not only the ability to inhabit a complex social game world with various groups but also insinuates to players the opportunity to shape the game world in accordance with their unique avatar.

Another way in which *Skyrim* creates a sense of agency is the system of rules that allows the player to move freely within the game world. This is a rendition of Tanenbaum and Tanenbaum's concept of agency as freedom – the "freedom to act upon the world without restriction" (3). Murray also finds spatial exploration essential to her experience of agency in video games: "As I move forward, I feel a sense of powerfulness, of significant action, that is tied to my pleasure in the unfolding story" (132). In the player community, the sense of freedom that *Skyrim* provides is highly valued. For example, reviewer Charles Onyett associates life in *Skyrim* with a "thrilling sense of freedom" (Onyett). This freedom manifests itself in the fact that players can access every zone in *Skyrim* from the start. Unlike more linear, campaign-driven games, there are no requirements or preconditions to unlock a zone. In *Skyrim*, the player can also choose not to do any of the quests and just roam the world. When travelling, the player is also not restricted to predefined paths: she can cross rivers and climb mountains. Onyett describes *Skyrim* as "absolutely stuffed with content and curiosities, making every step you take, even if it's through what seems like total wilderness, an exciting one, as something unexpected often lies just over the next ridge" (Onyett). Indeed, this openness of the gamespace and the possibility to freely travel set Skyrim apart from more linear games.

Finally, another game mechanism that implies player agency is giving the player the choice to side with various factions in the war. One of the main questlines in *Skyrim* is the civil war between the rebelling Stormcloaks and the ruling Imperials. The fact that players can choose a side provides them with the possibility to intervene in the gamespace: siding with one of the parties effects the gamespace. The main gameplay mechanism in the civil war questline centers around conquering cities and camps. Eventually, the appropriation of land and cities by players may imbue them with a sense of agency and accomplishment. Therefore, choosing a side in the civil war aims to give players the possibility to make an intervention in the narrative and in the gamespace.

All these aforementioned mechanisms and rules work together to produce a coherent procedural rhetoric in *Skyrim:* it uses a system of rules that allows the player to move freely within the gamespace, to choose a side within the civil war, and to shape the world according to their desires. In a telling statement journalist Tom Francis for *PC Gamer* enthusiastically asserts that "[t]he games we normally call open worlds – the locked off cities and level-restricted grinding grounds – don't compare to this. While everyone else is faffing around with how to control and restrict the player, Bethesda just put a f*cking country in a box" (Francis). In reviews, gamers themselves express similar sentiments. User Zalhum, for example, says: "It's exciting how much you can actually just be yourself and the world around you reacts to the very little details of your choices" ("The Elder Scrolls V: Skyrim User Reviews"). Another user named Nemmy finds *Skyrim* "the best rpg ever made in my opinion as far as freedom is concerned" ("The Elder Scrolls V: Skyrim User Reviews"). Gamer SilverDragon7 adds: "The best part about it is the free roam and the free choice which it gives to the player. [...] You can literally do anything you want to do" ("The Elder Scrolls V: Skyrim User Reviews"). These reviews are symptomatic for the players' general level of enthusiasm about the agency *Skyrim* provides, suggesting that the players indeed feel agency in *Skyrim*.[4]

Creating an Illusion of Agency in *Skyrim*

Despite such perceptions of agency, there are significant instances of procedural rhetoric that push the player in a certain direction in *Skyrim*, restricting player agency. The notion of procedural rhetoric is key here: procedural rhetoric exposes the ways in which rules and mechanisms impose a particular playing style. This section explores whether players have the agency to decide upon their own playing style, or, whether their play is regulated by procedural rhetoric. This analysis also allows for a reflection of the kind of agency that *Skyrim*'s procedural rhetoric advocates for, especially in relation to gamespace: the ultimate goal for the 'Dragonborn' appears to be the domination of each faction of *Skyrim*, and the procedural rhetoric encourages the player to exhaust the land of *Skyrim*, using the non-player characters, wild animals, and mythical creatures primarily as resources for the player to harvest.

While scholars such as Murray suggest that spatial exploration is one of the central ways in which video games provide their players with agency and per-

---

[4] These reviews decode *Skyrim* in what Stuart Hall would term a "hegemonic manner" (101–103). If a consumer decodes something in a "dominant-hegemonic position," he or she "takes the connoted meaning from, say a television newscast or current affairs program full and straight" (101). The gamers from metacritic.com seem to readily accept Bethesda's marketing of agency, hardly challenging the advertised message.

form "meaningful actions," this raises the question whether exploration always is an active choice of the player. Murray notes that for her "[c]onstruing space and moving through it in an exploratory way (when done for its own sake and not in order to find the dentist's office or the right airport gate) is a satisfying activity regardless of whether the space is real or virtual" (130). However, in the case of *Skyrim*, procedural rhetoric demands that the player roams the vast gamespace. Is exploring the gamespace truly a form of agency if the *Skyrim*'s game mechanisms leave no other option? *Skyrim*'s map and fast-travel mechanism both work to bar any other form moving around in the game world, leading to mandatory world exploration. Unlike other games in the same genre, such as *The Witcher III*, there is no actual map on display while moving in the game world. Instead, in *Skyrim* the player has a compass-assisted bar on top of the screen which points North, South, West, or East, and objectives are placed in between those indicators. If the player wants to go to a new location, she thus only knows the direction with no sense of distance or the intermediary landscape. While *Skyrim* gives players the possibility to look at the map, to do so the player must stop, press the menu button, and select the map. It can therefore happen that a player, while travelling straight towards a location, eventually finds herself facing a very steep mountain or ravine that cannot be passed and has to walk all the way around it. The game rules thus prevent the player from taking the shortest route and force her to roam the game world.

Another way the game encourages world exploration is through the fast-travel mechanism. It is impossible to fast-travel to an undiscovered location which means the Dragonborn must go there by foot or by horse. A possibility to travel by carriage exists, but carriage transport only goes from city to city, while many of the objectives are remote locations in the wilderness. Especially in the beginning, travelling from place to place necessarily takes a long time. Even though for players roaming the virtual world is not the same as finding the right airport gate or going to the dentist (to use Murray's comparison), quests are located at exact locations on the map, and *Skyrim* gives no opportunity to find them quickly, which can lead to annoyance. As other players ironically suggest, "[s]oak in every detail of the vast continent, as the lack of fast travel makes you explore it by walking, jogging, hiking, running, strolling, tiptoeing, roaming, marching and more hiking" (Smosh Games). The fast-travel option or rather its lack in *Skyrim* prevents the player from completing quests quickly and instead forces her to roam the game world.

Skyrim's procedural rhetoric insists not only on world exploration, but also prescribes a particularly exploitative relationship between the player and the game environment. The way in which the game environment functions in *Skyrim* allows us to interrogate the ideological implications of validating a game for its agency. In *Skyrim*, engagement with the game's landscape often ends with the exploitation or domination of the land, casting the player necessarily in an imperialist role.⁵ The interactivity of *Skyrim*'s game environment allows the player to use and harvest most of the items found: plants and insects can be used to make potions, animals give the player pelts, claws, or meat, dragons can be harvested for their bones and scales, and non-player characters (NPC) always carry items or gold to loot. To advance in the game (level up abilities, get stronger items), it is necessary to make use of the items found and to kill the animals, mythical creatures, and NPCs for their loot.

In a call towards a more realistic depiction of video game environments in an era of climate change, Media Studies scholar Alenda Chang condemns games that are "predicating player success on extraction and use of natural resources" (58). Player agency, Cheng argues, can be an obstacle to more environmentally oriented games, and potentially ecocritical play: "While I cannot discount the value of player agency, too often this kind of skill mastery merely equates to mastery of the external environment, and consequently games naively reproduce a whole range of instrumental relations that we must reimagine" (60). In *Skyrim*, the imperative is not only to master the external environment and extract the resources from the gamespace but also to dominate most of the civilizations that inhabit the land. At the end of the game, the Dragonborn can also be Thane (or leader) of each hold, Champion of each Deadra, Harbinger of the Companions, Guildmaster of the Thieves' Guild, and Archmage of the College of Winterhold. As such, in *Skyrim*, the relationship between the player and the game environment is based on exploitation and domination.⁶

While mandatory world exploration limits player agency, the most powerful mechanism undermining the sense of agency in *Skyrim* is giving the player quasi-choices. A quasi-choice is when neither choice is inherently good or bad and the consequences are merely aesthetic. As a result, players rarely make meaningful interventions in the gamespace. Arguably the largest quasi-choice in *Skyrim* is the decision to pick sides in the civil war, which is framed as a defining choice in the game's narrative. The land of *Skyrim* is torn between two factions: the ruling Imperials and the rebelling Stormcloaks, led by Ulfric Stormcloak. The opening scene sets the tensions for the game: the Dragonborn is

---

5 For a critical assessment of imperial themes in other video games (and the American literature tradition), see the essay "Owning Global Spaces and the Frontier in *Uncharted 4: A Thief's End*" by David Callahan in this volume.
6 For a reading of a less exploitative and environmental conscious approach to open-world design, see the essay "On Postapocalyptic Frontiers in *Horizon Zero Dawn*" by Nathalie Aghoro in this volume.

captured by the Imperial Army and rides in a cart alongside rebel Ulfric Stormcloak, who is accused of killing the High King. The Imperial Army tries to execute the Dragonborn, while there are no records of her committing any crime. Judging by this action, it would be logical to join the Stormcloaks but the question whether Ulfric Stormcloak is a traitor remains a judgement for the player to make and to this day sparks vivid discussions on game forums online. Furthermore, the Stormcloaks discriminate against all races other than Nords (a specific human-type race). Therefore, narrative-wise, neither choice seems inherently good or bad.

Remarkably, notwithstanding narrative elements, the gameplay for both sides is virtually the same. Both questlines consist of roughly similar activities: the basic premise is that the land of *Skyrim* must be conquered step by step. The first obstacle is the city of Whiterun, which the Imperials have to defend and the Stormcloaks must attack. The Dragonborn's alignment decides whether the city is taken or not. The remainder of the questline consists of taking over the forts of the enemy and eventually the headquarters of either the Stormcloaks (the city Windhelm) or the Imperials (the city Solitude). It inevitably ends in killing the leaders of either the Stormcloaks or the Imperials. After this is done, there are no major changes to *Skyrim*'s gamespace. The difference between the beginning and either ending of the game is purely cosmetic, as merely the uniforms of the guards in the big cities and the uniforms of the survivors of the losing faction in camps scattered around *Skyrim* vary.

Since gameplay and narrative are basically the same for both sides, the choice between the Stormcloaks and the Imperials is a *quasi-choice*. Picking sides in *Skyrim* thus epitomizes Adorno and Horkheimer's illusion of choice: the animated discussions consumers have about the advantages and disadvantages of each choice functions only to maintain "the appearance of competition and choice" (97). For *Skyrim*, the choice between the Stormcloaks and the Imperial army sparks heated debates online about which side players should join, for example on the forum of the Imagine Game Network (IGN Boards, see LegacyAccount). It is exactly this debate of enthusiasts that sells players an illusion of agency and the illusion of choice. The way in which *Skyrim* employs quasi-choices to get players to debate the supposed difference between the sides confirms Adorno and Horkheimer's premise that "difference is fundamentally illusional" (97).

Considering the other ways in which *Skyrim* employs quasi-choices, the experience of difference is similarly illusory. Decisions about what the avatar looks like have hardly any implications in the gameplay: the character traits that come with a specific race (or gender) are, above all, aesthetic, and if the player plays in the game in the first-person perspective, the avatar hardly features in the gameplay. While players are indeed free to roam the gamespace, the map and the fast-travel mechanism dictate this way of moving through space, making it impossible to move from one point to the next quickly. The choices that are framed as meaningful are, in fact, quasi choices. In these aspects, the agency that is encoded by *Skyrim*'s designers is limited. The case study demonstrates a clear discrepancy between the amount of agency encoded in *The Elder Scrolls V: Skyrim* and decoded by players. As players perceive a large amount of agency while it is often limited or cosmetic, this video game sells an illusion of agency. The way players perceive the game is exactly how the game is marketed.

Conclusion

The notion of agency has become a marketing buzzword for game producers, an aspect highly valued by video game players, and a fiercely debated topic for video game scholars. A game that supposedly gives its players a lot of agency, *The Elder Scrolls V: Skyrim*, fails to fulfill its promise. The game employs quasi-choices and procedural rhetoric to impose a preferred playing strategy based on spatial exploration and environmental exploitation. This analysis puts pressure on the definitions of agency by scholars such as Murray who define agency as "see[ing] the results of our decisions and choices" and perceive spatial navigation as meaningful action. A close analysis of *Skyrim*'s procedural rhetoric unveils an underlying ideological idea of what agency in video games should be, already setting up players for hegemonic decodings of agency.

The kind of agency Bethesda sells is closely connected to North American spatial discourses. David Noble's notion of the U.S. as a "timeless space" illustrates how some of the founding ideals of American identity relate to their experience of space, especially in contrast to the hierarchies of Europe. The "timeless space" of the U.S. offered Anglo-Americans the possibility to own private property by cultivating the land and fighting off indigenous populations. Through this 'conquering' of space and private property they would leave behind their European histories and become Americans (see 1–8). Bethesda's marketing strategies and the procedural rhetoric of *Skyrim* propose a similar relationship between the player and the gamespace: players are encouraged to exhaust the game environments' resources for their own gain by killing the 'enemies,' animals, and mythical creatures that inhabit the space. In a way, *Skyrim* is also a timeless space, as through the exploration and exploitation of the game environment players become their version of the Dragonborn and are momentarily free from the oppressive structures and hierarchies of the 'real world.'[7]

Bethesda's marketing strategy has been highly successful, as *Skyrim* is one of the best-selling role-playing games of all time, and the celebration of agency allows them to further consolidate their position in the video game industry and profit off players in new ways. When players assert their agency in other ways, the game industry finds ways to monetize and restrict their actions. Specifically, Bethesda robbed players of the possibility to mod the world of *Skyrim* to increase profits and online reactions suggest that this form of monetization crossed a line. Modding is a form of programming players use to change the code of the video game to fix bugs and errors in the game engine or to create a personalized experience, expand the main narrative, and alter the visual appearance of the world. *Skyrim* has an extensive modding community sometimes investing hundreds of hours to change the game in funny and unpredictable ways by, for example, replacing the dragons with cartoon figure Thomas the Tank Engine (see Lambo_96). While players usually share their mods online for free, Bethesda Game Studios commercialized the modding experience making players pay for these mods. Unsurprisingly, *Skyrim* players felt cheated, leaving angry comments and reviews on metacritic.com. MoshMonkey, for example, says: "[*Skyrim*] was one of my favourite games before corporate greed reigned supreme. Best mod workshop in all of steam [is] now hidden behind a paywall." The video game industry increasingly finds ways to make agency profitable.

Another question that arises from this analysis of agency in *Skyrim* is: how desirable is this focus on agency in video games? This paper has illustrated that the centering of agency in video games comes with uneasy ideological implications: it furthers a neoliberal ideology or, "the new spirit of capitalism" that promises workers agency but justifies capitalism's exploitative mechanisms. Furthermore, the use of quasi-choices highlights a consumerist idea of choice, where the choice is always between similar consumer products. Finally, the centrality of player agency in open-world games such as *Skyrim* promotes an imperialist logic, where the main aim of the player seems to harvest the resources of the game environment effectively and become the most powerful being in the game, exploiting the game environment and all its inhabitants. Therefore, what this chapter calls for is a more nuanced evaluation of the notion of agency as fundamental and as one of the core pleasures of video games.

---

7 The average *Skyrim* player spends 150 hours in its vast open world (see Suellentrop).

Works Cited

Bakie, Robert T. "A Brief History of Videogames" *Introduction to Game Development*, edited by Steve Rabin, Charles River Media, 2010, pp. 3–42.

Bakie, Robert T. "Games and Society" *Introduction to Game Development*, edited by Steve Rabin, Charles River Media, 2010, pp. 43–59.

Bogost, Ian. *Persuasive Games: The Expressive Power of Videogames.* MIT Press, 2007.

Boltanski, Luc and Ève Chiapello. *The New Spirit of Capitalism.* Translated by Gregory Elliott, Verso, 2007.

Clark, Steve. "Skyrim versus The Witcher 3, Which is the Best RPG?" *VG 24/7*, 26 October 2016. www.vg247.com/2016/10/26/skyrim-versus-the-witcher-3-which-is-the-best-rpg/. Accessed 29 January 2021.

Cohen, Nick. "*Elder Scrolls V: Skyrim* Review." *The Guardian*, 10 November 2011, www.theguardian.com/technology/gamesblog/2011/nov/10/elder-scrolls-v-skyrim-review. Accessed 29 January 2021.

Dyer-Witheford, Nick and Greig De Peuter. *Games of Empire: Global Capitalism and Video Games.* University of Minnesota Press, 2009.

"2019 Essential Facts About the Computer and Video Game Industry." *Entertainment Software Association*, May 2019, www.theesa.com/esa-research/2019-essential-facts-about-the-computer-and-video-game-industry/. Accessed 29 January 2021.

Fendt, Matthew, Brent Harrison, Stephen G. Ware, Rogelio E. Cardona-Rivera, and David L. Roberts. "Achieving the Illusion of Agency." *International Conference on Digital Storytelling*, Springer, 2012, pp. 114–25.

Francis, Tom. "The Elder Scrolls V: Skyrim Review" *PC Gamer*, 10 November 2011, www.pcgamer.com/the-elder-scrolls-v-skyrim-review/. Accessed 29 January 2021.

Frasca, Gonzalo. "Rethinking Agency and Immersion: Video Games as a Means of Consciousness-Raising." *Digital Creativity*, vol. 12, no. 3, 2001, pp. 167–74.

Goldberg, Harold. "How the West Was Digitized: The making of Rockstar Games' *Red Dead Redemption 2*" *Vulture*, 14 October 2018, www.vulture.com/2018/10/the-making-of-rockstar-games-red-dead-redemption-2.html. Accessed 29 January 2021.

Hall, Stuart. "Encoding, Decoding." 1973. *The Cultural Studies Reader*, edited by Simon During, Routledge, 1991, pp. 90–103.

Harris, Malcolm. *Kids These Days: Human Capital and the Making of Millennials.* Little, Brown, 2017

Harvey, David. *A Brief History of Neoliberalism.* Oxford University Press, 2005.

Hauntdos. "The Rise of the Video Game: Level 1." *YouTube*, 5 November 2012, www.youtube.com/watch?v=3u3Hc13wzHE. Accessed 29 January 2021.

Horkheimer, Max and Theodor W. Adorno. "The Culture Industry: Enlightenment as Mass Deception." 1947. *The Dialectic of Enlightenment.* Stanford University Press, 1972, pp. 95–136.

Howard, Todd. "Episode 6: Enter the Dragon." *The Bethesda Podcast*, 16 December, 2010. www.tunein.com/podcasts/Sports-Recreation-Podcasts/The-Bethesda-Podcast-p1134380/. Accessed 29 July 2021.

Jelfs, Tim. *The Argument about Things in the 1980s: Goods and Garbage in an Age of Neoliberalism.* West Virginia University Press, 2018.

Lambo_96, "Skyrim – Thomas the Tank Engine Mod (HD)." *YouTube*, 11 December 2013, www.youtube.com/watch?v=yNaTZV8qS1I. Accessed 29 January 2021.

LegacyAccount. "So do I join the Stormcloaks or The Imperial Legion?" *IGN Boards*, 20 November 2011, www.ign.com/boards/threads/so-do-i-join-the-stormcloaks-or-the-imperial-legion.206923225/. Accessed 22 March 2018.

Murray, Janet H. *Hamlet on the Holodeck: The Future of Narrative in Cyberspace*. Free Press, 1997.

Newman, James. *Videogames*. Routledge, 2004.

Noble, David, W. *Death of a Nation: American Culture and the End of Exceptionalism*. University of Minnesota Press, 2002.

Ocio, Sergio and Jose Antonio Lopez Brugos. "Multi-Agent Systems and Sandbox Games." *The Society for the Study of Artificial Intelligence and Simulation of Behavior Convention*, 2009, pp. 70–74.

Onyett, Charles "The Elder Scrolls V: Skyrim Review" *IGN*, 10 November 2011, www.ign.com/articles/2011/11/10/the-elder-scrolls-v-skyrim-review. Accessed 29 January 2021.

Pwnagemeister. "Should I join the Stormcloaks or Imperials." *Skyrim Forums*, 17 December 2011, www.skyrimforums.org/sf/threads/imperials-or-stormcloaks.3219. Accessed 22 March 2018.

Salen, Katie and Eric Zimmerman. *Rules of Play: Game Design Fundamentals*. The MIT Press, 2004.

Shaw, Adrienne. "Encoding and Decoding Affordances: Stuart Hall and Interactive Media Technologies." *Media, Culture and Society*, vol. 39, no.4, 2017, pp. 592–602.

Smosh Games. "The Elder Scrolls V: Skyrim (Honest Game Trailers)." *YouTube*, 3 May 2014, www.youtube.com/watch?v=rjTOF8IC528. Accessed 29 Jan. 2021.

Stuart, Keith. "Video Games Aren't About Power – They're About Agency." *The Guardian*, 16 October 2015, www.theguardian.com/technology/2015/oct/16/video-games-power-agency-control. Accessed 1 May 2018.

Suellentrop, Chris. "'Skyrim' Creator on Why We'll Have to Wait for Another 'Elder Scrolls.'" *Rolling Stone*, 21 November 2016, www.rollingstone.com/culture/culture-features/skyrim-creator-on-why-well-have-to-wait-for-another-elder-scrolls-128377/. Accessed 29 July 2021.

Tanenbaum, Karen and Joshua Tanenbaum. "Agency as Commitment to Meaning: Communicative Competence in Games." *Digital Creativity*, vol. 21, no. 1, 2010, pp. 11–17.

Tanenbaum, Karen and Joshua Tanenbaum. "Commitment to Meaning: A Reframing of Agency in Games." *Digital Arts and Culture*, 2009, pp. 1–10.

TheArtOfScience. "What Does 'Agency' Mean in Regards to Games?" *Gamers with Job*, 13 January 2010, www.gamerswithjobs.com/node/1270831. Accessed 29 Jan. 2021.

The Elder Scrolls V: Skyrim. Bethesda Game Studios. 2015.

"The Elder Scrolls V: Skyrim User Reviews." *Metacritic*, www.metacritic.com/game/pc/the-elder-scrolls-v-skyrim/user-reviews. Accessed 1 May 2018.

Thue, David, Vadim Bulito, Marcia Spetch and Trevon Romanuik. "A Computational Model of Perceived Agency in Video Games." *Association for the Advancement of Artificial Intelligence*, 2011, pp. 91–96.

Turkay, Selen, and Charles K. Kinzer. "The Effects of Avatar-based Customization on Player Identification." *International Journal of Gaming and Computer-Mediated Simulations (IJGCMS)*, vol. 6, no.1, 2014, pp. 1–25.

Part II

Damien B. Schlarb
Filling Out the Map: The Anxiety of Situatedness and the Topological Poesis of Cartographic Maps in Video Games

Cartographic maps in action-adventure video games afford a function that is increasingly hard to come by in games with large-scale worlds as well as in everyday life: oversight. Maps tell what lies ahead, what quests are available, which objectives matter, and which mountains may yet be too high to climb. The winning conditions of such games require players to situate themselves in the game world. Cartographic maps aid players in finding their ways through a game's multifarious diegetic and non-diegetic structures. Maps track players' physical movements and reveal their progression in the story by revealing more and more details about the game world and registering the effects of player actions. Vanquishing a boss may unlock a new region, picking up a new item may reveal a new class of collectible, now marked on the map. Filling out the map is a process that runs silently and in parallel to play, tying traversal and exploration to narrative and characterization. Functionally speaking, good game design, as Katie Salen and Eric Zimmerman note, inspires "meaningful play," that is, "the process by which a player takes action within the designed system of a game and the system responds to the action. The meaning of an action in a game resides in the relationship between action and outcome" (66). With regards to action games, meaningful play emerges as a function of purposeful movement through the game world as enabled by cartographic maps.

Designers must ask how wayfinding and traversal are enabled or hindered, which resources must be consumed, which obstacles cleared, and by what means. The answers to these questions define how meaningful play may be achieved. Transferred to the spatial analytical paradigm, design determines the utility of gamespace for players. Understanding spatiality in action-adventure games requires that we attend to the ways space is designed and navigated as well as to the manner in which such design links up with a game's narrative.

Games are notoriously difficult to define conceptually because of their multimodal mediality and generic variety. Any structural analysis has to tarry with the ways these modes and forms intersect. In 1974, more than a decade after *Space War!* (1962) appeared on the radar screens at MIT, spatial studies pioneer Henri Lefebvre argued that space is produced by sociocultural negotiations and at the time was "becoming the principal stake of goal-directed actions and struggles" (410). Years later, Digital Game Studies pioneer Espen Aarseth declared that such struggles are the essential concern of video games' "spatial representation and negotiation," and proposed that any "classification of computer games can be based on how they represent – or, perhaps, *implement* – space" ("Allegories of Space" 154; emphasis added). If we want to examine how game worlds, traversal, and stories intersect and influence each other, we must find an inflection point in their design, an area where these design elements and their interactions become legible. Embedded cartographic representations of gamespaces and objectives, or in-game maps, represent such an inflection point.

In this chapter, then, I discuss how cartographic maps in games enable meaningful action. Maps allow players to move with agency and purpose. As embedded media, maps afford a bird's-eye-view of a game's moral and material landscape, simultaneously signifying the terrain, game challenges, and practices players must adopt in order to progress. By mediating the virtual space of the game world, maps moralize – in the classic sense of describing human activity – the game's spaces. As with real-world maps, game maps mobilize activities of rendering familiar, unveiling, or colonizing, all of which emerge during play. Maps illustrate cultural spatial practices that generate the space they then mediate. The project of understanding game maps, I propose, warrants that we consult scholarship on colonial cartographic maps, specifically those of early America colonialism, as doing so can help us examine critically their semiosis and ideological commitments. In what follows, I deliberate on how third-person, open world action-adventure games represent and engender space through their in-game maps. I consider maps as embedded cultural artefacts that mediate the game world and, in doing so, expose its cultural politics of spatiality. Maps perform self-reflexive, topological poesis, a process of world-building that reflects its own underlying ethics. The self-reflexive doubling of the game world through maps, I contend, allows us to confront their spatial politics and the ideological commitment of the games that envelop them.

Capturing the representational ambivalence of game maps requires an interdisciplinary approach. American Studies, and in a wider sense Culture Studies, offers such an angle, because it avails itself of historical, structuralist, and semiotic analytical sensibilities. The discourses relevant to my discussion from both fields are part of the spatial turn in the humanities, that is, a discourse, as Doris Bachmann-Medick argues, that examines spatial thinking in various contexts "with respect to politicizations and depoliticizations, to naturalizations and symbolizations" (216). Research conducted in Early American Studies on colonial mapping and cartography can help us determine the nature of maps in games. My chief interest here is in the semiotic operations encoded in and made manifest through and on in-game maps. When I speak of an anxiety of situatedness, I refer to the implications of the game design as reflected by the cartographic representations of game maps – the mission objectives listed, the manner in which certain areas of the map are courted off for later parts of the game, etc. – rather than speculating about players' mental states.

Moving purposefully to gain the ground of the game world, analogously, is part of the central conflict, or argon, of open-world action games. In these games, maps visualize this struggle, as it becomes bound up with uncovering and rendering known the game world. Maps create and recreate the game world in the wake of play, allowing players to apprehend that world and their place in it at a glance, thus enabling the kind of analytical and transformative semiotic work that constitutes gameplay in the first place. We may also recall Aarseth's original definition of games as "ergodic literature" (*Cybertext* 1) a kind of text that needs to be traversed to unfold. Traversal and semiotic manipulation in games constitute practices of sense making that tie gamic space to meaning. "[G]ame spaces," Michael Nitsche argues, "evoke narratives because the player is making sense of them in order to engage with them. Through a comprehension of signs and interaction with them, the player generates new meaning" (3).

Disorientation arguably is the default subject position in action-adventure games. At the beginning of such games, the embryonic protagonist stands virtually defenseless facing overwhelming odds, often lacking the power and skills necessary to traverse a hostile world. Progressing in the game means progressing through the game world. In *Horizon Zero Dawn*, for instance, players first assume the role of Aloy, the game's protagonist, when she is a defenseless child wandering through a cave with only environmental cues to guide her. Aloy and the player's experiences become aligned, infantilized as they are while struggling to find their way through an unfamiliar world.[1] Game maps record this journey, chronicling player progression, character development, and narrative while alleviating the anxiety of situatedness, but they also shape play.

Like geographic maps, video game maps enable wayfinding by organizing information in ways conducive to meaning making (see Turchi 11). They allow players to traverse and change the game world, which in turn extends the map as a permanent record of both player knowledge and diegetic events. As traversal and wayfinding inform each other, maps become what Aylish Wood calls "recursive space" (88). Players use maps to apprehend and reconfigure the game world, and designers use different representational means to translate this process into semiotic activities. Players may disperse fog to reveal new sections of the

---

[1] For a detailed analysis of the role of space in *Horizon Zero Dawn*, see Nathalie Aghoro's essay "On Postapocalyptic Frontiers in *Horizon Zero Dawn*" in this volume.

map, transforming terra incognita into familiar stomping grounds. They may fill in blank sections of the map or capture enemy territory. But game maps also allow players to navigate a game's narrative as well as its non-diegetic systems (pause screens, inventory menus, etc.). In this sense, maps bridge the gap between narrative and design and make possible literal and figurative forms of traversal through the layered and intertwined systems of a game.

These processes of meaning-making are not disinterested, however. The actions that maps mobilize – orientation, traversal, and manipulation (of the game world) – have ethical vectors. They regularly require disposing hordes of enemies, pilfering hidden artefacts, and destroying cultural heritage. Filling out the map is anything but fun and games. Wayfinding and mapping in games come at a price for which maps arguably function as the moral ledger. Regarding video game maps as cultural artefacts that build worlds allows us to unearth their underlying cultural ethics. Game maps are part of human spatiality insofar as they signify the processes of spatial negotiation. Lefebvre and others have made the case that space is not a container occurring naturally in the world but a cultural and social construction (see 16). Affording an "interactive process of navigation" (82), as Janet Murray noted at the dawn of digital media studies, is what distinguishes digital from analog media. And so, maps are also communal spaces that enable interactions between players and designers, players and non-player characters (NPCs).

My argument here will be two-fold: first, I argue that maps can help us understand how that spatiality becomes bound up with narrative, design, and the activity of play in action games. Second, I contend that game maps reveal and seek to alleviate what I want to call an anxiety of situatedness but at the same time reproduce this anxiety. They reveal this anxiety by rendering the game world legible and navigable and by enabling players to find their way through the world. Two warrants underpin this argument: one, maps are essential for understanding the spatiality of action-adventure games, one of the most popular video game genres. Two, maps link video games to the larger discourses of cultural and human spatiality. This second point is particularly relevant, for considering games as part of human spatiality allows us to take what we learned about real-world maps and apply it to games, as I do below. Doing so may help us discover overlaps and incongruities between real-world and game maps.

I will begin my discussion by theorizing video game maps through the analytical lenses of history, design, and ideology. First, I situate game maps in a longer western media history of cartographic maps. I draw on Early American Studies and its work in colonial mapping and cultural cartography to show how geographical maps have always constituted arenas of spatial negotiation and speculation, both of which produce cultural and natural spaces. I then think more broadly about how game maps constitute video game spaces and about how they imply through their design an anxiety of situatedness. I turn to the analytical examples of *Horizon Zero Dawn* (2016) and *Assassin's Creed: Syndicate* (2015) to discuss how that anxiety morphs into political and ideological commitments expressed through design. In a semiotic reading, I examine the signification strategies the two game's respective maps deploy and how they integrate design, traversal, and narrative. I end by considering how these significations both alleviate and reinforce the spatial anxiety in games.

Historicizing Video Game Maps

Game maps are embedded, procedurally unfolding representations within media artefacts (games) that are themselves part representation (story, video sequences, design, etc.) and part multimodal, interactive, and procedurally generated simulations. This twofold mediatedness imbues them with a unique self-reflexivity. Given this reflexivity, game maps can help us understand spatiality in video games as well as the spatial politics that inform their design. By studying game maps through this constructivist lens, we may discover the ideological trappings and constitutive cultural practices – colonialist, exploitative, masochistic, but also reconstructive, collaborative, liberatory – they signify, revealing the cost and promise of wayfinding in games. Game design, as game scholar Patrick Jagoda observes, can serve as a platform for socio-political commentary and even activism (see 212). Armed with this knowledge, we may ultimately move on from discussing game maps and spaces to ponder how those in the cultural sphere of influence of the United States construe virtual spaces.

Historians have used maps as records of colonization and artifacts that reveal the colonialist imaginary. Early Americanist Martin Brückner argues that maps are "things whose social lives reveal in full their material and cultural utility and value" (3). Like early modern maps, for instance in colonial America, video game maps facilitate commercial and social circulation. Maps to art historian W.J.T. Mitchell are not hermetic systems, but function "as if they were environments where images live, or personas and avatars that address us and can be addressed in turn" (203). Maps set up virtual spaces in which spectators may not just encounter but engage virtual entities. Early Americanist Ralph Bauer argues that eighteenth-century colonial literature, specifically narratives of shipwreck and captivity, "narrativize the new forms of knowledge production" (9) about space that emerged at the end of the feudal colonialist era. Oliver Scheiding, in his examination of early modern maps of the New World, shows how theological and geographical discourses complement each other to remap America as a virtual space in terms of Europe's westward expansion and in the case of Anglo-Protestant colonialism. The new world occupies a purely symbolic function in the European imaginary, filling the role of a promised land in the scheme of Protestant millennial history and a "geography of salvation" (Scheiding 2). Mapping the continent in American letters, Literary Studies scholars Edward Watts, Keri Holt, and John Funchion remind us, always entailed a tension between the national expansionist narratives of manifest destiny and regional narratives that often contradicted this imperialist nationalism (see 5). Switching between maps and in-world actions in action-adventure games may reveal the same tensions between local and global contexts, and side quests may (inadvertently) voice criticism of players' colonizing conquest of the game world. Discussing the function of cartographic maps in strategy games for subaltern players, Souvik Mukherjee points out how such games evince in their map design a quasi-colonialist, ethnically essentializing logic when they try to adopt a culturally relativist outlook (see 508–509). That being said, he also acknowledges that a "game's map is also a space where alternative history(ies) are made possible. Here, it is possible to reverse the colonial process and conquer the erstwhile imperial powers" (Mukherjee 509). In video games as in cartography, making maps thus constitutes a socio-cultural practice, a kind of metagame surrounding the actual game.

Game maps are not projection screens that merely reflect game narrative. Communal and constructivist in nature, they mount cartographic narratives that may both complement and countermand a game's narrative. As cultural artefacts, they reflect and refract narrative, (re-)inscribing ideologies, specifically logics of conquest and extraction, that inform the cultures which produce the games. Like real-world, cartographic maps, they are part and parcel of these logics. Likewise, cartographic maps do more than represent topography. They tell stories, not the least of which are the culturally specific spatial politics they signify. Geographical maps, classicist Christian Jacob notes, are "tools of wayfinding" (10). They mediate space to facilitate the kinds of scope and perspective that is normally unachievable within the confines of human perception. Maps, he observes, actualize, by way of metaphor, the fantasy of a comprehensive bird's-eye view on the world (see 1). They are, in this sense, fictional. So, when Nitsche talks about the prospect of comprehending space and movement through video-game narrative (see 7), can the reverse be true as well? In other words, can we understand games, the stories they tell, the play they engender, the ideologies that they are entangled in, by examining the way they represent movement and space in cartographic forms? If literary maps, for instance, can clarify the large-scale implications of narrative, as literary studies scholar Franco Moretti argues, could we argue the same for video games (see 60)?

Game maps thus may enable reparative readings and actions even beyond the mere reversal of fortunes between parties locked in colonialist conflict. Gamespaces and traversal can be designed to enable appreciation and reverence and even connect players to experience collectively a sense of place and even community. *Assassin's Creed Origin* (2018) was the first entry in the long-running series to feature a traversal mode that lets players wander freely through the game's Egyptian setting without having to engage in combat. *Death Stranding* (2019) allows players to collaborate asynchronously on construction projects like roads to ease world traversal. Players never meet directly but can behold the effects of their collaboration in their respective game worlds. Meanwhile, in *Red Dead Redemption Online* players meet up for cross-country walks with soup trays in hand, adding to the emergent tradition of open world game cross-country walks (see Slonitram, Zwiezen).

Video Game Spaces and the Anxiety of Situatedness

Video games, argues Nitsche, resituate us in new geographies and identities: "[W]e are transformed," he says, "situated into a new context, and we 'know our place' in this situation. There are still many communication channels that do not depend on such relocation, but game worlds offer us digital realms that put the place back into our reach" (244). Part of the appeal of this experience, his comments imply, is that this relocation is not entirely pleasant, but unsettling. Thinking about space in this manner can help us conceive of maps as responding to the problem of wayfinding. Being thrown into the world, as Heidegger would have it, players are called upon to situate themselves in unfamiliar surroundings – wearing unfamiliar skins – and begin their journey through alien, potentially hostile environs. This anxiety of situatedness makes the game's conflicts spring to life.

Designers see in-game maps as an answer to the dilemma of world size and the player's anxiety of situatedness. Maps link the architectural vision of the designer with player activity. They express where players should go and what they should do. In this sense, maps signify what Stephan Günzel has called topology, a concept of utilitarian space (see *Topologie* 21). Maps situate players in the game's narrative and the sociocultural space of the game, but that process of situating is always already part of the conflict that drives the game. Günzel, in talking about first-person shooter games, claims that "[n]ot only do [player] perspective and topographic spatial representation correspond in video games, in the sense that the map represents the relation between individual gamespaces and the overall game [*Spielverlauf*], but they are also interlaced on the level of gameplay, insofar as players may switch between them at will and according to their requirements" ("Raum" 126; my translation). Players, he notes further, experience the game's spatiality precisely in the interstice between these two perspectives and only by way of their reciprocity (see "Raum" 128). Third-person games construct spatiality in similar manner, but afford a broader field of vision via drawn-back camera angels. They thus allow for more distance to the action and afford a level of defamiliarization of what are often violent actions. The sense of situatedness is built through the interplay between the map and the world, between localized actions in the world and the global vision of the game narrative and its central conflicts that the map affords. In this sense, maps perpetually frame the player's sense of place, both in the world and in the story, and thus exert a world-constituting poesis, a function that Robert Tally – harkening back to Gaston Bachelard's *Poetics of Space* (1958) – notes ultimately bespeaks the overall poetic nature of human-made space in general (see 116). The void or blank slate of the map players confront at the beginning of the game produces anxiety that is only alleviated by perennially moving forward and filling out the map in the process.

Maps are virtual spaces built by processes of cultural and social negotiation. Cultural constructivists like Lefebvre argue that spaces are always sites of contestation (see 17). Maps thus are tools of socio-cultural organization whose ideological and symbolic power flows from their ability to constitute worlds, rather than describing them impartially. They mark safe zones, cement territorial claims, and fence off no-man's lands. They indicate routes for travel and territorial dominion between rivaling state entities. While Nitsche notes that gamespaces bear a "architectoral quality" (3), it is important to remember that this quality is neither apolitical nor aesthetically disinterested. "Play," Dutch historian Johan Huizinga famously notes, creates order, "*is* order" (10; emphasis in the original), and in all games – not just digital games – instilling that order means designing a game world according to certain aesthetic and political programs. Like games, maps impose a somewhat arbitrary order on the world. Games and maps may have more in common than it initially appears, because they both frame processes of spatial construction as playful and ambivalent negotiations. Tally reminds us that maps are ludic in nature, assigning a playful and ambivalent character to the types of negotiations that constructivists apprehend in spaces (see 7). By comparison, action-adventure games project these dynamics covertly, yet in doing so they draw attention to the fact that traversing the game world is simultaneously an act of mapping entangled in colonialist implications. Maps here signify the consequences of conquest and the colonial gaze. They may thus allow us to ask ethical questions about what is required to transform the map. What kind of work do we perform to perfect the map according to its design?

The Ideology of Game Maps

Game maps in action-adventure games fill out as ludic actions and narrative plot unfold, revealing new objectives and topographical changes players wrought in the world through their actions. Understanding this recursive mechanism requires that we consider their referential other, game worlds, as well as their own malleability, i.e., the changes they undergo during the course of play. Maps administer what David Harvey calls "spatial organization," as a necessary panacea to "overcome space," i.e., the anxiety of unfamiliarity it imparts (see Harvey 145).[2] The maps in *Assassin's Creed Syndicate* and *Horizon Zero Dawn* respond to the anxiety of situatedness produced by the size of their game worlds.

Horizon Zero Dawn is set in a post-apocalyptic world where human society has reconfigured itself in neo-tribal communities. Players assume the role of Aloy, a young outcast who must discover her origins and uncover the mystery of how civilization ended in catastrophe and eventually got reset. The cataclysm that wipes out both humankind and the ecosphere occurs in the form of self-replicating robots that use biomatter as fuel. The machines, created by a weapons manufacturer called Faro Industries, eventually designate all of humankind their enemy and replicate until they consume the whole biosphere. This "Faro Plague" is an extinction event that ends life on earth. The game also makes a cogent argument about how technology is a double-edged sword that can yield creation or dole out destruction. A project called "Zero Dawn" effects the resurrection of humankind through a combination of cloning and automated education programs, all controlled by an artificial intelligence named GAIA. Once humans – now organized in tribes and in pantheistic religious systems – have sufficiently repopulated the world, their curiosity accidentally causes them to awaken the very war machines that extinguished them before.

The game is ambivalent in its messaging. On the level of story, it presents progressive gender ideals through its capable and independently-minded female

---

[2] On a more basic level, maps are quality-of-life amenities to players saving them from walking in the wrong direction or searching in vain for mission objectives for hours on end. Geographical growth coincides with increased playtimes. And while I will not focus on temporality in this essay, it bears mentioning that narratologists and Media Studies scholars like Marie-Laure Ryan remind us that time and space in digital media are inextricably linked and must be considered together (see Ryan 19).

protagonist – a source of controversy prior to its release. It also mounts a scathing critique of unfettered capitalism by allegorizing its self-destructive tendencies in its rapacious robotic antagonists. The game casts Aloy as a female, secular-messianic figure, who gets to step outside the religiously colored worldviews of her tribal peers. On the level of gameplay, however, Aloy too must extract resources by hunting wildlife, collecting medicinal herbs (that seem to regrow at infinitum), and salvaging parts from sentient, animal-like machines that GAIA uses to terraform the earth to make it inhabitable again. These actions serve not just her survival but conspicuously consumptive and speculative purposes: machine parts and animal skins can be sold or traded with the various merchants that linger around the world. Some machines have to be hunted to rank up in the so-called hunting lodge, a guild of machine hunters, or to curry favor with certain quest givers in the game. Players thus inadvertently reenact the very logic of resource extraction demonized by the Faro Plague, the storyline extinction-level event caused by corporate greed that killed of the biosphere.

Horizon Zero Dawn's map weaves these emancipatory and exploitative thematic strands into a narrative fabric. Technically, the map provides a stereoscopic view on the game world, making it appear like a miniature model with only minimal abstraction. It reflects the lore of the game's story by including dead machines alongside topographic characteristics of the world, making it a topological map. For instance, the mountain ranges skirting Aloy's home valley are shot through with tentacles of the now defunct kraken-like Faro war machines. They have become part of the environment and thus figure as part of the material history that confronts its inhabitants as a hieroglyph and that Aloy uncovers on her journey.

Initially, we find the map shrouded in fog, except for Aloy's home village. The vista that the map offers represents the compass of her world and the expanse of her understanding. This representation coincides with the knowledge level of players in this early phase of the game. As Aloy encounters other tribes and explores new areas, new sections of the map appear. Meanwhile, points of interest are represented as two-dimensional icons, these include story locations, collectible artefacts, and hunting grounds for machines and live animals, both become resources for upgrading gear and weapons. These icons appear on the map when players scale and hack giant machines called Tallnecks – think brachiosaurus with a head shaped like the saucer section of the *Enterprise* – in each area, to hack it and collect data on the area. The task is to disperse the fog and render the map fully visible.

Aloy's coming-of-age story allegorizes players' growing proficiency. Traversing the game world furthers Aloy's story, making available more and more areas on the map, as players become more adapt at managing the game's various role-playing submenus as they upgrade and refine Aloy's abilities and equipment. Traversal not only means moving across the game world but also exploring the depth of its systems. It is a multi-layered metaphor that signifies the connection between the game's diegetic and non-diegetic systems. While players grow accustomed to the control schemes and become literate in the game's visual language, Aloy gains competency and confidence as she learns to fend for herself and uncovers the mystery of her origins.

Both Aloy and the player experience and eventually overcome the anxiety of situatedness – in the environment, in the game menus – as they sally forth into the world. All these forms of traversal unfold in time and in doing so become intertwined and "co-implicated" (Massey 55). Aloy and the players journey from helplessness to competence, from innocence to shrewdness, from ignorance to knowledge. Insofar as this movement in and with maps produces space, narrative, and play, we may speak of games as examples of what Edward Soja calls "thirdspace," "a distinct mode of critical spatial awareness that is appropriate to the new scope and significance being brought about in the rebalanced trialectics of spatiality–historicality–sociality" (57).

A more obvious case of what may be called ludo-narrative dissonance – a somewhat trite term at this point – can be found in *Assassin's Creed Syndicate*. The series chronicles the perpetual fight of the individualist Assassins against the power-hungry and coercive Templars. In this iteration of the story, players organize a street gang to wrest control of the boroughs of London from the eponymous syndicate by violent means. Following such conquests, map sections change from red to transparent, yet the effects in the game world of these victories allegedly won in the name of personal freedom and self-determination are merely cosmetic: gang members don differently colored outfits, while the character models for non-player characters remain the same. Epistemologically speaking, such victories can turn out to be Pyrrhic, as conquering parts of the city floods the map with several new objective markers and collectible items. The space that has been unlocked and rendered familiar has not been rendered harmless. On the contrary, it instantly demands that players attend to several possible objectives. Even in its perfected state, the map reinforces the anxiety of situatedness here by pulling players every-which-way to new mission objectives.

The alleged autonomy connoted by non-linear design produces open game worlds and necessitates comprehensive in-game maps in the first place. Yet any oversight these maps afford comes at the cost of a second kind of spatial anxiety: Solving one task produces exponentially more. The map, in this case, emblematizes an overwhelming, potentially debilitating breadth of choice players face within open-world, action-adventure games. A recent article found that only about 25 percent of players finished *Assassin's Creed Odyssey* (2019), the latest entry in the series, which sports an even bigger game world than its predecessors (see Reese). And while the fact alone does not establish correlation between game size and completion rate – let alone map quality and completion rate – the same article lists higher completion rates for structurally linear games.

The previous example suggests that maps do not only facilitate wayfinding but may inhibit it by discombobulating players. Both processes coincide. While maps signify a game's innate tendency to create order, they also re-summon the specter of spatial anxiety. Video game scholar John Sharp argues that maps are part of imperfect information systems, as not all information about the game, its narrative, and its systems is available from the beginning (see 96). While the rules of the game may be known, players are called upon to make decisions based on incomplete information in order to forge ahead into unfamiliar territory. The reciprocal process by which players fill out the map and by which the map points the way can also be seen as a deliberate narrowing of players' perspective. Besides being cluttered, the map may obstruct the player's view in other ways (e. g. fog of war). Information is doled out with one hand and withheld with the other. What is not in the purview of the map is not in the purview of the game, this includes vistas, wild life, NPCs all of which populate the world. Map design, as I noted above, shapes gameplay. As part of a game's affordance ecology, maps function to propel progression, by simultaneously lessening the impact of their decision and thus the potential for emergent play. As games of progression, action-adventure games "have narrower spaces of possibility due to the constraints placed upon player decision-making by the narrative progression" (Sharp 97). Maps thus afford progression by inhibiting emergence; they open up and immediately restrict a thirdspace of possibility for player action.

If geographic maps lead social lives, video game maps may be said to lead ambivalent double lives. They flatten out the game world only to repopulate it with objectives, simultaneously banishing and calling forth what I have called the anxiety of situatedness. The technical purpose of the game is to complete it, i.e., to void it of its objectives, becomes emblematized in the map. Extending Günzel's point about the game taking place in the interstices between the map and the field of vision, we may argue that the objective of third person, open world action games is perfecting the map. Once all objectives markers on the map are cleared, the game ends. Maps must constantly change to accommodate the fact that their depictions are always preliminary. It is a blended, real-and-imagined space full of potentiality but it may seem an anxious, compulsive sort of play.

Conclusion

Video game maps can provide useful insights about spatiality in games and how it coincides and differs from spatiality constructed through geographical maps. As constructivist edifices, they constitute places of asynchronous spatial negotiation that allow players to confront in real time their own efficacy as well as the map-making process as such. Maps then integrate these other functions with the signification of a game's narrative, carving out a lacuna in the game that counteracts the fluidity of played and narrated events. At the same time, maps reconjure the anxiety of situatedness by displaying – again, at-a-glance – the sheer volume of tasks to be undertaken. This temporal concentration betrays a different kind of anxiety by displaying multiple vectors of activity that players may engage in at any moment. The map for players is both a codex of topographical information and a record of their semiotic manipulations of the game world. A cartographic reading of game maps could even argue that gameplay and story are subservient to the process of progression, i.e., filling out the map.

Playing through the game effectively duplicates the map, producing a second version of the world, in which all secrets eventually get disclosed and all objectives achieved. If the map players see at the beginning of their play session is always already a construction, filling out the map, completing quests and missions, lets them reenact the process of constructing the map and thus the gamespace. A process that arguably helps games perform what Gordon Calleja calls "incorporation" (177), the internalization of the game world into players' consciousnesses. Maps thus simulate progress through the game's geographic world, within the game's story, and players' evolving relationship with the game by tracing players' physical progression through the world and signify, through the structuring logic of their at-a-glance representation of the game world, the cathartic state of completeness.

Such completeness is necessarily ideational. Lefebvre notes that "the 'real' can never become completely fixed, that it is constantly in a state of mobilization. It also means that a general figure (that of the center and of 'decentering') is *in play* which leaves room for both repetition and difference, for both time and juxtaposition" (399; emphasis added). Games, meanwhile, *can* be completed (using maps) and as such afford the illusion of a world rendered fully transparent and familiar. This illusion begins and ends the moment the map is filled out and the game is over. The movement to this ideal state has spiritual connotations along the lines of what philosopher Charles Taylor in his discussion of pre-modern religious culture calls "fullness" (9). What I have called the anxiety of situatedness may thus be viewed, along a longer historical arc, as a longing for such fullness and as such may point to one of the fundamental characteristics of modernity. Hans Ulrich Gumbrecht has argued that modern representation is "not an act that makes 'present again' what, after having been present, is now absent. Rather, the word subsumes all those cultural practices and techniques that replace through an often complex signifier (and make thus available) as 'reference' what is not present in space or time" (11).

As cultural objects of modernity, maps may well be said to fulfill and signify that surrogate function for fullness and presence. Video game maps would likewise reflect that surrogate function in their signification: they involve players into their virtual worlds by mirroring back, narcissistically, the alleged immediacy and meaningfulness of their own semiotic actions. And because they are designed objects, game maps allow us to examine critically the semiotic, historicizing, and ideological strategies that mobilize this modern logic of substituting presence for reference. The epistemic potential of game maps for players and scholars runs deeper than this brief discussion can fathom, and more work will be necessary to sound these depths. Cartographic maps in action-adventure games, I hope to have shown, are dense sites of knowledge that simultaneously may situate us in the game world, the story, and within cultural history.

Works Cited

Aarseth, Espen J. "Allegories of Space." *Cybertext Yearbook 2000*, edited by Markku Eskelinen and Raine Koskimaa, Jyväskylä, Research Centre for Contemporary Culture, 2001, pp. 152–171.

Aarseth, Espen J. *Cybertext: Perspectives on Ergodic Literature.* Johns Hopkins University Press, 1997.

Assassin's Creed Syndicate. Ubisoft, 2015.

Bachmann-Medick, Doris. *Cultural Turns: New Orientations in the Study of Culture.* De Gruyter, 2016.

Bauer, Ralph. *The Cultural Geography of Colonial American Literatures: Empire, Travel, Modernity.* Cambridge University Press, 2003.

Brückner, Martin. *The Social Life of Maps in America, 1750–1860.* University of North Carolina Press, 2017.

Calleja, Gordon. *In-Game: From Immersion to Incorporation.* The MIT Press, 2011.

Gumbrecht, Hans Ulrich. *The Powers of Philology: Dynamics of Textual Scholarship.* University of Illinois Press, 2003.

Günzel, Stephan. "Raum, Karte und Weg im Computerspiel." *Game Over!? Perspektiven des Computerspiels*, edited by Jan Distelmeyer, Christine Hanke, and Dieter Mersch, transcript, 2008, pp. 115–132.

Günzel, Stephan. *Topologie: Zur Raumbeschreibung in den Kultur- und Medienwissenschaften.* Transcript, 2007.

Harvey, David. "The Geopolitics of Capitalism." *Social Relations and Spatial Structures*, edited by Derek Gregory and John Urry, Macmillan, 1985, pp. 128–163.

Horizon Zero Dawn. Sony Interactive Entertainment, 2016.

Huizinga, Johan. *Homo Ludens: A Study of the Play-Element in Culture*. 1949. Angelico, 2016.

Jacob, Christian. *The Sovereign Map: Theoretical Approaches in Cartography through History*. Translated by Tom Conley. English-Language Ed. University of Chicago Press, 2006.

Jagoda, Patrick. "Videogame Criticism and Games in the Twenty-First Century." *American Literary History*, vol. 29, no. 1, 2017, pp. 205–218.

Lefebvre, Henri. *The Production of Space*. 1974. Trans. by Donald Nicholson-Smith. Blackwell, 1991.

Massey, Doreen. *For Space*. SAGE, 2005.

Mitchell, W.J.T. *What Do Pictures Want? The Lives and Loves of Images*. University of Chicago Press, 2005.

Moretti, Franco. *Graphs, Maps, Trees: Abstract Models for Literary History*. Verso, 2007.

Mukherjee, Souvik. "Playing Subaltern: Video Games and Postcolonialism." *Games and Culture*, vol. 13, no. 5, 2018, pp. 504–520.

Murray, Janet H. *Hamlet on the Holodeck: The Future of Narrative in Cyberspace*. The MIT Press, 1997.

Reese, Tyler. "RDR2 and *Assassin's Creed* Data Reveals How Few People Complete Games." *GameRevolution*, 20 January 2019, www.gamerevolution.com/features/486029-rdr2-and-assassins-creed-data-reveals-no-one-completes-games-anymore. Accessed 21 July 2020.

Ryan, Marie-Laure, et al., editors. *Narrative Across Media: The Languages of Storytelling*. University of Nebraska Press, 2004.

Salen, Katie, and Eric Zimmerman. *Rules of Play: Game Design Fundamentals*. The MIT Press, 2003.

Scheiding, Oliver. "Mapping America and the Colonial Imagination." *A Companion to American Cultural History*, edited by Bernd Engler and Oliver Scheiding, WVT, 2009, pp. 1–26.

Sharp, John. "Dimensionality." *Routledge Companion to Video Game Studies*, edited by Mark P. Wolf and Bernard Perron, Routledge, pp. 91–98.

Slonitram. *Red Dead Online – Zoobz's Excellent Walk Meet*, 2019. www.youtube.com/watch?time_continue=158&v=bLp38io1Vec. Accessed 21 July 2020.

Soja, Edward W. *Postmodern Geographies: The Reassertion of Space in Critical Social Theory*. Blackwell, 1996.

Tally, Robert T. *Spatiality: The New Critical Idiom*. Routledge, 2013.

Taylor, Charles. *A Secular Age*. Harvard University Press, 2009.

T., Amanda, and Jim Drey. "Cutman's Stage." *Video Game Maps*. 18 August 2008. www.videogamemaps.net/maps/nes/megaman1/Cutman's%20Stage%20-%20Mephea.png Accessed 15 May 2019.

Turchi, Peter. *Maps of the Imagination: The Writer as Cartographer*. Trinity University Press, 2004.

Watts, Edward, et al., editors. *Mapping Region in Early America*. University of Georgia Press, 2015.

Wood, Aylish. "Recursive Space: Play and Creating Space." *Games and Culture*, vol. 7, no. 1, 2012, pp. 87–105.

Zwiezen, Zack. "A Large Group of *Red Dead Online* Players Tried to Carry Bowls of Soup across the entire Map." *Kotaku*, 29 September 2019. www.kotaku.com/a-large-group-of-red-dead-online-players-tried-to-carry-1838594087. Accessed 21 July 2020.

Juliane Borosch
Detroit: Become Human – Orientational Mapping in the City and (Hi)Story

> A very strong element of Detroit is that there is a lot of industrial wasteland – and a lot of nature, too – and for us, the graphic designers, it was an incredible playground: The destroyed zones, which we wanted to preserve, we appropriated them to turn into something else. Then, in the areas that needed to be rebuilt, we were able to imagine our Detroit of the future. We didn't want to make a science fiction universe, but a world of anticipation.
>
> Christophe Brusseaux, Graphic Director *Detroit: Become Human*
> ("Detroit Become Human – Art of Detroit," 01:02–01:26)

Detroit: Become Human (2018) is an interactive drama and adventure game played from a third-person perspective.[1] As the name gives away, the game is set in Detroit – in the not-so-distant future of the year 2038. By then, as is the premise of the game, the city will have turned into an 'Android City' in which humans and androids, AI robots that look like humans, live together. Originally created as aides for and servants of humans, androids have also replaced humans in many occupations. This continuous loss of human jobs to machines as well as the gradual spiritual awakening of androids are the central causes of conflict and the starting point of *Detroit Become Human*. The game's plot, similar to many TV shows, is divided into three story lines: Each revolves around a different android, Connor (a police android), Markus (a caretaker), and Kara (a housekeeper), offering three distinct android perspectives. Comparable to television shows, players also alternately play these three androids in different episodes. As the androids gain consciousness and emancipate themselves from their sole purpose as service machines to humans, one possible ending leads

---

[1] The production company Quantic Dream coined this genre designation for their games (see Schenk 190–191), as their focus is as much on the narrative as on the visual and technical aspects of a video game. The developers also use techniques from other audio-visual media to realize their game. As the storytelling is intermedial, researchers can also bring in analytical tools and concepts from different media, especially from Television Studies and Seriality Studies. As Sabine Schenk states, "[it] is a small leap from television to computers" (183), particularly since TVs are becoming smarter and offer more interactive experiences. Shane Denson and Andreas Sudmann in "Digital Seriality: On the Serial Aesthetics and Practice of Digital Games" (2017) further describe how "[s]eriality is a factor not only in explicitly marked game series, but also within individual games, as well as on the level of transmedial relations between games and other media." Henry Jenkins discusses this medial flux and overlap in various medial forms in *Convergence Culture: Where Old and New Media Collide* (2006).

https://doi.org/10.1515/9783110675184-010

to the three protagonists partaking in or, in the case of Markus, leading a successful androids' civil rights movement.

As an interactive drama *Detroit: Become Human* was conceptualized similar to other audio-visual media but in greater detail to account for its interactivity. Its story was developed over 4,000 pages of script instead of the about 45 to 75 pages used for an hour-long TV show. This size accounts for the extraordinarily great number of different gameplay options players can choose from via dialogue.[2] These decisions are one characteristic feature of the gameplay that gives players the agency to significantly alter the game's plot progression. The number of different characters and settings a player encounters also necessitate the very detailed script. Consequentially, all options had to be shot scene by scene with real actors using motion capture, performance capture, body-only shoots (for action scenes), and a distinct cinematographic presentation for each protagonist (see "The Making Of" 26:49). The viewing angles from which players see and experience the game are designed to simulate camera angles (see 25:45). Depending on the mode of the game, however, players can move and guide these camera angles themselves. This guarantees a realistic and immersive experience for players.

As technical advancements in digital game play progress, so do the storyworlds. Cities, as the "most enduring self-organized form of people living together" (Faßler 11, my translation),[3] frequently function "as the major sites and topics of cultural production and consumption as well as of cultural, social and political progress" (Buchenau and Gurr, "Urban American Studies" 399). They are, thus, the subject of "place-making texts" (Buchenau and Gurr, "On the Textuality" 2), narratives that occupy an important part in the process of shaping or commenting on the cultural identity of a place. Such place-making texts appear in various forms and media. However, scholarship has not studied video games as place-making texts. Yet, as the epigraph reveals, this is exactly what the producers of *Detroit: Become Human* are trying to create. The graphic director of the game describes Detroit as an "incredible playground" of vacant land that they "appropriated" to "imagine [their] Detroit of the future" ("Detroit Become Human – Art of Detroit" 01:00–01:26).[4] While also working to "preserve" and

---

[2] As actor Jesse Williams, who plays Markus, explains, "[e]very decision the player makes, it's going to open up 40 more pages of material" ("The Making Of" 13:30).

[3] In the German original, Manfred Faßler states that "Stadt ist die historisch robusteste Selbstorganisation menschlichen Zusammenlebens" (11).

[4] This treatment of the city or at least parts of the city as empty land devoid of meaning happens frequently in postindustrial Detroit. It is popular in urban imaginaries, but also appears in actual urban planning projects. Treating urban places as empty neglects to see their histories

"rebuil[d]" ("Detroit Become Human – Art of Detroit" 01:00 – 01:26), the makers of *Detroit: Become Human* added additional layers to the city's complex imaginary.

Cities in general, according to American studies scholar Klaus Benesch, are "open systems" with an "innate tendency towards continual self-transcendence" (12). Therefore, they have an infinite potential to expand and proliferate that seems "incalculable" (Benesch 12). Players of what I would describe as story-world-building games (similar to open world games but with a distinct focus on narrative exploration)[5] intuitively develop skills to cope with these elaborate spatial structures[6] – guided by the games' producers. However, players and scholars can also benefit from fixed analytical tools to uncover additional layers of meaning for these types of video games. One such tool is a technique I term orientational mapping.

While it may *seem* redundant to call a technique *orientational* mapping, this analytical term serves to highlight the actual function and active process of mapping. The *Oxford English Dictionary* defines the verb 'to map' as "to describe, outline, chart, or represent as if on a map" (*OED*) while 'mapping' is defined as "the drawing, making, or provision of a map or maps" (*OED*). The documentary function of maps seems to be predominant in the standardized definitions. In this chapter and with regard to the player agency in *Detroit: Become Human*, however, the focus lies on the personal, cognitive, and active function of mapping. For Robert J. Tally, video games – as narratives – necessitate this type of orientation but also offer guidance along the way. To him narratives are, in fact, actual "mapping machines" as they are "simultaneously something that maps and something to be mapped" (3). Taking these facets into account, I define orientational mapping as *the practice of finding your bearings, orienting yourself, or being oriented within a (fictional) space*.

Orientational Mapping can be experienced and analyzed in three ways: *visually*, *narratively*, and *temporally*. First, a visual analysis of recognizable landmarks and built features of Detroit within the game helps players to locate them-

---

and people, which can translate to plans that exclude or displace existing communities. For a detailed problematization of this see Sattler "Finding Words: American Studies in Dialogue with Urban Planning."

5 As lead game designer Simon Wasselin puts it: "There are games out there offering world exploration. We offer narrative exploration" (see "The Making Of" 13:00).

6 What Jason Mittell has determined for complex television shows also rings true for other media, such as video games: audiences need to have "formal memory" ("Previously On" 96) and "procedural literacy" ("Narrative Complexity" 39) to successfully orientate themselves within the storyworld.

selves within the city imaginary of *Detroit: Become Human*. Here, knowledge of real-life locations can enhance this experience. Second, the narrative exploration of *Detroit: Become Human*'s plot is aided by different modes in the game, namely the "mind palace" and an extensive tree diagram. Orientation within the visual and narrative setting of the game, finally, opens the possibility of adding depth to the depiction and experience of a fictionalized city by also anchoring it within its history. This is possible through the analysis of typologies and palimpsestic layers of Detroit's past in *Detroit: Become Human*'s city imaginary.

Visual, Narrative, and Temporal Mapping

Cities are highly complex in form and function. It is therefore impossible to experience, let alone depict a city in its totality. Writers, artists, or filmmakers need to find ways of coping with and visually mapping cities despite these limitations. One such strategy is "cityscaping" – described by Therese Fuhrer, Felix Mundt, and Jan Stenger as "the process through which an image of a city or an urban landscape is imaginatively constructed" (1). In *Detroit: Become Human*, such "cityscaping" mainly works through grounding the fictional Detroit of the video game in the real Detroit by depicting well known sights and landmarks of the city.[7] Since "only a few elements may be needed to create the [...] backdrop to an action or to situate some particular content," Fuhrer, Mundt, and Stenger explain, "the 'scenography' of a cityscape may be selective" (Fuhrer, Mundt, and Stenger 1).

This use of well-known "urban 'props'" (Fuhrer, Mundt, and Stenger 3) – boiled-down portrayals of characteristic landmarks that are also aesthetically appealing – to create a city imaginary is particularly characteristic of audio-visual media. When the rebelling androids of *Detroit: Become Human* march past the renowned statue of The Spirit of Detroit to campaign for civil rights, for example, any player of the game with a slight knowledge of Detroit can locate the ongoing action on the central road of downtown Detroit, Woodward Avenue. Similarly, accurate, yet 'futurized' depictions of landmarks exist of the well-known Monument to Joe Louis, St. Mary's Church, Belle Isle, and the Detroit Skyline. The game, however, also depicts important infrastructure decisive for the workings of the city, such as a monorail system, the Rosa Parks Transit Center, or well-known street crossings in the downtown area.

---

[7] For visual examples of the comparison between the real and digitally created Detroit, see "Detroit Become Human – Game vs Real Life Detroit" on YouTube.

Such "urban props" in audio-visual media work similarly to the "textual declarations" (91) that Marie-Laure Ryan discusses for narrative mapping in literature. In *Detroit: Become Human*, like in the narratives Ryan describes, these signposts and guidelines for readers' mental constructions of a storyworld function through "the import of information provided by internalized cognitive models, inferential mechanisms, real-life experience, and cultural knowledge" (91).[8] This experience differs from person to person, as everyone brings a different background and knowledge to the text.[9] The previous and contextual knowledge players are expected to bring to *Detroit: Become Human* can be deduced from the first glance at the game trailer: The decaying, sometimes even burned down (suburban) houses in the trailer directly reference the ubiquitous trope of Detroit as 'the city in ruins,' while the 2038 setting of the video game is referenced through futuristic downtown skyscrapers and a highline transport system. These instantaneous orientations are especially important for this game, as it is not an open world game. Instead, the player is dropped off in a limited part of the city for each episode.

Detroit as a location is important for the game. However, the focus lies much more on narrative space than on the physical or geographical space. Narrative space, in contrast to geographical space, describes the unfolding space given to the narrative elements of a video game, and the care dedicated to developing story over, for instance, setting. This distinction highlights the importance of different forms of orientational mapping within a game, not just the geographical kind.[10] Thus, the second form of orientational mapping in *Detroit: Become*

---

8 In this context, see also the "mental maps" city dwellers come up with to make sense of and navigate the city that are studied in behavioral geography (see Lynch).

9 Winfried Fluck explains that "what we actually see is shaped by the store-house of images in our imagination with which we approach the pictures. The transfer through which aesthetic experience is brought about thus entails a screening of the picture in terms of the images with which we approach it. In this process, we 'de-corporealize' the image in order to be able to link it with new experiences and meanings, so that we can make it 'our own'" (Fluck, "Playing Indian" 77) Therefore people's "aesthetic experience[s]" (Fluck, "Playing Indian" 74) are highly individual. Drawing on Wolfgang Iser, Fluck defines "imaginary transfer" as the "key formative aspect" ("Playing Indian" 74) of this experience.

10 It also alludes to the oftentimes neglectful treatment of the spatial dimension of a story compared to the temporal or narrative one. As TV scholar Jason Mittell attests for complex television shows, "[w]hile many fans will try to make sense of muddled chronology or plot continuity, such geographical incoherence in navigating a story space is typically only recognised by natives of a given city searching for spatial realism, suggesting that [...] temporal consistency trumps spatial coherence" ("Serial Orientations" 173). This is also true for *Detroit: Become Human*, whose creators have excelled in digitally recreating landmarks such as The Spirit of Detroit or 'The Fist' but have been criticized for failing to coherently connect and properly place the different set-

Human concerns the narrative within individual scenes and its overall structure. In times when narratives of any kind grow increasingly more complex it becomes essential for recipients to orient themselves within a story to find their way through it.[11] This suggests or even requires a more active interest of players in the form and medium of their narrative.[12]

In *Detroit: Become Human*, one feature of narrative orientation is learned in the very first scene:[13] By pressing the R2 button, players can access the so-called "mind palace," an analytical mode that presents the surrounding area in a grid system. In this mode, players can recap movements, find clues, and ascertain success rates for their actions. Similar to modern land surveying technologies,[14] the agency of mapping a place lies not in the actions and movements of the character, player, or land surveyor but in the fixed, given measurements of a machine, laser beam, or grid. While androids aim to *Become Human*, as the game's title suggests, the "mind palace" indicates that they still map and reconstruct narrative situations in a computerized way.

Narrative orientational mapping in *Detroit: Become Human* also works on the level of what Jason Mittell has called "orienting paratexts" ("Serial Orientations" 165) for television. These supplements to the actual narrative "exist outside the diegetic storyworld, providing a perspective for viewers to help make sense of a narrative world by looking at it from a distance" (165). Such "orienting practices" (165) thus give audiences guidance to general plot questions or for locating their current position within a narrative. In *Detroit: Become Human*, the "orienting paratext" (165) is an official part of the game in the form of a tree dia-

---

tings of the game compared to the actual Detroit (see Seppala). However, this is not necessarily a negative aspect: when reality is presented in a "fictional mode" (Fluck, "Aesthetic Experience" 416) it allows the medium to restructure and highlight or hide certain features. As soon as you no longer "insist[s] that reality is truthfully represented" you can "concentrate on other aspects and possible functions of the object" (Fluck, "Imaginary Space" 30) or place, allowing for artistic freedom to explore new perspectives, to express criticism, or to uncover things.

11 This increase in complexity happens because of a general high familiarity with different media and to motivate recipients to re-read, re-watch, or replay said narrative. For more information regarding the topic of 'rewatchability,' see e.g., Mittell "Narrative Complexity in Contemporary American Television" (2006).

12 This is, so to speak, a double-edged sword of interdependence, where increased media literacy allows for more medially complex narratives, but more complexity also asks for more active engagement with the narrative.

13 The developers of *Detroit: Become Human* themselves speak of 'scenes' in the game's "Making Of" rather than of 'levels' or 'sub-levels,' further underlining the game's structural and conceptual similarities to TV shows, movies, or plays.

14 For more on this, see Eric Haas' talk "Do We Have to Stick to the Script? … Cities, Surveys and Descripting" at The Mediated City Conference in Los Angeles, 1–4 October 2014.

gram.¹⁵ During and after each episode or level, players can track their progress or go back and unlock new options of continuing the storyline.¹⁶ While connected to the internet, they can also see how their choices are faring compared to other players worldwide.

This organization of the narrative in *Detroit: Become Human* can be described as what Christoph Bode and Rainer Dietrich define as "future narratives" (3). According to Bode and Dietrich, these are "narratives that have at least one nodal situation or node. A node [...] is a situation that allows for more than one continuation" (16). In *Detroit: Become Human* each scene within an episode (level) is such a nodal or decision point. There are multiple options on how to handle a task or problem. Depending on which action a player chooses to take, the game's plot – the causally connected sequence of events within *Detroit: Become Human*'s narrative – develops in a different way. This type of open, multi-option, interactive narrative suggests a special agency of the player, since "the essential narrative labor of connecting can be delegated to and be carried out by [him or her]" (Bode and Dietrich 5).¹⁷ In this highly complex game, players are granted a quasi-behind-the-scenes look at their own narrative labor in the form of a flow chart or tree diagram. From the very first scene, for each nodal point, they can map and track their choices, what consequences these had, and how many other options were available. For *Detroit: Become Human*, this official "orienting paratext" (Mittell, "Serial Orientations" 165) aids players in situating themselves within the narrative, increases re-playability of the game by laying open other plot options,¹⁸ and it ensures that players see the complexity of the game and the effort that was put into making it.¹⁹

---

15 For more on the literary concept of 'paratext' as well as its usability for other media, see Gérard Genette *Paratexts: Thresholds of Interpretation* (1997).
16 Compared to open world games where players are able to stroll around the storyworld to explore the entirety of the game, in *Detroit: Become Human*, the space to further discover the game world is narrative space, something the lead game designers specifically set out to offer (see "The Making Of" 13:00 – 13:04).
17 The writers of *Detroit: Become Human*, in fact, approached the game in a way where their "job [was] to provide a narrative context in which the player can write his own story. You are giving him this kind of narrative Lego that he can kind of snap together in his own shape" ("Making Of" 11:00 – 11:11).
18 Notably, in this context, the tree diagram only reveals that there were other options of action, thereby not spoiling the fun of revealing which options these are.
19 The inclusion of "future narratives" in video game narration may even have the potential to solve or at least lessen the problem that "[i]nteractivity and narrative seem to be incompatible with each other" (Schenk 184).

By using the visual and narrative mapping cues to situate their playable characters in the events happening in the fictional Detroit of 2038, players can also map the game's time and place in the succession of the city's history. Orientational mapping in the temporal contexts of *Detroit: Become Human* works as a typology as well as in the form a palimpsest. Typology is concerned with sets of types, while the metaphorical concept of the palimpsest is used to investigate layers, rewritings, and simultaneity. These forms of temporal mapping are not mutually exclusive but can function simultaneously.

Typology as "[t]he study of symbolic representation, esp. of the origin and meaning of Scripture types" (*OED*) is a helpful tool in mapping the temporal context of the video game. *Detroit: Become Human* refers to different historical and symbolic types when, for example, drawing on famous nicknames of Detroit or its image and reputation. Commonly, Detroit is denoted as the Motor City, or more recently as 'the city in ruins.' In *Detroit: Become Human*, the city now has the byname 'Android City.' While this does not cancel out the (visually still prevailing) city in ruins, the Android City draws a direct analogy to the Motor City moniker. The fictional Detroit of the future is once again the center of a mechanized work revolution, where the history of Fordism clearly shines through the new paradigm of 'Androidism' – from the basic premise of non-human optimization of labor down to the fears of replacement of and objections by the citizens of Detroit.[20] Thus, with this label, the game identifies its setting as a particular type of city: either the mechanized, industrial city devoid of humans or the city where machines are favored over humans.

The concept of the palimpsest as a piece of parchment that has been written on and scratched off several times with multiple layers still shining through has proven popular in urban studies to document and symbolize the different historical layers and stages of the material city.[21] However, the concept is also important for the imaginary of a city. According to Fuhrer, Mundt, and Stenger, the "value of the term 'palimpsest' is that it reminds us of the structural depth of images of cities and the simultaneous presence of diverging elements" (15).[22] This is what the temporal dimension of orientational mapping can highlight for *Detroit:*

---

20 This, by definition, is also a palimpsest.
21 For the concept behind the term palimpsest, see Genette *Palimpsests* (1997).
22 They further elaborate that "each text, each painting, each relief or film that represents an image of the city, overwrites to a greater or lesser degree, the previous mental representations of the city, with the result that the urban space is like a parchment that has been written upon several times. As each new model is laid over the previous ones, though without obscuring them entirely, the image of the city becomes inscribed with different layers of time and different cultural preferences and meanings" (15).

Become Human, here exemplified by the androids' "March to Freedom," which is the actual title of one of the episodes of the game. It combines the well-known March on Washington and the lesser-known Walk to Freedom, which took place in Detroit in 1963 and, thus, draws a line from the android emancipation and their civil rights movement to the historical Civil Rights Movement of ethnic minorities in the 1960s.

In a parallelism and problematic mixing that reaches further back historically, the game's plot is also linked to the struggle for freedom by African Americans: The different choices for protesting chants a player can choose from during the androids' march also allude to the fight to abolish slavery. The different buttons on the gaming controller offer the options "we are people," "no more slavery," "set us free," and "we are alive" respectively. Although the game here seems to (sometimes problematically) mix (up) different, yet related historical instances, players, who are familiar with this history, are still able to place and map the narrative actions in the real-life history and setting of Detroit.

The androids' march, for example, follows the same route down Woodward Avenue towards the river that the Walk to Freedom led by Martin Luther King took 75 years earlier. They visibly walk past the statue of The Spirit of Detroit, which is indeed on this route, and the place they are marching towards is also one of symbolic importance and consists of many historic layers: Hart Plaza is the alleged spot where in 1701 French imperial explorer Antoine Laumet de la Mothe Cadillac first landed and founded the colonial settlement that is now Detroit. Since 1975, it has been a public park that now holds statues for workers' rights, the Underground Railroad, and the Dodge family. It is also situated right next to the Cobo Arena (now TCF Center), the place where in 1963, Martin Luther King held an early version of his "I Have a Dream" speech at the end of the Walk to Freedom. This revelation casts the android Markus (played by Black American actor and activist Jesse Williams) as a 'civil rights leader' in a typological sense, as an android Martin Luther King. In fact, the game's narrative options dictate that only when the emancipation movement tries to practice non-violence, are they successful.

Thus, *Detroit: Become Human* places the android movement in direct succession of the Civil Rights Movement. The very last episode of the game, episode 32 "Battle for Detroit," is divided into three plot strings (one for each protagonist). Markus' storyline lends itself to tracing the history and symbolism of Detroit in it: It starts out with the 'Hart Plaza Freedom March' and potentially ends with revolution and a final rally that leads to a favorable public opinion towards androids. At the rally, Markus speaks to his people from an improvised stage on the battle-stricken Hart Plaza. There, the Dodge Fountain – a memorial to the 'industrial masters' – is thrown over while the androids are victorious, and the arches of the workers' rights memorial still gleam in the background. That Markus is cast as a leader in the tradition of Martin Luther King can also be concluded from the content of Markus' final speech: He stresses that the androids are "emerg[ing] from a long night" (*Detroit: Become Human*). This is a metaphor and motif employed by King and other civil rights speakers to describe the end of slavery, most prominently in King's "I Have a Dream" speech. In the speech, he describes the Emancipation Proclamation as "a joyous daybreak to end the long night of their captivity."

While it can be fascinating to immerse oneself in this enhanced narrative experience, the game also requires a cautious approach. Digital media and computing scholars Katie Salen and Eric Zimmerman explore how

> a player relates to a game character through the double-consciousness of play. A protagonist character is a persona through which a player exerts him or herself into an imaginary world; this relationship can be intense and emotionally "immersive." However, at the very same time, the character is a tool, a puppet, an object for the player to manipulate according to the rules of the game. In this sense, the player is fully aware of the character as an artificial construct. (453)

While players are thus used to treating their playable characters as "tool[s]" or "puppet[s]" (453), *Detroit: Become Human* personalizes a pressing current and recurring social and political issue through one protagonist without ever explicitly acknowledging or problematizing it.[23] Even though players need some historical knowledge to grasp the full extent of references, these allusions to historical events are not particularly subtle. Equating the Black Civil Rights Movement in the United States with a fictional emancipation movement of de-facto machines in *Detroit: Become Human* has highly problematic undercurrents: It not only could be said to remind of or even resume a treatment of African Americans as non-humans for dramatic emotional effect. It also generalizes the specific struggle of a specific people, especially when considering that the game also conflates the American Civil Rights and Abolitionist movements, thereby negat-

---

23 These are not the only issues *Detroit: Become Human* uses to uncritically equate divergent experiences of hardship and discrimination. As media and video game scholar Daniela Bruns describes, "*Detroit: Become Human* repeatedly refers to inhumane practices of slavery, racial segregation, and genocide. To name a few examples: the junkyard for androids evokes images of a mass grave; the division of public transport into compartments for androids and humans refers to the systematic suppression of the African American population in the United States; and triangle and armband of the android uniform induces associations of the forced labeling of the Jewish population with the Star of David during National Socialism in Germany" (181).

ing any progress made by Black Americans in-between those eras.[24] While Western societies today have not achieved ethnic and racial equality, the hard-fought progress and achievements of Black Americans toward this goal should not be overlooked or blurred in the name of a "social science fiction" (Bruns 173) gaming plot.

Conclusion

Orientation in space is not only important for movement in cities but also for playing video games. This chapter introduced the technique of orientational mapping, 'the practice of finding your bearings, orienting yourself, or being oriented within a (fictional) space,' to analyze the various forms of orientation in *Detroit: Become Human*. Not only is orienting oneself visually, narratively, and temporally helpful for the successful completion of the game, but it can "create a layer atop the programme to help figure out how the pieces fit together or propose alternate ways of seeing the pieces" (Mittell, "Serial Orientations" 165).

On a visual level, the use of "urban props" (Fuhrer, Mundt, and Stenger 3) helps to instantaneously locate oneself in exact locations within the city of Detroit. These locations can carry specific connotations that are important for the tasks that players have to complete, but with their detailed graphical realization, they can also allow a glimpse at a 'realistic' Detroit imaginary. Taking this technique even further, players or reviewers could look past the clear-cut "urban props" toward geographic inconsistencies in relation to the real-life city in a next step. Some locals looking for spatial realism have noticed these in the game. However, these inconsistencies (at least in this game) do not seem to affect the general geographic logic of the game.

Narrative orientation within *Detroit: Become Human* works on two levels: On the one hand, the "mind palace" mode of looking at scenes allows for a systematic tracing of the information needed to advance in the narrative. The paratextual tree diagram, on the other hand, reveals *Detroit: Become Human* to be a "future narrative" that gives players agency to design the game's plot. With their decisions, players activate different paths to advance in the game. The tree diagram allows players to locate themselves within the narrative progression but

---

24 In an essay with a larger scope or more specific focus on the portrayal of social justice issues in video games, one could further critically interrogate the implications of discussing the "double consciousness" (Salen and Zimmerman 453) of video game players in the context of Black Emancipation and Civil Rights Movements.

also reveals the possibility of other paths through the game, multilinear stories, and thus the potential re-playability of the game.

Building on the visual and narrative mapping within *Detroit: Become Human*, the game can also be mapped temporally. This does not mean tracing the narrative progression of the game but rather combines the information gathered about the place and plot to analyze this Detroit city imaginary for parallels to historical events within the city. For this purpose, the analysis of typologies and palimpsests can be employed. The game labels Detroit as the "Android City." This moniker designates a type closely connected to notions of Detroit as the Fordist City, the Motor City, and the city in ruins. On a palimpsestic level, *Detroit: Become Human* layers its narrative atop existing streets and landmarks and the historical significance of these locations. This form of orientation within the game depends on players' previous knowledge. Nonetheless, it offers the opportunity to learn about these types of movements and, if a player is 'in the know,' this temporal orientation can guide gameplay decisions towards a successful completion of the game's possible plots. However, players or researchers could also critically look at the temporal layering and grounding the game practices and the sometimes-inconsiderate allusions to the discrimination of minorities this entails.

In conclusion, the technique of orientational mapping as analyzed with regard to *Detroit: Become Human* therefore allows for an enhanced gameplay experience that works through visual, temporal, and narrative orientation. This gameplay experience exceeds the goal of mere successful completion of the game by enriching the fictional city imaginary of Detroit with features of its real-life location. Simultaneously, the players' awareness of the operational workings of the game is raised during the playing of the game.

Works Cited

Benesch, Klaus. "Concepts of Space in American Culture: An Introduction." *Space in America: Theory History Culture*, edited by Klaus Benesch and Kerstin Schmidt, Rodopi, 2005, pp. 11–23.

Bode, Christoph and Rainer Dietrich. *Future Narratives: Theory, Poetics, and Media-Historical Moment*. De Gruyter, 2013.

Bruns, Daniela. "When the Future Becomes the Present: *Detroit: Become Human* as Social Science Fiction." *Mixed Reality and Games: Theoretical and Practical Approaches in Game Studies and Education*, edited by Emir Bektic, Daniela Bruns, Sonja Gabriel, Florian Kelle, Gerhard Pölsterl, and Felix Schniz, transcript, 2020, pp. 173–185.

Buchenau, Barbara and Jens Martin Gurr. "On the Textuality of American Cities and their Others: A Disputation." *Projecting American Studies: Essays on Theory, Method, and

Practice, edited by Frank Kelleter and Alexander Starre, Universitätsverlag Winter, 2018, pp. 135–152.

Buchenau, Barbara and Jens Martin Gurr. "Urban American Studies and the Conjunction of Textual Strategies and Spatial Processes." *Spaces—Communities—Representations: Urban Transformations in the USA*, edited by Julia Sattler, transcript, 2016, pp. 395–420.

Denson, Shane and Andreas Sudmann. "Digital Seriality: On the Serial Aesthetics and Practice of Digital Games." *Media of Serial Narrative*, edited by Frank Kelleter, The Ohio State University Press, 2017, pp. 261–284.

Detroit Become Human. Quantic Dream, 2018.

"Detroit Become Human – Game vs Real Life Detroit." *YouTube*, uploaded by Dan Allen Gaming, 27 May 2018, www.youtube.com/watch?v=s98hGGwTSTw. Accessed 27 February 2021.

"Detroit: Become Human – Art of Detroit | PS4." *YouTube*, uploaded by PlayStation, 4 May 2018, www.youtube.com/watch?time_continue=19&v=QVcCNw7Qd_8. Accessed 27 February 2021.

Faßler, Manfred. "Umbrüche des Städtischen." *Urban Fictions: Die Zukunft des Städtischen*, edited by Manfred Faßler and Claudius Terkowsky, Wilhelm Fink Verlag, 2006, pp. 9–36.

Fuhrer, Therese, Felix Mundt and Jan Stenger. "Introduction." *Cityscaping: Constructing and Modelling Images of the City*, De Gruyter, 2015, pp. 1–18.

Fluck, Winfried. "Aesthetic Experience of the Image." *Romance with America*, edited by Laura Bieger and Johannes Voelz, Universitätsverlag Winter, 2009, pp. 409–432.

Fluck, Winfried. "Playing Indian: Aesthetic Experience, Recognition, Identity." *American Studies as Media Studies*, edited by Frank Kelleter and Daniel Stein, Universitätsverlag Winter, 2008, pp. 73–92.

Fluck, Winfried. "Imaginary Space; or, Space as Aesthetic Object." *Space in America: Theory History Culture*, edited by Klaus Benesch and Kerstin Schmidt, Rodopi, 2005, pp. 25–40.

Genette, Gérard with Gerald Prince. *Palimpsests: Literature in the Second Degree*. Translated by Channa Newman and Claude Doubinsky, University of Nebraska Press, 1997.

Genette, Gérard with Richard Macksey. *Paratexts: Thresholds of Interpretation*. Translated by Jane E. Lewin, Cambridge University Press, 1997.

Haas, Eric. "Do We Have to Stick to the Script?... Cities, Surveys and Descripting." *The Mediated City* Conference, 2 October 2014, Woodbury University, Los Angeles, CA. Conference Presentation.

Jenkins, Henry. *Convergence Culture: Where Old and New Media Collide*. New York University Press, 2006.

King, Martin Luther, Jr. "I Have a Dream." *A Call to Conscience: The Landmark Speeches of Dr. Martin Luther King, Jr.*, edited by Clayborne Carson and Kris Shepard, IPM/Warner Books, 2001, pp. 75–88.

Lynch, Kevin. *The Image of the City*. The MIT Press, 1960.

Mittell, Jason. "Serial Orientations. Paratexts and Contemporary Complex Television." *(Dis)Orienting Media and Narrative Mazes*, edited by Julia Eckel, Bernd Leiendecker, Daniela Olek, and Christine Piepiorka, transcript, 2013, pp. 165–181.

Mittell, Jason. "Previously On: Prime Time Serials and the Mechanics of Memory." *Intermediality and Storytelling*, edited by Maria Grishakova und Marie-Laure Ryan, de Gruyter, 2010, pp. 78–98.

Mittell, Jason. "Narrative Complexity in Contemporary American Television." *The Velvet Light Trap*, vol. 58, 2006, pp. 29–40.

"mapping, n." *OED Online*, Oxford University Press, March 2019, www.oed.com/view/Entry/113868. Accessed 16 May 2019.

"map, v." *OED Online*, Oxford University Press, March 2019, www.oed.com/view/Entry/113855. Accessed 16 May 2019.

Ryan, Marie-Laure. *Narrative as Virtual Reality: Immersion and Interactivity in Literature and Electronic Media*. Johns Hopkins University Press, 2001.

Salen, Katie and Eric Zimmerman. *Rules of Play: Game Design Fundamentals*. MIT Press, 2004.

Sattler, Julia. "Finding Words: American Studies in Dialogue with Urban Planning." *Projecting American Studies: Essays on Theory, Method and Practice*, edited by Frank Kelleter and Alexander Starre, Universitätsverlag Winter, 2018, pp. 121–134.

Seppala, Timothy J. "PS4's 'Detroit' Doesn't Take Place in the Motor City I Know." *Engadget*, 2 June 2018, www.tinyurl.com/4wp8f9fk. Accessed 2 Sept. 2019.

Schenk, Sabine. *Running and Clicking: Future Narratives in Film*. De Gruyter, 2013.

"typology, n." *OED Online*, Oxford University Press, March 2019, www.oed.com/view/Entry/208394. Accessed 16 May 2019.

Tally Jr., Robert T. "Introduction. Mapping Narratives." *Literary Cartographies: Spatiality, Representation, and Narrative*, edited by Robert T. Tally Jr., Palgrave Macmillan, 2014, pp. 1–12.

Stefan Schubert
'Playing for Space:' Negotiating and Narrativizing Space in *One Hour One Life*

Many narratives of early American settlement are characterized by metaphors of conflict and struggle over space, centrally implied in myths like 'manifest destiny' or the 'errand into the wilderness' (see Miller). Later reevaluations of these narratives equally highlight this understanding of space, for instance in Richard Slotkin's phrasing that "regeneration through violence" was "the structuring metaphor of the American experience" (5) or in Annette Kolodny's characterization of the frontier as "a multiplicity of ongoing first encounters over time and land" (13). Video games largely reiterate this imagination of space as something to be fought over, something that is constantly in conflict. In many strategy games, for instance, the predominant focus lies on the acquisition and defense of land against one or multiple enemies. For example, the *Steam* page for *Crusader Kings II* (2012) entices players to "[e]xpand your feudal domain" and to "defend against" and "struggle with" ("Crusader") different foes, and *Civilization VI* (2016) promises players "expansive empires" that "spread across the map like never before" ("Sid Meier's"). While the more recent critical reconsiderations of early America rightfully highlight the brutality and violence with which the continent was settled by Europeans, such perspectives more generally also deemphasize elements of spatial cooperation – of, for instance, the importance of a community of people coming together in establishing early settlements and towns.[1] Curiously, this dimension of space has remained similarly underdeveloped in video games and is also considered less frequently in scholarship than the myriad ways in which games imagine space as a competitive battlefield. In contrast, in this contribution, I want to explore possibilities of spatial cooperation and collaboration through a case study of *One Hour One Life* (2018), a game that provides players with the opportunity to settle and develop a new, 'untouched' land.

---

[1] In turn, earlier myths of U.S. settlement disregarded the violent encounters with the native population, yet they also rarely focused on communal aspects. In contrast, Frederick Jackson Turner's 'frontier hypothesis' famously highlighted the importance of individualism, alleging that the "most important effect of the frontier has been in the promotion of democracy" since "the frontier is productive of individualism," and this "frontier individualism has from the beginning promoted democracy" (6).

To do so, I will first introduce *One Hour One Life* in some more detail, especially pointing to its features as a multiplayer game focusing on social interaction. This rather lengthy and more general look at the game seems warranted since no scholarship exists on it so far. While it is a relatively little-known indie game, its specific gameplay elements make it particularly interesting to investigate in an American Studies context. Afterwards, I will specifically examine the game's depiction of space and in which ways space figures into its gameplay. From that, I will extrapolate a few thoughts on the idea of what I call 'playing for space,' which highlights cooperation and negotiation rather than competition. Finally, I will scrutinize some of the community interactions the game has engendered in its online forum and contextualize these within an ecocritical perspective. Taken together, I thus argue that 'playing for space' is the central anchor around which community is negotiated in *One Hour One Life*, fostering an online community around efforts of negotiating and narrativizing the manipulable space available to players.

One Hour One Life

One Hour One Life was released in 2018 for the PC, originally only available via the website of the developer but since November 2018 also via *Steam*. It is an indie game developed and published by one person, Jason Rohrer, and it is continuously being updated with new content, balance adjustments, or bug fixes (usually weekly). In terms of genre, it is a massively multiplayer online (or MMO) survival game. Its most original mechanic is that each player always only lives for a maximum of 60 minutes – players begin the game as a newborn and then become a teenager, an adult, and eventually an elderly person, dying after 60 minutes, which equate to 60 years of having lived. After that, if they want to play again, they will spawn as a different character, often in a very different part of the map. They are born either as a child to another player or, in rarer cases, in the wild as a young adult, a so-called 'Eve,' who can start a new life somewhere.[2] The controls primarily work via the mouse, by clicking

---

[2] If players are not born to another player, they thus always start as a female. As such an Eve, the color of their skin is randomized, instead of being the same as one's 'mother' if players are born to someone else. Similarly, it is random whether they are born as a male or a female child to someone else. How the game simulates these markers of identity in a multiplayer setting is also highly relevant for how communities engage with such categories of difference (for instance, often, female children are valued more highly than male ones, since only they can give birth to other players), warranting further studies.

on things players want to interact with and then clicking on another object to combine something or use something on. The keyboard is mostly used for typing, specifically to search for how to combine or make certain items and to talk to other players, even though the number of characters one can type is restricted by how old one is, to simulate the process of language acquisition. Similar to games like *Don't Starve* (2013), the main mechanic to play against is hunger, since players continuously have to find food. Additionally, maintaining the right body temperature (neither too cold nor too hot) also affects one's rate of hunger. Yet what players will actually struggle to accomplish in the game is to build some kind of 'civilization,' cooperating with other players to get a fire going, acquire clothing, establish more sustainable sources of food, create tools to gain access to higher tiers of items and equipment, etc.

Writing about *One Hour One Life* is made difficult due to two factors in particular: One concerns its inherently communal nature, as a game that makes little sense to try to play on your own, without interacting with other players. In the past few years, there has been "an increasing interest in *social* multiplayer gaming activities from [...] the gaming industry, the audience, and academia" (Quandt and Kröger, "Introduction" 3; emphasis in original), yet most academic investigations of multiplayer games come from sociological and media studies (see, e.g., Quandt and Kröger, *Multiplayer*; Kowert and Quandt). Partly because multiplayer games often focus less on linearly presented narrative elements than many single player titles (see Joseph and Knuttila 211), they have been less frequently studied from a Literary and Cultural Studies perspective. In this contribution, however, I want to investigate how communities of players narrativize certain aspects of space in a game like *One Hour One Life* – which by itself features few explicitly narrative elements – partly by tracing players' discussions and interactions on the game's official forum. Secondly, many of *One Hour One Life*'s gameplay elements are constantly in flux, since the game is being updated on a weekly schedule. Often, new aspects and items to interact with are introduced, but core gameplay aspects also change from time to time. This ephemeral quality of the game's internal rules makes it especially difficult to focus or agree on a kind of static 'object' or 'textual artifact' when discussing the game. However, the changes that have been implemented throughout the development cycle also become noteworthy in themselves for how they evidence an interaction with the community and their discussions, how they showcase shifts in gameplay philosophies, and how they can be interpreted as wanting to foster different engagements with space in the game. Hence, while I will mainly focus on the latest version of *One Hour One Life* at the time of this writing (update #78 from October 26, 2019), I will at times also make reference to past iterations of the game.

As with many survival games, one particular appeal of *One Hour One Life* is also inherently spatial: the idea of building, or reliving, 'civilization,' of starting from scratch in an apparently untouched 'wilderness.' Such idealized imaginations strongly correlate with the ideological assumptions inherent in the myth of the frontier and related notions.[3] So far, the technology in the game stops mostly with early historical civilizations, up to the Iron Age, but more recent updates have also added modern inventions, such as a form of radio communication and a rudimentary way of flying. By focusing on the earliest inventions of humanity and setting the game in a 'natural' landscape, part of *One Hour One Life*'s aesthetic and gameplay appeal also touches on simple-living movements, encapsulated in literary classics like Thoreau's *Walden* (1854) just as much as in popular *YouTube* channels like *Primitive Technology*. In this sense, the game tries to be 'realistic' in order to correctly simulate some of the difficulties of not having modern-day luxuries at one's disposal, and it provides the pleasure of being the first to settle a new land, in the Walden-esque sense of 'going back to nature.'[4]

While these mechanics are quite similar to a number of survival games, they gain increased importance due to the game's multiplayer context coupled with

---

[3] On such ideological underpinnings of spatial imaginations in video games, see especially Murray 160–176.

[4] As an example of the game's appeal to a realist mode, making fire, which in many games can be achieved through one click or one button press, involves several individual steps in *One Hour One Life:* Players start by picking up a round stone from the surrounding area and then smash it on a big hard rock to turn it into a sharp stone. They then pluck a straight branch from a maple tree and turn that branch into a long straight shaft with the help of the sharp stone. Afterwards, they have to use a fire bow drill on that shaft. The drill is made from a small, curved branch plucked from a poplar tree, turned into a small, curved shaft with a sharp stone, with an added rope and a short shaft, made from another long straight shaft. The rope is made from two threads, created by combining two milkweed stalks harvested from a milkweed plant in the environment. Once players use the fire bow drill on the long straight shaft, they then take a leaf from a nearby tree to transfer the ember to juniper tinder from a juniper tree. After five seconds, they can add kindling to the burning tinder to get fire. Kindling can be made by using a stone hatchet on wood. A stone hatchet, in turn, is made from combining a sharp stone with a tied short shaft (which consists of rope and a short shaft). Players then have to keep the fire alive with more kindling or other wood. To be able to accomplish this properly, players need to have the tools ready beforehand and should have the material around them – and, importantly, they actually need the space to put all these things somewhere, since every object takes the same amount of space, one square. Other players might also randomly come by and take away a piece of tinder for something else. Figuring out these exact steps through experimentation is rather laborious and difficult, thus simulating the creation of fire by early humans; once learned, it is thus important to pass on this knowledge to other players, which partly happens in-game and partly extradiegetically, in the forum or on wikis.

Fig. 1: Making fire in *One Hour One Life*.

the fact that players only ever live for a maximum of 60 minutes. From the first minute on, they thus depend on other people and on an overall community. For instance, as a newborn baby, there is little players can do, and for the first three minutes (or years) in the game, they are quite helpless. They will continuously be hungry, so in order not to die, they have to be fed by another player, their 'mother,' through breastfeeding. Alternatively, they can also be handed food by somebody else, but they cannot yet interact with anything in the world themselves.[5] There is also only a rudimentary tutorial for the game, so in order to learn the precise ins and outs of what the gameplay options offer, especially newer players often have to depend on other people, either observing what they do or explicitly asking them to teach them something.

In this way, the game tries to foster a sense of community, since there is only so much that a single player could achieve on their own in sixty minutes. For instance, working alone to produce an upper-tier tool like a steel axe in a community with barely any infrastructure in place can take a whole lifetime. In order to make an impact on the world and have a legacy – which cannot be achieved if, after producing that tool, nobody can ever use it because the settlement has been deserted – players also need to focus on a family of other players. *One Hour*

---

5 Initially, players can only type one character, and it has been established in the community of the game that typing "F" (for food) indicates that their avatars are hungry and need to be fed.

One Life encourages this idea of a legacy through family trees that are automatically created on the game's website.[6] At the same time, so-called 'griefing' is also possible, i.e., a playing practice during which a player does not try to help but harasses other players.[7] This can range from small annoyances, like misplacing somebody's tools or putting out a fire, to more drastic measures, like using a knife to kill somebody else. In a tight-knit community, there are ways to try to counteract that with advanced medicine and attempts to enforce order and laws (so that aspect of the game also tries to simulate how a society in general might think about ordering, structuring, and protecting itself). Overall, while the specific mechanics of the game are somewhat in flux due to the weekly updates, *One Hour One Life* already offers a unique simulation of living in a community, specifically through the feature of 'permadeath' after 60 minutes. Other survival games usually do not limit how long a player can try to keep their character alive but might make that effort progressively more difficult, thus challenging players to maximize their survival efforts. In *One Hour One Life*, no matter how well a player might live their life, they always die after 60 minutes. The social dynamics the game creates through these features can be studied in a variety of ways, and in the following, I specifically want to focus on the representation and the subsequent narrativization of space, which encourage players to 'play for space' rather than to compete over it.

'Playing for Space'

Space figures into the game in a variety of ways. On one level, the way space is generally represented in *One Hour One Life* is significant, as players view their avatar and their surroundings from a top-down perspective. This relatively limited point and field of view makes the world players cannot see more dangerous, since bears, wolves, or rattlesnakes might kill them if they venture too quickly through the land.[8] On another level, interacting with the represented space through the game's controls is also slightly unusual, since players only ever click on one item, pick it up, and click on another item they want to combine

---

6 If players spawn as an Eve, they can give themselves a last name, and when they hold a child, they can give him or her a first name, thus marking them as part of their family. The gameplay function of the family trees thus also encourages the idea of developing a lasting legacy.

7 For a larger study of such practices in video games, see Meades, who understands them as forms of 'counterplay.'

8 At the same time, they provide a better sense of the players around them, making it more difficult, for instance, to be murdered in an attack from behind.

or use it with. There is no inventory in the usual sense: If players want to put on a hat, they click on the hat, then on themselves to put it on; if they have a backpack on them to store at least a few items, they also click on these and then precisely on the backpack. These controls can be quite finicky, particularly when trying to click on very small items such as a berry or a needle, and they can thus be understood to be purposefully part of the difficulty of the game as well, mirroring some of the complexity inherent in the tasks that the avatar can perform.

As a third aspect, the space of the represented fictional world is crucial for the gameplay in terms of where a community is started and how, in turn, objects within that location are placed. Most immediately, this concerns the placement and building of a community. The different biomes of the world all have their unique advantages and disadvantages, and the procedurally generated world can mix these various zones and their potential objects to create more or less hostile areas to live in. Once players start building or planting the first few objects, space continues to be crucial in terms of where they position parts of their settlement. Early on, this includes, for instance, the planting of berry bushes or rows of carrot seeds; later, it is a question of where to put a well or how to best construct a sheep pen or walls and floors for an enclosed building to provide shelter. Some of these actions can be reverted but, more importantly, some cannot. For example, players can construct an oven out of adobe, and when they add another piece of adobe to it, it permanently turns into a kiln, which has different functions (one is used for baking, the other for blacksmithing). If they add bellows to the kiln, it becomes a forge, with yet different purposes. A kiln cannot easily be returned to its oven state once the extra adobe has been added, so if a town placed these different elements strategically (e.g. for a baking era), it would be a mistake to accidentally add another piece of adobe to it – yet, since most of the items in the game do not belong to any specific character, any player could do just that. The manipulation of space is of similar importance for objects such as berry bushes, ponds, certain walls, roads, and others.[9]

Due to this importance of space in *One Hour One Life*, I suggest a reading of the game less focused on immediate needs such as hunger and warmth as the primary gameplay incentive but, instead, on a practice that could be called 'playing for space.' This is meant as a variation on the more common phrasing 'com-

---

9 Different versions and updates have changed some of these dynamics. For instance, a steel mining pick can deconstruct a kiln. Wrongly interacting with a pond, berry bush, or milkweed plant used to invalidate them, which eventually entailed moving a settlement to a different place if all of the natural resources had been consumed. In later updates, ways to (slowly) replenish such resources were implemented, although more recently, the game's developer included measures to make resources more finite overall.

peting for space' (or 'fighting over space'), which certainly describes an important element of a lot of video games. In a discussion of the role of players in relation to video game space, Michael Nitsche notes that "the player is a performer but can participate in the game world in more than one role" (203), and I would see competing for and playing for space as two such different roles. In multiplayer games in particular, "the inscription of self on the space becomes a socially mediated experience. Through action, communication, and being in relation to others, users come to find themselves 'there'" (Taylor qtd. in Nitsche 207–208). In this sense, the feeling of being in a specific space – and hence the notion that this space 'exists' in the first place – can be heightened by the spatial interaction with other players. In many multiplayer video games, this happens through competition: instead of trying to shoot another player or being faster than them, players compete directly for the space that is represented, for instance in sports or strategy games.[10]

Whereas most gameplay scenarios understand space as something to be fought for competitively, the phrasing 'playing for space' suggests using space cooperatively. Of course, players still need to make use of space strategically. In *One Hour One Life*, they strive to achieve the best possible outcome together not out of the goodness of their heart but out of necessity, because only playing by themselves while ignoring others will not get a player very far in a maximum of a 60-minute lifetime. The multiplayer setting thus also encourages a negotiation of (or over) space: While in a competition-heavy game, the use of space might be enforced through violence (i.e., attacking or killing another player), in a game focused on spatial cooperation, violence might only be a last resort, and will often entail additional side effects.[11] Instead, communicating with another player about the optimal utilization of space will often have more desirable results, also because *One Hour One Life* requires multiple players to collaborate in order to produce or construct most elements in the game. Since the avatar only lives for a maximum of one hour, this mechanic overall de-emphasizes the im-

---

10 For instance, in *Civilization VI*, scouting ahead and finding suitable locations for one's cities to spread one's empire is particularly important. If another player settles an important spot more quickly, this is significant not only because it entails a loss of resources but also because the occupation of space itself is crucial in the game, in the form of extending one's overall civilization. In that way, while players of *Civilization* also directly fight with their enemies' units and have other means of aggression, one of the most decisive aspects is this competition for space.
11 For instance, in *One Hour One Life*, there is a system in place to 'curse' a player who unscrupulously murders others, potentially banishing that player to a separate realm.

portance of characters – instead, a player's lasting impact in the world is spatial, providing something that future generations can build on.[12]

For example, this dynamic comes into play in the rearing of new-born children. Whenever a newborn is hungry, it makes a loud, quite annoying crying sound (surely meant to deliberately disturb and unnerve players). If a child is born to a player, they, as its mother, are often its only guardian. The child cannot protect itself and it cannot feed itself, so to remind others that they have to feed it, it cries.[13] In a larger community, however, child-rearing is often a centralized task: When a child is born, a player may bring it to a central meeting point, where other players, who chose childcaring as a task, make sure to feed the child and keep it warm. However, how best to achieve the right temperature can be difficult to determine. Standing next to a fire or wearing clothes increases the child's warmth, which in turn slows down their hunger bar (even though the values of this mechanic have been changed throughout the game's history). Since players with adult characters do not know the actual temperature or warmth of a child and the child players cannot properly communicate their status, arguments about the right clothing or the correct position to a fire may ensue. Scenarios in which a player might argue with another adult player for where best to position their children or in which players might scold a child to stay in place thus illustrate how playing for space highlights the cooperative nature of trying to optimize communal living spatially.

Narrativizing Space

This focus on spatial cooperation – rather than competition – engenders and encourages community efforts to narrativize that space. By this, I mean that, since players recognize the importance of space in the game and of using and manipulating it efficiently, their experience of that space creates distinct stories, and

---

12 Certain objects in the game also encourage this idea, such as the bell tower, which places a marker for players in the vicinity, directing them to the position of the tower. Since it takes multiple generations to build, it will usually only be found in well-developed settlements, attracting more players to an already established village.

13 This is also meant to elicit an emotional reaction: Depending on how many people want to play the game at a given moment, a player can be frequently giving birth to other players, which can become too many to handle, both for that player and for the specific community in terms of the food it can produce. Similarly, if players are currently roaming around in the wilderness to collect something, having to suddenly carry a baby as well might become too much of a burden to them – so they might be tempted to abandon their child. To counteract this dynamic, the babies' pleading cries and their cute design try to appeal to players' sense of empathy.

Fig. 2: Child-rearing in *One Hour One Life*.

their negotiation of space also forms communities. As Sebastian Domsch notes, against the background of contemporary video-game trends towards both elaborate narratives and vast open worlds, the "challenge for the game designer who wants to combine open worlds with narrative potential is therefore to find new forms to 'narrativise' space" (103). *One Hour One Life* features such narrativizations through what Henry Jenkins has called "emergent narratives," which "are not prestructured or preprogrammed, taking shape through the game play" (128). The game's official forum thus features retellings of the sixty-minute lives by some of the players in posts and threads labeled "User Stories." The high stakes implied in the gameplay – e.g., the irreversibility of some of the actions and the danger of dying to starvation or wildlife – generally afford a high degree of "tellability," i.e., "features that make a story worth telling" (Baroni 447). Moreover, the fact that players, after their death, cannot easily communicate again with the other players they just interacted with also increases the impetus for some of them to use the game's forum to retell the events of their played life.

In addition to this focus on enacted stories, *One Hour One Life* also encourages players to communicate with each other about strategies, best practices, or 'rules' for specific behavior. This happens partly in-game (where communication is more difficult) and partly extradiegetically, on the official forum. This creation of communities is, again, especially engendered by the game's use of space. Such a dynamic was most notable in the weeks immediately after the game's release, when all players still struggled to optimize gameplay strategies and discussed which ways might be best to teach new players how to optimally make use of the game's world. One particularly prominent idea from those days was to spread the so-called 'four laws':

THE FOUR LAWS
NEVER VIOLATE
EVEN TO SURVIVE
1. ONLY PICK FRUITING MILKWEED
FRUITING MILKWEED regrows and gives seeds
2. NEVER EMPTY PONDS
Ponds refill if not DRY. Refill ponds if dry.
3. ONLY HUNT FAMILY ANIMALS
Lone animals don't respawn. Family animals come back.
4. DON'T PLANT BERRY BUSHES
Berry bushes waste fertile soil. Only plant if composting
THE COROLLARY:
TEACH YOUR CHILDREN THE LAWS. ("Sustainability Laws")

All of these 'laws' more or less related to questions of space: For instance, players were supposed to watch the state of milkweed to pick only fruiting ones, since picking them at other stages would not make them regrow, wasting the space they occupy. While some of these mechanics have been changed in later updates, it is still noteworthy how the relatively small community of players early on recognized the importance of carefully 'playing for space' in the game, and how they formed rules around it. In other examples, such laws also resemble the Ten Commandments, here referred to as the 'seven tenets,' among them to "LIVE LIGHT UPON THE LAND" ("THE TENETS") as well as tribes that try to organize how to settle the land (see "Milkweed People").[14] Yet other posts focus on 'min-maxing,' i.e., making the most out of the resources and the space that is available to players, e.g. by discussing ideal placements and designs for towns (see "Town Design Guide"). These, too, can be understood as discussions of how to optimize the use of space.

In this sense, playing for space affords community building through negotiation, and it leads to a community of players forging their own narratives around their efforts to transform the land and build small towns. On one level, this kind of playing encourages ecological thinking, taking into consideration the impact players have on the land and thinking of ways to make that sustainable by reduc-

---

14 In-game, in more advanced communities, rudimentary communication can also happen via radio messages and paper notes that can be left for later generations, potentially including hints and 'laws' for how to use the land as well, even though this happens much more prominently on the forum.

ing the effects of a developing civilization on the natural land. The 'four laws' cited above, for instance, all refer to questions of sustainability. From an ecocritical perspective, parts of the game's player base could thus be understood as forming "participatory communities" that develop "unanticipated environmentalist perspectives" (Chang and Parham 7). On the other hand, however, for the longest time, the game repeated the central myth of the frontier and westward expansion: That there is an almost unlimited vast amount of empty land just waiting to be 'conquered' and settled, since the procedurally generated world can always continue to expand. If an area's environment truly got ruined due to barren berry bushes and empty ponds, players could always try to build a new settlement further west – or east, north, or south. At least to some extent, this also reduces the need for community-induced rules that focus on the preservation of land, discouraging this part of the narrativization of space. In more recent changes to *One Hour One Life* (started in July of 2019), the game's developer has adjusted and reduced this infinity of resources through the introduction of 'rifts' in the world, which limit the available map space, and via the focus on 'arcs' of play, i.e., states in the world that need to be reached in order to reset the map and begin again. This possibility of a restart limits, of course, the game's (and almost any game's) ecocritical potential, yet within one specific arc, this change highlights the importance of playing for space even more, as the area of land that can be occupied is limited, forcing players to newly negotiate how to use the space available to them.

Conclusion

In this contribution, I have used *One Hour One Life* as a case study to muse about the uses of space in video games and their correlation with spatial myths and imaginaries in American Studies. I focused on only a few of the many gameplay elements and potential community interactions of the game, and its unique simulation features certainly invite further scholarly inquiries. Still, rather than tackling my overall question from a more theoretical angle, I thus hope to have also demonstrated the merits of using primary texts – in this case, a lesser-known indie video game – as a potential starting point for more abstract discussions of matters such as space in both American Studies and Game Studies.

The way in which *One Hour One Life* foregrounds playing for space as a means of fostering a (narrative) community is certainly a dynamic present in other games as well, even if less prominently so. Yet, it remains understudied when compared to the omnipresent understanding of and focus on space as something to be fought over. In that sense, such an approach might lend itself especially well to other multiplayer games that emphasize both a fight for survival and the importance of interacting with space, such as *Minecraft* (2011), *Rust* (2013), or *Don't Starve Together* (2014). While such games all include competitive elements (or might allow for players to 'grief' – i.e., irritate – each other by deliberately destroying or misusing another person's constructions), they also centrally revolve around making strategic and efficient spatial decisions together. As the example of *One Hour One Life* has shown, it is thus not just anger over how another player might have ruined one's playing experience that can trigger further engagement in discussion forums and similar venues but also a conscious community effort at coordinating how best to play for space.

Works Cited

Baroni, Raphaël. "Tellability." *Handbook of Narratology*, edited by Peter Hühn et al., de Gruyter, 2009, pp. 447–454.

Chang, Alenda Y. and John Parham. "Green Computer and Video Games: An Introduction." *Ecozon*, vol. 8, no. 2, 2017, pp. 1–17.

"Crusader Kings II." *Steam*, store.steampowered.com/app/203770/Crusader_Kings_II/. Accessed 28 October 2019.

Domsch, Sebastian. "Space and Narrative in Computer Games." *Ludotopia: Spaces, Places and Territories in Computer Games*, edited by Espen Aarseth and Stephan Günzel, transcript, 2019, pp. 103–124.

Jenkins, Henry. "Game Design as Narrative Architecture." *First Person: New Media as Story, Performance and Game*, edited by Noah Wardrip-Fruin, The MIT Press, 2004, pp. 118–130.

Joseph, Daniel, and Lee Knuttila. "Single-Player/Multiplayer." *The Routledge Companion to Video Game Studies*, edited by Mark J. P. Wolf and Bernard Perron, Routledge, 2014, pp. 211–219.

Kolodny, Annette. "Letting Go Our Grand Obsessions: Notes Toward a New Literary History of the American Frontiers." *American Literature*, vol. 64, no. 1, 1992, pp. 1–18.

Kowert, Rachel and Thorsten Quandt, editors. *New Perspectives on the Social Aspects of Digital Gaming: Multiplayer 2*. Routledge, 2017.

Meades, Alan F. *Understanding Counterplay in Video Games*. Routledge, 2015.

"Milkweed People." *One Hour One Life Forums*, www.onehouronelife.com/forums/viewtopic.php?id=206. Accessed 29 October 2019.

Miller, Perry. *Errand into the Wilderness*. 1952. Harvard University Press, 2009.

Murray, Soraya. *On Video Games: The Visual Politics of Race, Gender and Space*. Tauris, 2017.

Nitsche, Michael. *Video Game Spaces: Image, Play, and Structure in 3D Worlds*. The MIT Press, 2008.

One Hour One Life. Jason Rohrer, 2018.

Quandt, Thorsten, and Sonja Kröger. Introduction. *Multiplayer: The Social Aspects of Digital Gaming*, by Quandt and Kröger. Routledge, 2013, pp. 3–9.

Quandt, Thorsten, and Sonja Kröger, editors. *Multiplayer: The Social Aspects of Digital Gaming*. Routledge, 2013.

"Sid Meier's Civilization VI." *Steam*, store.steampowered.com/app/289070/Sid_Meiers_Civilization_VI/. Accessed 28 October 2019.

Slotkin, Richard. *Regeneration Through Violence: The Mythology of the American Frontier, 1600–1860*. 1973. University of Oklahoma Press, 2000.

"Sustainability Laws." *One Hour One Life Forums*, onehouronelife.com/forums/viewtopic.php?id=161. Accessed 29 October 2019.

"THE TENETS." *One Hour One Life Forums*, onehouronelife.com/forums/viewtopic.php?id=195. Accessed 29 October 2019.

"Town Design Guide." *One Hour One Life Forums*, onehouronelife.com/forums/viewtopic.php?id=4074. Accessed 29 October 2019.

Turner, Frederick Jackson. "The Significance of the Frontier in American History." 1893. *National Humanities Center*, nationalhumanitiescenter.org/pds/gilded/empire/text1/turner.pdf.

"User Stories." *One Hour One Life Forums*, onehouronelife.com/forums/viewforum.php?id=9. Accessed 29 October 2019.

Greta Kaisen
There is no Place like *Gone Home*: Exploring Gothic Settings in Video Games

In Horace Walpole's novel *The Castle of Otranto*, which was originally published in 1764 and is considered the first Gothic novel, the setting is the origin of all the uncanny occurrences in the story and so crucial to the plot that it serves as the novel's eponym. Secret trapdoors, unknown passageways, and hidden manuscripts about to reveal a dark family past have since been the formulaic ingredients of many Gothic plots. Gothic hero-villains that keep innocent heroines enclosed in obscure chambers are the characters that usually inhabit those Gothic settings. Heroines like Jane Eyre in the novel of the same name by Charlotte Brontë (1847) have to explore their surroundings in order to reveal secrets that will further the narrative. Gothic literature is thus often about the exploration of a place and about movement within space. According to Angela Wright, "buildings are as important as the protagonists in Gothic romance" (36). They impose themselves on the narrative becoming the antagonists that provide challenges to a romance plot. Only when the castle Thornfield Hall burns down, and with it the burdens of hero-villain Edward Rochester's past, can he and Jane Eyre be together.[1]

Surprisingly, scholars have recently argued that video games have many characteristics in common with the traditional Gothic novel. Summarizing Fred Botting's take on the subject, as argued in *Limits of Horror* (2008), Michael Hancock states that, "both are the center of moral panics and controversy; both are known for their somewhat formulaic and mechanical structure; both emphasize intense emotion and violent shock" (166). I suggest that they have yet another thing in common: Traditional Gothic stories unfold and develop through and are triggered by their settings – and this can also be said about Gothic narratives in video games. According to Game Studies scholar Espen Aarseth, "[t]he defining element in computer games is spatiality" (44). He continues that "[c]omputer games are essentially concerned with spatial representation and negotiation, and therefore the classification of a computer game can be based on how it represents or, perhaps, implements space" (44). If space is equally important to

---

[1] One of these 'burdens' is his marriage to Bertha Mason, a character that inspired the literary theme of 'the madwoman in the attic,' a term first used in Sandra Gilbert's and Susan Gubar's *The Madwoman in the Attic: The Woman Writer and the Nineteenth-Century Literary Imagination*, published in 1979.

both the creation of the Gothic as well as to video games, the question arises how games remediate the Gothic mode.

As an example of a Gothic video game, I am going to take *Gone Home*, an independent first person exploration game published by the Fullbright Company in 2013, into account. The walking simulator is set in 1995 and the player assumes the role of Kaitlin Greenbriar, a 21-year-old that comes home to a rural area – fictional Boon County in Oregon – from her gap year in Europe only to find out that her family is gone. The setting is an old inherited mansion that her family has moved into during her absence. By walking through the house, the player-character will discover many rooms, out of which not few are locked. Hidden passageways lead to other, more secluded parts of the house. It is the player-character's quest to find out what happened in the past by looking at every object in the house. From marital problems, her father's struggle as a failed author and his abusive childhood to her sister's queerness and secret relationship with a girl in her class, Kaitlin encounters many secrets throughout her exploration of the house.

After its publication in 2013, *Gone Home* has received considerable critical attention. For example, Sercan Şengün has argued that the game as a walking simulator fosters "ludic voyeurism" (2017) by limiting interactivity and agency for players. Robin J. S. Sloan has read the game as a commodified nostalgic simulation with its many references to '90s popular culture – a "Baudrillardian restoration" (537) rather than a historical representation. *Gone Home* has also received great interest as a queer and feminist video game: Rowan Tulloch, Catherine Hoad, and Helen Young have called it "a piece of riot grrrl art" due to its employment of the movement's feminist strategies and its "resistance to norms of masculinity and heterosexuality" but also pointed out how its progressive potential is, similar to the '90s Riot Grrrl scene, limited by "its tacit adhesion to white racial normativity" (338). Bonnie Ruberg looks beyond the representational by examining the "potential for queer movement in *Gone Home*" and its "straightening" by the highly structured mode of storytelling as well as speedrunners "who play the game along the straightest possible paths" (632–633). Furthermore, the use of horror tropes in the game has been pointed out by some (see Kopas; see Tulloch, Hoad, and Young), but its particular Gothic qualities have not received much attention – except by Naiara Sales Araújo and Ludmila Gratz Melo. By exploring intertextual references to eighteenth and nineteenth century British Gothic literature, they argue that *Gone Home* is expressive of a modern female Gothic. While Araújo and Melo position *Gone Home* in a Gothic literary tradition, they leave much to be said about the media-specific ways in which *Gone Home* can be considered an American Gothic video game.

From its aesthetic outset, *Gone Home* can already be considered a Gothic game – and the Gothic mode primarily manifests itself in the setting. The old mansion has a mysterious past, a dark basement, and a closed attic. When Kaitlin arrives at one a.m., a thunderstorm rages outside and the branches of the surrounding trees are vaguely visible as shadowy shapes behind the windows. The player-character can, however, never leave the house, which is reminiscent of the Gothic trope of a heroine confined in a castle. The sound design of the game plays into the Gothic atmosphere as well: Kaitlin's steps, startling sounds of the creaking wooden floor, mysterious, low music, and sudden thunderclaps contribute to the eerie scene.

However, I argue that the exploration of the setting creates a Gothic mode specific to video games. It is an example of how games give Gothic settings a new, distinct quality in that a Gothic mode is not only created by the setting's impact on the narrative(s), but simultaneously by the player's interaction with the setting. Going home seems to be a nostalgic act of reminiscence but by exploring and discovering its secrets, the nostalgic feeling gives way to the uncanny realization that the home is gone. Ultimately, this chapter argues that the game is not only an example of how video games remediate Gothic settings but also of a specifically American Gothic setting.

The Gothic Mode in Video Games

Video games tell their narratives by spatial exploration and thus through "environmental storytelling" (Jenkins 57). Video games scholar Michael Nitsche calls the elements with which the player can generate meaning while moving through the gamespace "evocative narrative elements" (37). These elements "can be anything and any situation encountered in a game world that is structured to support and guide the player's comprehension" (37). In *Gone Home*, the player has to examine everyday items, letters, or notes as well as audio- and videotapes, magazines, or books that provide information about the characters and their story but also often include references to U.S. pop culture of the 1990s.[2] This creates a sense of having gone home to a place of a specifically American past and clearly distinguishes the setting from the old castles of the traditional European Gothic. The tension between a nostalgic homecoming to an American past on the one

---

[2] Items that include references to 1990s' U.S. pop culture are, among others, magic eye pictures, videotapes of the first season of the TV show *The X-Files* (1993–2002), and magazine covers featuring *Nirvana* front man Kurt Cobain.

hand and the feeling of some secrets haunting this seemingly functional family is what makes the game an American Gothic setting.[3]

The 'home' that at first might foster those longings, will soon become "unhomely" (Freud 134) or uncanny, which is one of the key concepts of Gothic literature. In his essay "The Uncanny" (1919), Sigmund Freud states that "the uncanny is that species of the frightening that goes back to what was once well known and has long been familiar" (124). He continues that "the uncanny element is actually nothing new or strange, but something that was long familiar to the psyche and was estranged from it only through being repressed" (147). While *Gone Home*'s game world, a 1990s American family home, might seem familiar to players, its underlying secrets inevitably lead to the emergence of uncanniness.

One of the game's mechanics responsible for the creation of its Gothic mode is movement through the gamespace. The player can only act within the fixed set of rules of the game world. For example, she can walk through the house, pick up objects, and crouch in order to contemplate things on the ground. However, what she cannot do is regulate her speed. The relatively slow movement through space condenses the Gothic atmosphere: Walking down a long corridor slowly attains an uncanny quality as walls, doors, and furniture obfuscate the view. Thus, the player cannot be sure of what lies ahead. Gothic texts often foster these feelings of uncertainty and unreliability rather than aiming at a radical confrontation with danger. According to Botting, they create suspense by "prolonging the interplay of anticipation and apprehension" (*Gothic* 5). In walking simulators like *Gone Home*, the Gothic mode thus comes into play perfectly: As opposed to a reader of a novel, the player has to actively navigate through the gamespace. Not being able to move quickly through the house prolongs feelings of anxious anticipation.

The division of the gamespace into rooms and corridors, and the interplay of light and darkness intensify this effect. Nitsche argues that "[c]omplete spatial presentation in fact reduces the dramatic effect of spatial exploration because it removes elements of surprise and suspense that can be triggered by a gradual revealing of the game space" (38). He continues that "[d]ramatic moments and references such as suspense and surprise depend on the nonvisibility of certain elements within the game space" (38). Upon entering a dark room, the player often has to first find a light switch in order to be able to make sense of her sur-

---

[3] The American Gothic comes closer to home. According to American Gothic specialist Alan Lloyd-Smith, "[t]he house, not the castle, becomes the site of its trauma; its terror deriving from the familiar inmates instead of some external threat" (75).

roundings. This presents itself as difficult in the darkness, and thus, the player is likely to lose orientation. These moments contribute to a Gothic aesthetic, not only in that the Gothic mode possesses, according to Fred Botting, "negative aesthetics" (*Gothic* 1) informed by an "absence of light" (2), but also because they create suspense. By only gradually revealing the gamespace to the player, *Gone Home* evokes the Gothic mode with means specific to the medium of video games.

However, these aspects are still exemplary of how the setting limits the player in her actions – which is in its nature still very similar to the workings of settings in traditional Gothic novels. In video games, the player can actively engage with her environment. This creates new dynamics between the setting and the player. These dynamics become apparent when looking at the specific way the player interacts with the setting.

While the player sees the house through Kaitlin's eyes, the game provides little information about her and, crucially, about her feelings regarding the family's secrets. The player can only guess her reactions when finding out about Samantha's struggles at school, her coming out, or her parents' estrangement. By moving the cursor over the objects in the house, the player can sometimes read Kaitlin's thoughts on the screen. This is, however, mainly a means to provide context for those objects and not to enrich Kaitlin's character with a backstory or with personal motives. Kaitlin is a *tabula rasa* onto which the player can inscribe herself (see Şengün). Since she does not know how Kaitlin relates to her family members after learning their secrets, the player is able to fill in that void with her own interpretations. In this way, Kaitlin's task becomes the player's quest and provides a justification for the player to unlock doors, find out locker combinations, read hidden journals and discarded papers in bins, and look under beds and in odd corners of rooms. Consequently, the game has a decidedly voyeuristic element, which the player has to accept if she wants to fulfill her quest (see Şengün). The player might find herself noticing that her actions could, in real life, fall into morally gray territory.

This voyeuristic element and its resulting dynamic between player and character fosters the Gothic mode further in *Gone Home*. This is especially apparent when Kaitlin examines objects that are explicitly marked as private. Michael Hancock goes so far as to describe video games generally as "inherently gothic" (166), because a "game pushes the player to identify with the avatar, to accept its actions as a surrogate for the player's actions within the game world, making it a candidate for the gothic double, or doppelgänger" (167). However, he acknowledges that players are often so used to these dynamics that they only notice them in explicitly Gothic game situations (see 169). Yet, he maintains that "[v]irtually any action performed in the context of a video game that, if it occurred in the outside world, would have legal or social repercussions, could arguably fall under art-evil" (177). Furthermore, he contends that "through playing art-evil, players can establish their avatars not just as their doubles, but their overtly evil doubles" (177) and concludes that "[t]he video game exposes the gothic self" (181). Even though the player cannot exert physical violence over other characters in *Gone Home*, I argue that there is an element of art-evil, nonetheless. The quest of the game can only be achieved by constantly going through the family members' belongings. By shedding light on places that have been in the darkness before, the player is thus not only transgressing spatial but also moral boundaries. This becomes especially apparent since she cannot hide behind Kaitlin's character but finds herself alone in the mansion making the choice to continue playing – and thus to transgress these boundaries.

These transgressions become apparent in the act of revisiting rooms. The player has the option to put all objects back into their place, but if she does not feel like cleaning up after herself in a video game, she will be confronted with their chaotic state when she returns to them. Her previous actions have thus become visible in the gamespace as if she had inscribed herself onto it. Consequently, she is not only limited by the setting but can interact with it as well. As opposed to traditional Gothic novels, in which the setting imposes itself on the narrative, the player of *Gone Home* imposes herself on the setting and, in doing so, makes hidden secrets visible. However, rather than creating more clarity, this leads to chaos. By looking back at her individual imprint on the setting, the player will be confronted with her previous intrusion into private spaces. The game world, which might remind a player of her own past with its many allusions to 1990s culture, is visibly altered. The nostalgic experience of the gamespace is disrupted as the player-character realizes that by the act of going back home, she de-familiarizes it in the process. In this manner, the player becomes her own antagonistic and uncanny doppelgänger, not only being confronted with fictional secrets of the family members but also with the actions of her past self.

So far, I have established that by providing little information about Kaitlin, the game facilitates the player's immersion in the game world as herself or at least as her own doppelgänger instead of playing the game as the character of Kaitlin. Actions that fall under art-evil then also become the player's actions rather than Kaitlin's. The player may only realize this dynamic when she finds a crumbled piece of paper in the basement which reveals a recollection of her sister Samantha's first sexual encounter with her girlfriend. Journals, letters, and personal notes can usually be read undisturbed by Kaitlin's thoughts. However, the paper crumbles together after a few seconds so that the player has no chance of reading the whole text. Kaitlin's thoughts appear on the screen: "Okay, not reading any more of that" (*Gone Home*). By repeatedly clicking on the paper, the player will only read more of those refusals. In this instance, "Kaitlin's role as a *tabula rasa* is temporarily forfeited and her presence reasserts itself" (Şengün, emphasis in original). She refuses to act on the player's demand, thereby breaking the strong immersion for a moment. While the player is constantly transgressing spatial and moral boundaries within the game, here, the game is setting boundaries and thus limiting the player from knowing everything. Furthermore, *Gone Home* calls out the player for her actions – ironically so, since the game can only be completed by transgressing those boundaries in the first place. Here the idea of the art-evil doppelgänger is evoked explicitly. The player-character, previously having experienced the setting itself as a Gothic antagonist, now becomes the Gothic antagonist herself wandering through the darkened corridors of her family's mansion, leaving behind chaos, uncovering secrets, and opening doors that were meant to be shut.

The element of interactivity is thus what creates a Gothic experience specific to video games. While the Gothic mode is always about the transgression of boundaries, here the player actively decides to take the first step by physically pressing her keyboard or buttons on a controller. According to Nitsche,

> [t]he player in a video game is both reader (of the computer's output) and producer (via input) of events. For video game spaces, this means the player not only enters the game worlds but also changes them and their ingredients. These event-shaping features separate interactive access from the experience of traditional media and pushes interactive game worlds beyond Barthes *readerly* and *writerly* texts. (31, emphasis in the original)

Admittedly, the degree of interactivity possible in *Gone Home* is subtle and the player will not be able to change the outcome of its narratives. According to Sercan Şengün, the player of *Gone Home* holds a position of *"passive spectatorship, trapped between the temporality when the narrative takes place and when it is being discovered"* (emphasis in the original). Reflecting on the dynamics between narration and interactivity in walking simulators, Şengün further argues that "[t]he story they present is not interactive; however, the process of discovering of that story is." In *Gone Home,* this interactive process of discovery is ultimately what makes players create their own narrative at each playthrough, and what informs their own experience of the game's stories. The player's actions have no impact on the narrative, but she is far from being passive – she is leaving her traces in the game world and is confronted with (albeit minor) choices or the imagination of choice (in the instance of Samantha's diary entry) – a possibility not available in traditional Gothic novels. In those early novels, settings are as important as the protagonists. They stay as important as the protagonists in Gothic video games. Yet, the interactivity of games allows for new Gothic modes.

Since spatiality is a key factor in Gothic fiction, the Gothic mode becomes especially potent for a remediation in games. As demonstrated before, this presents itself in its interactive qualities, which is closely related to notions of agency. Furthermore, the interaction of setting and player is, in some ways, a physical one in video games. When playing a record player in Kaitlin's father's room, the player has to actively set the tone arm on the vinyl in order to listen to the song. This is done by actively using the computer mouse or the controller. Without the player's input that is registered in the game world, the game would not play music. In his book *Cybertext: Perspecties on Ergodic Literature* (1997), Espen Aarseth defines ergodic literature as texts that require "non-trivial effort [...] to allow the reader to traverse the text" (1). Specifically in the context of video games, Nitsche summarizes the act of "ergodic participation" as "any physical input that can be registered by input devices and has an effect on the video game world" (32). The act of clicking on the tape and thereby inserting it in the tape player has an immediate impact on the gamespace.

This ergodic participation, which has a decidedly corporeal quality, is especially fruitful for the emergence of Gothic moments. According to James Ash, "[f]rom a phenomenological perspective, senses such as touch and hearing are as important as sight in understanding how players engage with video games" (122). He continues that "[t]hinking about the corporeal aspect of video games is important as it opens up new ways to think about the spatiality of video games as spatiality produced through the body" (122). Thus, a video game mediates different sensory stimuli with sound, visual impressions, and even touch in the "meta-medium computer" (Nitsche 1) and thereby informs the spatial experience of the player. The player's affective response caused by such an interaction might in turn manifest itself in the gamespace. According to Ash, "[w]hereas one can be scared by the actions of a character in a film, in a video game this fear manifests itself in a direct response to what is happening in the game" (123). For example, the player's fear of encountering an unknown situation in the game might influence her ability to navigate the avatar through the ludic challenges the game provides. In *Gone Home*, this might result in a momentary loss of orientation. In other, often more fast-paced games, it can have an impact on the narrative of the played experience.[4] The act of ergodic participation is

---

[4] Affective responses to the Gothic like fear, anxiety, and shock, then, influence the story in video games. Thinking of rumbles in game controllers and even VR headsets, the Gothic mode might develop an increasingly corporeal aspect in video games.

thus another crucial element in the creation of a Gothic mode that is specific to video games.

Exploring *Gone Home* shows that video games create a specific Gothic mode. As video games are a spatial medium, the Gothic mode is also created spatially: The slow movement through space and the interplay of light and darkness reveal the gamespace only gradually and thus create feelings of uncertainty in *Gone Home*. Even more characteristic of the Gothic in video games are moments in which the player inscribes herself onto the setting. In *Gone Home*, the player interacts with the game world through spatial exploration. She becomes her own art-evil doppelgänger in the process, as she voyeuristically explores the family's mansion. As I am going to show in the final part of this chapter, these Gothic moments disturb the game's inherent nostalgic aesthetics.

Nostalgia and the American Gothic

If nostalgia is a "melancholic longing for a space in time" (Sloan 529), the white middle-class American home of the 1990s in *Gone Home* may offer a remedy for this yearning for some.[5] It seems not only to transport the player back in time but equally to a specific *place* in that time: Kaitlin's sister Samantha's room has a basketball hoop and a bulky cupboard adorned with magic eye pictures, and her father's office has a desk with a typewriter and many handwritten sticky notes. In other parts of the house, the player can find fanzines and V.H.S. tapes of the first season of the TV show *The X-Files* (1993–2002) and even listen to songs by Riot Grrrl punk bands such as *Heavens to Betsy* and *Bratmobile*. With its references and memorabilia, the game may seem like an interactive museum of the past.

It is important to note that even some of the game's Gothic elements – like the sudden creaking of the wooden floor, flickering lights, and the frequent allusions to ghosts – contribute to a nostalgic aesthetic in that they are serving a nostalgia for stock Gothic elements. For example, the board game "Escape

---

5 Nostalgia does not actually refer to a place in the past but rather to a place that is constructed by individual or cultural memories of that past. The video game can thus only foster nostalgic longings for the place in time it simulates, if nostalgia for that place has existed in the first place. For example, if the player has no cultural association with white middle-class American (pop-)culture in the 1990s, she might not actually feel nostalgia at all. Without understanding or caring for the cultural nostalgia artifacts and cues in *Gone Home*'s space, objects, and themes, the player might be immune to both the nostalgia and the haunting elements the game tries to evoke.

from Ghost Mansion," which the player can find hidden in a closet, is emblematic of *Gone Home* as a video game: the idea of ghosts is evoked but rather belongs to the realm of "game" and "play." These elements do not seem to have the potential to actually scare the player. I suggest that this remediation of the Gothic displays a self-referential nostalgia instead, which plays with Gothic tropes such as ghosts. Consequently, even though I have described this aesthetic as the first aesthetic layer of the Gothic mode inherent in the game, I contend that the game's source of terror lies rather in those elements of the game that the player does not immediately identify as Gothic.

In the end, the many secrets the player discovers while playing the game – revealing the dysfunctionality behind a seemingly harmonious family life – are far more haunting than the fictional ghosts hinted at by objects such as board games or Ouija boards.[6] What is truly frightening is only revealed by the player's interaction with the gamespace: By exploring the house, the player-character not only discovers those family secrets, but is confronted with her own art-evil doppelgänger: Kaitlin is the Gothic ghost who brings them out into the open. In this way, she haunts the nostalgic world of *Gone Home*. The setting repeatedly turns from a nostalgic to a Gothic one, layering the idea of having gone home: By going through her family's belongings, Kaitlin goes 'home' to the past of her own family. Playing the game could also potentially be seen as an act of going home for a player who might nostalgically long for the many allusions to America's pop culture in the 1990s. By interacting with the setting, the uncanny feeling arises that the home the player might have thought to have accessed through the screen like an interactive museum, has been an illusion after all. Going home implies the nostalgic act of revisiting a place of the past that one has been absent from through spatial or temporal distance. Isabella van Elferen argues that "[i]f nostalgia is characterized by the retrospective creation of an idealized homeland, the Gothic renders this very homeland uncanny by perverting its idyllic quality" (5). If *Gone Home* is a nostalgic homeland, it is turned uncanny by the player's interaction with the game world.

Another layer of the act of going home is the fact that Kaitlin comes home to the U.S. after having spent a year in Europe. However, Europe, the place of early Gothic novels, does not turn out to be the setting that creates an uncanny experience: it is the American home that she returns to. The tension between a nostalgic homecoming to an American past on the one hand and the feeling that

---

6 Those fictional ghosts, at times, and in truly Gothic fashion, come to represent those very real family secrets, as in the case of Terrence Greenbriar's abusive uncle Oskar Masan, who might not actually haunt the mansion as a ghost (as assumed by Samantha and her girlfriend Lonnie), but his memory seems to haunt Terrence in his adult life.

there are some secrets underlying this seemingly functioning family is what makes the game an American Gothic game. According to Alan Lloyd-Smith, "[t]his is the distinctive theme and deepest insight of American Gothic, the sense that there is something *behind*, which may not be, as in European Gothic, the Past, but some perpetual and present Otherness, hidden within, behind, somehow below the apparently benign 'natural' surface" (86, emphasis in the original). Even though the player-character uncovers past secrets while going through the house, in the end, there is the realization that she herself is the one revealing them in a voyeuristic manner, uncovering what lays *behind* her American family home. This reflection is what makes *Gone Home* an American Gothic game, unsettled by a decidedly spatial Gothic mode that is specific to video games.

Works Cited

Aarseth, Espen. "Allegories of Space: The Odyssey of Spatiality in Computer Games." *Space Time Play: Computer Games, Architecture and Urbanism: The Next Level*, edited by Friedrich von Borries, Steffen P. Waltz and Matthias Böttger, Birkhäuser Verlag, 2007, pp. 44–47.

Aarseth, Espen. *Cybertext: Perspectives on Ergodic Literature*. John Hopkins University Press, 1997.

Araújo, Naiara Sales, and Ludmila Gratz Melo. "O Gênero Gótico Em *Gone Home*: Uma Análise à Luz Da Intertextualidade." *Itinerários: Revista de Literatura*, vol. 47, 2018, pp. 119–132.

Ash, James. "Video Games." *The Ashgate Research Companion to Media Geography*, edited by Paul Adams, Jim Craine and Jason Dittmer, Ashgate Publishing, 2014, pp. 119–136.

Botting, Fred. *Limits of Horror: Technologies, Bodies, Gothic*. Manchester University Press, 2008.

Botting, Fred. *The Gothic*. 2nd ed., Routledge, 2014.

Elferen, Isabella van. "Introduction: Nostalgia and Perversion in Gothic Rewriting." *Nostalgia or Perversion? Gothic Rewriting from the Eighteenth Century until the Present Day*, edited by Isabella van Elferen, Cambridge Scholars Publishing, 2007, pp. 1–10.

Freud, Sigmund. "The Uncanny." *The Uncanny*. 1919. Edited by Adam Phillips, translated by David McLintock with an introduction by Hugh Haughton, Penguin Classics, 2003, pp. 132–162.

Gone Home. The Fullbright Company, 2013.

Hancock, Michael. "Doppelgamers: Video Games and Gothic Choice." *American Gothic Culture: An Edinburg Companion*, edited by Joel Faflak and Jason Haslam, Edinburgh University Press, 2016, pp. 166–184.

Kopas, Merritt. "On *Gone Home*." *Queer Game Studies*, edited by Bonnie Ruberg and Adrienne Shaw, University of Minnesota Press, 2017, pp. 145–149.

Lloyd-Smith, Allan. *American Gothic Fiction: An Introduction*. Continuum, 2004.

Nitsche, Michael. *Video Game Spaces: Image, Play and Structure in 3D Worlds*. MIT Press, 2008.

Ruberg, Bonnie. "Straight Paths Through Queer Walking Simulators: Wandering on Rails and Speedrunning in *Gone Gome*." *Games and Culture*, vol. 15, no. 6, 2020, pp. 632–652.

Şengün, Sercan. "Ludic Voyeurism and Passive Spectatorship in *Gone Home* and Other 'Walking Simulators'." *Video Game Art Gallery*, 2017, www.videogameartgallery.com/vga-reader-articles/ludic-voyeurism-and-passive-spectatorship-in-gone-home-and-other-walking-simulators. Accessed 31 July 2021.

Sloan, Robin J. S. "Videogames as Remediated Memories: Commodified Nostalgia and Hyperreality in *Far Cry 3: Blood Dragon* and *Gone Home*." *Games and Culture*, vol. 10, no. 6, 2015, pp. 525–550.

Tulloch, Rowan, Catherine Hoad, and Helen Young. "Riot Grrrl Gaming: Gender, Sexuality, Race, and the Politics of Choice in Gone Home." *Continuum: Journal of Media and Cultural Studies*, vol. 33, no. 3, June 2019, pp. 337–350.

Wright, Angela. *Gothic Fiction: A Reader's Guide to Essential Criticism*. Palgrave MacMillan, 2007.

Florian Deckers
Exploring the Digital Land of the Dead: Hybrid Pan-Latinidad in *Grim Fandango*

Apart from its innovative design as one of the first 3D rendered point-and-click adventures, there is one thing that was and still is even more ground-breaking about LucasArts' *Grim Fandango* (1998), especially from a Cultural Studies perspective: It is one of the first games which focuses on a story and gaming experience that revolves around Latinx culture and (re-)constructs a hybrid pan-Latinx identity.[1] Even today, more than 20 years after *Grim Fandango* was first published and republished in a remastered version in 2015, games that center on Latinx experiences are scarce. In their study "The Virtual Census: Representations of Gender, Race and Age in Video Games," Dimitri Williams et al. find that only about three percent of video game characters can be recognized as Latinx and less than five percent of those are actually playable. This seems at odds with the fact that Latinx children and teenagers play more hours per day than children of any other ethnic group in the U.S., according to studies by the Henry J. Kaiser Family Foundation and by the Pew Research Center.[2] Thus, they represent a large part, if not the largest, of the group of potential players. Nevertheless, the representation of Latinas and Latinos in video games still tends to be largely stereotypical. Most commonly Latinas and Latinos are either depicted as hyper-masculine, violent, and potentially criminal men, or as over-sexualized, objectified women.[3] Arts and humanities scholar Frederick Luis Al-

---

[1] Like other ethnic markers, the term used by members of the group as well as outsiders to describe the part of U.S. population that is from Latin American descent has changed over the years and will continue to do so. In this text, however, I will use the word 'Latinx' as a gender inclusive term for the group. The 'x' stands in for both genders, that would otherwise be denoted by an 'a' or 'o' at the end of a nationality or other group name. Further it includes identities that do not adhere to or identify with one of these genders. Referring to material that predates the use of the 'x' to denote this inclusive understanding of gender and identity, I will apply the gendered endings of 'a/o' or 'as/os' for national and ethnic groups, such as, for example, Chicana/o.
[2] For information on the demographics of gamers in the U.S., see the study of the Henry J. Kaiser Family Foundation (available online at www.kff.org/disparities-policy/press-release/daily-media-use-among-children-and-teens-up-dramatically-from-five-years-ago) and the Pew Research Center's study (available online at www.pewresearch.org/fact-tank/2015/12/17/views-on-gaming-differ-by-race-ethnicity).
[3] On the prevailing sexism in video games, see Anita Sarkeesian's video-blog "Tropes vs. Women in Video Games" available online at www.feministfrequency.com/series/tropes-vs-women-in-video-games.

dama characterizes these enduring problematic practices in the relatively young medium of video games as follows: "When not a marauding gang in need of a good pummeling, urban-set, single player and multi-player video games typically place Latinos in the background streetscape for a verisimilar ghetto look" (242).[4] These overly simplistic constructs can, as Aldama argues, even lead to "exclusionary practices [towards Latinx people] in the real world" (256).[5]

In sharp contrast, *Grim Fandango* offers another perspective on Latinoness, or *latinidad*, wrapped in a detective story inspired by film noir. The player takes over the role of Manuel 'Manny' Calavera, who is dead – as are all other characters in the game. Manny works for the "Department of the Dead" and it is his job to sell tickets to newly deceased for their journey through the Land of the Dead to the next stage of their afterlife. Depending on the virtuousness during their lifetime, they either travel in a luxury train, a cruise-ship, or, if less righteous, on foot. Manny has hit a slump in his job as travel agent / grim reaper and needs to make some successful deals in order to also be able to leave this stage of existence behind. He suspects that his boss, Don Copal, and his co-worker, Domino Hurley, are behind his failures at work. When a woman whom Manny serves as an agent, Mercedes 'Meche' Colomar, suddenly disappears, he starts to investigate and embarks on a journey through the Land of the Dead in search for the perpetrators. It is noteworthy that the game's version of the afterlife combines the idea of an active existence in the hereafter that appears to be rooted in indigenous mythology, which attributes a very active role to the deceased (see Marchi), with a capitalist logic that is ingrained in U.S.-American ideology and which strongly resembles the world of the living: including nine-to-five jobs, bureaucracy, and other real-life institutions one might hope not to encounter in life after death.

Not only the plot, however, might be a direct adaptation of a film noir movie, with the obvious exception that all characters are skeletons and demons. The clothes that the characters wear as well as the objects they interact with and

---

[4] As Mastro, Behm-Morawitz, and Ortiz point out, Latino/a television portrayals resemble their video game counterparts in rareness of appearance as well as in their stereotypical construction, "consistently confining Latinos to a narrow set of roles, such as that of the Latin lover, buffoon, and criminal" (348).

[5] Also compare Dimitri Williams et al.'s study: "Although there are no race data for older game players, we do know that Latino children play more video games than white children, so it is conceivable that they play more as teenagers and adults. Nevertheless, Latinos are unlikely to see representations of their ethnic group among game characters and never as primary characters. According to social identity theory (Tajfel, 1978), this lack of appearance is a direct signal to Latinos that they are relatively unimportant and powerless compared to more heavily present groups. In addition, perceptions about Latinos may change for members of other groups" (828).

the Art Deco interior of the buildings evoke the 1920s to 1940s, which was the heyday of film noir. Meche, for example, wears a hat no flapper girl would be ashamed of and the pin-stripe suits of the male characters equally fit the fashion of the time. Candlestick telephones with a rotary dial and separate ear- and mouthpieces and numerous other objects equally add to the game's noir atmosphere. In interviews, director and writer Tim Schafer mentions that *Casablanca* (1941) was a huge inspiration for *Grim Fandango*. This becomes particularly apparent in the second chapter of the game in which Manny owns a casino in a small harbor town called Rubacava. This intertextual reference or even homage clearly alludes to the character of Richard 'Rick' Blaine and his Café Américain in the famous movie featuring Humphrey Bogart. This chapter of the game features the highest ratio of locations the player can visit, including a beatnik café, a racetrack, a police station, a tattoo parlor, and a factory, among others, which creates a dense urban atmosphere. The urbanity, which the gamespace reproduces, is also a distinct part of film noir (see Christopher).

As can already be deduced from this short introduction to the game, its plot and motifs are inspired by Latin American as well as U.S.-American sources, or in other words, the game amalgamizes elements from multiple Latin American cultures and U.S. culture into one hybrid form. This implies an understanding of hybridity that "has long left behind the negative implications and connotations of inferiority, contamination, miscegenation and perversion, which it had had in nineteenth-century racist scientific discourses" (Raab and Butler 1) and sees the term as "a most useful metaphor for conceptualizing and analyzing cultural contact, transfer and exchange" (1). This is very much in the vein of postcolonial scholar Homi K. Bhabha's understanding of hybridity. Bhabha quotes the Chicana/o performance artist Guillermo Gómez-Peña and his metaphor for emerging hybrid identities in the Mexican dish *menudo chowder*. This perception of identity interprets the contact and exchange between people of different cultural or ethnic backgrounds as a process in which something new forms without the complete dissolving of its parts. Those elements, which are incommensurable, remain as discernable "stubborn chunks (Asians, Blacks, Latinos & Native Americans)" (Gómez-Peña 71) in the soup that is society – while also being "condemned merely to float" (71).[6] Comparable to the metaphorical *menudo chowder*, hybridity offers an option for the creation of an identity that can be a completely

---

[6] As indissoluble markers of ancestry, the "stubborn chunks" (Gómez-Peña 71) refuse to cave in to assimilating concepts of Americanness such as the melting pot, which Gómez-Peña characterizes as a biased and romanticized concept: "[T]hat particular romance [American romance with immigration] had always been selective, and [...] the promise of the 'melting plot' [sic] was strictly meant for 'white' immigrants" (71).

new thing blending several others without destroying them in the process. Along these lines, I argue that *Grim Fandango* – although produced and developed by a primarily Anglo- and Asian-American team – iterates a hybrid pan-Latinx identity: (1) on a visual level this occurs through the construction of the city including its architectural style, (2) on an auditory level via language as well as music, and (3) through the incorporation and transformation of religious and mythologic motifs, narratives, and characters.

Spatial, Audiovisual, and Cultural Pan-*Latinidad* in *Grim Fandango*

The hybrid identity *Grim Fandango* substantiates itself on the level of architecture most noticeably in the way in which the capital of the Land of the Dead is constructed. For instance, the city's name, 'El Marrow,' is a hybrid of a Spanish article and an English noun. And like marrow is at the center of the bone, the eponymous city is at the center of the game – with two of the game's four chapters taking place in it (the first and the last chapter take place in this city, which frames the adventure and emphasizes its central role in the game). This digital urban center is based on the paradigmatic U.S. metropole, New York City, hybridized with numerous markers of Latin American culture. For example, in the first part of *Grim Fandango*, whenever players can look out of the window or in the few scenes in which they enter the streets, they encounter buildings that resemble famous landmarks such as the Chrysler Building, the Empire State building, or the Eldorado apartment building.[7] These visual references to New York City simultaneously construe a connection to various Latin American nations since the Latinx community of the city is very heterogeneous – with the largest proportion of Puerto Ricans, Dominicans, and Cubans.[8] The same heterogeneity can be found when examining New York's demographics at the smaller level of the neighborhood. While Latinx neighborhoods in, for example, Los Angeles, are very homogenous and the city and its Latinx community is primarily perceived as Mexican or Chicanx, in New York City "Latino neighborhoods have large

---

7 While this Upper West Side's luxurious apartment building with its double towered structure might not be one of the most famous sights of New York it is still a clear reference to the city as well as to the myth of El Dorado, which was first believed to be a golden chieftain, then a city, and later even a land of gold (see Silver).

8 See the 2010 census report for New York City which is available online at: www1.nyc.gov/assets/planning/down-load/pdf/data-maps/nyc-population/census2010/t_sf1_p8_nyc.pdf.

non-Latino minorities (African-American, Asian, Black Caribbean, new European, etc.) of 30 to 45 percent" (Davis 41). In a game that otherwise relies heavily on cultural practices and symbols stemming from Mexican and Chicanx culture as, for example, in the Day of the Dead motif, the reference to this particular city substantially contributes to the production of a pan-Latinx identity.

Further, the game does not leave the city unchanged or try to simulate New York City as closely as possible, emulating streets, buildings, and places, as numerous other games do. The *Grand Theft Auto* series, for example, is well-known for its architecturally 'realistic' representation of the Big Apple called "Liberty City." Along these lines, communication scientist Antonio Corona describes modding projects that generate a "Mexican-based *GTA* game" (464) based on *GTA: San Andreas* (2004) as a "sort of hybrid representation, in which the gamespace is an amalgam of U.S. and Latin American spaces, and which, similar to border settlements, requires active discrimination on the part of the player to be read as the national representation it aims to be" (464). While the resulting hybridity that Corona identifies in these GTA-mods might be unintentional or even unwanted in those mods, in *Grim Fandango* it is a clear motif of the game. The players' perception of the Land of the Dead as a hybrid of Latin America and the U.S. indeed appears to be one of its implied readings.

Refraining from a 'simple' digital mimesis, *Grim Fandango* transforms well-known landmarks or whole neighborhoods and latinizes them by altering their shape. The first street that the player enters, for example, appears to be directly rendered after a picture of the Meatpacking District – including the typical red brick houses, the iron fire escape ladders, and wooden rooftop water towers. Yet this impression only lasts for the duration of a first glance. By placing several markers of indigenous culture in this urban setting, such as obelisks and buildings that call to mind Mesoamerican temples and step pyramids, the game generates a hybrid city that is at once U.S.-American and Latinx as well as modern and pre-Columbian. The game further emphasizes this hybridization via another architectural marker of indigenous American culture – ornaments embedded in the outer walls of skyscrapers that depict monsters or animal faces based on indigenous stonemasonry and artworks such as the Maya calendar.[9] This Mesoamerican artwork features iconographic faces of animals, deities, or humans of religious or mythological significance engraved or chiseled into them. The major-

---

[9] The artist Peter Chan, who was responsible for a lot of the original artwork and design in the game, features some of this work on his website, available online at www.peterchanconceptart.com.

ity of buildings in the game feature such signifiers and thus immensely contribute to its particular (hybrid) atmosphere.

At first glance, one might argue that the constant usage of these icons and symbols by the non-Latinx developer team presents a form of exoticism, or just plain commodification of indigenous culture. Following the comparatist Joseph Theodoor Leerssen's definition, exoticism is the appreciation of another culture but "exclusively in terms of its strangeness; it is reduced to the aspects wherein it differs from the domestic standard" (325). In other words, exoticism is a process of reduction of complexity comparable to that of stereotyping or Othering.[10] In *Grim Fandango*, however, the depiction of indigenous symbols seems crucial to the creation of a game experience which transports a complex vision of Latinoness and recreates a positive hybrid U.S.-Latinx identity. Thus, *Grim Fandango* does not use Latinx culture to Other but provides an actual hybrid game world – which can positively affect the auto- as well as the hetero-image of the Latinx population.[11] This is in stark contrast to most contemporaneous, and even contemporary, video games which tend to focus on either the image of the luchador[12] or the stereotypical figure of the Latino gangster. Despite the stereotypical nature of this figure, most producers of action titles resort to this stereotype in a harmful attempt at 'authenticating' their product.

In addition to creating a hybrid cityscape, *Grim Fandango* also generates a hybrid pan-Latinx identity through its use of language. The first instance of this hybridity already occurs in the game's title, which is a compound of the English word *grim*, as in the Grim Reaper (Manny's job), and the Spanish word *fandango* which is the name of a song and dance originating from the Iberian Peninsula. The title thus combines the Anglo-American version of personified death with the Latinx couple dance. While death is a male figure in many Western mythologies and religions (for example, in Greek mythology or Christianity), in those based on Roman languages, it is most commonly a female figure, matching

---

[10] 'Othering' is a part of the process of identity construction, in which the self is defined by demarcation from a supposed 'Other' (see Hall 128). However, by Othering an individual or a group of people their status is subjugated from that of subjects to mere objects and as such they cannot participate in the discourse that negotiates their identity and position within society (see Pickering 71).
[11] Those terms refer to the perception of a group or nation from within (auto-image) and from the outside (hetero-image). For a detailed description of the comparatist understanding of the terms see Beller and Leerssen (343).
[12] A Latinx wrestler or *luchador* character, which are easily identifiable by their typical mask, can be found in almost every Fighting Game (such as the *Street Fighter* or *Tekken* series) but also in the Metroidvanian *Guacamelee! 1* and *2* in which the player takes over the role of the luchador Juan Aguacate to save the day.

the feminine gender of its Spanish designation, *la muerte*. The term *fandango* appears to be equally equivocal and has come to connote more than just a specific dance in Texas and California "[s]ince at least the early eighteenth century" (Castro 103). In the context of Chicana/o culture, the word describes a public place for a party or dance as well as gambling. Thus, the establishments that offered their patrons the opportunity to gamble, dance, and have a party were called "*fandango* houses" (Castro 104; emphasis in the original). The game's narrative more or less directly refers to both meanings of the word. Not only does Manny run a casino or *fandango* house during his time in Rubacava, the romantic dance for two could also be interpreted as a metaphorical description of Manny's quest to find Meche and the evolving love story between them.

Another detail which fosters this sense of hybrid identity on an auditive level in the original English-language version of the game is the repeated insertion of Spanish phrases into the mainly English utterances of the characters. This clearly marks their Latinx background. At the same time, those utterances are still easily decipherable for players who do not speak the language, which plays a large role in regard to the marketability of the game. The fact that Manny is voiced by the Cuban American actor Antonio 'Tony' Plana – who played in ABC's *Ugly Betty*, *CSI*, *Deep Space Nine*, and numerous other shows and movies – further underlines the mixture of several Latin American cultures that are combined in the game's inclusive vision of pan-*latinidad*. An additional auditive marker of this pan-Latinx identity is the pan flute motive appearing several times in the score, titled "Ninth Heaven," which is a clear reference to South American music from the Andean regions of Peru and Bolivia. In addition, the score also includes elements of Jazz and Swing music, both originally U.S.-American genres. With its music as well as its dialogues, the game amalgamizes various national influences on an auditory level, thus conveying yet another facet of Latinx and U.S.-American hybridity.

One of the characters who embodies the game's specific version of hybrid *latinidad* is Manny's sidekick Glottis. The non-player character (NPC) is depicted as a large yellow creature with a dog-like face and a profound love for automobiles, which fits his job as Manny's driver and mechanic. Only with the help of this NPC sidekick can the player travel from one stage to another. And, like every good sidekick, Glottis provides comic relief throughout the game. The character's appearance is directly inspired by U.S.-American hot-rod culture and in particular by Rat Fink and other monsters designed by Ed 'Big Daddy' Roth, one of the most famous hot-rod cartoonists. This reference to Ed Roth's comic hot-rod creatures is emphasized, when the large yellow dog-monster builds a hot-rod called the 'bone-wagon,' with flames painted on the sides of the car and a large chrome exhaust – which fits the way "in which young [working class] people modified or 'hot rodded' the cars of domestic brands and raced them" (Gartman 172–173) in California starting in the 1940s. Indeed, the character combines this typical U.S.-American hot-rod culture with pre-Columbian mythology in the form of the Aztec deity *Xolotl*.[13] The word *Xolotl* stems from the language Nahuatl and translates to "divine dog" (Carrasco and Sessions 48). The character's intertextual connection to the Aztec deity becomes apparent when looking at their functions in their respective narratives. *Xolotl* is a deity connected to death and the underworld, where he helps the dead to reach the next world across a seven-armed river, comparable to the five rivers in the ancient Greek underworld, Hades. In Aztec mythology, it is also *Xolotl*'s task to guide and guard the sun on its journey through the underworld every night, "so that it may exit the Underworld and be reborn each morning" (Maffie 207). Like his Mesoamerican predecessor, Glottis accompanies Manny on his travel through the Land of the Dead, the underworld, and helps him to reach the next stage of existence.

As yet another direct reference to Aztec philosophy, *Grim Fandango*'s plot unfolds over four years on four consecutive Days of the Dead. In Aztec and other Mesoamerican peoples' belief systems there are several spheres of existence, split up into three main stages. In this system *Mictlan* is the name of the underworld – a space the soul has to traverse to reach heaven. The Aztecs believed that this journey takes a soul four years; the same time that it takes Manny to complete his adventure and leave the Land of the Dead behind.[14] The Day of the Dead, however, is not only the major topos of the game and an important festivity for large parts of the Latinx community in the United States, it also is a prime example for the hybridity of cultures and their constantly changing nature. The holiday itself is based on the veneration of a family's deceased members, which is common in numerous Latin-American cultures and can be traced back to pre-Columbian times. Media studies scholar Regina Marchi

---

13 One of the depictions of the deity with a dog's head can be found in the Codex Fejérváry-Mayer, named after the Hungarian collector Gabriel Fejérváry and the English antiquarian Joseph Mayer, who owned the artefact. Today the codex is kept at the World Museum in Liverpool. The archeologists Maarten Jansen and Gabina Aurora Pérez Jiménez argue in favor of renaming the calendar document as Codex Tezcatlipoca after the deity that is depicted in the center of its first page (see 61). Such a renaming process could be read as a powerful anti-colonial sign, shifting the attention back to the indigenous culture that created the artefact and away from the colonizing power that still possesses it.

14 The only exception to this rule were warriors who died in battle and mothers who died during childbirth, they directly reached heaven, called *topan* or *ilhuicatl* (although in Aztec mythology the concept is separated into 13 distinctive forms of heaven). The middle world, inhabited by the living, is called *cemanahuatl* or *tlalticpac*. For a detailed account of the various stages of existence of the Aztec philosophy, see Maffie.

explains the handling of death, which interconnects and integrates the world of the dead into the day-to-day life of the living, as follows:

> In the worldview of the Aztecs, Maya, Olmecs, Mixtecs, Zapotecs, Aymara, Quechua, and other agricultural-based aboriginal peoples of the Americas, maintaining harmony between the worlds of the living and the dead was a crucial spiritual belief before the arrival of Europeans to the hemisphere. Festivals to honor the dead via the construction of harvest altars were held throughout the calendar year in conjunction with harvest cycles, as the dead were thought to have powers to enhance or thwart agricultural and reproductive fertility. (276–277)

El Día de los Muertos also incorporates Catholic traditions that were brought to the Americas by Spanish colonizers and missionaries and that were forced upon the indigenous population.[15] In their contemporary form, the celebrations present an amalgamation of Catholic holidays with the particularly indigenous form of worshiping the deceased. It is particularly noteworthy that, "[i]n contrast to official All Saints' Day and All Souls' Day observances, filled with thoughts of suffering and mournful supplications to free souls from their purgatorial incarceration, Day of the Dead celebrations in Indigenous regions of Latin America manifest feelings of happy reunion between heavenly and terrestrial relatives" (Marchi 277).

Another marker for the hybrid nature of modern Day of the Dead festivities is their contemporary form of street processions – closely resembling U.S.-American celebratory parades such as the Macy's Thanksgiving Day Parade in New York City or the Mardi Gras Parade in New Orleans. These processions are a comparably new invention of Latinas and Latinos within the United States. In most Latin American countries people used to celebrate by visiting the graveyard and bringing special foods and drinks as offerings to enjoy with their family or by building altars with fresh or hand-cut paper marigolds to honor the deceased. The flowers are believed to help guide the souls on their way from the Land of the Dead to the realm of the living with their bright color and their strong scent.[16] However, as Marchi points out, "United States Day of the Dead events

---

[15] The Catholic Church regularly used existing religious places, practices, and festivities and incorporated or rather re-labelled them and thus facilitated the transition of the indigenous people from their original beliefs to Christianity in Europe as well as in the Americas and the rest of the world. This specific strategy of Christianization is known as *Interpretatio Christiania* (see Eberlein).

[16] Marchi emphasizes the importance of these activities in strengthening the community's cohesion: "In Latin America, rituals such as refurbishing gravesites, constructing altars, or preparing special foods for the holiday require the collaboration of extended networks of family and

are not simply Latin American celebrations transferred to a new location. They are hybrid formations that communicate vastly different meanings than do celebrations with the same name in Latin America" (274). She traces this transformation and the intertwined rise in popularity of the holiday in the U.S. back to the year 1972. In that year, Chicana/o artists and activists in San Francisco and in East Los Angeles were the first to organize processions, in which they dressed as skeletons and marched to the nearest cemetery (see Marchi 281). The Californian Chicana/o activists further developed the existing traditions not only to create group cohesion within their communities but also to popularize their culture and festivities among the rest of U.S.-American society.[17]

Today, the festive processions draw a heterogeneous crowd from all ethnic groups in the U.S. and have even been exported back to numerous Latin American countries.[18] Mexico City, for example, did not have a Day of the Dead parade before 2016. Only after the opening sequence of the James Bond movie *Spectre* (2015) had imagined such festivities in Mexico City, which were up to that point primarily found within the United States, did city planners identify the potential of such a parade to attract tourists and generate revenue. In addition, these developments embody the constant hybridization of societies as well as the travelling of cultural practices accelerated through the media. In this vein, the Day of the Dead processions constitute a case of 'Latinization' of American mainstream but simultaneously also a case of 'Americanization' of mainstream culture in Latin American countries.

Conclusion

The version of a pan-Latinx identity, which *Grim Fandango* iterates, can be read as relativizing national backgrounds, which is not an unproblematic stance regarding assimilation and loss of culture, or as Latinx studies scholars Clara Ira-

---

friends who come together to pray for the deceased, visit each other's altars to pay respects to the dead, share festive food, and reaffirm collective identity and solidarity" (284).

17 The historian Eric Hobsbawm identified the process of inventing new traditions as a means of generating solidarity for a certain group. Hobsbawm further pointed out the tendency within these social processes to incorporate older traditions or to refer to "history as a legitimator of action and cement of group cohesion" (12).

18 Marchi specifies the rising popularity of the Day of the Dead procession in San Francisco today as "attract[ing] an estimated 20,000 participants spanning all ages, races, and ethnicities – making it the largest Day of the Dead processions in the United States. The procession is not only pan-Latino, but Pan-American, reflecting the many diverse cultures coexisting in San Francisco (and the United States)" (282).

zábal and Ramzi Farhat describe it, the "homogenization of [...] communities" (221). Despite those dangers, Irazábal and Farhat strongly argue in favor of this interpretation of *latinidad* in a U.S.-American context, stressing its community-building potential:

> In general, the further consolidation of a post-national or pan-Latino identity has been a boost to the fortunes of urban Latinos. This convergence, in many ways, reflects the fact that Latino communities in the United States face common challenges such as coming to terms with Americanization, developing a sense of citizenship, enduring the migratory experience, and positively utilizing aspects of transnational memory and identity [...] Predictably, this has enabled the formation of a larger, more visible group that can better gain recognition and entitlements from the state. (220)

The implicit complications of a pan-Latinx identity should not be left unmentioned: tensions between groups within a larger "imagined community" (Anderson 6) such as among Latinx people in the U.S. persist and will not be resolved by a video game – a task it is not fit to fulfill nor sets out to accomplish.[19] It is arguable, however, whether these limitations outweigh the positive ramifications an "immersive [gaming] experience" (Penix-Tadsen 176) can have for the process of identity construction for members of the in- *and* out-group – that is players that would consider themselves to be Latinx as well as players who affiliate with another ethnic identity.

Along these lines, I further argue that in spite of issues regarding exoticism and cultural appropriation, *Grim Fandango* construes a hybrid version of *latinidad* that incorporates Latinx and U.S.-American traditions in a pan-Latinx or even pan-American gaming experience that is unique in its medium. While the line between appropriation and celebration of a culture can be a thin one, particularly when the cultural artifact is also a product which is designed to generate profit, as it is the case with video games, it would be wrong to assume that this artifact cannot be efficacious in regard to a group's identity construction just

---

[19] I am using Benedict Anderson's term here, who argues that every nation is an 'imagined community,' due to the fact that it is impossible to know each and every member of that group: "In an anthropological spirit, then, I propose the following definition of the nation: it is an imagined political community – and imagined as both inherently limited and sovereign. It is *imagined* because even the members of the smallest nation will never know most of their fellow-members, meet them, or even hear of them, yet in the minds of each lives the image of their communion [...] In fact, all communities larger than primordial villages of face-to-face contact (and perhaps even these) are imagined" (6, emphasis in the original). The word *imagined* in this context obviously does not denote that a community is not 'real.' Indeed, imagined communities are bound through shared common values, language, norms, and, of course, narratives.

because it has been produced within a capitalistic system. In this vein, the game can be interpreted as a positive factor in the complex process of identity construction of Latinas and Latinos in the U.S. by generating group cohesion comparable to Day of the Dead celebrations and other shared traditions. Of course, this happens within the limits of its medium, but especially when keeping in mind the demographics of gamers in the U.S., who are to a large percentage Latinx, the role of video games in this process of (re-)negotiating identity should not be underestimated. Simultaneously, *Grim Fandango* can contribute to a positive hetero image held by other ethnic groups in the country and elsewhere as one of the few non-stereotypical representations of *latinidad* in video games.

Ideally, the game might further have a continuing impact on its genre and particularly on the way in which ethnicity is (re-)constructed in video games. In its creation of an immersive hybrid U.S.-American and Latinx world, it sets a positive example by managing to do without simplistic stereotypes and Othering. As has been demonstrated, the game generates this hybridity through, among other things, its characters. For instance, those characters fuse Aztec mythology with U.S. subculture, as is the case with Glottis. Also contributing to this hybridity are the game's auditory elements. The score, for example, consists of a mixture of typical U.S.-American elements as well as Latinx elements, including pan-flute music, which is a clear reference to musical traditions stemming from the Andean region of South America, as well as Jazz and Swing music. Possibly one of the most immersive factors through which *Grim Fandango* realizes this hybrid world, however, is through its digital spaces. The player can explore the game's spaces and encounter sites and buildings that have markers of Latinx culture as well as markers of U.S.-American culture at all stages.

Works Cited

Aldama, Frederick Luis. "Getting Your Mind/Body *On:* Latinos in Video Games." *Latinos and Narrative Media: Participation and Portrayal*, edited by Frederick Luis Aldama, Palgrave, 2013, pp. 241–258.

Anderson, Benedict. *Imagined Communities: Reflections on the Origin and Spread of Nationalism*. Verso, 1983.

Beller, Manfred and Joseph Theodoor Leerssen. *Imagology: The Cultural Construction and Literary Representation of National Characters*. Rodopi, 2007.

Bhabha, Homi K. *The Location of Culture*. Routledge, 1994.

Carrasco, David and Scott Sessions. *Daily Life of the Aztecs: People of the Sun and the Earth*. Greenwood Press, 1998.

Castro, Rafaela G. *Dictionary of Chicano Folklore*. Abc-Clio, 2000.

Christopher, Nicholas. *Somewhere in the Night: Film Noir and the American City*. Shoemaker and Hoard, 2006.
Corona, Antonio. "Video Games." *The Routledge Handbook to the Culture and Media of the Americas*, edited by Wilfried Raussert, Giselle Liza Anatol, Sebastian Thies, Sarah Corona Berkin, and José Carlos Lozano, Routledge, 2020, pp. 462–467.
Davis, Mike. *Magical Urbanism: How Latinos Reinvent the US City*. Verso, 2000.
Eberlein, Johann Konrad. "Interpretatio Christiana." *Brill's New Pauly: Encyclopaedia of the Ancient World*, edited by Hubert Cancik, Helmuth Schneider, Christine Salazar, Manfred Landfester, and Francis Gentry, 2006, doi.org/10.1163/1574-9347_bnp_e1406540. Accessed 27 August 2020.
Gartman, David. *Auto Opium: A Social History of American Automobile Design*. Routledge, 1994.
Gómez-Peña, Guillermo. *Dangerous Border Crossers: The Artist Talks Back*. Routledge, 2000.
Hobsbawm, Eric. "Introduction: Inventing Traditions." *The Invention of Tradition*, 1983, edited by Eric Hobsbawm and Terence Ranger, Cambridge University Press, 2010, pp. 1–14.
Irazábal, Clara and Ramzi Farhat. "Latino Communities in the United States: Place-Making in the Pre-World War II, Postwar, and Contemporary City." *Journal of Planning Literature*, vol 22, no. 3, 2008, pp. 207–228.
Jansen, Maarten and Gabina Aurora Pérez Jiménez. *The Mixtec Pictorial Manuscripts: Time, Agency and Memory in Ancient Mexico*. Brill, 2011.
Maffie, James. *Aztec Philosophy: Understanding a World in Motion*. University Press of Colorado, 2014.
Marchi, Regina. "Hybridity and Authenticity in US Day of the Dead Celebrations." *The Journal of American Folklore*, vol. 126, no. 501, 2013, pp. 272–301.
Mastro, Dana, Elizabeth Behm-Morawitz, and Michelle Ortiz. "The Cultivation of Social Perceptions of Latinos: A Mental Models Approach." *Media Psychology*, vol. 9, no. 2, 2007, pp. 347–365.
Penix-Tadsen, Phillip. "Latin American Ludology: Why We Should Take Video Games Seriously (and When We Shouldn't)." *Latin American Research Review*, vol. 48, no.1, 2013, pp. 174–190.
Pickering, Michael. *Stereotyping: The Politics of Representation*. Palgrave, 2001.
Raab, Josef and Martin Butler. "Introduction: Cultural Hybridity in the Americas." *Hybrid Americas: Contacts, Contrast, and Confluences in New World Literatures and Cultures*, edited by Josef Raab and Martin Butler, LIT, 2008, pp. 1–18.
Silver, John. "The Myth of El Dorado." *History Workshop*, no. 34, 1992, pp. 1–15.
Williams, Dimitri, Nicole Martins, Mia Consalvo and James D. Ivory. "The Virtual Census: Representations of Gender, Race and Age in Video Games." *New Media and Society*, vol. 11, 2009, pp. 815–834.

Part III

Michael Nitsche
Breaking Worlds Three Ways

Like other cultural spaces, such as temples, theaters, or workplaces, video game spaces are both a creation and reflection of our human condition. The fact that they are enacted and culturally produced only emphasizes their importance. That is why we so often (and rightly) turn to cultural tropes to describe and discuss "narrative" spaces or "cinematic" worlds with "immersive" or "creative" qualities. Game worlds readily connect back to these fields and have been debated across and in-between them. Focusing on the moment of production of space, the jump off point for this section will be Performance Studies, a field that emerged as a discipline somewhat in parallel to the digital revolution. It grew out of related fields such as Communication, Drama Studies, and Anthropology and it centers on the productive activity of performing itself. In performance, it is the "act" that counts (see Schechner), and scholars often combine critical reflection on such an act with their own experimental exploration and social engagement. As a field, Performance Studies constantly adjusts to include new principles, such as mediation (see Auslander), digital technologies (see Dixon), or media theory (see Kember and Zylinska, "Creative Media"). Thanks to this flexibility Performance Studies stays interdisciplinary and easily transcends domain boundaries in practice. This – and the staunch focus on the action itself – recommends it as a powerful field of reference for Video Game Studies.

Video games' growing role in cultural production started at a demo day in 1958 at the Brookhaven National Laboratory when William Higinbotham invited visitors to play *Tennis for Two* and it has exponentially exploded since. From the sprawling game worlds of open world AAA blockbusters to the re-imagination of physical worlds through GPS and locative devices to the introduction of Augmented and Virtual Reality, gamespaces take countless forms and reach ever wider audiences. To expand the notion of space in video games, however, this essay will not attempt a purely historic breakdown. Instead, it will step through three examples from past experiments in virtual and hybrid spaces to isolate key points of performative space in video games. Those themes are opened up in the hope that they can reflect some of the theory discussions behind debates on

---

Note: The projects mentioned in this chapter were conducted at or collaborations involving the Digital World & Image Group. They received funding from: Informatix Inc of Tokyo (for *Mindstage*), Google, and GVU/ Georgia Tech (for *UrbanRemix*), and the NEH (#PR-253380–17) (for *Archiving Performative Objects*). Any views, findings, conclusions, or recommendations expressed in this essay do not necessarily reflect those of the supporting institutions.

https://doi.org/10.1515/9783110675184-014

video game spaces by connecting them back to Performance Studies. The goal, here, is to emphasize the diversity of approaches toward game worlds and highlight the value of gamespaces for academic critique, experimentation, and media philosophy alike.

The narrative loosely follows a historic timeline in its three-step argument. It starts from an exploratory mind-space, built to support mnemonic structures through spatial design. These designs are compared to the workshop format in performance, building on Schechner. As examples for research through design, they focus on experimentation and allow for the development of concepts that probe new and emerging spatial and interaction designs. Spatial design itself is malleable and experimental. Second, we turn to socially constructed spaces supported by locative media. These environments still utilize game design structures but emphasize the shared making of space through social interaction in particular contexts. The notion of trajectories, adapted from Benford and Giannacchi, helps to shine a light on this integration of physical and virtual spaces through media design. Finally, we look briefly at spaces that build on a more-than-human principle. Puppetry and material performance serve as guides into a view of gamespaces that are not centered on the human alone anymore but merely include them in their operations. Relating to Bell's work on material performance, we look at the role of gamespaces and their design for the material turn.

Along these three steps, the story roughly identifies a focus on the promises of the mind, one on the social production, and one on the turn to new materialism. Each step will be supported by one short example project from the author's research group to consolidate the more conceptual points. The three central points are ultimately accumulative and should not be understood as conceptual divisions. They are presented here to exemplify the richness and different perspectives toward gamespaces. As such, they do not attempt any concluding answers but try to sketch opportunities in a field that is ever expanding with the growth of the underlying art form.

Workshops

The idea of game worlds as mnemonic spaces is not new. It was one of the promises suggested by cyberspace visionaries to design worlds accessible to everyone, equally supporting all without regard of social barriers of any kind, forming a deterritorialized knowledge space as "civilization's new horizon" (Levy 8). These spaces offered a malleability that allowed for exciting new opportunities that were embraced enthusiastically.

Mindstage (2003–04) was a project that centered on a lecture given by the British production designer Christopher Hobbs and implemented by Paul Richens, Michael Nitsche, and Jonathan MacKenzie with advice from Maureen Thomas at the Digital Studios at the University of Cambridge – almost 20 years ago. Christopher Hobbs worked, among many other titles, on the BBC's *Gormenghast* series, one of their most ambitious projects at the time. He shared his knowledge on set design through an extensive lecture that used videos as well as still images to develop key concepts such as the use of perspective or texture in film design. The *Mindstage* project aimed to take this linear presentation and translate it into a virtual space for visitors to explore and interact with. Based on a recording of his talk, we designed various environments for the central themes of his talk. Each of them anchored particular subjects in designated spatial constructs. A section on Gothic-inspired film design included 3D models and videos of Ridley Scott's *Blade Runner* (1982) and – at the same time – was hosted in a cathedral-inspired game level. The surrounding world design itself was part of the means of communicating Hobbs' core topics. In that way, *Mindstage* provided a combination of a mind palace and a virtual museum tour through Hobbs' talk (see Nitsche and Richens). It featured the videos and still images he would use in a regular presentation and arranged them in the 3D spaces. But it also included customized architectural design that allowed visitors to step into a set, a range of evocative objects such as virtual reconstructions of miniature shots or additional material, such as screenplay excerpts. All of these were open to visitors to explore and play with as they follow the talk through its spatial progression from topic to topic. It even experimented with multiplayer options and spatial notations that visitors could mark for themselves along their individual explorations. The overall design exploration combined concepts of narrative space (see Jenkins, Thomas and Penz) with educational functions. Around the same time, the online world of *Second Life* launched, which quickly grew into a lively virtual space full of rapidly changing spatial constructs formed by its users. These included educational spaces and at some conferences, the question was posed why dinosaur systems such as brick and mortar universities still try to stand against the tide of the times which obviously was drawing us into ever-more elaborate immersive 3D places to teach and learn.

We see virtual heritage projects and even commercial game titles, such as *Assassin's Creed Odyssey* (Ubisoft 2018) that include educational tours in virtual landscapes. But when the Covid pandemic hit in 2020 and educational institutions all over the world had to rely on digital teaching, they largely turned to video meetings. Video streaming has proven far more efficient, and these kinds of custom-built environments are left to large institutes or have gone the way of the procedural. But that does not devalue the need for experimental

Fig. 1: Mindstage (Richens, Nitsche, MacKenzie) sample view of the "Gothic" section.

Fig. 2: Start of the lecture and avatar selection.

spaces such as *Mindstage* or the unhinged story of *Second Life*'s online universe. Building and exploring a virtual mind space such as *Mindstage* offers a valuable design experiment, a look into the possibilities of game worlds and players' cognitive connections to them. We need to build experimental spaces like these that test the sometimes-preposterous promises associated with game worlds to expand, evaluate, and re-think their designs. These worlds might not deliver as products on a large scale, but they are irreplaceable research through design instances. They are not a critical look back at existing virtual landscapes but an experimental step forward in pushing their boundaries. By definition, these instances are not conclusive, but they are productive as prototype research endeavors. A long history of research through design in Human Computer Interaction (HCI) attests to the necessity of such probing work (see Zimmerman, Forlizzi, and Evenson) and supports their role as necessary petri dishes for the development of new design and interaction principles.

In terms of performance practice, these instances are not the main act. These are earlier stages of what Schechner termed "proto-performance" (225). In this proto stage, we train, build, experiment, rehearse. The format of such experimentation is the workshop. As Schechner explains,

> [t]he workshop is a way of playing around with reality, a means of examining behavior by reordering, exaggerating, fragmenting, recombining, and adumbrating it. The workshop is a protected time/space where intra-group relationships may thrive without being threatened by intergroup aggression. In the workshop special gestures arise, definite sub-cultures emerge. The workshop is not restricted to theater, it is ubiquitous. In science, it is the 'experimental method' the laboratory team, the research center, the fieldwork outpost. In psychotherapy, it is the "group," the rehabilitation center, the "therapeutic community." In living styles, it is the neighborhood, the commune, the collective. (68–69)

We need such workshop-like space explorations because the way we encountered digital spaces was not comparable to the discovery of a new land – even though it is sometimes portraited as such. These were not pre-existing ecosystems that we would colonize. Instead, we designed the spaces as we moved into them. The operation of these spaces might depend on very real material conditions, such as power grids, CPU performance, or network speeds but the procedural logic of these spaces is left to us. The spatial constructs and interaction design for *Mindstage*, as well as those of countless other game worlds that live in this experimental approach, emerged through the practice of design, implementation, and through iteration and experimentation. In these cases, the construction of space is part of the experiment. The process is "reordering, exaggerating, fragmenting, recombining, and adumbrating" gamespace. It is integrating spatial design and practice into the explorative nature of a workshop. We built these laboratories and allowed for the emergence of sub-cultures and "special gestures." Foundational questions such as whether movement in a virtual world should be conducted by linear progression or teleportation, whether virtual visitors can communicate with each other or not, whether one can step through walls or not, which visual perspective one might take in relation to the game universe – remain open in game worlds and they all require our design explorations.

This design work was part of a spatial workshopping. We built explorative spaces and experiences within them, provided for emergent play practices in a shared workshop setting, where space itself was not a given but a variable to explore. Much like actors develop roles, behavior, and conflict in a performance workshop, we developed narrative space, educational mind spaces, and community spaces to engage with. Not unlike actors who work on their relationship to a role, we enter the spaces we designed, experience them, alter and iterate them. The design, implementation, and encounter with these worlds opens up the opportunities within this new form. Some of those experiments were lucid (like the cyberspace dreams of a society living away from the bodies in eternal equality), some were dystopian (there are countless end-of-world scenarios), but they all combined dynamics of spatial and behavioral designs in the making of such worlds to envision our possible futures within them.

Trajectories

The second sample case, *UrbanRemix* (2010–2012), was a collaboration with my colleagues at Georgia Tech, Jason Freeman and Carl DiSalvo. The project centered on the use of locative sound for hybrid performances. Unlike the experi-

Fig. 3: UrbanRemix (DiSalvo, Freeman, Nitsche) mixing sound on Google maps.

Fig. 4: Recording on Times Square.

mental workshop worlds that readily re-arranged and re-invented virtual gamespaces, *UrbanRemix*'s focus on locative media rooted the project in the already existing surroundings of physical environments. Its main technical components were a cellphone app and a customized Google map visualization (see Freeman, DiSalvo, Nitsche, and Garrett). The app and the online visualization were freely available but most *UrbanRemix* events involved workshops with specific communities. In these events, we would provide an introduction to the project and distribute Android devices pre-loaded with the app to the participants. Then, participants would use the *UrbanRemix* app to collect sounds and images from the immediate surroundings. These sounds would later be re-used in different performance pieces. Usually, each workshop ended with a live performance where a local musician would mix the sounds collected in a public music performance on location. A second instance of the remixing was performed by the workshop participants themselves.

Workshop participants would scavenge for sounds, record them with the app, and upload them to a central server. Their uploads included the GPS coordinates of each sound source and we used this information for a form of spatial remixing. Each sound source was automatically positioned on a Google map according to its real-world locations. In that way, each workshop generated a cacophony of sound markers spread all over a particular neighborhood. The sound was mapped from the participants' daily "lived" space onto a digital map.

Once this map was populated with all the sounds collected in the particular event, participants could mix their own sound walks across the digital landscape using this map. Drawing a path across the map would define a spatial-acoustic walk through the spatialized sound markers. It defined a soundtrack as much as a virtual passage through the mapped space. Playing with a traversal of mapped space included playing with a journey through the acoustic space produced by the field recordings and any virtual path turned into a sound mix. The project included a number of additional components, such as looping, or on-location mixing of sound that used the orientation of the cell phone, but here we will focus on the recording and re-use of sounds in the virtual map space. As participants laid out their acoustic paths across the map, defined their loops, and mixed them together in a kind of virtual map exploration, they experimented with the digital space designed and provided for them in advance. At the same time, they re-encountered their own daily environments anew.

The spatial construct itself was not as malleable as the virtual game worlds discussed above. Instead, the project is an example of dynamic "trajectories" as suggested by Benford and Giannacchi. They develop the concept of trajectories in a discussion of their own work, which often included other forms of locative media in collaboration with *Blast Theory*. Trajectories are formed as a designer provides the means to connect across hybrid structures, but any realization of such a connection depends on the activity of participants and how they actually experience the hybrid spaces and the events that unfold in a mixed reality performance: "The foundation of this theory is that we can express how artists design, and participants experience, mixed reality performance in terms of multiple interleaved trajectories through complex hybrid structures of space, time, interfaces, and roles that establish new configurations of real and virtual, local and global, fact and fiction, personal and collective" (Benford and Giannachi 1).

This approach is not about the infinite malleability of digital space but about designing interdependencies. We encounter the hybrid space, interweave the available components through the interaction design made possible by the developers, and form our own pathways through the events and conditions. The results of these pathways are trajectories. Benford and Giannachi list space, time, interface, and role as forming an "own particular ecology" (229) that one traverses. This movement – often quite literally a physical movement – creates trajectories which interconnect the different layers. In the case of *UrbanRemix*, the relationships between the mapped sound sources, their physical origin spaces, and the virtual pathways/ loops that can be arranged on the map form such trajectories.

Benford and Giannachi emphasize that a key quality of these trajectories is coherence (see 230). But coherence is not given, it is constructed through the interaction. Because these spaces include our physical environments infused by our daily lives and because their design interweaves them with digital layers, we are dealing with an alteration of lived social space. The results cannot be detached from a pre-existing spatial ecology, but they can form their own combined histories. Accordingly, Benford and Giannachi differentiate between canonical (designer-implemented), participant (player-realized), and historic trajectories (recorded-and-play-back of a performance). Mapping out possible trajectories is messy business (see Benford and Giannachi 238–242) but in their turn to "historic trajectories" we already see the construction of social spaces and the emergence of a canon through activity. These spaces inscribe themselves onto the existing ones through the emerging trajectories.

In this second instance of gamespace iterations, the temporary magic circles of the workshop spaces collide with existent spatial practices. These spaces have to deal with given limitations and recognize their dependencies.

UrbanRemix opened up existent spaces to the participants of the various events. They might re-encounter spaces that were lost or hidden from their awareness. One student in an event at New York's Times Square "discovered" the sound of a fountain near their school building. Even though they had passed this fountain countless times before, it took the special condition of the *UrbanRemix* event to realize the presence of that water feature. The design of the project had changed the role of the student from a commuter on their way to school to a neighborhood explorer. It created an opening for a spatial discovery that unfolded in the recording and in the subsequent remixing. But at the same time, the recorded pieces have a "historic" trajectory. One of the first events conducted for *UrbanRemix* happened along the Atlanta Beltline, a huge development area that is currently an open access park-like sprawl but that will eventually include a new transit rail line surrounding central Atlanta. The space is changing with the slow but ongoing development of the neighborhoods along this massive urban transportation project. When we conducted our workshop there it was largely a wild park and the sounds recorded for that event will differ from those days when trains will pass through the same location. They are confirmations of existing space realized by participants but growing into historic trajectories of the location and the time they are from.

In a trajectories-informed spatial encounter, play evolves from an experimental encounter and it contributes to social, spatial, and temporal construction. What started as the specialized – spatially distanced magic circle – becomes cultural production within and for the community. The construction of these spaces is consolidating. This consolidation is not a turning away from the physical space but an embrace of it. Critically reflecting on such consolidation is as important as it was to open these worlds up in the first place.

UrbanRemix was built on Google maps and ubiquitous computing via cellphone integration and networking. Part of its operation builds on the fact that the former novelty of Google maps has become a default for the way we encounter our cities and how we traverse them. Pathbreaking GPS technologies have become part of everyday life and their impact on our spatial experience is not a technological edge anymore but part of our daily lived environments. *UrbanRemix* extended this consolidation of the hybrid space into the acoustic space and inspires participants to create novel interconnections – trajectories – between them.

Posthuman

The *Center for Puppetry Arts* in Atlanta features multiple stages as well as a recently renovated museum that hosts – among many other puppets – a wide range of Jim Henson's *Muppets*. Like most archival spaces, it can only display a fraction of the material actually available in storage. *Archiving Performative Objects* (2017–19) aimed to digitize sample puppet objects to make them available as interactive 3D characters in online form as well as in Virtual Reality (VR). For this project, the team around Pierce McBride, Michael Nitsche, and Veronica Spencer 3D-scanned a range of historic puppets specially selected from the archive, optimized the 3D models for use in a real-time 3D engine, rigged them, textured them, and re-created their control mechanisms in a virtual game world. This turned historic hand puppets, marionettes, rod puppets, found objects, and shadow puppets into 3D objects that mimicked their performative qualities in virtual spaces. A version of one of the Center's stages was re-created as the main performance space to interact and play with these virtual puppet objects.

Even though the puppets and the virtual stage were modeled as close as possible to the existing material conditions, we cannot claim that we re-created the exact conditions. The digital versions lack force-feedback and most of the tactile details that a traditional puppet would provide. Controlling a virtual puppet is not the same as controlling its physical original. But it offers a remediation (see Bolter and Grusin) of traditional puppet control schemes to give users access to the manipulation of these objects. The project included various elements that dealt with archival access, such as a sample 3D web representation and object data storage, but here we will focus on the VR visualization of those puppet objects and their control mechanisms (see Nitsche and McBride).

The import of the historic puppets into VR and their interaction design focused on the accurate adaptation of their object qualities and their manipulation schemas into a digital condition. By definition, the design was not about the realization of the human expression but about empowering the cooperation of puppet object and human puppeteer.

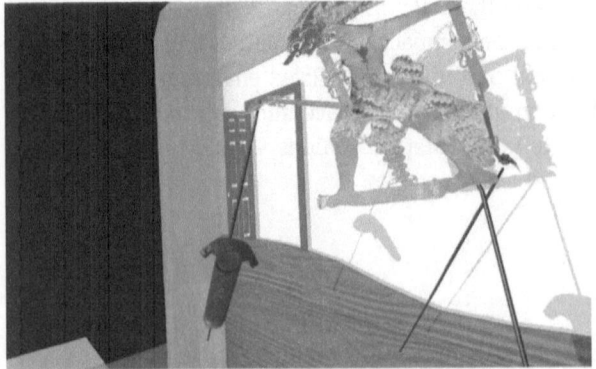

Fig. 5: Archiving Performative Objects (Nitsche and McBride) controlling a shadow puppet in VR.

Fig. 6: Example detail of textured puppet object.

Working with spaces for a third object – a puppet – transcends the construction of a social space as a space mainly for fellow humans. Puppetry lives in the collaboration of the human and the non-human, in the turn to the spaces in-between the two. Puppetry reminds us that the moment we incorporate our own bodies, we automatically incorporate the bodies of other things and beings. Looking at puppetry as a field, Bell argues, "first, that to understand puppetry is to understand the nature of the material world in performance; and second that the material world in performance is the dominant means by which we now communicate" (*American Puppet Modernism* 2). Following his turn to materialism, puppetry as a performative practice opens up our realization of game worlds as more-than-human.

It is largely accepted that game worlds require us to "enact" them and that this depends on a form of embodied interaction (see, for example, Dourish). Such embodied interaction always happens in context and in relation to one's surroundings. Yet, we still seem to focus on the "experience" and the "agency" of only the human actor in this web of interdependencies. Puppetry presents a more-than-human model in which "puppets and other material objects in performance bear visual and kinetic meanings that operate independently of whatever meanings we may inscribe upon them in performance" (Posner, Orenstein, and Bell 5). The materiality of a puppet is not simply supporting the human operations, but it has foundational functions in and of itself. The wood of a Pinocchio puppet, the fabric of a Kasperl hand puppet, the strings of a Harlequin marionette, the leather of a Wayang Kulit shadow puppet are all integral participants in the performance and in the creation of the performative enacted space. They produce a different kind of negotiation space, not one of an arena (as implied by the magic circle of an experimental workshop) or of a social space on location (as implied by locative media spaces) but one that fundamentally challenges the dominance of the human and shifts the attention to nonhuman participants.

Interpreting human interactions within gamespaces as a form of puppetry is not new. In fact, it was one of the earliest metaphors developed for Human Computer Interaction (see Walser) and it continues to shape our designs for game controls and controllers. This line of thought has followed an association via control schemes and representation in game worlds. It concerned the representation of the human body – as an avatar – in the game world or the design of the controllers – as ergonomically efficient input devices – in the hands of the player. In contrast, the material turn has made it clear that we also have to recognize the agency of every other contributing actor to the unfolding encounter. The puppet object is not a powerless tool for human expression but provides an active voice itself. "The essence of puppet, mask, and object performance (as countless puppeteers have said from their own experience) is not mastery of the material world," Bell notes, "but a constant negotiation back and forth with it. Puppet performance reveals to us that the results of those negotiations are not at all preordained and that human superiority over the material world is not something to count on, especially since *we* all eventually end up as lifeless objects" ("Playing with the Eternal Uncanny" 50).

Game worlds remain valuable performance spaces in this turn to the more-than-human space. They realize virtual puppets and their interaction design can emphasize the importance of Haraway's notion of response-ability between all active partners. This speaks to the turn to new materialism and the renegotiation of the human-non-human borderlines through performative qualities in these spaces. These spaces are not the setting for a representational event for humans to express themselves anymore, but every element in that situation becomes equal part of the unfolding performative construction process. For Barad, "[t]his will require an understanding of the nature of the relationship between discursive practices and material phenomena, an accounting of 'nonhuman' as well as 'human' forms of agency, and an understanding of the precise causal nature of productive practices that takes account of the fullness of matter's implication in its ongoing historicity" (810).

This integrates gamespaces into the debates inspired by feminist technoscience (see Haraway) and materialism in media studies (see Kember and Zylinska, *Life After New Media*). In this case, gamespaces like the virtual stage of *Archiving Performative Objects* provide unique qualities to inform the much-needed debate about a re-positioning of humanity's role. If the designs of workshop-inspired worlds emphasized our experiments in the expansion of human consciousness and the trajectories-based worlds realized social "lived space" in hybrid conditions, then these more-than-human spaces reduce the role of the human individual as well as that of the social community and emphasize material agency instead.

Fragments

This text set out to shine a light on some of the inherent richness in gamespaces and our critical encounters and experiments with them. It traced three different approaches and connected all of them to particular notions adapted from Performance Studies. First, the notion of gamespaces as part of a workshop event emphasized the experimental nature of our spatial design and novel experience in game worlds. In this case, spatial and functional designs are as important as experience and interaction. Space making is driven by a research through design philosophy that aims to push boundaries of cognitive engagement ever further. Second, the notion of gamespaces as entangled phenomena emerged from the trajectories that participants form as they traverse them. Here, the designed digital worlds are in direct dialogue with the lived-in spaces that we construct in our daily routines, which means that their operation is affected by those everyday world activities. In return, our digital environments shape the lived spaces they are connected to. Third, the essay examined the notion of gamespaces as performative realization of a new materialist inter-species and inter-material engagement. These worlds are not detached or representational anymore but form in the encounter of human and non-human contributors and can advance debates in Science and Technology Studies and media philosophy, which aim to adjust the role of the human in this world we live in. All three notions offer infinite levels of depth within themselves. All three are accumulative and non-exclusive. The experimental workshop vision might ultimately feed into a more-than-human space design, just as the material-focused vision always includes the construction of social space. Breaking space across these three axes does not fragment game worlds but only shows three example lenses in a rich multi-prism of approaches to game worlds. They offer three fragments of different perspectives that help us to discuss gamespaces at large.

As every proposal for critical perspectives does, this one only produces more problems, more open challenges. The three sample projects, *Mindstage*, *Urban-Remix*, and *Archiving Performative Objects* were covered only in parts but hopefully provided tangible examples to support the theoretical angles proposed here. It is one of the most powerful qualities of game worlds that they allow us an amazing degree of freedom to explore, after all this is why we created them in the first place.

Work Cited

Auslander, Philip. *Liveness: Performance in a Mediatized Culture.* 2nd ed., Routledge, 2008.
Barad, Karen. "Posthumanist Performativity: Toward an Understanding of How Matter Comes to Matter." *Signs*, vol. 28, no. 3, 2003, pp. 801–831.
Bell, John. *American Puppet Modernism: Essays on the Material World in Performance.* Palgrave Macmillan, 2008.
Bell, John. "Playing with the Eternal Uncanny: The Persistent Life of Lifeless Objects." *The Routledge Companion to Puppetry and Material Performance*, edited by Dassia N. Posner, Claudia Orenstein, and John Bell, Routledge, 2014, pp. 43–53.
Benford, Steven and Gabriella Giannachi. *Performing Mixed Reality.* The MIT Press, 2011.
Bolter, Jay David and Richard Grusin. *Remediation: Understanding New Media.* The MIT Press, 1999.
Dixon, Steve. *Digital Performance: A History of New Media in Theater, Dance, Performance Art, and Installation.* The MIT Press, 2007.
Dourish, Paul. *Where the Action Is: The Foundations of Embodied Interaction.* The MIT Press, 2001.
Freeman, Jason, Carl DiSalvo, Michael Nitsche, and Stephen Garrett. "Soundscape Composition and Field Recording as a Platform for Collaborative Creativity." *Organised Sound*, vol. 16, no 3, 2011, pp. 272–281.
Haraway, Donna J. *Staying with the Trouble: Making Kin in the Chthulucene.* Duke University Press, 2016.
Jenkins, Henry. "Game Design as Narrative Architecture." *First Person: New Media as Story, Performance, and Game*, edited by Pat Harrington and Noah Wardrip-Fruin, The MIT Press, 2004, pp. 118–131.
Kember, Sarah, and Joanna Zylinska. "Creative Media: Performance, Invention, Critique." *Interfaces of Performance*, edited by Maria Chatzichristodoulou, Janis Jefferies, and Rachel Zerihan, Ashgate, 2009, pp. 7–23.
Kember, Sarah, and Joanna Zylinska. *Life After New Media: Mediation as a Vital Process.* The MIT Press, 2021.
Levy, Pierre. *Collective Intelligence: Mankind's Emerging World in Cyberspace.* Plenum, 1997.
Nitsche, Michael and Pierce McBride. "Manipulating Puppets in VR." *2020 IEEE Conference on Virtual Reality and 3D User Interfaces, 22–26 March, 2020, Atlanta, GA*, IEEE, 2020, pp. 10–17.
Nitsche, Michael and Paul Richens. "Telling Stories through Space: The Mindstage Project." *Technologies for Interactive Digital Storytelling and Entertainment*, edited by Stefan Göbel, Rainer Malkewitz, and Ido Iurgel, Springer, 2006, pp. 61–71.
Posner, Dassia N., Claudia Orenstein, and John Bell, editors. *The Routledge Companion to Puppetry and Material Performance.* Routledge, 2014.
Schechner, Richard. *Performance Studies. An Introduction.* 2nd ed., Routledge, 2002.
Schechner, Richard. *Performance Theory.* Routledge, 2003.
Thomas, Maureen, and Francois Penz, editors. *Architectures of Illusion: From Motion Pictures to Navigable Interactive Environments.* Intellect, 2003.
Walser, Randy. "Elements of a Cyberspace Playhouse." *Proceedings of the National Computer Graphics Association*, 1990.

Zimmerman, John, Jodi Forlizzi, and Shelley Evenson. "Research through Design as a Method for Interaction Design Research in HCI." *Proceedings of the SIGCHI Conference on Human Factors in Computing Systems, April 2007, San Jose, CA*, edited by Mary Beth Rosson and David Gilmore, Association for Computing Machinery, 2007, pp. 493–502.

Maria Sulimma
Surviving the City: *Zombies, Run!* and the Horrors of Urban Exercise

Exercising in public, densely populated areas can be horrible for anyone – especially if one does not conform to narrow standards of athleticism; or if one's body is not granted the right to take up space. This chapter argues that a playful engagement with the formulaic narratives of the multimedia horror genre may make such horrors of urban exercise more bearable. I am interested in the ways the running app *Zombies, Run!* (*ZR*) enables its users to cognitively transcend their actual surroundings and to imagine running in a post-apocalyptic landscape infested by the living dead. The contribution proceeds through three stages: The first part introduces *ZR* and some of the complex cognitive maneuvers it requires its users to perform regarding space; the second part zooms in on a significant demographic of the game – female runners in urban spaces – and the empowering potentials the app carries for users struggling with harassment and scrutiny during their workout. Lastly, the contribution places *ZR* within the larger cultural phenomenon of zombie apocalypse preparedness – thereby, it complicates the possible empowerment of the app by situating it within a neoliberal framework of self-optimization.

Working out Zombies, Run!

First released in 2012 for iOS and Android smartphones, the app *ZR* is developed by independent game developer Six to Start. To many observers, the British app's success, particularly within a U.S.-American market, is indicative of a "Kickstarter revolution" (Walton) because the game was the most backed crowdfunding project in 2012. With almost 4 million downloads, the indie app is one of the highest-grossing apps in the category of Health and Fitness (see Hon "Five Years of Zombies, Run!"). It embeds the tracking functions of conventional running apps within an audio-based survival narrative set in a post-apocalypse storyworld in which the player has to run from zombies and gather supplies.[1]

---

[1] In addition to its roots in West African and Haitian folklore, the zombie as a cultural figure often takes on specific cultural meanings in U.S.-American popular culture. Following the films of cult director George A. Romero, most prominently *Night of the Living Dead* (1968), the U.S.-American zombie is taken as embodying a critique of capitalism and mass consumer cul-

https://doi.org/10.1515/9783110675184-015

Notwithstanding the collaborative production processes of electronic games, programmer Adrian Hon and novelist Naomi Alderman act the roles of creators or author figures for *ZR* – with Hon representing the technical side of the app, and Alderman taking credit for the creative, storytelling-related aspects of production. Alderman's feminist science fiction bestseller *The Power* (2016) further contributed to the success of the app. For *ZR*, the novel serves as an example of what media scholar Jonathan Gray calls an "entryway paratext" (10–11) because it leads readers to the exercise app and manages their initial expectations of the game, as I will explore in more detail in the second part.

Alderman prominently became a mentee of author Margaret Atwood through the Rolex Mentor and Protégé Arts Initiative in 2011. Atwood's own female-centric dystopian bestsellers include *The Handmaid's Tale* (1985), *The Year of the Flood* (2009), or *The Testaments* (2019). Atwood has a cameo in the episode "Canada" (2013) of *ZR*'s second season in which even tough survivalist Janine (Eleanor Rushton) turns into a babbling fangirl when speaking to Atwood in a radio transmission. This segment demonstrates the occasional humor and lightness of *ZR*, the ways the app imagines the cultural savviness of its users, and its self-aware position in popular culture.

> Janine: [laughs nervously] I suppose you never saw this coming, despite your many novels on potential future environmental apocalypses.
>
> Margaret Atwood: Novelists aren't soothsayers [....] we have some useful intel you may be able to deploy over there. We've discovered that the zombies respond very strongly to some Canadian pop music. They like Justin Bieber, but they can't stand Céline Dion!

But it is not only in regard to its production history, marketing, and intertextual references that *ZR* hits the cultural zeitgeist. The app further seems another instance of the much-proclaimed dynamic of gamification which our current culture appears to be increasingly following. A wide variety of apps utilize game-related pleasures to, for instance, help their users do their banking, drink more water, or even garden (see Haef's contribution in this volume). Because *ZR* seeks to gamify exercise habits – running or walking – it can be grouped within the genre of so-called exergames which begins with Konami's arcade hit *Dance Dance Revolution* (1998) and prominently includes various fitness installments of

---

ture: the mindless, shambling zombie is likened to the mindless consumer. While this cultural (after)life of the zombie is relevant for the app's appeal, as I have written elsewhere, "the zombie possesses infinite possibilities to become a cultural allegory. Academic research has struggled to pin down the zombie's proliferating cultural meanings and in the process appears to create ever new zombie metaphors" (Sulimma 200).

Nintendo's Wii, or *Pokémon Go* (2016). Countless studies in health sciences, medicine, or media studies are dedicated to the question of whether exergames lead to more active, healthier lifestyles; yet the verdict varies from study to study. What is more relevant for my purposes than this concern, is how exergames collectively brand physical exercise as boring and hard, as something that cannot be pleasurable of itself, and therefore, users need the game to make exercise fun or entertaining as well as easier to pursue.

Even though *ZR* is often likened to *Pokémon Go* (2016), it offers no augmented reality or even location-based gameplay. The app does not evolve with or react to locations in the physical world. Instead, it takes a rather minimalist approach to gaming: *ZR* is no cohesive game but an amalgamation of different components. The most prominent aspect of *ZR* is a serialized audioplay of eight seasons and 340 missions or episodes. These episodes consist of audio clips that are layered over the music that a user listens to through an external music player while running (see screenshot fig. 1). Each episode is tailored to last for roughly thirty minutes, making the app's total running time – as its creators proudly boasted on several occasions – much longer than that of the expansive television series *Game of Thrones* (2011–2019). The comparison with this show is fitting because *ZR*'s kind of audioplay is indeed reminiscent of serialized television shows, radio plays, or fictional podcasts series – with one significant exception: the app makes players 'earn their fun,' it requires the player to begin another episode/running session to find out how the story continues. Serialized media consumption thus is linked to regular, ritualized exercise. Unlike other examples of gamified practices, *ZR* seeks to make exercise entertaining by introducing users to the narrative scenario of the zombie apocalypse and by giving their exercise fictional purpose in the app's storyworld.

ZR complicates any clear differentiation between ludology and narratology that some parts of Game Studies are so hung up on (see Denson and Jahn-Sudmann for a helpful overview). Whether one accepts the contested notion of gamification for *ZR* or not, this exercise app's turn to gaming is only possible with a simultaneous turn to narrative. By this I mean that its kind of gamification goes hand in hand with what could be called a narratification or fictionalization of formerly non-fictional cultural artifacts and practices. In *ZR*, ludic pleasures and goals are inseparable from its emphasis on story: Human survivors form communities which depend on runners to gather resources, information, and lead away zombie hordes from their settlements. These runners, who have no supernatural abilities but are exceptionally athletic, are celebrated by their communities. Like athletes in team sports, the runners do not go by names but by assigned numbers. Their numbers contribute to the runners' iconic status but also to their expendability and replicability: The user of *ZR* takes up the perspec-

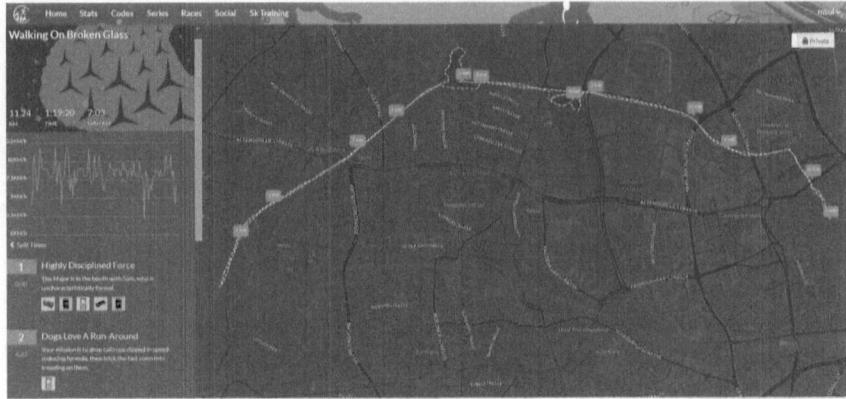

Fig. 1: This screenshot of my run in the city of Essen shows different segments of the audio-play and supplies collected at during the run.

tive of the silent, genderless, generic but charismatic Runner 5 who joins a settlement called Abel Township after the death of its previous Runner 5.[2] Playing this avatar, users of the app run missions, collect supplies, and uncover the secrets which surround spies from other settlements, the origins of and a possible cure for zombies as well as the evolution of different species of zombies. The app develops elements of alternate reality when items which the player automatically picks up during runs reveal email addresses or Twitter accounts, or characters send 'letters' to Runner 5 through the user's email address.

Because *ZR* relies exclusively on the auditory mode, users can keep running while listening and do not have to stop exercising to interact with the game manually. *ZR* thus finds a way to avoid one of the fundamental issues of exergames: how to incorporate plots when players may not be able to react to or process extensive narrative information during physical activities (see Lu 22). *ZR*'s audioplay transports all narrative information through the speech of other characters, either of other runners whom Runner 5 accompanies and encounters, or the various inhabitants of Able Township who communicate via headset with Runner 5 and employ radio transmission, scanners, or surveillance videos to inform the player of fictional surroundings and occurrences. Official social media accounts and fan art circulate visual illustrations of the large, diverse cast of characters

---

[2] Abel Township is a telling name in several ways. It emphasizes not only the (physical) abilities of the gamer (as able to run) but also – through a reference to the biblical Abel – the exceptional position of its inhabitants as the narrative's 'good guys.'

whom players otherwise only encounter via their voices. Among these characters, the settlement's communications operator, the sympathetic and nerdy Sam Yao (spoken by Phil Nightingale), stands out as the most frequent (homodiegetic) narrator instance.[3] It is Sam with whom the player interacts in the first episode, who names the player, and introduces them to the storyworld: "Hey, uh, listen ... I'm gonna call you Runner 5. Um, just 'cause ... well, I don't know your name, and we just lost a runner, in that same hospital you're running through now" ("Jolly Alpha Five Niner"). Because a user's run may be longer than an episode, after each mission Sam hands the mike to the Radio Abel DJ team, the gay couple Jack (Rhys Jennings) and Eugene (Nathan Nolan), who offer insight into life in Able Town and host the player's playlist.

Most users seem to prefer to use the apps' GPS mode over a time-based mode made for treadmill use because GPS allows for one of the app's most compelling, immersive components: zombie chases.[4] These chases provide interval running training; they occur two or three times an episode. When zombie growls are layered over the music a player is listening to, they have to pick up their speed by 20 percent to escape the zombies supposedly tailing them. However, Runner 5 is never in danger of dying, when zombies catch up to the player, the only punishment is dropping items collected – supplies necessary to build Abel Township. The effects of the zombie chases may also be unintentionally hilarious, for instance, when growling zombie sounds overlay an upbeat song.

Aside from the dominant audioplay, the app also includes a miniature sandbox game that allows players to put to use supplies they have automatically gathered during runs to build up Abel Township (see screenshot fig. 2). By completing different missions, players can unlock more features to build up their settlement and improve the lives of its population similar to classic city-building games such as *SimCity* (1989). The gaming pleasures of this component of *ZR* are remarkably different from the audioplay because the driving dynamic is not immediate survival and the uncovering of plot mysteries but the gradual re-

---

[3] Sam's name implies a British East Asian ethnicity and thus allows for an intertextual reference to another popular serialized zombie narrative: *The Walking Dead*. One of the central characters of the large cross-media franchise is charismatic Asian American Glenn Rhee who similarly uses radio transmission to save an unknown stranger, protagonist Rick, from zombies in early installments of the television show and comic book series.

[4] The app has expanded to serve various other running needs: Virtual races with standalone stories allow players to run a longer race within a specific time frame; the app *Zombies, Run! 5K* trains players to be able to run longer time spans and distances for the main app; and during the global COVID-19 pandemic, *ZR* released "The Home Front"-exercise missions for users in lock-down or quarantine.

Fig. 2: The user can build Abel Township from supplies gathered during runs.

building of society through the building of Abel. Aside from a defense tower, housing, or farms, players may choose an outdoor movie theater, a swimming pool, a tequila shack, a pottery kiln, or memorials for deceased fellow runners. The miniature Abel Town includes settings described by characters in the missions but does not depict any characters. This city without (visible) people is the counterpart to the audioplay's emphasis on characters describing surroundings for the player. Further, while the audioplay episodes by nature occur outside of Abel Township when Runner 5 embarks on various missions, this city building allows players to visually explore a space they otherwise have only heard of and yet are supposed to feel invested in protecting and improving.

Both the zombie chases and the city building component of *ZR* point to the interesting tension between visual space, that is a player's actual surroundings while running, the virtual or rather auditory space described by the characters during the missions, and the complex practices which users perform to reconcile these two spaces. For instance, scholars have sought to describe their changed perceptions of public spaces while using the app. Sociologist Emma Witkowski notes how

> moving with (and away from) zombies tuned my footwork and awareness toward the quirks and possibilities within local space, where straight pathways and regular running circuits were switched out for escape trails, unpopulated terrain, and eerie environments. My alertness and experience of geographical space was enriched through a playful attention toward moving through it. (154)

Theater studies scholar Kris Darby recalls a run in a graveyard as a similarly playful, but more self-conscious experience:

> I instinctively shut the gate behind me, ensuring that its catch was in place. Seeing someone in the distance, I quickly ducked behind a gravestone. On reflection, I am uncertain as to whether such an action was motivated by my fleeing of zombies or whether I was embarrassed about being caught in the act of roleplaying. (232)

These runners-cum-scholars' experiences demonstrate that *ZR* is not merely a non-interactive audiobook with gimmicky minor game components. Instead, by acoustically layering a narrative space on top of the player's actual surroundings, the app enables cognitive maneuvers that users perform to imagine themselves as runners within a dystopian zombie apocalypse. This does not mean that such maneuvers do not require significant cognitive efforts and are easily available to players. To help users project the storyworld onto their specific surroundings, the missions keep descriptions of spaces purposefully generic to allow for the cognitive transfer of the zombie apocalypse into as many settings as possible. Even though the app is a British production and the majority of characters have British accents, it only rarely makes explicit references to specific locales. Even though the setting of Abel Township is just outside of London, this narrative fact is seldom mentioned, and any references to buildings and landmarks are vague enough to work for most environments.

Despite such attempts at general spatial applicability, the app does appear tailored to urban or suburban runners. A trailer released in 2015 to promote season four exemplifies this because it visually showcases deserted postindustrial spaces, parking lots, and hypermodern corporate headquarters after business hours overlaid with soundbites from the app (see *Zombies, Run!*). Such an imagining of the surroundings which its users turn to when running with the app highlights the appeal of postindustrial and urban cityscapes as the most interesting backdrops for the story. Just as Witkowski describes in the above quote, users of the app may change their previous exercise routes to accommodate its narrative affordances in a playful manner. In the next section, I turn to the ways female runners make use of this playful appropriation of urban space as a simultaneous space of exercise and playing field to counter the sexualized hostility they encounter during runs in populated areas.

Running in the City "While Female"

Even though running is frequently hailed as the most democratic of sports – for requiring little equipment or a specialized skill set, like any sport, running is a particularly embodied activity effected by a person's intersectional situatedness in a society. Race, gender identity, socio-economic status, and many other factors influence how and possibly even if one runs. In general, black runners and runners of color encounter particular forms of discrimination and exclusion. For instance, sports scholarship has explored how distance running is constructed as a "white space" (Walton and Butryn 2, 4, et passim) in the cultural imaginary. The tragic case of Ahmaud Arbery, an African American runner who was attacked and murdered by two white supremacists while exercising in Georgia in February 2020, serves as a painful reminder of the white privilege connected to running. Arberry's death and the authorities' negligence in persecuting his murderers fueled the Black Lives Matter demonstrations in the summer of 2020 and the hashtag #IRunWithMaud which runners continue to use to express remembrance, solidarity, and – for black runners and runners of color – racialized experiences of running. Despite its characters of different ethnicities, ZR appears to be most popular with white players – but there is no robust data to support this impression.[5] In contrast with ZR's imagining of its users as ethnically diverse, discrimination impact runners differently. In the following, I want to think more about the specific experiences of white urban female runners as a demographic segment which prominently presents itself as players of ZR on social media.

Female runners often report various inconveniences, harassment, and assault which are mostly unheard of by white, cis-male runners. Best-known examples reach from the Boston Marathon organizers attacking Kathrine Switzer, the first woman to run the marathon in 1967, to the backlash against Kiran Gandhi

---

[5] Neither Six to Start nor the scholarship on ZR provides current statistics of who uses the app. Previously, female users slightly outweighed male users across almost all age groups (see Hon "Two Million Runners Five").

who 'dared' to run the London Marathon while visibly menstruating.⁶ Far from specific to organized races, *Runners World*'s Georgia Scarr and Michelle Hamilton found that 46.5 percent of women have experienced harassment on their runs – a figure that varies in-between 40 to 60 percent in other surveys, but that always diverges extremely from the single-digit percentage of male runners who have experienced harassment. Such figures increase by 10 to 20 percent in urban settings (see Scarr and Hamilton). Many female runners in cities have written about their specific experiences:

> It feels almost pointless to say, but I was frequently catcalled, as every female runner has been. The experience of being catcalled is always unsettling. It forces your brain into overdrive. You quickly review every possible threat and create an escape plan. *Do I acknowledge the harasser? Run faster? Stop running?* (Dooley; emphasis in the original)

> We have also adapted to the realities – and risks – of running while female. Just as our bodies learned how to sprint around the curve of a track, our muscles learned to tense up when men honked their horns as they passed us. And just as we learned to use that nervous feeling in our gut before a race to propel us across the finish line, we also recognized the gut feeling that told us a trail wasn't safe to run on alone. (Minsberg)

These quotations indicate how deeply embedded experiences of everyday sexism are in the routines of female runners, how these runners even anticipate harassment, and develop strategies to respond to it.⁷ Because, as the many female-authored think pieces and articles published under titles such as "Running While Female" or "Running as a Woman" tend to agree, to stop running altogether or solely run on the treadmill in a gym are not a solution for the individual authors.

A telling example of one such protective strategy is the kind of resisting mindset which a female running coach from New York puts forward in her interview with the lifestyle website *Refinery29:* "I think every female runner is a feminist [...]. I think if you run in New York City and you're getting catcalled and

---

6 Remarkably, tampons are among the items which users can collect during their runs in ZR. The app diverges from other zombie narratives in which male-centric survival plans and scenarios do not consider issues surrounding menstrual hygiene during a zombie apocalypse.

7 Gendered street harassment has long been and continues to be a momentous concern of various women's movements. In the U.S., feminist activists of the second wave formed initiatives under the slogan "take back the night" and problematize the exclusion of women* in public spaces. A prominent example of a recent campaign is the viral video "10 Hours of Walking in NYC as a Woman" created by advocacy group Hollaback!. The video features actor Shoshana Roberts silently walking through Manhattan and getting catcalled more than 100 times. It was heavily criticized for its racial bias because the condensed clip mostly showed the harassment by men of color. As of writing it has been viewed 49 million times.

you're just like I don't give a shit like I'm in booty shorts and a sports bra and I'm owning this in the world and if you get distracted that's your problem and not mine" (Huntington). That the person uttering this commentary is white, normatively beautiful, and stylishly dressed intensifies some troubling implications of this postfeminist rhetoric of empowerment. As an analytical term established in the intersection of feminist media studies and cultural studies, postfeminism critically describes the complex ways that popular culture simultaneously affirms and disavows feminism. Postfeminist co-options of feminism are subject to change but often involve a set of themes, among them an emphasis on individualism and a rhetoric of choice that are embedded in neoliberal practices of consumption, (self)-surveillance, and self-discipline (see Gill; Sulimma). Like many other scholars of postfeminism(s) in popular culture, Rosalind Gill finds current representations of feminist empowerments to "turn attention away from social transformation onto individual entrepreneurialism. Choices celebrated in postfeminist inflected media are those such as 'the freedom to run in heels' and the 'right to wear red lipstick'" (624). The insistence on the 'right to run in booty shorts' is easily recognizable as a variation of such a depoliticized emphasis on choice. Correlating with the sexist trope of the short skirt when survivors of sexualized violence face 'victim-blaming,' the running coach seems unaware that not every person who experiences street harassment while running does so while wearing booty shorts and a sports bra. Nonetheless, this female urban runner's refusal to accept being shamed out of running in public, crowded urban spaces is relevant because it demonstrates an insistence to take up this space and her search for strategies in order to safely and sanely do so. Overall, the interview with the running coach develops a postfeminist fantasy of an individualized fix to a larger societal problem concerning access to public space.

An important paratext for *ZR*, the novel *The Power* by Alderman, provides an interesting take on female movement in public spaces without the fear of harassment. It develops an exaggerated fantasy of such a postfeminist fix: *The Power* begins with one of its protagonists, the teenager Roxy, refusing to run from violent attackers. Instead, Roxy discovers that her body possesses the ability to develop a powerful electrostatic force that she can wield to fight off assailants. In her review for *The New York Review of Books*, scholar Elaine Showalter finds the novel's depiction of female violence as a response to sexist dystopian societies to diverge significantly from the nonviolent tradition of female-authored feminist science fiction. Alderman herself has explained that the desire to live a life free of fear and harassment is at the core of the new "power" that the novel imagines as an empowerment for women: "If you were able to live your life as if you were able to cause hurt when you needed to [...] your life would be so different, even if you never ever had to do it. That makes you less afraid all the time" (qt. in Showalter). Thus, *The Power* spins one such fantasy to fix gendered harassment, discrimination, and abuse.[8] Female users of *ZR* may be drawn to the app through Alderman's (and the novel's) sensitivity toward the fears and insecurities that running "while female" may cause as well as the app's potential to develop a similar narrative scenario to 'fix' harassment temporarily.

In her interviews with users of the app, Jamie Henthorn found that most players of *ZR* "actually have very little interaction with their own communities while playing the game" (175). This strategic detachment through the narrative scenario of the zombie apocalypse likely amounts to the app's main appeal. *ZR* enables female runners to appropriate (urban) spaces for their exercise in the name of the game's postapocalyptic pleasures. The app's fictional narrative drive to escape chasing zombies, to bring relevant supplies to Abel Township, or to explore a fictional setting for clues to the mysteries of the zombie epidemic become much more cognitively interesting to players and thus allows them to blend out possibly discriminatory surroundings. Rather than sources of threat or distraction, obstacles such as crowds and even catcallers become obstacles for the user of *ZR* to quickly master and evade. In this manner, the maneuvers of *ZR* users recall the spatial practices of parkour. Lieven Ameel and Sirpa Tani argue that the playful, childlike behaviors of those practicing parkour reconfigure and loosen up urban public "tight space" (17) not intended for sports. Like users of *ZR*, these athletes experience "feelings of liberation when they realized that they did not have to obey the conventions for the use of space, or the limitations imposed by urban planners" (22). Similarly, in her research on female users of *ZR*, Emma Witkowski finds that the playful engagement fostered through the app allowed her interviewees to enter seemingly risky spaces – deserted parks, tunnels, or parking lots – without the worries about personal safety so often attached to such locales (see 164–169).

Feminist scholarship on such risky spaces highlights a troubling paradigm shift in urban planning and building, a paradigm shift away from the historically violent exclusion of women from public space to now instilling in women fears of public spaces in which they may encounter violence (see Becker 61–64). In a reframing of responsibilities, this shift emphasizes female fears rather than male

---

[8] However, the novel's treatment of this theme is much more complicated than my argument reproduces here. While like many other female characters, Roxy uses her new ability to protect herself and those she loves, however, at large, the now physically stronger women exert their powers to systemically oppress, violate, and subordinate men – effectively re-creating a mirror image of patriarchy. The novel also at moments reflects on the problematic binary gender dichotomy of its narrative scenario, when not all female-identified characters possess 'the power,' and some male-identified characters acquire it surgically.

violence. In urban planning and building, the conception of risky spaces for women is often used to legitimize security policies that aim at surveillance, regulation, and control rather than the access of female users to public space (see Becker 69). For (white) female runners, the horror genre becomes a means of dealing with their own horrific gendered experiences during exercising, specifically through their playful re-appropriation of seemingly risky, urban environments. In this regard, female users of *ZR* behave similarly to the NYC running coach and refuse to view themselves as vulnerable and potential victims of harassment or assault. Instead, these app users "revel in the fear factor of the horror narrative tied to their movement into space with new orientations within it" (Witkowski 167). Accordingly, the hostile catcaller can be reframed as a hungry zombie, not a threatening display of the male entitlement to judge female bodies in public space but an undead creature non-discriminatorily hungry for any kind of human flesh. A socially ingrained fear of 'risky' environments can become fictionalized as playful fear of zombies which may propel one to enjoy running faster.

The new sense of spatiality that the narrative scenario of *ZR* allows these runners to develop becomes such an effective tool for female runners due to its playful approach to urban surroundings. Miguel Sicart has productively described "play" and "playfulness" as related, yet conceptually different: "[P]lay is an *activity*, while playfulness is an *attitude* [which is] a stance toward an activity – a psychological, physical, and emotional perspective we take on activities, people, and objects" (*Play Matters* 22; emphasis in the original). *ZR*'s achievement is allowing runners to take up a different perspective or mindset on urban running, one that is fundamentally playful and rooted in the narrative pleasures of the zombie genre. For urban runners countering harassment and taking up space, such a playful mindset follows a long tradition. Again, in the words of Sicart: "[P]layful engagement with urban environments has been a constant mode of resistance and appropriation of cities for their citizens" ("Play and the City" 27). Such engagements "strive to create (or construct and reconstruct) new ways of imagining and experiencing the city [...] whose everyday rules and norms can become unhinged – and thus productive – through the activity of play" (Ackermann, Rauscher, and Stein 8). The use of *ZR* as fictionalized horror to mask the sexualized horrors of running in the city is one such new way of experiencing the city.

However, the ability to employ *ZR* as such a fictional and playful aid to encounter harassment is again deeply racialized – despite the app's desire to attract diverse users. In *The New York Times*, philosopher George Yancy struggles to explain to a white friend why he prefers to exercise on the treadmill rather than run in public: "It never occurred to her that walking through white neighborhoods in the South was an act I experienced through the lens of a murderous history that filled me with fear and a sense of deep trepidation" (Yancy). Like the users of ZR, Yancy experiences how the surroundings he exercises in become cognitively infiltrated by and linked to a narrative – not an entertaining, fictional zombie horror story but a horrific history of actual racial violence. Yancy's account vividly demonstrates how ZR's 'resisting' mindset and use of space is not open to all potential users.

Zombie Survivalism as a Cultural Phenomenon

Frequently zombie preparedness takes the form of a desire to stock up on emergency rations. Such practices are not exclusively pursued by masculinist prepper cultures but also the goal of various educational campaigns on disaster preparedness aimed at a wider public. Specifically in 2011 and 2012, U.S.-American institutions on federal and local levels (as well as universities and the Centers for Disease Control and Prevention) relied on the zombie apocalypse as a narrative tool to prepare for potential disasters. But the cultural phenomenon of zombie apocalypse preparedness also involves 'zombie workout' as a culturally pervasive and less obviously detectable symptom.

Like many commercially successful artifacts of popular culture, ZR has a kind of origin story: Alderman frequently shares how the inspiration for the app stemmed from her attending a running class in which one participant joked about wanting to learn to run to "escape the zombie horde" (Orin). Most horror aficionadas and aficionados will have encountered a similar comment at some point. The cultural phenomenon of zombie survivalism easily incorporates practices of personal fitness and physical activity. Aside from ZR, there are zombie-themed exercise classes with names such as "Zombie Fit" and "Zombitsu," and various role-playing races with volunteers made up as zombies. More implicitly, zombie narratives like the television show and comic books series *The Walking Dead* (2010-present; 2003–2019) also undertake an idealization of able-bodiedness, physical health, and endurance (see Sulimma).

In this television show's action sequences, the killing of zombies is represented as a kind of physically exhausting, yet also rewarding work – or rather workout. Its fighting scenes mostly take the form of close physical combat, in which characters utilize their surroundings to manage large groups of zombies by picking them off one by one. For example, in episode 7.12 ("Say Yes"), a group of seventy zombies chases protagonists Michonne and Rick on a deserted fairground. Both characters remain calm and confident, strategize how to most efficiently separate the zombies, and dispatch their attackers with calculated blows. As the zombies' bodies fall one by one, the human survivors' bodies are splattered with blood and drenched in sweat. Even though such fighting scenes are gory and bloody, the athletically attractive bodies of the survivors shape a pleasing aesthetic of survival as a workout. Emblematic of aspirational sportswear commercials, such scenes show experienced athletes engaged in well-practiced routines necessary for them to maintain their level of sports(wo)manship. Taking the form of rewarding labor, zombie workout enables these defined, lean bodies to maintain their attractive forms and is celebrated as an individual character/actor's achievement – to be emulated by audience members.

While in audiovisual media such as *The Walking Dead*, fighting to survive looks like a workout, in *ZR*'s audioplay working out becomes the only way to fight the zombies. The app mostly does without any descriptions of fighting scenes, and users outrun the zombies in the interval mode. Zombies are solely represented through their collective growls or the descriptions of other characters. In accordance with the horror genre's interest in bodily metamorphosis and destruction, *The Walking Dead*'s action scenes centralize questions of materiality through the juxtaposition between the bodies that serve as obstacles to be disposed of and the bodies that become active agents mastering other bodies; between the visually decaying, stumbling bodies of zombies and the defined, controlled bodies of human characters. In *ZR*, this differentiation is taken to a new extreme: because zombies only growl, users do not build any emotional connection to them and cannot do more than treat them as obstacles to outrun.

Framing such practices of fighting as an enjoyable zombie workout disturbingly helps to conceal the neoliberal logic of optimization, productivity, and self-regulation that exert influence on bodies. Generally assumed to have taken hold in Western societies from the 1980s onward, neoliberalism becomes a catch-all phrase to describe a complex economic and political undertaking that subordinates all political and social areas under a logic of the presumably free market – including the increasingly globalized deregulation of economies, the privatization of formerly public sectors, and the acceleration of capitalist synergies. Feminist political scientists have long argued that bodies not only make politics, that is, the bodies of political actors and institutions, but that politics also inscribe themselves into the bodies of human actors. Within neoliberal agendas, bodies are sought to be emancipated from any 'flaws' or 'deficiencies' through self-management. Addressing an "autonomous, calculating, self-regulating subject" (Gill and Scharff 7) neoliberal body politics emphasize self-monitoring and optimization.

The app's social media accounts cleverly celebrate the confessionals and stories of users who express that they felt too self-conscious and aware of public harassment or judgment to exercise in public (see screenshot fig. 3). According to

Fig. 3: This screenshot of the official ZR Twitter account celebrates the diversity of its implied users.

their own assessments, these users do not conform to the narrow, normative construction of athleticism and profess to having discovered exercise through the app. This is quite a remarkable achievement for an app with a zombie apocalypse setting to pull off because it is a staple of zombie narratives to adhere to normative constructions of athleticism, which is to consider people with nonconforming and specifically fat bodies to have little chance at survival. For example, in the first minutes of the movie *Zombieland* (2009), a voice-over of protagonist Columbus relates "Cardio" as the "First Rule of Survival" overlaying an image of zombies chasing a fat person. Through such fat-shaming, zombie narratives continue societal prejudices that mistakenly assume that fat bodies are incapable of athletic achievement and that all slim bodies are. *ZR* does allow for a wider, more inclusive understanding of public performances of athleticism – one that emphasizes that any body is capable of exercise and that the pleasures to be found in exercising outweigh possible harassment on the part of others. Such a more inclusive understanding of athleticism does, however, leave the goal of self-optimization and efficiency of the body in place. Occasionally, in their social media posts, users with diverse body types share pictures in the sensationalist 'before and after'-fashion, showing their current slimmer and smiling selves in workout clothes. Rather than comment on these users' increased adherence to normative body ideals, other users laud these runners for 'looking after themselves' and appearing happier and healthier. Such posts demonstrate *ZR*'s repositioning of not only the horrors but also the hard *work* of working out as fun and entertaining yet aspiring to the same purposes and results of non-fictionalized workout.

Conclusion

The contribution traced how *ZR* allows (white) female runners and runners with non-normative bodies to gamify sexism, gendered discrimination as well as the hard labor of workout by overlaying such horrors with the narrative scenario of the zombie apocalypse. In other words, the auditory space of *ZR* thus enables runners to claim freedoms of movement in their actual surroundings. This playful and entertaining engagement with hostile surroundings does not consciously force runners through a didactic of de-tolerization but instead acknowledges the fears and insecurities that (white) female runners may carry with them. By turning the catcaller into an undead obstacle to run away from and by running in seemingly risky spaces otherwise avoided, runners appropriate urban public spaces for their exercise.

If the zombie apocalypse serves as such a productive, didactic setting within which we are taught values, practices, and norms that serve the stabilization of the current neoliberal marketplace, what do we make of the ways female users of the app employ its narrative to playfully deal with harassment and occupy risky spaces? Similar to the postfeminism of the urban running coach discussed earlier, such considerations develop fantasies of an easy fix to issues of access to public space. At closer sight, the individualizing, depoliticized component of such narrative aids reveals itself and highlights how little compatible they appear to be with larger systemic changes. First and foremost, these fantasies are detrimental to more extensive social change because of the racialized white privilege inherent in the spatial practices that they encourage. An optimistic view could emphasize that by individual runners routinely taking up public space, potentially the routines of urban spatial assignments can be changed 'in the long run.' It is remarkable that an app like *ZR* enables urban runners of all body types (but not all skin colors) to appropriate spaces for their exercise. Instead of celebrating an app, a game, or other commercial artifacts for their liberating potentials, however, we need to remain aware of their limitations.

Despite all empowering potentials and narrative-ludic pleasures, the app allows for the responsibility to cope with sexism to be tied to the individual affected by it. Thus, the app shifts attention from the responsibility of the larger society to interrogate the ways we construct and valorize certain kinds of masculinity, athleticism, resilience, and self-reliance as well as the access to public spaces connected to these constructions. And finally, such gendered understandings of space and access extend beyond the urban space as a site of running back to the virtual space of gaming, too, as GamerGate has demonstrated.[9]

Works Cited

Ackermann, Judith, Andreas Rauscher, and Daniel Stein. "Introduction: Playin' the City – Artistic and Scientific Approaches to Playful Urban Arts." *Navigationen: Zeitschrift für Medien- und Kulturwissenschaften*, vol. 16, no.1, 2016, pp. 7–23.

Ameel, Lieven, and Sirpa Tani. "Parkour: Creating Loose Spaces?" *Geografiska Annaler: Series B, Human Geography*, vol. 94, no. 1, 2012, pp. 17–30.

Becker, Ruth. "Angsträume oder Frauenräume? – Gedanken über den Zugang von Frauen zum öffentlichen Raum." *Street Harassment: Machtprozesse und Raumproduktion*, edited by Feministisches Frauenkollektiv, Mandelbaum, 2008, pp. 56–74.

Darby, Kris. "Our Encore: Running from the Zombie 2.0." *Studies in Theatre and Performance*, vol. 34, no. 4, 2014, pp. 229–35.

Denson, Shane, and Andreas Jahn-Sudmann. "Digital Seriality: On the Serial Aesthetics and Practice of Digital Games." *Eludamos. Journal for Computer Game Culture*, vol. 7, no. 1, 2013, pp. 1–32.

Dooley, Tatum. "On Running in the City as a Woman." *Outside Online*, Outside Magazine, 26 Nov. 2018, www.outsideonline.com/2367496/running-city-woman-haruki-murakami. Accessed 8 September 2020.

Gill, Rosalind. "Post-Postfeminism? New Feminist Visibilities in Postfeminist Times." *Feminist Media Studies*, vol. 16, no. 4, 2016, pp. 610–630.

Gill, Rosalind, and Christina Scharff. Introduction. *New Femininities: Postfeminism, Neoliberalism and Subjectivity*, edited by Gill and Scharff, Palgrave Macmillan, 2011, pp. 1–17.

Gray, Jonathan. *Show Sold Separately: Promos, Spoilers, and Other Media Paratexts*. New York University Press, 2010.

Henthorn, Jamie. "Rewriting Neighbourhoods: *Zombies, Run!* and the Runner as Rhetor." *Social, Causal and Mobile Games: The Changing Gaming Landscape*, edited by Tama Leaver and Michele Willson, Bloomsbury, 2016, pp. 165–177.

Hollaback! "10 Hours of Walking in NYC as a Woman." *YouTube*, uploaded by Rob Bliss Creative, 28 October 2014, www.youtube.com/watch?v=b1XGPvbWn0A.

Hon, Adrian. "Two Million Runners Five." *Medium*, Medium, 13 Oct. 2015, www.medium.com/@adrianhon/two-million-runners-five-cdb53cd793a1. Accessed 8 September 2020.

Hon, Adrian. "Five Years of Zombies, Run!" *Zombies, Run!*, 27 Feb. 2017, blog.zombiesrungame.com/2017/02/27/five-years-of-zombies-run/. Accessed 8 September 2020.

---

9 The real-life harassment and misogynistic entitlement to certain spaces that female runners describe, echoes GamerGate, the vicious harassment campaign against women in video game culture from 2012 to 2014. See Shaw and Chess for an overview of the chronology of GamerGate and the violent practices that targeted feminist critic Anita Sarkeesian, independent game developers Zoë Quinn and Brianna Wu, and other female gamers and game designers (see 280).

Huntington, Jacki. "Why Every Female Runner Is a Feminist." *Refinery 29*, Refinery 29, 3 April 2016, www.refinery29.com/en-us/robin-arzon-running-motivation. Accessed 8 Sep. 2020.

"Jolly Alpha Five Niner." *Zombies, Run!*, Story Missions, Season 1, Episode 1, Six to Start, 2012.

Lu, Amy Shirong. "Narrative in Exergames: Thoughts on Procedure, Mechanism, and Others." *Games for Health Journal*, vol. 4, no. 1, 2015, pp. 19–24.

Minsberg, Talya. "Running While Female." *The New York Times*, The New York Times, 28 Aug. 2018, www.nytimes.com/2018/08/28/well/move/running-while-female.html. Accessed 8 September 2020.

Orin, Andy. "Behind the App: The Story of *Zombies, Run!*" *Lifehacker*, 10 Sept. 2014, lifehacker.com/behind-the-app-the-story-of-zombies-run-1632445358. Accessed 8 September 2020.

Scarr, Georgia, and Michelle Hamilton. "Running While Female." *Runner's World*, 3 March 2017, www.runnersworld.com/uk/a775643/running-while-female/. Accessed 8 September 2020.

Shaw, Adrienne, and Shira Chess. "Reflections on the Casual Games Market in a Post-GamerGate World." *Social, Casual and Mobile Games: The Changing Gaming Landscape*, edited by Tama Leaver and Michele Willson, Bloomsbury, 2016, pp. 277–290.

Showalter, Elaine. "Imagining Violence: 'The Power' of Feminist Fantasy." *The New York Review of Books*, 26 Feb. 2018, www.nybooks.com/daily/2018/02/26/imagining-violence-the-power-of-feminist-fantasy/. Accessed 8 Sep. 2020.

Sicart, Miguel. *Play Matters*. The MIT Press, 2014.

Sicart, Miguel. "Play and the City." *Navigationen: Zeitschrift für Medien- und Kulturwissenschaften*, vol. 6, no. 1, 2016, pp. 25–40.

Sulimma, Maria. *Gender and Seriality: Practices and Politics of Contemporary US Television*. Edinburgh University Press, 2021.

Walton, Mark. 2012. "The Story of *Zombies, Run.*" *Gamespot*, 19 June 2012, www.gamespot.com/articles/the-story-of-zombies-run/1100-6382310/. Accessed 8 September 2020.

Walton, Theresa A., and Ted M. Butryn. "Policing the Race: U.S. Men's Distance Running and the Crisis of Whiteness." *Sociology of Sport Journal*, vol. 23, no. 1, 2006, pp. 1–28.

Witkowski, Emma. "Running with Zombies: Capturing New Worlds Through Movement and Visibility Practices with *Zombies, Run!*" *Games and Culture*, vol. 13, no. 2, 2018, pp. 153–173.

Yancy, George. "Ahmaud Arbery and the Ghosts of Lynchings Past." *The New York Times*, 12 May 2020, www.nytimes.com/2020/05/12/opinion/ahmaud-arbery-georgia-lynching.html. Accessed 8 September 2020.

Zombies, Run! "All-New Zombies, Run! Trailer." YouTube, uploaded by Zombies, Run!, 13 May 2015, www.youtube.com/watch?v=QXV5akCoHSQ.

Elisabeth Haefs
"#Gameüse:" Planting the Digital Garden

The advent of digitalization has significantly changed gardening traditions and practices. Not only can digital technology influence cultivation itself, but it can also simulate cultivation in the form of gaming. An important forerunner of the digital gardening trend is Zynga's well-known game *FarmVille* (2009), a social-network browser game that was usually played on *Facebook*. The game lets its users simulate agriculture and offers related activities such as plowing, planting, and harvesting. A romanticization of the pastoral[1] is probably an important factor for the success of *FarmVille*: As Alenda Chang puts it, "the humble farm game convinced millions to [...] log on regularly, in order to colonize the pastoral frontier of the social web" (159). In an unusual take on the pastoral vision, the Berlin-based company *IPGarten*[2] seems to be a real-life manifestation of *FarmVille* by offering a gamified process for planting and ordering vegetables. "Ordering" is used here in the double sense of structuring the arrangement of vegetables on the plot, and at the same time buying them.

This chapter analyzes the design and the workings of the *IPGarten* ordering process from the perspective of American Studies. As a result, inherent notions of what I call pastoral surveillance characterize this combination of online gardening and grocery shopping.[3] While analyzing this process, it is important to note that *IPGarten* is guided by the principles of the *Gemeinwohlökonomie* (an economy for the common good), an economy model proposed by the author and political activist Christian Felber. Thus, *IPGarten* does not aim to gain considerable economic profit, which complicates their ongoing quest for funding (see Kruszka 2020b).[4]

IPGarten offers a service which resembles *FarmVille*, with the exception that plants are grown on actual fields, roughly 78 miles from Berlin. One plot of 16

---

[1] The pastoral here refers, in a broad sense, to art forms that portray an idyllic country life, usually with the shepherd watching over the sheep, or the idealized farmer. According to the *OED*, the pastoral is a "literary work portraying rural life or the life of shepherds, esp. in an idealized or romantic form." See Empson for a detailed discussion of the pastoral; for a discussion of the pastoral and the counter-pastoral in connection to farming games see Chang 158–165.
[2] The *IPGarten* hashtag "Gameüse" is a pun combining "game" with the German word for vegetables (*Gemüse*). The company's online gardening is currently only available to customers from Berlin.
[3] While this chapter does examine certain processes employed by *IPGarten*, it is not aimed at criticizing this form of gardening or the people who use it.
[4] Martin Kruszka is the founder of *IPGarten*.

https://doi.org/10.1515/9783110675184-016

square meters can be rented for €395 per year, on top of roughly €40 for gardening services (see Thiemig 242). Similar to a remote control, the client-gardener (or player) gives commands or orders while navigating the digital plot, and the farmer executes them. Thus, a veritable playing field emerges where gardening and gaming meet: the plants cultivated on the virtual plot are later sent to the client-gardener. On top of this, *IPGarten* offers "unique transparency" (243) in the form of surveillance through on-site cameras. These elements establish a tension between a pastoral vision and notions of surveillance: this pastoral surveillance enabled by the camera in the garden is made up of contesting perceptions of being in control and being controlled.

IPGarten and Pastoral Surveillance

The company's self-branding is represented by a short advertising video which depicts gardening as an enjoyable and easy enterprise, accentuated with cheerful and slightly childlike music (see "IPGarten in 40 Sekunden"). In this video, satisfied customers are shown using the *IPGarten* software at home while someone else tends to the physically separate, rented plot. The vegetables on the plot are spotless and colorful. When gardeners' hands are shown in the video, they are either tidy or in gloves; one early shot shows an already clean pair of hands being washed. The apparent naivety encoded in this advertisement coincides with a simplified pastoral vision in the form of the garden as idealized escape from the city; it capitalizes on the fast and work-oriented lifestyle of Berlin's urban dwellers, promoting the sense of being able to grow one's own vegetables even if you do not have the time to "put your hands in the ground" ("IPGarten in 40 Sekunden"). This video and the *IPGarten* software seem to draw on *FarmVille*, which make use of a similarly playful, green, and clean aesthetic.

Apart from being, as *IPGarten* suggests, a playful activity, gardening itself has many more connotations, such as contact with nature or hard physical work. *IPGarten* implicitly invokes the "return to nature"-trope, stating that it wants to bring young and old people "back to the garden" (*IPGarten* website).[5]

---

5 "Wir wollen keine Konkurrenz zum eigenen Gemüsegarten sein. Vielmehr wollen wir junge wie alte Menschen über die 'Brücke' IPGarten wieder *zum Garten zurückführen*" (*IPGarten* FAQ; emphasis added). "We do not want to compete with the personal vegetable garden. Rather, we want to bring young as well as old people *back to the garden* using the 'bridge' that is IPGarten" (trans. E.H.; emphasis added). Adding more bridges, Boris Thiemig, a member and executive manager of *IPGarten*, suggests that the company builds a "digital bridge" between city and country, between clients and organic farmers, and between client and garden (see Thiemig

Gardening can be a necessary and self-sufficient form of food production in the form of strenuous physical labor, a utopian playground, or a leisurely pastime. Most importantly, gardening implies a fundamental ambivalence in its relation to nature: it can denote a humble 'return' to nature, but at the same time, it is a cultivating appropriation and domestication of nature. A similar ambivalence also defines the pastoral vision: "The pastoral as a mode [...] expresses a feeling which oscillates between a longing for peace and harmony on the one hand and for an improved civilized world on the other" (Grewe-Volpp 155).[6]

To bring forth the pastoral connotations of *IPGarten*, Thomas Jefferson can be invoked: As Jefferson puts it, those "who labor in the earth are the chosen people of God" (678). Jefferson, as Henry Nash Smith notes, is known for positing the "cultivator of the earth, the husbandman who tilled his own acres, as the rock upon which the American republic must stand" (128). Blurring the line between garden and farm, Smith also states that the American "master symbol of the garden embraced a cluster of metaphors expressing [...] growth, increase, and blissful labor in the earth, all centering about the heroic figure of the idealized frontier farmer" (123). This frontier farmer, according to Leo Marx, is an embodiment of the pastoral "literary shepherd" (130).[7] This male figure of the frontier[8] farmer-shepherd has an important function in the *IPGarten* software, as we shall see.

In the American garden metaphor, the figures of gardener, farmer, and shepherd often seem to blend into one, and coincidentally, *IPGarten* is a prime example of how the terms "garden" and "farm" are sometimes used interchangeably.[9]

239–241). However, the divide between city and country thus emphasized (see, for instance, Williams; Conn) is too wide a topic to be discussed in the frame of this chapter.
6 Ecocritic Lawrence Buell proposes that "'pastoral' has become almost synonymous with the idea of (re)turn to a less urbanized, more 'natural' state of existence" (31). At the same time, the "natural environment as empirical reality has been made to subserve human interests, and one of these interests has been to make it serve as a symbolic reinforcement of the subservience of disempowered groups" (21). Countering this idea of nature's "subservience," ecofeminism, for instance, can advocate "a human collaboration with nature as opposed to the domination of nature" (White 18).
7 More precisely, Marx proposes to reveal the "noble husbandman's true identity: he is the good shepherd of the old pastoral dressed in American homespun" (127).
8 Partly reminiscent of the frontier narrative, a 2019 *IPGarten* advertising campaign emphasizes the "pioneering" quality of IP gardening (ipgarten.de, see also Thiemig 244).
9 As Crawford puts it, "[u]nspoken hierarchies of class, gender, and race are at play in the definitions, too. To call someone's farm a garden (with its feminized connotation), a hobby farm (with its elitist connotation), or subsistence farm (with its impoverished one) can carry a whiff of superiority." Moreover, she points out that the "marketing potential of the word *farm* is significant – having a farm attached to one's business can raise its profile as well as its prof-

Its name suggests the activity of gardening, and the employees are mostly called gardeners. However, growing food which is to be sold is a common denominator of farms (see Crawford), and the United States Department of Agriculture defines a farm as "any place from which $1,000 or more of agricultural products were produced and sold, or normally would have been sold, during the year" ("Farm"), a sum which *IPGarten* easily surpasses. The general direction of this distinction is mirrored by environmental scholar Robert S. Emmett, who states that, at least in American history, food gardens were mainly connected to subsistence, while farming became more and more industrialized (see 34) in the twentieth century. This might explain why *IPGarten* prefers the term "garden," as it implies small-scale local production, trustworthiness, and accessibility.

To return to the American garden metaphor and to cite another important American thinker, gardening, according to Henry David Thoreau, is "civil and social, but it wants the vigor and freedom of the forest and the outlaw. There may be an excess of cultivation as well as of anything else, until civilization becomes pathetic. A highly cultivated man, all whose bones can be bent! whose heaven-born virtues are but good manners" (55). "Vigor" here denotes an "[a]ctive physical strength as an attribute or quality of living things" (*OED*). In humans, vigor apparently is threatened by what Thoreau calls "an excess of cultivation" (55), a removal of humans from nature, establishing a divide between human 'nature' and cultivated civilization. Following Thoreau, gardening thus denotes a "civil and social" taming or domestication of (human) nature. However, within this tamed form, gardening still contains a – maybe fundamentally American[10] – yearning for "vigor and freedom" as indicated by the formulation "[gardening] wants the vigor and freedom" (Thoreau 55), which is to be understood in the sense of gardening as 'lacking vigor and freedom.'

At first sight, the service offered by *IPGarten* seems to interact harmoniously with both Jefferson's idealized agrarian farmer and Thoreau's notion of the desirability of "freedom and vigor." This service makes it possible for everyone, even busy urbanites, to become a farmer and a gardener of sorts. It allows for freedom and vigor in the form of being free to do the gardening in one's own time, without having to depend on weather, specific locations, or other physical restrictions.

On the other hand, *IPGarten* enables surveillance and works with commands; it creates a mechanical, maybe restrictive vision of gardening which

---

its." Interestingly, *IPGarten* seems to do the opposite thing in calling its patchwork field of plots a "garden."

10 According to Marx, the "pastoral ideal has been used to define the meaning of America ever since the age of discovery" (3). The garden metaphor is tied to this pastoral ideal.

runs counter to ideas of freedom and vigor and seems to embody something which Thoreau would criticize as "excess of cultivation" (55) in the form of controlled virtual gardening with no physical contact to the outside world. This controlling environment is embodied by the drag-and-drop movement of planting crops, virtually pulling radishes across the screen, and putting them in the digital ground. This movement implies direct control and total command of the crops – without putting any effort into it, unlike the process of physical planting. Therefore, it "wants vigor:" the client-gardener sits at home and can do the gardening without having to move much at all.

IPGarten also offers the possibility of not doing any digital planting at all if the autopilot mode is selected. Since this system works with commands, it automatically establishes a hierarchy. The player uses the software to give orders and request vegetables: everything that is planted in the digital plot results in a direct email with a corresponding order to the gardeners outside of Berlin who carry out the planting and further "gardening services" (Thiemig 241, "gärtnerische Dienstleistungen," trans. E.H.). This way, the client-gardener seems to be in control of the plot. However, they are not able to virtually move around or navigate the gamespace: there is no mobile avatar, only the plot and the cursor. This way of ordering and buying vegetables suggests a hierarchical system, because the person in the field, who carries out the clients' commands and can be an employed gardener or an organic farmer who cooperates with *IPGarten* (see Thiemig 241, 243), then seems subjugated to and controlled by the on-site cameras.[11]

The aspect of control is further enhanced by the words chosen for the platform. To plant the crop, the player can use a so-called "planting matrix" (trans. E.H.).[12] In an etymological sense, the matrix denotes a "supporting or enclosing structure" (*OED*) in the form of the maternal womb which enables growth. It thus seems well-suited to gardening.[13] However, the plant matrix also carries with it a calculating approach to gardening – in the sense of a matrix as an organizational, enclosing, and structuring grid. With the "plant matrix," the sense of ordering

---

11 In an American context, this slightly problematic part of the *IPGarten* system might even allude to questions of the agrarian ideal and slavery, a relationship most famously embodied by Thomas Jefferson. I wish to thank Dietmar Meinel for this observation. Correspondingly, the apparent *IPGarten* hierarchy might call into question the "happy classless state" (Marx 127) of the Jeffersonian pastoral ideal as well as *IPGarten*'s self-promoted sense of the economy for the common good.

12 "Pflanzmatrix" (ipgarten.de)

13 As a side note, the idea of the plant matrix emphasizes the overall staked-out, rectangular shape of the 'little plot.' This parceling of land calls to mind historical American references such as the Homestead Act of 1862 which granted land to individual farmer settlers.

as structuring, as commanding, and as placing a request at the same time becomes evident. This grid to plant the crops then guides and restricts, and thus controls, the planting process. Now, the client-gardener might still have the illusion of being in control but is in fact following the game's rules. The text and images accompanying the various gardening services posit and personify plants as conscious beings which try to "escape" as, for instance, the "pumpkin grows into the neighboring plot," or "pumpkin, zucchini, and the like try to run away from your plot" (trans. E.H.).[14] On the website, this text box is accompanied by an image of a dip net capturing a plant. Thus, the client-gardener gains a feeling of being able to control these plants which seem to have a mind of their own.[15] The plants must be kept in line, which is achieved by the commands of the client-gardener.

Control is also conveyed through the figure of the optional gardening guide, who is called *Landwirt*, a slightly sophisticated German word for "farmer." Thus, gardening knowledge is provided to the client-gardener in the form of a (white, male) guide, whose function is comparable to a Non-Player-Character (NPC) in video games. This valuable knowledge must be paid for. In the form of a speech bubble, the guide then tells the client what kinds of plants he or she can plant next to each other to ensure beneficial growth and equal distribution of nutrients. This benevolent pastoral farmer supervising the gardener's activity can be compared to Jefferson's idealized agrarian frontier farmer, a white male who is experienced in agrarian work such as tilling, planting, and harvesting and who, in Jefferson's view, builds the backbone of the nation (see Smith 128). In the *IPGarten* software, this type of farmer is installed in the form of the guiding and controlling *Landwirt*, who is a farmer and a shepherd at the same time. The *Landwirt* resembles a 'kind uncle,' while he also has supervising and controlling features.[16] The client-gardener, depending on experience level, is dependent on the knowledge provided by the *Landwirt*.

---

14 "GEMÜSE FANGEN. Der Kürbis wächst ins Nachbarbeet. [...] Kürbis, Zucchini und Co. machen schon mal 'lange Arme' und reißen gerne aus deiner Parzelle aus. Du kannst dein 'junges Gemüse' aber wieder einfangen lassen." (ipgarten.de)
15 On the other hand, the plants must also be protected from bugs, mosquitoes, and weeds. The activity of weeding has, for instance by Zygmunt Bauman, frequently been connected to a violent process of clearing a (garden) space from unwanted 'contamination' (see Bauman 30–39). In the *IPGarten* app, weeding is another service that can be easily commanded and ordered for an extra fee.
16 In a planned software update, the *Landwirt* will also display emotions, for instance a sad facial expression, if the client-gardener forgets to water the plants. The updated *Landwirt* will also be able to learn and conserve established gardening knowledge (see Kruszka 2019).

In contrast to being supervised by the *Landwirt* farmer guide, the client-gardener can keep everything the gardening employees on the field do under surveillance. There are more than 400 cameras on site which constantly show what is happening on the field. This stream is updated every 60 seconds, and the cameras also have night vision. Moreover, there are soil sensors in the ground, and drones take pictures of the plot from above. As stated in the company's FAQs, this is also one of the reasons why *IPGarten* does not wish visitors to walk on the field, because the company cannot guarantee any kind of privacy or data protection due to the live-streamed camera content.[17] At first sight, this does not matter when it comes to their own field workers. However, employees can cover the cameras if they do not want to be filmed (see Kruszka 2020b), and it is nearly impossible to recognize a face through the webcams (see Kruszka 2020a).[18] Interestingly, as Kruszka notes, the company's service would also work without the use of cameras. According to a survey, roughly half of their clients would support a version of *IPGarten* that works without cameras (see Kruszka 2020b). Still, the atmosphere of possible surveillance and the advertised "transparency" seem deeply at odds with the harmonious pastoral activity that is sold by the company. On the other hand, it simply mirrors what is already engrained in gardening – the cultivation (and thus, also the surveillance) of nature to make it fit one's own needs.

The possible surveillance of gardening employees and of the field itself via the camera shows how *IPGarten* intersects with a culture of surveillance and with social media. The camera is watching the pastoral landscape. However, by watching the field on a screen, the client-gardener can also be considered part of the camera. The surveillance of the field employed here brings a detached, dispassionate element into the process of gardening that seems at odds with the way the company brands itself, namely as a green activity that is beneficial to both city and country, that promotes diverse cultivation, and that adheres to standards of the economy for the common good. Surveillance is called "transparency" and is used to emphasize that, in opposition to common supermarket vegetables, the origin of *IPGarten* products is completely transparent. This way, the client-gardener gains the illusion of being in control once more. This apparent transparency also coincides with the clean look of the advertising video, where exhausting and dirt-related digging is turned into a clean and, virtually,

---

17 "Der Datenschutz kann nicht immer gewahrt werden, denn Kameras filmen und streamen ins Internet." (ipgarten.de)
18 This raises the question whether it is socially acceptable for the employees to cover the camera, or if this act creates the impression that they might 'have something to hide.'

see-through enterprise (see "IPGarten in 40 Sekunden").[19] In fact, surveillance and 'harmless,' enjoyable browser games seem to go hand in hand: Eric Schewe states that "[s]ocial media, in fact, have integrated free-to-play multiplayer gaming apps into their platforms to attract users and to establish regular habits." According to him, these regular habits seem designed to "lull us into accepting surveillance" through "pleasure." *FarmVille*, which shares the aesthetics of the *IPGarten* software, seems an adequate example of such gaming apps. Therefore, it is possible that users of *FarmVille* and similar games might be especially attracted to the aesthetics and the functionality of the *IPGarten* software.

Once again, gardening – and especially pastoralism itself – can denote a form of surveillance, viewing the shepherd or gardener as surveyor of sheep, landscape, or plants. Read this way, *IPGarten*'s webcam enables the online gardener to become a shepherd to the physically distant plot. This controlling notion of the pastoral can also be found in Michel Foucault's concept of pastoral power: Taking the figure of the Christian pastor as shepherd caring for his flock, Foucault argues that the modern democratic state exerts pastoral power instead of absolute sovereign power. Thus, pastoral power constitutes a supposedly tender and caring form of power (see Foucault 782–784). To care for the flock, still, the flock must be observed and monitored – correspondingly, the garden plot is observed by the gardener (in this case: on screen, via a monitor).[20]

The contesting layers and directions of control inscribed into the *IPGarten* process – in the form of governing one's own plot but somehow being manipulated at the same time – are also embodied by the figure of the pastor-shepherd: Graham P. Martin and Justin Waring state that "[o]n the one hand, the pastor is a 'relay' of surveillance and discipline; on the other, the pastor promotes self-reflexive, self-governing subjects" (1298).[21] Therefore, the *IPGarten* camera in the field embodies the pastor-shepherd. On the other hand, the pastor-shepherd is explicitly represented by the *Landwirt*. However, the latter appears to have a

---

19 For contemporary treatises on transparency in the realms of the social, the political, and in literature, see Docherty; Schneider; or Berger and Owetschkin.

20 Additionally, although the pastoral seems contrary to the sublime (see Fay 12), the notion of the sublime might shed a new light on the camera in the garden, if viewed in the sense of a "technological sublime" (Nye xiii).

21 The authors suggest that "Foucault's nascent concept of pastoral power offers a route to a better conceptualization of the relationship between discourse, subjectivity and agency, and a means of understanding the (contested, non-determinate, social) process through which governmental discourses are shaped, disseminated and translated into action" (Martin and Waring 1292).

less tangible form than the camera, because this figure does not always appear and must be paid for.

In this atmosphere of surveillance, the digital and the physical garden space merge into one; the screen conveys a simulation of the garden that caters to a desire for an authentic gardening experience. Coming back to Thoreau's statements on gardening, this process can also be read as an inversion. The *IPGarten* software suggests being in touch with an ideal nature in the form of the garden plot – via the double function of feeling in touch and using a *touch*screen or a *touch*pad – while in fact encouraging more spatial distance between plant consumer and plant origin than is characteristic of conventional gardening. Thinking that they are going back to nature, the customer physically, and frequently, returns to a screen – the opposite of what a gardener would call nature. Thus, the screen is where Thoreau's vigor (of physical exercise in the form of gardening) and freedom (of choice as in planting what the customer desires) are simulated but in fact undermined – this happens especially through surveillance and the game rules analyzed above, rules of structuring and commanding which create contesting notions of being in control and being controlled.

If gardening is, as Thoreau states, "civil and social," then IP gardening could even be posited as a caricature of Thoreau's statement. At first sight, *IPGarten* does not seem civil and social. It apparently emphasizes an individual, digitized approach to gardening over a community-based effort. However, *IPGarten* does support organic farmers, it adds to an increase of regional produce and denotes a departure from harmful monocultural farming in times of climate change and related droughts in central Europe (see Thiemig 243). IP gardening might also lead to an increased awareness concerning food sources and agricultural processes (see Thiemig 244).[22] Moreover, *IPGarten* creates above minimum wage jobs in the country; superfluous produce can be donated; and *IPGarten* has been integrated into a class teaching syllabus (see Thiemig 244–245). On top of this, each rented plot contains one so-called Soli-square meter,[23] which

---

[22] Thiemig here refers to a research group that investigates *IPGarten* from the angle of environmental psychology at the University of Magdeburg (see "Projekt IPGarten"). Moreover, projects like *IPGarten* could have beneficial effects concerning individual environmental education and decision-making (see WBGU 226).

[23] "Die Natur ist nur schwer zu berechnen und sucht sich oftmals ihre eigenen Wege. So kann es auf ganz natürliche Weise zu Ernteausfällen kommen. Doch die Gemeinschaft steht hierfür ein. Ein Quadratmeter von jeder Parzelle 'gehört' allen und wird geteilt. Somit haben wir die Möglichkeit auf Ernteausfälle zu reagieren, und niemand muss leer ausgehen. Es wird im Bedarfsfall lediglich 1/16 deiner Gesamternte einbehalten und der Gemeinschaft zur Verfügung gestellt." (ipgarten.de) "Nature is unpredictable; it finds its own ways. That is why crop failures can simply come as part of a natural process. But the community is ready for this: One square meter of every

even calls to mind the pre-industrial form of the commons: common land used by farmers. One square meter of every plot belongs to the community of IP gardeners, to be shared collectively in the case of crop failure or other incidents. This solidarity square meter is a major factor that supports *IPGarten*'s claim of promoting the economy for the common good. They prioritize solidarity and economic sustainability rather than economic profit, while still working to build up the necessary reserve funds to run the business (see Kruszka 2020b). However, these notions seem to clash with the uncritical way that hierarchical control is suggested through mechanisms of surveillance. The laudable solidarity square meter also raises the question of how far the company invokes the current trend of urban community gardening as a vehicle for its own vegetable production.

Conclusion

IPGarten is a service that works with contesting levels of control which seem to empower the client-gardener only to locate control in the software itself (the company) in the following step. The question of who controls whom is probably not answerable. However, the pastoral surveillance embodied by the visual axis from screen to camera to garden strongly suggests that control is not in the hands of the person doing the physical part of gardening; thus, control lies either with the client-gardener or the company itself. Since these analysis results are mainly concerned with the software and design of *IPGarten*, the company's community-oriented properties and its work for environmentally friendly and not-for-profit agriculture should not be overlooked. The concept and the design of *IPGarten* house a variety of oppositions and unclear relationships, such as surveillance and transparency, community and individualism, control and freedom, vigorous exercise and relaxed convenience as well as the garden and the farm. In fact, what this company offers might have more in common with farming than with gardening. Mirroring the conflation of garden and farm inherent in the influential American garden metaphor, the imagined garden refuge which the company advertises is indeed a farm or an agricultural field: the garden plots outside of Berlin make up one big field that does not look like a garden at all. All these ambivalences show that a complex process underlies online gardening and

---

plot is 'owned' by the community and will be shared. This way, we can react to crop failures and no one is left out. In this case, only 1/16 of your harvest will be withheld and given to the community." (trans. E.H.)

farming, a process that stands in contrast to the supposedly easy and innocent activity sold by *IPGarten*.

Works Cited

Bauman, Zygmunt. *Modernity and Ambivalence.* Polity Press, 1991.
Berger, Stefan, and Dimitri Owetschkin, eds. *Contested Transparencies, Social Movements and the Public Sphere: Multi-Disciplinary Perspectives.* Palgrave Macmillan, 2019
Buell, Lawrence. *The Environmental Imagination: Thoreau, Nature Writing, and the Formation of American Culture.* The Belknap Press of Harvard University Press, 1995.
Chang, Alenda Y. *Playing Nature: Ecology in Video Games.* University of Minnesota Press, 2019.
Conn, Steven. *Americans Against the City: Anti-Urbanism in the Twentieth Century.* Oxford University Press, 2014.
Crawford, Andrea. "What's the Difference Between a Garden and a Farm?" *Slate*, 12 February 2014. www.slate.com/human-interest/2014/02/farm-vs-garden-the-definition-depends-on-whether-you-ask-the-usda-or-the-waldorf-astoria.html. Accessed 12 September 2020.
Docherty, Thomas. *Confessions: The Philosophy of Transparency.* Bloomsbury, 2012.
Emmett, Robert S. *Cultivating Environmental Justice: A Literary History of U.S. Garden Writing.* University of Massachusetts Press, 2016.
Empson, William. *Some Versions of Pastoral.* New Directions, 1974.
"Farm." *United States Department of Agriculture Glossary*, 27 November 2019, www.ers.usda.gov/topics/farm-economy/farm-household-well-being/glossary.aspx#farm. Accessed 29 September 2020.
FarmVille. Web. Zynga, 2009.
Fay, Elizabeth A. *Becoming Wordsworthian: A Performative Aesthetics.* University of Massachusetts Press, 1995.
Felber, Christian. *Change Everything: Creating an Economy for the Common Good.* 2011. Zed Publishing, 2015.
Foucault, Michel. "The Subject and Power." *Critical Inquiry*, vol. 8, no. 4, 1982, pp. 777–795.
Grewe-Volpp, Christa. "The Machine in the Indigenous Garden." *Rereading the Machine in the Garden: Nature and Technology in American Culture*, edited by Eric Erbacher, Nicole Maruo-Schröder, and Florian Sedlmeier, Campus Verlag, 2014, pp. 148–166.
IPGarten. www.ipgarten.de/. 05 May 2019.
"IPGarten in 40 Sekunden." *YouTube*, uploaded by IP Garten, 30 July 2018. www.youtube.com/watch?v=amBy3tr9E84. Accessed 7 October 2019.
Jefferson, Thomas. "Notes on the State of Virginia." 1781–1785. *The Complete Jefferson*, assembled and arranged by Saul K. Padover, Duell, Sloan and Pearch, Inc., 1943.
Kruszka, Martin. Telephone interview. 15 May 2019.
Kruszka, Martin. "Re: IPGarten." Received by Elisabeth Haefs, 9 September 2020.
Kruszka, Martin. Telephone interview. 28 October 2020.
Martin, Graham P. and Justin Waring. "Realising Governmentality: Pastoral Power, Governmental Discourse and the (Re)constitution of Subjectivities." *The Sociological Review*, vol. 66, no. 6, 2018, pp. 1292–1308.

Marx, Leo. *The Machine in the Garden: Technology and the Pastoral Ideal in America*. 1964. Oxford University Press, 2000.
"Matrix, n. 1." *OED Online*. Accessed 20 November 2020.
Nye, David E. *American Technological Sublime*. The MIT Press, 1994.
"Pastoral, II. 3.a." *OED Online*. Accessed 1 October 2020.
"Projekt IPGarten." *Otto-von-Guericke-Universität Magdeburg*, 16 April 2018. www.ipgarten.ovgu.de. Accessed 9 September 2020.
Schewe, Eric. "How Pleasure Lulls Us into Accepting Surveillance." *Jstor Daily*, 28 June 2018. www.daily.jstor.org/how-pleasure-lulls-us-into-accepting-surveillance/. Accessed 7 May 2019.
Schneider, Manfred. *Transparenztraum: Literatur, Politik, Medien und das Unmögliche*. Matthes & Seitz, 2013.
Smith, Henry Nash. *Virgin Land: The American West as Symbol and Myth*. 1950. Harvard University Press, 1973.
Thiemig, Boris. "IPGarten – der erste Onlinegarten der Welt mit echter Ernte." *Smart City – Made in Germany*, edited by Chirine Etezadzadeh, Springer Vieweg, 2020, pp. 239–248.
Thoreau, Henry David. *A Week on the Concord and Merrimack Rivers*. 1849. Houghton Mifflin, 1906.
"Vigour, n. 1.; 1.c." *OED Online*. Accessed 7 May 2019.
White, Monica M. "Sisters of the Soil: Urban Gardening as Resistance in Detroit." *Race/Ethnicity*, vol. 5, no. 1, 2011, pp. 13–28.
Williams, Raymond. *The Country and the City*. 1973. The Hogarth Press, 1985.
Wissenschaftlicher Beirat der Bundesregierung Globale Umweltveränderungen (WBGU). *Hauptgutachten: Unsere gemeinsame digitale Zukunft*. WBGU, 2019.

Kirsten Möller and Anna Kpok
Performative Playground: Narrative Spaces in Theater Games

In recent years, theatrical performances based on game structures and their narrative techniques have caught some attention in the independent theater scene of Germany. Among others, the performance collective Anna Kpok has developed unique formats inspired by the digital story telling of old-school jump-and-run games as well as by contemporary narrative adventures. An important aspect is the translation of the immersive experience of a digital game and its narrative strategies into performances. In this process of analogization, new features of performance and theater are combined with the rules and settings of gaming as a social situation. Thus, a distinctive experience is created that turns the spectators into participants.

Who is Anna Kpok?

Anna Kpok is an artist group of about eight steady members founded in 2009 in Bochum. They create theater, performances, and games and work mainly in the Ruhr region, especially at the *Ringlokschuppen.Ruhr* in Mülheim an der Ruhr. They have also showed their work in Dortmund, Bochum, Hannover, Cologne, Munich, and Berlin. Anna Kpok cooperates with a broader network of affiliated creators: artists, scientists, coders, game and interaction designers, and many more. They create common spaces of interaction and performative playgrounds, understanding theater as an experience created by producers and audience cooperatively. Anna Kpok aims to turn the audience members into actively involved participants or players. In contrast to a common understanding of theater, the spatial and conceptual separation of spectators and performers is repealed. Instead, players interact with performers or interactive objects in the room to unfold the story and develop the narration together. A performance of Anna Kpok is a participatory art-experience.

What is a Theater Game?

In 2013, Anna Kpok created their first series of theater games, a new subgenre they labeled *live jump-and-run games*. It is not the only kind of performance they work on but has been a large part of their recent works. It all started with the question: How is it possible to transfer parts of a digital video game into analog theater situations?

An important step was to transfer the concept of the avatar from the digital world into the physical world. A performer embodies a virtual figure and is controlled by the audience members. Starting with simple movements available in 2D sidescrolling games, Anna Kpok developed the concept further so that the avatar was not only able to jump and run but also to carry objects and solve quests as in adventure games. The group of players shares the same space with the performers as if they were sitting in front of a gaming device pushing buttons, but they also walk around with their avatar at the same time. Playing in this hybrid stage comes with some limitations. The group of players are only allowed to interact with their surroundings (the game-space) via the performer, i.e. they are not allowed to move or touch anything by themselves. To add some level of empathy and confusion, the avatar is also called "Anna Kpok," like the performance group.

Instead of using an electronic device, players control the performer with voice commands. Each player has control over two "buttons," functions that enable them to move the avatar around the space or interact with their surroundings. The episodes in the series of live jump-and-run games included commands such as "start – stop," "left – right," "jump – duck," "collect – use," "attack – defend," and "examine – zoom in." Together the five players function as a game controller sharing the different commands – or buttons – to move their avatar through the stage setting that oscillates between the virtual and physical world. Players can only use their two commands until the end of the game. If a player tries to break the rules and voices a command of another player, the performer does not react. That means the performer also needs to stay very attentive, especially at the beginning of the game, when the commands are handed out to each player. The performer needs to memorize each of the five voices with the corresponding command for they will not always be able to look at the player giving the command.

The first three gaming performances in this fashion were site-specific works. They were not performed at a theater stage but an old air raid shelter, an empty office building, and the backstage of a theater house including the catacombs under the revolving stage. The second game, for example, took place in a building over three floors. When audience members entered the building, they became players and thus entered the world of the game. As the whole building was transformed into a derailed office with traps and bizarre employees, everything inside was set to become part of the story.

To smooth the transition from the "real" or physical world into the gaming experience, a "threshold room" was installed. Here the (usually) five players were assigned the various voice commands, learned about the rules and the story, and could choose one of three avatars. Afterwards, they entered the first floor and followed a parkours passing riddles, enemies, and obstacles. The game always ended with an epic boss fight. While controlling an avatar in an unfamiliar situation may sound daunting at first, players quickly understood the theater game mechanics. Simple rules, such as colored lines on the floor which indicated boundaries the avatar could not cross, did not have to be verbalized. The game rules were generally quickly accepted by the players if seen performed by the avatar, though avatar gestures had to be large and exaggerated as players tended to overlook small hints due to the unusual surrounding and the amount of information they had to process. In the site-specific versions of the series, the setting made it obvious most of the time where the players had to go to follow the narrational path. Comparable to an old side-scrolling jump-and-run, it was only possible to walk forward while returning to the first parts of the game was not an option. In addition, players were also supervised by a second performer who provided support for the players by showing information about the avatar's health and their collected bonus points as well as by providing hints when necessary. In true gaming tradition, this performer functioned as a living tutorial, a helper making themself noticeable when the group of players was stuck or to celebrate with them.

These first three games of the series of live jump-and-runs were framed by a continuing narrative, also deriving from classic video game settings: Anna Kpok's friend, a little zombie, was kidnapped and disassembled into different pieces. Anna Kpok had to defeat evil scientists, sinister bureaucrats, and virtual beings to get parts of their zombie friend back. These themes and the location predefined the stage design while moments of irritation and irony abounded. For example, in the Silver Lake Room, in which players had to figure out that all commands were reversed, they could only control the reflection of their avatar visible in a large mirror at the backwall of the room. These site-specific games focused on the immersive experience of being "inside" an old video game as well as on the interactive situation between the players and the avatar. Moreover, the group dynamics made up a large part of the experience. The game was developed to make all voice commands important (even if they differed in frequency of usage) thereby fostering a high level of coordination within the group so that every single player had to be highly involved.

Changing the Focus

The next phase in the exploration of the potential of these kinds of inclusive, interactive gaming performances was to complexify the stories and change the narrative character to resemble multi-linear, open-world digital games while keeping the restriction of the voice command controls and thus the experience of a group collaboration to achieve a common goal. This task had to overcome various obstacles as became clear in conversations with players of the first games. The immersive framework and the concentration they had to maintain trying to keep their avatar alive or avoid it being stuck resulted in a lack of attentiveness to things that were not relevant to this goal, such as projected video footage containing additional background story or subtle narrational fragments scattered across the rooms. As players submerged into the game world, they tended to forget that they controlled a human being and not an actual (that is, digital, super-human) avatar. As a result, players tried to have the avatar jump higher than humanly possible by shouting (as in "pressing the button just hard enough" in a digital game). Afterwards, players talked about the atmosphere of the theater game and how they got drawn into the experience but could not exactly reproduce why they even went on the initial quest they so intensely tried to solve.

While jump-and-run games usually provide little narrative context for their adventures, to develop a more story-driven theater game required additional planning and designing. To figure out how to include narrative elements into the gaming structure itself, Anna Kpok organized several workshops and was part of the artistic research residency program *flausen*. Whereas the jump-and-run scenarios relied on (a succession of) quick and immediate reactions to threats in the game world or small puzzles that could be solved within a few minutes, narrative-driven theater games would allow players to discover the story step by step by interacting with the game world. Objects in the gamespace further heightened attentiveness and created situations where players were challenged to make their own decisions and react to the information they discovered. Both aspects led to a more in-depth reflection on the relationship between the players, the avatar, and their surroundings.

This approach was combined with a broader spectrum of possible ways to play the game. Players were free to decide what to do first, how to react to parts of the story, and how to enact their roles as players as well as to influence how the avatar should react to what they were confronted with during the game. Inside the gameworld they could go wherever they pleased. This shift reduced the linearity in the narrative as well as in the actual gaming. This opening of the gameplay corresponded to a reduction of the gameworld from an entire building to a single room – from a site-specific location back to a theater space. Through this shift the key elements in the game could become responsive to the group's behavior. The boundaries of the world, for example, were not marked by lines on the floor anymore but with the use of lighting and by the performer. Transferring the gameworld onto a classical theater stage has some advantages as well: it allowed Anna Kpok to tour with the game and thus offer the experience to more people. Also, the potential audience expanded to include a more classical theater audience often less experienced with gaming formats in general.

Real Reality

Real Reality was the first full-length game created by Anna Kpok for a theater space. It premiered on 18 September 2018 at *Ringlokschuppen.Ruhr* in Mülheim an der Ruhr as a coproduction with Theater Dortmund and *Schaubude* Berlin. During the development of the theater game, the performance group was particularly interested in researching the functionality and problematic usage of online profiling and the resulting online identities. The project specifically engaged with the phenomena of the so called "digital twin" or "data double" – online representations of people that consist of all the collected data of an individual created when, for example, shopping online, using social media platforms, or simply visiting a website (with its tracking functions). These datasets are often combined with data from the physical world, so that, for example, the address of a person is linked to the credit score of their neighborhood, which can have severe consequences and disadvantages particularly for marginalized groups (data collectors include, for example, the "big five" internet corporations – Google, Amazon, Microsoft, Facebook, Apple – as well as governments and their agencies). *Real Reality* wanted to show the possible consequences of the supposedly virtual existence of a data double on the whole physical life to challenge clear-cut distinctions between notions of "real life" and "virtual life" or "real world" and "virtual worlds" in the digital age.

The story of *Real Reality* takes place in an unspecified but not too distant future, where all the current world problems – such as climate change, ecological destruction, growing world population – have not been solved but have increasingly shaped the lives of billions of people. Those who can afford the expenses live in gated urban communities. In this scenario, a company called RealReality promises a unique living experience. People can choose to live anywhere on the planet for however long they prefer but the apartments RealReality provides are exactly the same everywhere: completely furnished and digitalized modern smart homes with an AI assistant that knows everything about the inhabitants from their daily habits to their deepest desires.

To let the audience experience this future, a whole smart home was installed on the theater stage containing, for example, a smart table with different news feeds and music accounts, a friendswall (a large screen with messages and videos), a game zone, and an ultimate dream machine which provides users with an efficient night of eight hours of sleep in only 30 seconds. The whole stage setting was interactive and responded directly to the actions of the players and the avatar. At the start of the performance, players had to choose one of five profiles and backstories for their avatar, so that the smart home could adjust to the specific needs of its costumer (these premediated profiles were inspired by the practices of advertising companies as well as social scientists to categorize with the help of their data double). Every profile consisted of a different set of news, messages, videos, music, and even light settings as well as a unique outfit and exactly one specific drink and meal. This living concept, although functional and comforting at first sight, turned out to be problematic as players began to realize the confinement and restrictions their avatar actually endured. Eventually, they were tasked to hack the smart home system to circumvent the constrains of the profile they had chosen in the beginning. Players also had to pass a (reversed) Turing Test to prove their identity and their humanness in order to confirm they were not a robot or a virus. Depending on the players' actions throughout the game and their decisions in the Turing Test, *Real Reality* had four different endings (although audiences could only experience one of them in a performance). Comparable to video game design, *Real Reality* offered a gaming experience open to numerous possibilities and interactions with the aim of balancing the narrative elements of the story and the ludic elements of play.

Four Aspects of Game Theater

As creators of theater games, Anna Kpok faces the same questions designers of video games encounter, namely, how to balance narrative and ludic elements. Particularly when dealing with open-world scenarios, it is pertinent to understand how to build a space that offers as many different choices as possible without the players getting lost in it. How is it possible to intertwine the elements of space and narration within the gameplay, so that players have fun exploring a room, discovering its clues, and thereby unravelling the story? These questions are not only important for many video game designers but are also essential aspects of staging a play from developing a dramaturgy to deciding on the perspectives of the story.

In the following, we want to detail specifically the four main aspects informing Anna Kpok's approach to developing a new format in theater gaming: interactive spaces, enacted narration, multi-linear storytelling, and participation. Some of them are similar to video game designing, but all of them have to do with the special relation between space and audience in a live situation. Eventually, we hope to show how digital culture and games shape new ways of storytelling in theater.

Anna Kpok tries to create interactive spaces where the stage setting and the scenery – the complete surroundings of the audience – acts as another play-actor within the game and is able to react directly to the actions of the audience. The scenery is crucial for the worldbuilding and has to be coherent to support, advance, and tell the story of the game. In this context, coherent does not mean the same as naturalistic, since players and theater audiences accept a minimalistic or fantastic design as long as the individual elements fit together. This can be achieved easier in a theater space, where artists can actively control the placement of every object and design the stage, than in a site-specific environment, where the existing building and a lot of its interior are already set. Because players try to use and make sense of almost every element they see, a stage allows for a more controlled and deliberately designed environment than a site-specific set. Consequentially, theater spaces permit an intensified focus on the story and its embedment within the narrative space.

Site-specific projects, on the other hand, face a unique set of challenges on their own. The main aspect to consider is the fact that the building and its interior predefine many aspects of the setting, the (possible) narration, and the play. The site-specific jump-and-run performances by Anna Kpok therefore focused much more on the action and the gameplay. As a result, these performances shifted the balance to the ludic dimension of the production providing only a basic story and offering only short glimpse into the world players inhabited.

Since games like *Real Reality* are multi-linear, players do not follow a single straight path through the game and do not encounter one "right" ending. Instead, the different conclusions depend on how players act within the game. Since many players inquired after their playthrough of *Real Reality* whether they won or lost the game, Anna Kpok explained from the start that participants cannot simply win or lose the game. More importantly, the theater game included various moments of decision-making to let players experience (part of) the multi-linear narrative throughout the game. As players became aware of the different narrative endings, they were subtly encouraged to speculate about the consequences of their actions during the gaming experience.

Embedded narrative elements within the gameworld, such as responsive stage settings, enable players to find their own way through the story. The latter, however, decide themselves what they are interested in or how deep they want to dive into the narration and discover the world behind the space. In staging an explorable narrative environment, the creation process of theater games like *Real Reality* involves aspects video game scholar Henry Jenkins describes as "environmental storytelling" (122) in his work. He argues for an understanding of game designers less as storytellers and more as narrative architects. In his view, "[e]nvironmental storytelling creates the preconditions for an immersive narrative experience [...] [as] spatial stories can evoke pre-existing narrative associations; they can provide a staging ground where narrative events are enacted; they may embed narrative information within their mise-en-scene; or they provide resources for emergent narratives" (123).

Depending on their decisions and their interactions with the setting, players take different paths through the game or a specific chapter. At the same time, narrative bottle-necks exist within the dramaturgy of the game to bring dividing storylines back together at various points during the game and to allow for a smooth transition from chapter to chapter. In this dramaturgy, strict if-then gates (binary functions that determine if A happens than B is triggered) still exist as every action triggers a new event and continues the storyline. Similarly, Jenkins speaks of "two kinds of narratives – one relatively unstructured and controlled by the player as they explore the game space and unlock its secrets; the other pre-structured but embedded within the mise-en-scene awaiting discovery" (126). Consequentially, players are not totally free to do whatever they like as they move and act within the gamespaces and structures. But how they act within these constructed situations, how they interact with the environment and, of course, their avatar differs from game to game (and every round of the game that is played). In their essay about the "Decision Turn" in Game Studies Tobias Unterhuber and Marcel Schellong argue that even the smallest actions have an impact on the unfolding of the game, from facing away from the avatar for a brief moment to small changes in light and sound atmosphere, even including hesitations or non-reactions by players (see 25). The game depends completely on the players' behavior, their skills, and their mode of playing and thereby shapes their sense of immersion. As *Real Reality* is directed live by a game-leader and includes technicians on the set, it is always possible to intervene in the "algorithm" (the predefined reaction of avatar, projections, sound, light, in short, the environment) as well to reward unusual solutions or sanction the players' behavior.

Comparable to the development of new video games, each show and live performance necessitates creating "a mixture of enacted and embedded narrative elements [that] can allow for a balance between the flexibility of interactivity and the coherence of a pre-authored narrative" (Jenkins 127). Consequentially,

Anna Kpok had to consider questions about player freedom not only in the development process but also during the course of every game: What agency do players really have in any given situation? What kind of decisions do they make and how powerful are they? Do player actions have consequences? Given the unpredictable nature of the live performance, the creators have to carefully balance what they want to keep in their own hands and what they can leave open or unplanned within the game.

Playgrounds for new Social Interactions

Anna Kpok aims to build performative playgrounds where the audience can rehearse new tactics and strategies for different (social and political) realities. In these theater games, mixed groups of up to 30 people participate. Sometimes these people know each other, but often they meet for the first time and have to form a group, although they are of different age, come from various social backgrounds, and possess varying degrees of game literacy. In a very short time, participants have to become a team that works together in solving problems and riddles as well as finding successful strategies of how they want to play the game. Comparable to the theater, they have to accept and share the illusion the game presents to take part in the performance. Therefore, they have to be open to its story and particularly its rules. Sometimes even the avatar becomes part of this social experiment when, for example, players take responsibility for them (whether players identify with the avatar or the person playing them, however, cannot be decided definitively).

The social interactions and interpersonal bonding produced by theater gaming is thus comparable to urban gaming. As Judith Ackermann notes for the latter, shared experiences and memories are able to build temporary communities among players – even between total strangers (see 6). In this way, playing together in urban spaces or the theater also means working together, engaging people with different perspectives, experiences and backgrounds, and making decisions together. Theater gaming underlines the social dimension of both playing and storytelling. In *Performing Stories* (2014), Nina Tecklenburg similarly highlights the importance of playful storytelling as a process of community creation in which the audience is able to participate actively in the narration and is invited to enact and even question the social contexts as well as the game rules (see 121).

Playing is the most relevant feature of the new genre of theater gaming. Crucially, both are fundamentally relational and social, creating novel spaces for interpersonal encounters and temporary communities. As Ackermann suggests, the experience of one's own agency within a playful situation can increase the awareness of (the possibilities of) agency in everyday life – and can furthermore lead to a transmission of this playful attitude (see 5). Since the gamespace is detached from everyday life, it thus enables participants to recognize and test out new tactics while also experiencing other points of view. In these situations, and in the genre of theater games in general, the boundaries between experienced situations and fictional narration, real and virtual spaces, and performers and avatars are blurred and overlap.

Works Cited

Ackermann, Judith. "Urban Gaming: Formen und Auswirkungen des Spielens mit und in der Stadt." *PH Lesenswert: Onlinemagazin des Zentrums für Literaturdidaktik. Kinder Jugend Medien, Special-Issue: "Spiel-Kunst,"* vol. 1, 2016, pp. 2–8.
Jenkins, Henry. "Game Design as Narrative Architecture." *First Person: New Media as Story, Performance, and Game*, edited by Noah Wardrip-Fruin and Pat Harrigan, The MIT Press, 2004, pp. 118–130.
Tecklenburg, Nina. *Performing Stories: Erzählen in Theater und Performance*. Transcript, 2014.
Unterhuber, Tobias and Marcel Schellong. "Wovon wir sprechen, wenn wir vom Decision Turn sprechen." *I'll Remember This*, edited by PAIDIA, Verlag Werner Hülsbusch, 2016, pp. 15–27.

Lauren Kolodkin and Ryan Linthicum
Museum Space Invaders: Video Gaming at the Smithsonian American Art Museum

In 2012, the Smithsonian American Art Museum (SAAM) opened the exhibition *The Art of Video Games*, one of the first major exhibitions to explore the evolution of video games as a narrative art form. The exhibition, guest-curated by Chris Melissinos, former Chief Evangelist and Chief Gaming Officer for Sun Microsystems and founder of PastPixels, featured graphics or sequences from more than 20 different consoles spanning a period from the late 1970s through 2011. The installation also included five playable titles: *Pac-Man* (1980), *Super Mario Brothers* (1985), *The Secret of Monkey Island* (1990), *Myst* (1993), and *Flower* (2009). Critics and visitors praised the exhibition, focusing on the importance of having video games presented at the Smithsonian (see O'Brien). Designed to be "an exhibition in easy mode" (Schiesel), *The Art of Video Games* was a broad introduction to some of the most influential artists, designers, and titles throughout the history. The exhibition garnered high visitation at SAAM and was extremely popular as a traveling exhibition – it traveled to ten different museums between 2012 and 2016. The exhibition also marked the beginning of the Smithsonian American Art Museum's commitment to the preservation, study, and interpretation of video games as part of the story of American visual culture.

The challenge that followed *The Art of Video Games* was twofold: how to keep audiences that had first been engaged by that exhibition coming to SAAM, and how to maintain the prevailing notion that SAAM had positioned itself as a museum that was open to including video games in the canon of American art. Since its inception in 2014, SAAM Arcade has attempted to address these challenges. In the last five years, it has become one of the SAAM's signature programs, transforming the museum's courtyard into an arcade primarily centered around an indie developer showcase and challenging visitors to experience video gaming as a form of experiential art. Initially presented with American University's Game Lab and then with the assistance of independent scholars and industry experts, indie developers are invited to submit a game to the museum for review and, if selected, show that game at the museum for a short pe-

---

Note: We have to give thanks to our colleagues Laura Baptiste, Sara Snyder, and Kayleigh Bryant-Greenwell for their support and assistance in making this project possible. Also, special thanks go out to all the participants of the 2018 SAAM Arcade Indie Developer Showcase, but especially Don Schmocker, Benjamin Poynter, and Robin Baumgarten.

https://doi.org/10.1515/9783110675184-018

riod (usually one to two days, depending on certain constraints). The original organizers of the program brought in other vendors to supplement the indie games with more recognizable titles via consoles and arcade cabinets.

After successes in 2014 and 2016, SAAM sought external grant funding to expand SAAM Arcade; with that grant in hand, they created a program in 2017 that was a massive two-day showcase that brought 20,000 people into the museum. The program's success presented new challenges, both in maintaining a connection to the museum's overall mission and sustaining engagement with the gaming audience between Arcades. One of the chief complaints we received in 2017 from participants at the Arcade was that the game *Flower* – which had been in *The Art of Video Games* and was displayed in the museum's time-based media arts galleries during previous Arcades – was not on view during the 2017 program. Despite having forty indie developers, a day-long e-sports tournament, two different musical acts, and special coding workshops, people wanted to see the game that started it all: Jenova Chen and Kellee Santiago's *Flower*. We realized that we had inadvertently created a pilgrimage to a specific art video game; audiences expected an annual opportunity to revisit specific experiences at each SAAM Arcade, when our aim was to create a sustained, ongoing, and varied exploration of the complexities of video games as an art form.

Thus, when we began planning for the 2018 Arcade, the first decision we made was to narrow our focus from a massive two-day video game takeover to an arts-focused, one-day video game showcase. The overwhelming success of the 2017 program, we believed, would make it possible for us to have a more focused program in 2018; our audience felt solid, and we felt that narrowing the pool of indie developers would only help us highlight the elements of gaming that bridged the gap between art and experience. We released an application on our website that focused on the concept of "gamespaces," asking applicants to consider how their game fit into three categories under the theme: the use of physical space in gameplay, the creation of digital space within the game itself, and the creation of social space through group or independent play.

Ultimately, the museum hosted fourteen indie developers alongside a selection of vintage computer classics, modern consoles, and arcade cabinets. The selection of indie games offered authentic experiences for both knowledgeable and inexperienced gamers – and each game demonstrated a unique approach to the concept of "gamespaces." We worked with Chris Totten, author and video-game developer (who has advised us about this event since 2015), to focus the indie developer showcase around a theme. In years prior, the Arcade had accepted a huge number of different developers to showcase their work, but the plethora of developers meant that the content varied greatly, which provided great diversity in gameplay experience. We wanted to work toward a cohesive presentation of the most artfully developed games. By selecting a theme that could be interpreted by the developers as a framework and by the museum as a guide for assessing applications, the indie developer showcase could be narrowed in terms of scale as well as intention. Architecture – and, by extension, the idea of physical space – was an organic choice to connect gaming and art on a more conceptual level. The games featured in the 2018 showcase conceptualized level design in an inventive way, transformed the real-world space in which they were played, or drew inspiration from a strong community or social space.

The exploration of space provided a framework for the Arcade, but it also served as a lesson in how museums conceptualize and prioritize artistic space. SAAM Arcade provides an example of how museums can be transformed into a place where visitors are free to explore the boundaries between video games and art. For many years, SAAM Arcade has been the museum's only annually recurring program focused on video games as time-based media art. In 2012, the museum organized GameFest, a three-day event that included lectures, panel discussions, performances, and playable games. Subsequent iterations of this video game-centered program rarely moved beyond celebrating the games; the Arcade has since grown to encompass more of the museum's creative, curatorial, and logistical energy with an emphasis on a critique of an issue explored through gaming. The early iterations of the Arcade focused on bringing games into the museum to advocate for their presence in the collection, but by 2018 we realized that the program had achieved those early goals and both the museum and the Arcade's audience were ready to consider more focused and nuanced questions about video games and their role in visual culture. The Arcade was in fact a platform where we could demonstrate the validity and richness of the nontraditional art experience that video games offer. The question became, "so what next?" In 2018, we began to explore that question.

Our new thematic approach linked video games to art, architecture, and the museum as a space for creativity, discovery, and engagement, but it also allowed us to ask more of ourselves, the indie developers, and vendors who participated in the program. SAAM has been working to position itself as a leader in exploring the impact and artistry of video games since 2012. Even now, more curatorial and programmatic support is being directed towards the museum's ongoing commitment to the conservation, study, interpretation, and promotion of video games as part of national visual culture. Prior to 2018, SAAM Arcade had not organized its selection of indie games with an art-historical analysis in mind. The concept of space allowed us, for the first time, to present a critically positioned group of developers whose work challenged the notion of "space" and threw into sharp relief the ability of the museum to act as a venue for debate and cultural authority.

Video games create compelling participatory and social spaces, imagined by artists and designers and activated by players, whose individual interactions are required to complete the experience. Every iteration of SAAM Arcade has emphasized this aspect of video game appreciation by encouraging hands-on engagement and in-person exchanges between indie developers, gamers, and new audiences. To understand how video games could create compelling and participatory experiences in an art museum, we had to define gamespaces from a museological perspective. In the most basic sense, gamespaces are the field of play in which the game takes place. This includes the game's boundaries, tasks, and outcomes (see Salmond 30). These parameters directly affect the player, non-playable characters, or levels, and are designed using a system of vectors within a set of dimensions. The term gamespaces for us came to be described in three general principles: level architecture, physical spaces, and social spaces.

We used the term "level architecture" to describe the design and building of a video game, drawing on Chris Totten's explanation of "level design" in the introduction to *An Architectural Approach to Level Design*, as "the thoughtful execution of gameplay into gamespace for players to dwell in" (xxiv). Michael Nitsche characterizes level architecture spaces into additional categories of movement beyond the standard two-and three-dimensional modes (up and down, left and right, forward and backward). First, interface abstraction is the movement through virtual space and a specialized manipulation of elements within that virtual space (see Nitsche 31). Examples of this type of movement might be building a virtual urban environment in *SimCity* or chatting in *Counter-Strike*. Second, structuring multilayered access, is characterized as the movement of the players through the three-dimensional virtual world and their interaction with objects (see Nitsche 33). Not only can an object within the game be controlled, but the camera and viewpoint of the player can be manipulated.

The second principle, physical space, refers to the place where the game is played (such as an arcade, a living room, or a museum). In our description of space, we acknowledged that the game itself is not necessarily affected by the location, but a player's experience in a physical space can create new contexts for that game. For example, playing the games in a museum seemed to intensify the players experience because of the museum authority as an art institution. In 2017, many museum visitors commented on how their experience of video games was changed dramatically simply by playing them inside an art museum at SAAM Arcade or other related exhibitions. Though the game's design and mechanics are the same, a player's understanding and appreciation of that game changes with the simple act of placing it in a new environment. One visitor to a recent SAAM Arcade wrote, "I love playing video games. It was so much fun playing them in a museum! Really made me think about the art of it all." This contextual effect can also be attributed to location-based game design; some of the games submitted to SAAM Arcade in 2018 required players to move around the physical world to play. With the rise of mobile gaming, these types of experiences are becoming more and more accessible and familiar; examples of location-based games include *Pokemon Go* (2016), *Urban Tapestries* (2003), and *Amsterdam RealTime* (2002). Unlike games that use an avatar represented on a computer, television, or mobile device, these location-based games engage the player by their physical surroundings (see Leorke 18). In an art museum, this type of game facilitated direct interaction with artworks in gallery spaces, something that could not have happened in a different spatial context.

The concept of "gamespaces" can also be applied to the immediate physical world in which one plays the video game; for instance, players act as "both reader (of the computer's output) and producer (via input) of events" (Nitsche 31) through physical interfacing with the game console and controller. For video gamespaces, this means that "players not only enter the game worlds but also change them and their ingredients" (Nitsche 31). This type of space can be defined as the player's interaction with the game's mechanisms. In *Cybertext: Perspectives on Ergodic Literature* (1997), Espen Aarseth describes playing video games as "ergodic," meaning that "non-trivial effort" (1) is required to process the text of the game – in this case, its parameters for play. Although the question of ergodicity in games is up for debate, in defining physical gamespaces we felt that all non-trivial movement in the physical world must be included in our definition of space. Because video games encourage hand-eye coordination through the translation of a physical movement – i.e., a mouse click or pressing buttons on a controller – into a virtual result, they can have a profound effect on the physical space in which they are played, depending on the skill, physical ability, and intent of the player.

Finally, we described gamespaces as social environments. Gaming is often thought of as an isolated activity, but gaming is mostly a dynamic engagement between a player and a variety of other actors, including other players, NPCs, developers, etc. A study done in 2006 looked at more than 5,800 messages sent from within an online multiplayer game – researchers wanted to determine whether the messages were socioemotional or task-oriented. Interestingly they found that there more than 3.2 times as many socioemotional messages as task-oriented (see Fishman). Different types of gamespaces create different gaming experiences, and this is absolutely true of social spaces. Online multiplayer games engage players cognitively, socially and intellectually. Including social space as part of our three-pronged definition of gamespaces also allowed us to seek out games that were based on examples of social space outside of the standard video game culture; an art museum regularly interfaces with various communities by showcasing (or omitting) their art from the museum, but video games are not often held to the same critical standard for considering how ethnicity, nationality, and culture can affect interactivity and representation. By allowing for social space to be as important an element of gamespaces as physical space or level architecture, SAAM Arcade was open to submissions that challenged the notion of what could be gamified.

Of the 14 games selected for showcase at the 2018 SAAM Arcade, we would like to discuss three of them in the context of this chapter. We felt that these three games best represented the theme(s) we were trying to express to our audience:

FAR: Lone Sails (2018) presents ideas about space in a more diegetic way than other entries; although gameplay is structured as a standard two-dimensional scrolling platformer, the player is presented with ideas of space in three layers. First, there is the space within the large vehicle that the player operates to traverse the landscape; second, the landscape being traversed, which the player must occasionally adapt (via puzzles) to accommodate the vehicle's transit; and third, the larger, non-traversable landscape that provides the isolated, post-apocalyptic narrative to the game (which otherwise has no dialogue).

In the context of its presentation at the museum, *FAR: Lone Sails* presents an interesting challenge in terms of interpretation. Unlike *Line Wobbler* (discussed later in this essay), which very obviously subverts our ideas about games and space, *FAR* feels like a more typical video game and without interpretive help, it might be easy to write it off as a "tranquil adventure game." *The Washington Post*'s review of the game – which was published two months before it was shown at SAAM Arcade – emphasized its tonal tranquility and bustling gameplay but failed to pick up on the more haunting elements that the game's use of space implies. As a lone figure building a huge, rumbling vehicle from scrap parts, the player is often faced with vast swaths of empty land; the player encounters the abandoned ephemera of a once-robust society (it must have been, to have left behind such massive pieces of engineering) that the hybrid vehicle traverses. The developers describe their game as a "zombie-free" apocalypse narrative. Even the huge distance between the player and the protagonist could be interpreted as a use of space to complicate the narrative of the game; is the protagonist an adult or a child? Human or alien? The distance encourages speculation and unease – if it is a child, where is its family? If it is an alien, why does this landscape seem so hauntingly Earth-like?

As the sun rises and sets over the dry seabed, the use of space engages the audience by forcing them to grapple with it at both the micro and macro level. The interior of the vehicle must be kept fueled and running to advance; the world around the vehicle must be scoured for obstacles and necessary supplies; and the larger landscape must be contemplated, during moments of peace, as either a great relic of something long dead (making the journey futile) or evidence of a hastily abandoned world (with the hope of survivors at the end of the journey).

These uses of space – internal, external, two-dimensional, and three-dimensional – allow for extraordinarily broad interpretations. In some ways, the game is evocative of great American landscapes of Albert Bierstadt or Thomas Moran, which feature tiny humans or animals in the distance; the awesomeness of the landscape is thrown into sharp (and perhaps terrifying) relief by juxtaposing insignificant humans and monumental mountain. There is a romantic notion of venturing into an unknown that is both physical and metaphysical embedded in the spatial scheme of *FAR: Lone Sails*, in that the game continuously confronts you with the lonely emptiness of the world while also preventing you from seeing what lies ahead until you are in the midst of it.

Doors to the City (*DTTC*, not released) has a similarly multi-dimensional approach but employs adaptive technology to enhance the experience. Rather than move along a 2D pathway, *DTTC*'s levels are each self-contained spheres that the player progresses through on a skateboard (mimicked by the adapted Tech-Deck controller). Suspended in a vast, star-speckled space, the player progresses through the game by collecting memories, leaping from sphere to sphere, and skating through an inverted, looping urban landscape. Created by Benjamin Poynter in conjunction with musician Josh Craig, the game's protagonist is based on Craig's likeness and the narrative includes his experiences of city life. As the virtual version of Craig, the player moves around the city and, according to the developer, "monologues to himself in reflection of what 'the city' means to him and where is home when everywhere is always."

Layered on top of the internal messaging about space – namely, regarding ideas of home and the nature of urban environments – is the physical gameplay through both an adapted controller – the Tech Deck, a 1/8 scale replica skateboard toy designed to recreate skate tricks with your fingers – and a holographic interface. Unlike *FAR: Lone Sails*, *DTTC* emulates an art experience in that it feels specifically experiential to the museum; at SAAM Arcade, the vast majority of participants had never used the Looking Glass 3D display system, let alone used a customized controller made from a nostalgic children's toy. In a museum space, this work could be installed seamlessly in a gallery and approached as a work of immersive or interactive art (unbound from the moniker of "game"). However, it is a game – its creator describes it and promotes it as a game, and its similarities in gameplay mechanics to the *Tony Hawk's Pro Skater* series (1999 – 2020) are unmistakable. *DTTC* takes a very familiar series of early-2000s objects and experiences – the Tech Deck, Tony Hawk, skateboarding, HipHop music – and combines them into a larger narrative about urban space and personal experience of that space.

It would be easy to contrast Robin Baumgarten's *Line Wobbler* (2014) with the two previously discussed games by focusing entirely on how this game takes up physical space wherever it is installed; however, we found ourselves truly engaged by the internal space of the game, the imaginary dungeon represented by a line of LED lights. Because he flattens the play space completely – *Line Wobbler* is a one-dimensional game – Baumgarten subverts expectations about the development of gaming and what constitutes engaging play. While most games layer more and more aesthetic and mechanical elements onto a game to make a dynamic experience, *Line Wobbler* simplifies its interface, from controller to "screen" to create a game that is as much a spectacle for a crowd as it is an individual play experience.

On Baumgarten's website, he describes the game as "a one-dimensional dungeon crawler game with a unique wobble controller made out of a door-stopper spring and a several meter long ultrabright LED strip display." The LED strip can be oriented around objects, along walls, or into free-standing shapes (such as a Christmas tree). The game can change depending on the orientation of the LED strip; at SAAM, we had the game as a free-standing piece in our courtyard, but it was recently shown at the Victoria and Albert Museum running up the wall of the exhibition space. It invites conversation, from its super bright lights to the physicality of the controller. Michael Nitsche notes that "freedom of spatial practice supports a bending or redefinition of given goals" (28) for players – and, as *Line Wobbler* proves, for developers as well. If play requires rules to provide focus, then those same rules can also be flouted in the pursuit of other elements of play – namely, surprise and pleasure.

Line Wobbler also acts as a bridge of sorts between interactive gaming and installation art, which has been present in the museum space since the mid-twentieth century. In this case, we are comparing *Line Wobbler* specifically with the work of artists such as Dan Flavin and Leo Villareal, whose works use light as a sculptural medium to engage the viewer with the piece and the space in which it is installed. Mark Rosenthal defines installation art as "an arrangement that is an integrated, cohesive, carefully contrived whole" (26). Like works by Villareal or Jenny Holzer, who uses scrolling LEDs to communicate challenging messages in public spaces, *Line Wobbler* asserts itself in space. *Line Wobbler* is a complete, *gesamtkunstwerk*-like, multivalent experience; from the sight of the LED strip, to the feel of the spring-based controller, to the sound of the gameplay (a soft trilling noise as the player works their way up the LED strip dungeon). Luminism was not conceived as an art form tied to gaming, but it certainly finds expression in *Line Wobbler* and other gaming experiences like *Dance Dance Revolution* (2010) or elaborate pinball machines. The experience of play is augmented by the inclusion of flashing lights and brightly colored, glowing interfaces that create an ambiance for the player and their surroundings. In many ways, *Line Wobbler* expands experiential space by diminishing the diegetic environment.

In some ways, these games represent all three of the elements of "space" we asked developers to focus on. All three present extraordinary examples of level architecture and design, and both DTTC and *FAR: Lone Sails* evoke a sense of isolation and exploration of the self in the scope of a larger landscape, while *Line Wobbler* – by the force of its presence in a space – creates a space for social engagement and a literal beacon for congregation (despite being exclusively single-player). The amount of physical space taken up by the games increases gradually; *FAR: Lone Sails* is contained within the standard spatial configuration of gamer and game, but *DTTC* modifies this by adapting the controller and incorporating new technology to modify the visual experience of the game. *Line Wobbler* then takes the adaptation of physical space to its most extreme with the complete subversion of physical interplay between the two agents.

The purpose of SAAM Arcade is to bring video games into the museum as artworks and invite people to recognize their important contributions to American visual culture. We recognize, however, that though this vision is beginning to be shared by other museums such as the Museum of Modern Art and the Victoria and Albert Museum, traditional art museum visitors continue to struggle with the idea of showing popular culture content alongside traditional fine art objects. It is not a question that the development of games requires artists and designers to create an aesthetically interesting product; there are also artists working today who create video games as part of their artistic practice, such as Porpentine Charity Heartscape and Steph Thirion. This is not a new phenomenon, either: In the 1970s, sculptors such as Peter Campus, Bruce Nauman, and Dan Graham wanted to bridge the space between art and video games by creating installations that played perceptual tricks with their own electronically altered images. Nam June Paik explored the idea of interactive media in *Good Morning, Mr. Orwell* (1984), which used a two-way satellite link between New York and Paris that transmitted live performances between the cities. Lynn Hershman Leeson's 1989 *Deep Contact* used an interactive console to allow viewers to interact with a virtual woman.

At the Smithsonian American Art Museum, we have explored this question through exhibitions such as *The Art of Video Games* and *Watch This! Revelations in Media Art* as well as SAAM Arcade. Our aim is to continue to challenge notions of what qualifies as American art aesthetically, philosophically, and socially. With the exhibition *The Art of the Video Games*, guest curator Chris Melissinos wanted visitors to understand the many artistic aspects required to create a video game; when asked if he thought video games were art, Chris responded,

> [a]ll video games include classic components of art – striking visuals, a powerful narrative, a strong point of view. What's new is the role of the player. Video games are a unique form of artistic expression through, what I call, the "three voices:" the voice of the designer or artist, the voice of the game and its mechanics, and the voice of the player. A designer can craft an experience that follows a pre-determined arc to a set conclusion, while allowing the player the ability to laterally move and experience the game world. This retains the authoritative voice of the creator, yet allows each player to have a unique experience. There is no other form of media that allows for these three distinct voices to combine and present themselves as the output of expression. (Eye Level, Blog "The Art of Video Games: Five Questions for Chris Melissinos")

The 2019 SAAM Arcade addresses sociocultural barriers within the video game industry; in the future, we are discussing new thematic approaches that we hope will challenge our visitors to seek their own answers and in turn inspire us with new questions.

Since 2012, other museums have exhibited video games, accessioned them into their collections, and generally grappled with how games can fit into the museum space, both physically (conservation and preservation are of great concern to time-based media specialists) and philosophically. SAAM Arcade acts as the Smithsonian Institution's largest ongoing contribution to the conversation, particularly through a lens of art and American visual culture. SAAM exercises its authority as a museum by using its physical and metaphorical spaces, as well as its staff, to grapple with these questions. In prioritizing video games – and then, in 2018, further subjecting games to a critical lens for organization and interpretation – the Smithsonian American Art Museum continues to be at the forefront of museums dedicating programmatic resources to video games as an artistic medium and advocating that video games can – and should – be dissected, analyzed, and considered with the same academic rigor as a work of film, sculpture, or painting.

Works Cited

Aarseth, Espen J. *Cybertext: Perspectives on Ergodic Literature.* The Johns Hopkins University Press, 1997.

Antonelli, Paola "Video Games: 14 in the Collection, for Starters." *Museum of Modern Art,* 29 November 2012, www.moma.org/explore/inside_out/2012/11/29/video-games-14-in-the-collection-for-starters/. Accessed 2 September 2020.

Antonelli, Paola. "Treat Design as Art." *TED,* March 2007, www.ted.com/talks/paola_antonelli_treats_design_as_art/up-next?language=en. Accessed 2 September 2020.

Baumgarten, Robin. "Line Wobbler." *Wobbly Labs,* www.wobblylabs.com/projects/wobbler.

Byrd, Christopher. "FAR: Loan Sails' a Tranquil Adventure Game." *Washington Post,* 18 June 2018.

Clarke, Andy, and Grethe Mitchell. *Videogames and Art.* Intellect Books, 2007.

Eye Level. "The Art of Video Games: Five Questions for Chris Melissinos," AmericanArt.si.edu, 18 August 2011. www.americanart.si.edu/blog/eye-level/2011/18/799/art-video-games-five-questions-chris-melissinos.

Far: Lone Sails. Okomotive Games, 2018.

Fishman, Andrew. "Video Games are Social Spaces: How Video Games Help People Connect," *Psychology Today,* 22 January 2019, www.psychologytoday.com/us/blog/video-game-health/201901/video-games-are-social-spaces. Accessed 2 September 2020.

Goldberg, Harold. "How the Smithsonian Screwed up its Video Game Exhibition." *NPR,* 26 March 2012.

Leorke, Dale. *Location-Based Gaming.* Palgrave MacMillan, 2018.

Mondloch, Kate. *Screens: Viewing Media Installation Art.* University of Minnesota Press, 2013.

Nitsche, Michael. *Video Games Spaces: Image, Play and Structure in 3D.* The MIT Press, 2008.

O'Brien, Jane. "Video Game Art Gets the Gallery Treatment." *BBC News,* 16 March 2012, www.bbc.com/news/magazine-17373879. Accessed 2 September 2020.

Poynter, Benjamin. "Doors To The City." *Benjamin Poynter,* www.benjaminpoynter.com/WELCOME.php.

Rosenthal, Mark. *Understanding Installation Art: From Duchamp to Holzer.* Prestel Publishing, 2003.

Salmond, Michael. *Video Game Design: Principles and Practices from the Ground Up.* Bloomsbury Publishing, 2017.

Santiago, Kellee. "Are Video Games Art?" *YouTube,* uploaded by USC Stevens Center for Innovation, 29 July 2010, www.youtube.com/watch?v=6GjKCnPQlSw.

Schiesel, Seth. "An Exhibition in Easy Mode." *New York Times,* 15 March 2012.

Totten, Christopher W. *An Architectural Approach to Level Design.* CRC Press, 2014.

Victoria and Albert Museum. "Video Games: Design/Play/Disrupt." *Victoria and Albert Museum,* www.vam.ac.uk/exhibitions/videogames. Accessed 2 September 2020.

Soraya Murray
Coda: Disoriented in the Field of Play

> Disorientation can be a bodily feeling of losing one's place, and an effect of the loss of a place: it can be a violent feeling, and a feeling that is affected by violence, or shaped by violence directed toward the body. Disorientation involves failed orientations: bodies inhabit spaces that do not extend their shape, or use objects that do not extend their reach. At this moment of failure, such objects 'point' somewhere else or they make what is 'here' become strange.
>
> Ahmed, *Queer Phenomenology* 160

Sometimes, something odd happens when I enter a gamespace that is new to me. I gravitate toward narrative games in highly articulated, open worlds. Often, they take a long time to load. I wait. I stare at the progress bar. I am full of anticipation. The game begins. Then, not knowing yet what I am supposed to do, or which way I am to go, I become disoriented. I notice the feeling, which passes almost instantly. I orient myself, finding my bearings, and push forward into the game world as if it were my space.

That brief disorientation I experience could be thought of as a mere behavioral quirk, or a moment of indecision, but I think it points to something else: a momentary disjuncture between the spatiality presented by the game and my personal spatial orientation. In that moment, I graft my sense of spatiality onto that of the game. But that means there exists a difference between the two. That difference appears as an ideological gap that must be bridged, in order for me to give sense to the space as a player who finds herself 'out of place' in a social construction inconsistent with her own. That gap has been an object of discomfort, a turbulence in the otherwise smooth transition of mapping one's self onto the technological space of a game. As a critical game theorist, I find these disorientations – these moments of failed orientations to gamespace – useful rather than merely extraneous moments of noise or friction that should be omitted. They point to someplace else, and because they flout the insistent imperative toward immersion – they keep the space strange. And in keeping it strange, they point to the limitations of the space with which we have been presented – which is invaluable because worldbuilding can be so alluring.

Space and spatiality have always been my main access points into the profundity of video games as a medium. Upon becoming drawn to games as objects of scholarly study, I first began thinking about what their spaces mean, how they signify, and the connection between the in-game aesthetic experience and an embodied perception of the lived world (see Murray, "High Art/Low Life"). This focus has run parallel to my interest in a sense of Americanness as being completely bound up in particular conceptions of space, or more precisely a conception of one's orientation within and command of space as an extension of a more generalized mode of consumption, possession, and predatory intention (see Murray, "Landscapes of Empire"). This is easily confirmed by the program of ideologically framing the American landscape to serve U.S. nation-building in ways that have been already very accurately captured in several of the included essays. These important writings tackle the propensity of video games for reproducing the industrial civilizing of the West, and more generally an imperial gaze connected to mapping, treasure hunting, and colonial adventuring.

The overall critical project of *Video Games and Spatiality in American Studies* operates at the intersection of American Studies and Critical Games Studies, with a focus on the theorization of space – American conceptions of space and place. Games can create spatial frictions that start to communicate, on a deeply aesthetic level, things that are unutterable, are never said, or do not occupy the narrative dimension. Increasingly, I am convinced their primary mode of communication is rooted in their engagement with the embodied and the affective. The self-awareness of political feeling or political affect, what Ann Cvetkovich identifies as the "relations between the emotional, the cultural and the political" as it relates to "the everyday experience of sensation and embodiment as ways of tracking [the] intersection of the social and the psychic" (Staiger, Cvetkovich, and Reynolds 5–6), can provide a means to break the smooth hailing of the player by the logics of the gameworld. Their complex manifestations can, across a duration of play, begin to gather up a particular affective experience within the worldbuilding of the game – but which is ultimately informed by larger cultural, social, and political intensities at work in the lived world. This can be conveyed through game rules, mechanics, texture, touch, temporality, narrative, atmosphere, mapping, aesthetics, and in many cases the borrowing of visual literacies from pre-existing media.

The writings collected in this intellectual project have certainly taken up some of the most critical intellectual threads in an ongoing conversation about the spatial from an American Studies perspective of games. But many possibilities for such a conversation in both game design and critical Game Studies still remain untapped. Much of the critical games scholarship on space and worldbuilding has retained some connection to the origins (and perhaps more precisely the original sin) of the U.S.A. as a nation, in terms of its troubled spatial politics. For example, in 1995, Henry Jenkins and Mary Fuller were already making implicit connections between the construction of the virtual and the rhetorics of software innovation and the reproduction of colonial paradigms and frontier ideologies (see 57–72). This is all true: progress in many games is demarked through the discovery and clearing of territories, the gathering of resources, and the construction of space as existing solely for the purpose of its use-value to the player (see Murray, "The Work of Postcolonial Game Studies").

What possibilities exist for imagining other futures through speculative spaces that break from the presumptive narratives we have been telling ourselves about space? And, just as significantly, how can we understand such dynamics as functions of the present, not merely the past? That is to say, it is not only about the past as it bears upon the present, but also the ongoing ways in which space, in an American context, becomes central to one's conception of what might be possible in the present and future. Here I am thinking of the present conditions of spatiality within the U.S., for those whose bodies, subjectivities, and orientations do not move in the same direction as the spaces they occupy. How can space be understood in the context of the use of music – early hip-hop, for example – in personal devices as well as thumping car speakers, to create a sonic envelope that makes space within the public sphere for those who might not otherwise feel they command it? What ethics of a right to take up space – to occupy it – can be simulated? What raced, gendered, sexed, and ableist inflected notions of space shape contemporary lived American spaces? Who can be the bearer of space, who commands it, who may own it, and who may build intergenerational wealth on account of it? I am thinking of a now famous article on housing discrimination, in which author Ta-Nehisi Coates maps the systematic denial of equitable home ownership and its profound impacts on the African American community across time (see Coates). These nuanced encounters with spatiality in the U.S. context are broadly experienced but under-recognized.

Truly, the great story of the United States of America – with the exception of Native Peoples – is the story of arriving from someplace else and making space for one's self in the nation. And in the interim, it is a story of orientation toward a homeland, disorientation, being out of place, being put in one's place, learning to find a place, existing as a conditional guest, or perhaps an unwanted entity. Sara Ahmed has considered the situatedness of particularized bodies in these terms, theorizing a queer phenomenology that seeks to understand the ramifications for a spectrum of "orientations" in space and time:

> for bodies to arrive in spaces where they are not already at home, where they are not "in place," involves hard work; indeed, it involves painstaking labor for bodies to inhabit spaces that do not extend their shape. Having arrived, such bodies in turn might acquire new shapes. And spaces in turn acquire new bodies. So, yes, we should celebrate such arrivals. The "new" is what is possible when what is behind us, our background, does not simply ground us or keep us in place, but allows us to move and allows us to follow something other than the lines we have already taken. (Ahmed 61–62)

Ahmed's work theoretically engages queerness as sexual orientation, but also as departure from the normative – and the positionalities that result from occupying space under such conditions. It is inflected by the particularities of what it means to be out of place as someone biracial and, as an immigrant, not at home. But these "arrivals" to places in which bodies are "not already at home" or "in place" articulates a different experience of space, and one that seems potentially very rich in terms of the new understandings of space that might emerge. Queer and trans bodies, multiracial bodies, bodies that in some way cannot be readily assimilated, open up other ways of engaging with space.

For instance, Ahmed writes of how race functions to orient bodies in space: "[I]t [racism] works as a way of orienting bodies in specific directions, thereby affecting how they 'take up' space. We 'become' racialized in how we occupy space, just as space is, as it were, already occupied as an effect of racialization" (24).[1] This describes an experience that would immediately sound familiar to someone whose racial designation others them within a public sphere or an institutional space. This is also a very North American experience of not belonging in space, if one is not considered fully American, or fully normal, or of the proper class. Yet, this is also not an experience of space that is rare – in fact it is an extremely common experience. This is a useful orientation for both affective and phenomenological understandings of gamespaces. Because, of course, a body is never just "a competent body wrapped around an input device: hands tapping at a keyboard, waving at a motion sensor, clutching a joystick, smearing a touchscreen, or, more often than not, wrapped around a gamepad" (Keogh 108). It is all of these things, but in excess of this, it is also a subjective body with a positioning that shapes how meaning in a video game evolves for an individual player and for culture.

Another instance: the gathering U.S.-based nationalist turn has been agitated in a constituency who feels that the country (their place) has been taken from them and that, as true patriots, it is their duty to reclaim it. This invokes the notion of a 'heartland' space that is 'traditional' (i.e. normative and white-identified) though it is not exclusively white. The unrest and major political turmoil around the identity of the United States, specifically the browning of national space, which is almost never overtly discussed, underlies the anxieties of the alt-right, who feel as though traditional America has died (see Hsu). This is

---

[1] Brendan Keogh's work provides some of the most valuable observations of how haptic dimensions of the human-computer interface and sensorial perception inform a meaningful experience of embodied gameplay. However, the phenomenological tradition of scholarship to which this work contributes is not specifically engaged with subject position and how that may influence perception and affect.

most recently evident in the 6 January, 2021, storming of the U.S. Capitol, which has quickly become a Trump-era moment of intense rupture within the nation but was fomenting for decades. One journalist characterized the Capitol riot as "an attack on multiracial democracy" against those whose inclusion and freedom was "less inalienable than those of their countrymen" (Serwer). In the live news footage, it appeared as a reassertion of particular people in command of a symbolic national space and the forcing out of other people whom they feel should be pushed out of place. Their own feelings of having lost their place led to a violence directed to both a symbolic space and a political body. But these things I am saying are not insightful. Anyone who lives the United States knows this about American space, because we live it, and if anything, these spatial relations are so overdetermining as to limit the scope of our imaginations.

An expanded notion of spatial paradigms has not yet been deeply investigated within video games. There are some exceptions, such as the personal games of Anna Anthropy, like her 2012 game *Dys4ia*, which engages with the being-in-the-worldness of gender dysphoria and hormone replacement therapy, or *Queers in Love at the End of the World* (2013), in which fraught temporality challenges normative notions of time. *Lim* (2012) by Merritt Kopas, with its apparent blocky non-spaces, uses reductive but extremely poetic design to point to the ways space can be perilous when one's body does not seem to be in place. Of the same year, *Mainichi* by Mattie Brice, operates in a similar way, engaging with personal experiences of what it means to be a queer body in normative space. *Hair Nah!* (2017) by Momo Pixel pointedly critiques the lack of respect accorded to black bodies in the public sphere through the simple gamic objective of swatting away probing white hands from a black woman's hair. Tracy Fullerton and the USC Game Innovation Lab's *Walden, a Game* (2017) simulates Henry David Thoreau's famous experiment in living at Walden Pond to contemplate self-reliance and living in balance with nature through slow (rather than frantic) forms of engagement with gamespace. Games such as these begin to signal what possibilities are made manifest when one's experience with disorientations begin to point to other places. There is a wealth of untapped opportunity in game design and critical game scholarship for polymorphous understandings of space.

I want to make clear that this is not a plea for representing 'other' spaces in the hopes of currying facile sentiment and generating empathy for the subaltern. In the context of the utopian rhetorics around VR, Lisa Nakamura has warned of an "identity tourism for the 21st century" that peddles a vision of how "racial and gendered otherness can be bridged by 'virtuous' VR that puts you in the shoes of marginalized and threatened bodies" (48). As she explains, it functions as a pernicious liberalism which supposes that in moving about the space of socially defined minorities, by feeling present in their space, one can somehow witness, know, and commiserate with their suffering. This is equally problematic for video games that mobilize a kind of "toxic empathy" (47) as Nakamura calls it, that confuses identity tourism for authentic empathy and compassion – and even worse – parades as political activism. What I am suggesting is something else; it is about the opportunity of what can be made possible when an enhanced understanding of space and spatiality finds expression in games criticism and theory. This extends to the phenomenological experience of playing the game which is specifically connected to a player's subjectivity or their positionality in relation to the spaces of the game through which they move. But this is all a way of suggesting that there are many prospects for a great untapped conversation, yet to be had, in a language of space that can embrace a queer phenomenology of displacements, being out of place, new lines of movement, disorientations, and other positionalities in space and time. I would point to the exploitation of glitches in games, speedruns, and playing it 'wrong' as glimmers of how a video game can be queered, repurposed, or manipulated into producing other kinds of space.[2]

The social production of space that goes on in video games should not be taken for granted as being about some things and not about others. In fact, one of the key roles of critical Game Studies is to meticulously record displacements and disorientations, divergences and idiosyncratic experiences. It is the documentation of how such spaces are made strange to its players, and what that strangeness means. For those who are not 'at home' in video games, this disorientation can be an asset to mining the political spaces of potential that get arranged within a game. It is the friction between the tool at hand (the video game) and positioned player that can start to become useful.

To break through to what specific video games as cultural objects mean, it is necessary to engage with the phenomenological experience of their spaces. After all, these games are practice-based in the sense that one must play them, and it is through an extended engagement with them that one comes to gather up a sense of their intensities of feeling. This happens through the experiential, through 'being there' in the game for long enough to follow around the affective cues that tell a player what they are to be doing, and how they are to be doing it. As I have written elsewhere, often the most intense experiences players have with games issue from the durational – from engaging with the game for long periods of time and having deeply affective spatio-temporal experiences of the gamespace (see "'America is Dead. Long Live America!'"). These games require

---

[2] For example, see Bonnie Ruberg "Playing to Lose" (2017) or *Video Games Have Always Been Queer* (2019).

players to know spaces, to unlock an understanding of key game mechanics, and to learn to take up space in the game through the proper orientation.

An incredibly valuable feature of critical Game Studies remains the documentation of many and varied experiences of what it means to experience a given video game. One early example of this, David Sudnow's obsessive account of playing Atari's *Breakout* (1976), called *Pilgrim in the Microworld* (1983), predicts one critical pathway for understanding how games work on us and in effect slows down and plants markers that re-orient a player to the intense ways we engage with them. Sudnow's ability to capture the minutia of his zealous fixations with the game, interspersed with personal subjective experience of its role in his life, inaugurated a kind of video game phenomenology. At first, he was not 'at home' in video games. The book catalogues his slow orientation toward *Breakout*, his being out of place in the physical arcade space of games, and the flat in-game space itself, as well as the failures and the frictions of his attempts to engage. Importantly, he gave voice to his own disorientation when encountering with the video game form and provided a sustained narrative of what it meant to be lost and sit with that disorientation.

Like him, I often find myself in an affective experience of being sustained in a worldview foreign to my own. While playing, I follow around the affective cues that tell me what I am to do, and how I am to be doing it. I notice how the spaces push and pull me, attempting to shape me, and that there are moments of disjuncture where the game and I never seem to entirely meet.

Capturing the affective, even mundane aspects of experiencing the game, inclusive of idiosyncratic dimensions of positioning, illuminates meanings and the ways in which it may become constantly revised through our ongoing engagement with them. Much of Game Studies seems to harbor unspoken expectations that its forms of knowledge production have more value if they can be distilled to general rules and assertions. Perhaps, it is wrong to traffic in too many generalizations when it comes to understanding gamespaces. The idiosyncratic interpretation and the 'oppositional' look that creates friction with the space of a game, can open up how the game's sensations and engagements with embodiment contribute to potent political affective intensities (see hooks 115–132).

For example, Jamil Jan Kochai wrote a fictionalized account of playing *Metal Gear Solid V: The Phantom Pain* (2015), an iconic mainstream video game that is part of a more than three-decade legacy. The first part of the game takes place in Afghanistan in the 1980s. From his position as part of an Afghan immigrant family, and son to a village farmer who served as a member of the mujahideen, his perspective melds a fanboy love of the game with shame and his sense of deep immersion in its impressive spaces:

> [T]he fact that nineteen-eighties Afghanistan is the final setting of the most legendary and artistically significant gaming franchise in the history of time made you all the more excited to get your hands on it, especially since you've been shooting at Afghans in your games (*Call of Duty* and *Battlefield* and *Splinter Cell*) for so long that you've become oddly immune to the self-loathing you felt when you were first massacring wave after wave of militant fighters who looked just like your father. (Kochai)

The writing begins with this orientation, as recognizable observations of a fraught subject position in relation to in-game representations. But increasingly it bends toward irrational fantasies connected to the narrator's trauma and longing projected into the space of the game: "Here is what you're going to do," Kochai writes, "before your father is tortured and his brother murdered, you are going to tranquillize them both and you are going to carry them to your horse and cross Logar's terrain until you reach a safe spot where you can call a helicopter and fly them back to your offshore platform: Mother Base" (Kochai).

Ultimately, the historical record should not only consist of efficient, smooth encounters with gamespace.[3] Critical insight also lies in capturing the phenomenological, the affective, the contemplative, the working-through of it, or the friction that occurs in gameplay.[4] It lies in realizing that you do not like how a game makes you feel. It is about what games make you dream of. It is about understanding the pivotal role of the player's subjectivity in the affective exchange that takes place. One's disorientations are incredibly useful, and certainly nothing to be shaken off as extraneous to legitimate game experience or mastery.

Rather than rejecting these spaces, or feeling ejected by them, go toward them. Sustain yourself in the spaces you do not like, be where you do not belong, sit with the friction, and refuse to be worn down by it. Figure out what is bothering you in games and bump up against their boundaries and strictures. Share what a game's affective impacts generate in you as a subjective player – what it makes you feel in your body. Document everything. Take up space. Point us someplace else.

---

[3] Of interest here is Braxton Soderman's critique of flow as a central concept of game design, *Against Flow* (2021).

[4] I want to point here to the important work of Patrick Jagoda (2018) who theorizes difficulty and affect in video games. Jagoda identifies three forms of difficulty: mechanical, interpretive, and affective. He writes: "we might think of difficulty not simply as a problem to overcome but an ambivalent space from which to experiment with our historical present through critical play. In this formulation, difficulty becomes an active practice rather than a mere obstacle" (232).

Works Cited

Ahmed, Sara. *Queer Phenomenology: Orientations, Objects, Others*. Duke University Press, 2006.

Coates, Ta-Nehisi. "The Case for Reparations." *The Atlantic*, June 2014, www.theatlantic.com/magazine/archive/2014/06/the-case-for-reparations/361631/. Accessed 22 June 2021.

Fuller, Mary and Henry Jenkins. "Nintendo and New World Travel Writing: A Dialogue." *Cybersociety: Computer-Mediated Communication and Community*, edited by Steven G. Jones, SAGE Publications, 1995, pp. 57–72.

hooks, bell. "The Oppositional Gaze: Black Female Spectators." *Black Looks: Race and Representation*, South End Press, 1992, pp. 115–132.

Hsu, Hua. "The End of White America?" *The Atlantic*, 2 February 2009, www.theatlantic.com/magazine/archive/2009/01/the-end-of-white-america/307208/. Accessed 22 June 2021.

Jagoda, Patrick. "On Difficulty in Video Games." *Critical Inquiry*, vol. 45, no. 1, 2018, pp. 199–233.

Keogh, Brendan. *A Play of Bodies: How We Perceive Videogames*. The MIT Press, 2018.

Kochai, Jamil Jan. "Playing Metal Gear Solid V: The Phantom Pain." *The New Yorker*, 30 December 2019, www.newyorker.com/magazine/2020/01/06/playing-metal-gear-solid-v-the-phantom-pain. Accessed 22 June 2021.

Murray, Soraya. "High Art/Low Life: The Art of Playing Grand Theft Auto," *PAJ: A Journal of Performance and Art*, vol. 27, no. 2, 2005, pp. 91–98.

Murray, Soraya. "Landscapes of Empire in Metal Gear Solid V: The Phantom Pain." *Critical Inquiry*, vol. 45, no. 1, 2018, pp. 168–198.

Murray, Soraya. "The Work of Postcolonial Game Studies in the Play of Culture." *Open Library of Humanities*, vol. 4, no. 1, 2018, pp. 1–25.

Murray, Soraya. "'America is Dead. Long Live America!' Political Affect in *Days Gone*." *Video Games and/in American Studies*, vol. 16, no. 3, 2021, pp. 1–23.

Nakamura, Lisa. "Feeling Good about Feeling Bad: Virtuous Virtual Reality and the Automation of Racial Empathy." *Journal of Visual Culture*, vol. 19, no. 1, 2020, pp. 47–64.

Ruberg, Bonnie. "Playing to Lose: The Queer Art of Failing at Video Games." *Gaming Representation: Race, Gender, and Sexuality in Video Games*, edited by Jennifer Malkowski and TreaAndrea M. Russworm, Indiana University Press, 2017, pp. 197–211.

Ruberg, Bonnie. *Video Games Have Always Been Queer*. New York University Press, 2019.

Adam Serwer, "The Capitol Riot Was an Attack on Multiracial Democracy." *The Atlantic*, 7 January 2021, www.theatlantic.com/ideas/archive/2021/01/multiracial-democracy-55-years-old-will-it-survive/617585/. Accessed 22 June 2021.

Soderman, Braxton. *Against Flow: Video Games and the Flowing Subject*. The MIT Press, 2021.

Staiger, Janet, Ann Cvetkovich, and Ann Reynolds. Introduction: Political Emotions and Public Feelings. *Political Emotions*, by Staiger, Cvetkovich, and Reynolds, Routledge, 2010, pp. 1–17.

Sudnow, David. *Pilgrim in the Microworld*. Warner Books, 1983.

Contributors

Nathalie Aghoro is an Assistant Professor of North American Literary and Cultural Studies at the Catholic University of Eichstätt-Ingolstadt with an interest in auditory culture, postmodern and contemporary literature, media theory, and social justice. Her book *Sounding the Novel: Voice in Twenty-First Century American Fiction* (Universitätsverlag Winter, 2018) examines the sonic mediality of voice in the works of Richard Powers, Karen Tei Yamashita, Jennifer Egan, and Jonathan Safran Foer. She is the co-editor of the 2017 JCDE special issue on *Theatre and Mobility* (with Kerstin Schmidt), and her publications include essays on postmodern novels, contemporary literature, and Afrofuturism in music. Lately, she keeps coming back to *The Pathless* in her quest for just the right mix of puzzle challenge and flow.

Juliane Borosch is a doctoral candidate at the University of Duisburg-Essen. She is a member of the University Alliance Ruhr graduate research group *Scripts for Postindustrial Urban Futures: American Models, Transatlantic Interventions*. Her dissertation project investigates the conjunction of creative and sustainable urban development in a transnational comparison of Detroit and the Ruhr Area. Juliane's research interests include American Urban Studies, popular audio-visual culture as well as the historical layering and complexity of the (post)Industrial. Due to persistent motion sickness, Juliane had to exit the world of video gaming when graphics evolved past the Game Boy Color. She is now a gamer by proxy and enjoys watching her siblings play the *Assassin's Creed* and *Uncharted* franchises, which is also how she experienced *Detroit Become Human*.

David Callahan is Associate Professor of English at the University of Aveiro, Portugal. His work has mostly dealt with postcolonial issues, in journals from *Interventions* to *Game Studies*. He has also published many book chapters on subjects as varied as "American Postcolonial Shame, Fiction and Timothy Bewes" and "Rotting, Blistered, Staggering Bodies and the Last of Ethnicity." His most recent publication is the co-edited *Body & Text: Cultural Transformations in New Media Environments* (Springer, 2019). At present he is learning the limit of his proprioceptive abilities by being unable to fly a plane in *Far Cry V*.

Florian Deckers is a doctoral candidate in the research group *Scripts for Post-Industrial Urban Futures: American Models, Transatlantic Interventions* at the University of Duisburg-Essen. His main fields of interests are transnational American Studies, contemporary popular culture, Media Studies, and Urban Studies. In his dissertation project *Raising Ethnic Voices: Counterscripts in the Contemporary Cultural Scene of New York City,* he investigates contemporary approaches of Latinx artists and activists in New York City and how these artists rewrite a vision of American society in music, art, and literature, claiming the fastest growing minority's right to the city. Exploring digital urban spaces has fascinated Florian ever since he stole his first car in *Grand Theft Auto*, which is why he decided to analyze the remastered *Grim Fandango* and visit all the hybrid places in the Land of the Dead.

Greta Kaisen is a research assistant and Ph.D. candidate at H.U. Berlin, Germany. In 2019, she completed a combined M.A. in American Studies and Literature and Media Practice from the University of Duisburg-Essen with a thesis on the Gothic mode and nostalgia in video games. As part of the research project "Liminal Whiteness: Southern Rednecks, Hillbillies, and Crackers in American Culture," her dissertation investigates representations of liminal white characters in Southern Gothic literature, film, and video games. While haunted houses are probably the video game settings where she feels most at home, she increasingly enjoys venturing out into all kinds of genres and aesthetics.

Elisabeth Haefs is a doctoral candidate at the University of Duisburg-Essen. As a member of the graduate research group "Scripts for Postindustrial Urban Futures: American Models, Transatlantic Interventions," she explores narratives about community gardening that circulate in urban planning documents from the U.S. and Germany. Her research interests include British and Postcolonial Studies as well as the field of Literature and Science. Unfortunately, her experience with video games is limited to Monolith Production's *Claw* (1997), but this one she has almost perfected.

Lauren Kolodkin is on the staff in the department of External Affairs and Digital Strategies at the Smithsonian American Art Museum (SAAM) in Washington, D.C. Since 2017, she has been acting as co-coordinator of SAAM Arcade, the museum's signature program highlighting video games as art objects and developers as artists and makers. She has a Masters in Art History from Boston University, where she studied American folk art and the ethics of collecting. She has played *Legend of Zelda: Breath of the Wild* at least three times, and she will probably do it again.

Ryan Linthicum earned her Master's degree in history at Simmons University in Boston, Massachusetts. In 2014 she finished her thesis "The Three Faces of Motherhood: Representation of Women in American Hollywood Films from 1970–1979." She went on to work at the Smithsonian American Art Museum from 2015 to 2020 where she managed the museum film programs and co-managed the museums video game public program SAAM Arcade. Now she is an independent researcher, museum professional, and public historian. Her fields of study include film, museum, and women's history. While she is not an avid gamer, she loves alternative ways of using museums to invite all communities through its doors.

Dietmar Meinel is currently working as a postdoctoral researcher in American Studies at the University of Duisburg-Essen, Germany. He has published in English and German, and his articles have appeared in journals *European Journal of American Culture* to *NECSUS: European Journal of Media Studies*. His monograph *Pixar's America: The Reanimation of American Myths and Symbols* (2016) has been published by Palgrave MacMillan. Together with Elena Furlanetto he also edited *A Poetics of Neurosis: Narratives of Normalcy and Disorder in Cultural and Literary Texts* (2018). He is currently pursuing a book project about failure in antebellum America. During the pandemic, he has found solace in the post-apocalyptic worlds and the cooperative play of *Remnants: From the Ashes*.

Kirsten Möller is a doctoral candidate at Ruhr Universität Bochum, game designer, and dramaturge at Schauspiel Dortmund. As part of the performance group *kainkollektiv*, she was involved in numerous national and international projects, in the preparation of the *Afro-Tech Fest* at Dortmunder U (2017) with medienwerk.nrw as well as the festival *Blue Skies – Bodies in Trouble* at PACT Zollverein (2019). As a member of the collective Anna Kpok, she has been developing installations, performances, and game theater since 2011, including *realReality*

(2018) or the city parcours *Walking in Someone Else's Shoes* (2019, in cooperation with Mercator Research Group). She is doing her Ph.D. on the concept of encounter in participatory formats of contemporary arts and is working on non-linear storytelling and interactive theatre forms. As a theater maker she is interested in narrative games like *Life is Strange* and is currently exploring the possibilities of collaboration in couch co-op games such as *A Way Out*.

Soraya Murray is an Associate Professor in the Film and Digital Media Department at the University of California, Santa Cruz. She holds a Ph.D. in Art History and Visual Studies from Cornell University. Her writings on art, media, and video games are anthologized widely and published in journals such as *Third Text, Art Journal, Film Quarterly, The Journal of Cinema and Media Studies, Feminist Media Studies,* and *Critical Inquiry.* Murray's book, *On Video Games: The Visual Politics of Race, Gender and Space* (I. B. Tauris, 2018), considers video games from a visual culture studies perspective. Recently, she edited a special focus on game space and landscape for *Art Journal* (2020) called "Horizons Already Here." She has also completed new writings on games and political affect. Along with TreaAndrea Russworm, Murray is currently co-editing an anthology on anti-racist futures in games, play, and the speculative imagination. Murray is currently re-experiencing the wonder of the classic *Shadow of the Colossus* for a forthcoming project.

Andrei Nae is Assistant Lecturer at the Faculty of Foreign Languages and Literatures where he teaches the M.A. course "Video Games and Cultural Identity" and the elective course "Introduction to the Study of Video Games as Narrative Media," alongside seminars in translation and American literature. Since 2019 he has been the manager and principal investigator of the research project "Colonial Discourse in Video Games" financed by the Executive Unit for Financing Higher Education, Research, Development and Innovation (UEFISCDI). Andrei Nae has published several books, chapters, and articles including the monograph *Immersion, Narrative, and Gender Crisis in Survival Horror Video Games* released by Routledge in 2021. He wishes contemporary AAA games were shorter so that he could have more time to write.

Hanne Nijtmans is a Ph.D. candidate at the American Studies department of the University of Groningen. Her project titled "Podcasting Paranoia: Aesthetics, Politics and Community in American Fictional Podcasts" focuses on the centrality of conspiracy narratives in fictional podcasts between 2012 to 2020. Beyond this project, her research explores the ways new media, including video games, podcasts, and interactive narratives construct different, and at times illusory, forms of agency. Lately, she and her boyfriend are very much enjoying the unique game mechanics of co-op game *It Takes Two*, which may be somewhat ironic since the game's narrative is aimed at fixing the protagonists' relationship.

Michael Nitsche is Associate Professor in Digital Media at the Georgia Institute of Technology, where he directs the Digital World & Image Group. His work combines elements of performance and craft to explore creative approaches to digital media. He has mainly published in the fields of Game Studies and H.C.I. and is co-editor of the journal *Digital Creativity.* His book projects cover the role of video game spaces and (together with Henry Lowood) Machinima as one form of digital expression. He cannot let go of the beautiful world of *Horizon Zero Dawn* and has high hopes for the sequel.

Damien B. Schlarb works as an Assistant Professor (limited term) at Johannes Gutenberg-University, Mainz, Germany, where he teaches courses in American Studies. He earned his Ph.D. from Georgia State University in Atlanta, G.A. His research interests include American literary romanticism, literary post-secularism, and Digital Game Studies. He has served as layout editor for *South Atlantic Review* and managing editor for *Amerikastudien / American Studies*. His book *Melville's Wisdom: Religion, Skepticism, and Literature in Nineteenth-Century America* (Oxford University Press, 2021), explores Herman Melville's engagement with biblical moral philosophy. He is currently working on a book on video games. He plays *Super Mario Odyssey* every Sunday morning under the supervision of his little son.

Sören Schoppmeier completed his Ph.D. with a dissertation titled "Playing American: Open-World Videogames, Ambient Operations, and the Reproduction of American Culture" at Freie Universität Berlin in 2021. His published and forthcoming academic writing has dealt with a variety of video games and franchises, including *Grand Theft Auto*, *Watch Dogs*, *Red Dead Redemption*, *Far Cry 5*, and *Pony Island*. While he fondly remembers the perfect open world of *Gothic II* and the quirky humor and sundry settings of *No One Lives Forever*, two of his all-time favorites, his interest has since shifted to narrative exploration games like *Gone Home*, *Firewatch*, and *Everybody's Gone to the Rapture*, as well as anything else that plays on his heartstrings.

Stefan Schubert is an Assistant Professor at the Institute for American Studies at Leipzig University, Germany. His dissertation on *Narrative Instability: Destabilizing Identities, Realities, and Textualities in Contemporary American Popular Culture* was published in 2019. He is co-editor of *Poetics of Politics: Textuality and Social Relevance in Contemporary American Literature and Culture* (2015) and *Video Games and/in American Studies: Politics, Popular Culture, and Populism* (2021; special issue of *European Journal of American Studies*), among others. His published articles cover topics such as video-game poetics and politics (e.g. in *BioShock Infinite*, *Alan Wake*, and *Heavy Rain*), contemporary U.S. popular culture, and narrativity. While living through the COVID-19 pandemic, he developed a troubling fascination with the (post)apocalyptic spaces imagined in games like *Death Stranding* and *The Last of Us Part II*.

Maria Sulimma is the Postdoctoral Researcher in the research group "Scripts for Postindustrial Urban Futures: American Models, Transatlantic Interventions" at the Department of Anglophone Studies at the University of Duisburg-Essen. Her research spans literary and cultural studies, urban studies, and feminist media studies. She is the author of *Gender and Seriality: Practices and Politics of Contemporary US Television* (Edinburgh University Press, 2021). Her current book project is on literature, gentrification, and urban pastimes of the nineteenth and twenty-first centuries. Since becoming a commuter (by train), she has rediscovered the point-and-click adventure games of her childhood, such as *Sam & Max Hit the Road*, *Day of the Tentacle*, or *Monkey Island* – but finds herself a much less patient gamer today (which may also be because online videogame walkthroughs were not available to her in the mid-nineties).

Felix Zimmermann is a doctoral candidate at the a.r.t.e.s. Graduate School for the Humanities Cologne at the University of Cologne. His research interests include the depiction of history in popular culture, concepts and use of historical authenticity and representations of traumatic history in digital games. He is also interested in non-functional and atmospheric spaces and imaginations of nature and environment in digital games. His publications include the anthology *History in Games: Contingencies of an Authentic Past* (with Martin Lorber, 2020), the article "Historical Digital Games as Experiences: How Atmospheres of the Past Satisfy Needs of Authenticity" (2021) and the journal special issue *Democracy Dies Playfully: (Anti-) Democratic Ideas in and Around Video Games* (with Eugen Pfister and Tobias Winnerling, 2020). A full list of publications is available at felix-zimmermann.net. When he first scored an aerial goal in *Rocket League*, his understanding of what constitutes the perfect multiplayer experience changed forever.

Index

agency 53, 115, 118–125, 159, 218–220
ambience 38, 53, 63, 66–67
American exceptionalism 14–18
American gothic 183–184, 190–191
anxiety 138–139, 140–141, 143–144, 148–149
Art of Video Games, The 263, 271
audioplay 225, 236

Barad, Karen 219
Bode, Christoph and Rainer Dietrich 159
Bonner, Marc 59–62

cartography see map
colonial gaze 106, 108, 144
colonialism 11, 14, 40–41, 102, 106–107, 109–111, 115, 138, 141–142
communism 111
community 168, 171–173, 177–178
conquest 17, 73, 76, 81, 108, 142
cooperation 167–168, 174–175, 217
Cooper, James Fenimore 87–88, 90, 96–98

Detroit 153, 156–157, 161
Dia de los Muertos 201
disenchantment 114–115

ecocritical 12, 54, 67, 80, 129, 178
economy 41–42, 46–47, 120–121, 241
ecosystem 54, 72, 81
encoding/decoding 123–125
environment 8–9, 12, 20–21, 64–68, 80, 81–82, 128–129, 131–132, 220, 234, 259–260, 267
exergames 224–225, 226
exotic spaces see space
exoticization 198
exploration 7, 71–72, 73, 80, 108, 119–120, 127–129, 131, 183, 211, 213

farm 243–244, 250
FarmVille 241, 248
Fluck, Winfried 157–158 nn.9-10

frontier 13, 14–16, 17, 37, 45, 54, 71–72, 73–74, 80, 87–89, 90, 92, 97–98, 167, 178, 243

Galloway, Alexander R. 38, 53
game theater 258–261
garden 15–16, 56, 242–243, 249, 250
gender 85, 91, 102, 104, 145, 230–235, 238, 279
gothic settings 181, 183, 187
Guerilla 71

history 36, 37, 40–41, 48, 59, 88, 95, 142, 160–161
horror 182, 234–235, 236, 238
hybridity 112–114, 195–196

identity 110, 117, 195–196, 202–204, 27
illusion of choice 119–120, 130
imagination 37–38, 47–48, 157 n.9, 167
imperialism 11, 18, 86, 107, 109–112
indie game 168, 223, 263–264, 266
interactive 4, 78–79, 124, 154, 259, 269
interactivity 120, 129, 182, 187–188
invisibility 114
IPGarten 241–243

Jefferson, Thomas 243, 244–245, 246

Kruszka, Martin 241, 247

Latinx 193–194, 196–197, 198–199, 202–204
locative media 210, 213–214
LucasArts 193

male adventure 86, 89, 97
male gaze 102
manifest destiny 107, 110, 113–115
map 11, 14, 80, 107, 128, 142, 214–215
– cartographic maps 137–138, 141–142, 149–150
– in-game maps 138, 143–144, 147–148

mapping 155, 157–158, 160, 163–164
Marx, Leo 15, 54, 56, 57 n.6, 59, 243
Mittell, Jason 155 n.6, 157 n.10, 158
multiplayer 168–170, 174, 267
myth 105, 114, 167, 198, 200
myth-and-symbol school 13, 15–16, 18,

narrative 6–7, 9–10, 20, 102, 130, 139–141, 142, 155–156, 157–159, 163–164, 176–177, 183, 187, 238, 256, 259–260
– future narratives 159
narrativization 5, 172, 178 see also narrative
neoliberal ideology 120 - 121, 132, 236
New Americanists 18
new materialism 219
nostalgia 189–190

open world 36, 51, 53, 60–63, 67, 119, 147–148

pan-Latinidad 196, 199, 202–204
past 33, 43–44, 48, 183
pastoral 15, 56, 59, 63–64, 66–67, 241–243, 248
patriarchy 102, 103–106, 110, 115
performance 218–219, 253, 256, 260–261
performance studies 209–210, 212
place 33, 38, 40, 43–44, 45, 47–48, 76, 154, 189 n.5, 277–278
politics of representation 4, 10, 12
postapocalyptic 72, 74, 78
postfeminism 232, 238
procedural rhetoric 107, 119–120, 125, 127, 131
public space see space
puppetry 217–219

Quantic Dream 161 n.1
queer games 182, 278–279

Regeneration Through Violence 16 n.18, 37
regeneration through violence 37–39, 46, 167
research through design 210, 212, 220
Retrotopia 33
retrotopia 33, 45–47

revisionist scholarship 16–18
risky space see space
rural 42, 44, 45–47, 56

Schafer, Tim 195
Schechner, Richard 210, 212
scripting 20–21
scripts 20–21
Smithsonian American Art Museum 263, 265, 271–272
space
– exotic spaces 89, 98
– public space 229, 232, 233–234, 238
– risky space 233–234, 238
– time-space 76–77
– virtual space 5, 75, 78–80, 141–142, 211–213, 215, 266
spatial turn 2, 4, 8–10, 12–13,16–19, 21, 138
storytelling
– environmental or spatial storytelling 6–7, 10, 183, 260
– intermedial storytelling 153 n.1
surveillance 242, 247–250
survival game 168, 170, 172
survivalism 235–238

terraforming 80–81
theater games 253–255, 258–261
Thiemig, Boris 242 n.5, 249 n.22
Thoreau, Henry David 244–245, 249
time-space see space
topological poesis 138
transnational turn 19

Uncanny, the 184, 190

virtual reality 209, 217
virtual space see space

wilderness 15, 53–54, 60, 63–64, 77
wilderness vs civilization 37, 39, 45, 57, 72–73

zombie 235–236

www.ingramcontent.com/pod-product-compliance
Lightning Source LLC
Chambersburg PA
CBHW020223170426
43201CB00007B/294